T0211721

Lecture Notes in Computer Science 9071

Commenced Publication in 1973
Founding and Former Series Editors:
Gerhard Goos, Juris Hartmanis, and Jan van Leeuwen

Editorial Board

David Hutchison
Lancaster University, Lancaster, UK
Takeo Kanade
Carnegie Mellon University, Pittsburgh, PA, USA
Josef Kittler
University of Surrey, Guildford, UK
Jon M. Kleinberg
Cornell University, Ithaca, NY, USA
Friedemann Mattern
ETH Zurich, Zürich, Switzerland
John C. Mitchell
Stanford University, Stanford, CA, USA
Moni Naor
Weizmann Institute of Science, Rehovot, Israel
C. Pandu Rangan
Indian Institute of Technology, Madras, India
Bernhard Steffen
TU Dortmund University, Dortmund, Germany
Demetri Terzopoulos
University of California, Los Angeles, CA, USA
Doug Tygar
University of California, Berkeley, CA, USA
Gerhard Weikum
Max Planck Institute for Informatics, Saarbrücken, Germany

More information about this series at http://www.springer.com/series/7411

Mari Carmen Aguayo-Torres · Gerardo Gómez
Javier Poncela (Eds.)

Wired/Wireless Internet Communications

13th International Conference, WWIC 2015
Malaga, Spain, May 25–27, 2015
Revised Selected Papers

Springer

Editors
Mari Carmen Aguayo-Torres
ETSI Telecomunicación
Malaga
Spain

Gerardo Gómez
ETSI Telecomunicación
Malaga
Spain

Javier Poncela
ETSI Telecomunicación
Malaga
Spain

ISSN 0302-9743   ISSN 1611-3349   (electronic)
Lecture Notes in Computer Science
ISBN 978-3-319-22571-5   ISBN 978-3-319-22572-2   (eBook)
DOI 10.1007/978-3-319-22572-2

Library of Congress Control Number: 2015946067

LNCS Sublibrary: SL5 – Computer Communication Networks and Telecommunications

Springer Cham Heidelberg New York Dordrecht London
© Springer International Publishing Switzerland 2015
This work is subject to copyright. All rights are reserved by the Publisher, whether the whole or part of the material is concerned, specifically the rights of translation, reprinting, reuse of illustrations, recitation, broadcasting, reproduction on microfilms or in any other physical way, and transmission or information storage and retrieval, electronic adaptation, computer software, or by similar or dissimilar methodology now known or hereafter developed.
The use of general descriptive names, registered names, trademarks, service marks, etc. in this publication does not imply, even in the absence of a specific statement, that such names are exempt from the relevant protective laws and regulations and therefore free for general use.
The publisher, the authors and the editors are safe to assume that the advice and information in this book are believed to be true and accurate at the date of publication. Neither the publisher nor the authors or the editors give a warranty, express or implied, with respect to the material contained herein or for any errors or omissions that may have been made.

Printed on acid-free paper

Springer International Publishing AG Switzerland is part of Springer Science+Business Media
(www.springer.com)

Preface

On behalf of the WWIC committee members, we welcome you to the proceedings of the 13th International Conference on Wired & Wireless Internet Communications (WWIC 2015), which was held in Malaga, Spain, during May 25–27, 2015.

WWIC is a well-established conference in all Internet communication aspects held in the late Spring. This year's 3-day event provided a dynamic platform to exchange ideas, research findings, innovations, best practices, lessons learned, and challenges encountered on wireless network technologies and their applications related to the Internet, in order to designate future research efforts and directions.

The 13th edition focused on the efficient integration of new network approaches with the traditional wired infrastructure. WWIC 2015 addressed research topics such as the design and evaluation of protocols, the dynamics of integration, the performance trade-offs, the need for new performance metrics and cross-layer interactions. The goal of the conference is to present high-quality results in the field.

The WWIC 2015 call for papers attracted submissions from 20 countries (Europe, North Africa, North America, Asia) on the major areas of next-generation services, resource management, wireless and wired networks, and network architectures and applications. Finally, 25 papers were selected out of 42 submissions, and they were grouped by topic into six technical sessions distributed throughout the event. The area of wireless and wired networks aroused more interest, with nearly half of the papers being on this topic.

We would like to thank our keynote speakers, Preben Mogensen (Aalborg University, Denmark) and Joerg Widmer (IMDEA Networks, Spain), for accepting our invitation. Their interesting talks introduced us to the forthcoming 5G generation radio technologies and the challenges and possible solutions for networking in the millimeter wave-band. The conference also held five invited papers from relevant research groups in the field, which addressed issues for optimization of link and network mechanisms. The accepted papers were organized in six sessions.

We thank all authors for contributing to the technical excellence of WWIC 2015. We would also like to thank all the members of the Technical Program Committee as well as the additional reviewers for their effort. Thanks also to our sponsors, in particular the School of Telecommunications Engineering (ETSIT), the University of Malaga (UMA), and the International Federation for Information Processing (IFIP).

We expect all attendees enjoyed the scientific and social program, and look forward to welcoming you at WWIC 2016!

May 2015

Mari Carmen Aguayo-Torres
Gerardo Gómez
Javier Poncela

Organization

Technical Committee

Khalid Al-Begain	University of South Wales, UK
Onur Altintas	Toyota InfoTechnology Center, Japan
Vangelis Angelakis	Linköping University, Sweden
Bigomokero Bagula	University of Western Cape, South Africa
Kamel Barkaoui	Cedric Cnam-Paris, France
Paolo Bellavista	University of Bologna, Italy
Fernando Boavida	University of Coimbra, Portugal
Malika Bourenane	University of Senia, Algeria
Wojciech Burakowski	Warsaw University of Technology, Poland
Scott Burleigh	JPL, California Institute of Technology, USA
Maria Calderon	Universidad Carlos III de Madrid, Spain
Paulo Carvalho	Centro Algoritmi, Universidade do Minho, Portugal
Ana Cavalli	Telecom SudParis, France
Ken Chen	University of Paris 13, France
Marilia Curado	University of Coimbra, Portugal
Boubaker Daachi	University of Paris-East, France
Aïssani Djamil	LAMOS, University of Bejaia, Algeria
Lefteris Mamatas	University of Macedonia, Greece
Ognjen Dobrijevic	University of Zagreb, Croatia
Scott Fowler	Linköping University, Sweden
Paul Gendron	University of Massachusetts Dartmouth, USA
Yassine Hadjadj-Aoul	University of Rennes 1, France
Haffaf Hafid	University of Oran, Algeria
Petr Hanacek	Brno University of Technology, Czech Republic
Jarmo Harju	Tampere University of Technology, Finland
Sonia Heemstra de Groot	Eindhoven Technical University, The Netherlands
Said Hoceini	UPEC, University of Paris-Est Creteil Val de Marne, France
Muhammad Imran	KSU, Saudi Arabia
Malika Ioualalen	USTHB, Algeria
Bouabdellah Kechar	University of Oran, Algeria
Ibrahim Korpeoglu	Bilkent University, Turkey
Francine Krief	University of Bordeaux, France
S.A. Kumar Kumar	Delhi Technological University, India
Abderrahmane Lakas	UAE University, UAE
Sekhri Larbi	University of Oran, Algeria

Vassilis Tsaoussidis	Democritus University, Greece
Pascal Lorenz	University of Haute Alsace, France
Chung-Horng Lung	Carleton University, Canada
Christian Maihöfer	Daimler AG, Germany
Christian Makaya	IBM Research, USA
Eva Marín-Tordera	Technical University of Catalonia, UPC, Spain
Xavier Masip-Bruin	Universitat Politécnica de Catalunya, Spain
Ahmed Mehaoua	University of Paris Descartes, France
Paulo Mendes	COPELABS, University Lusofona, Portugal
Enzo Mingozzi	University of Pisa, Italy
Edmundo Monteiro	University of Coimbra, Portugal
Hassnaa Moustafa	Intel, USA
Liam Murphy	University College Dublin, Ireland
Rakesh Nagaraj	Amrita School of Engineering, India
Ioanis Nikolaidis	University of Alberta, Canada
Panagiotis Papadimitriou	Leibniz Universität Hannover, Germany
Nikolaos Pappas	Linköping University, Sweden
Ioannis Psaras	University College London, UK
Jean-Pierre Richard	Ecole Centrale de Lille, France
Dimitrios Serpanos	University of Patras, Greece
Farhan Siddiqui	Walden University, USA
Vasilios Siris	Athens University of Economics and Business, Greece
Harry Skianis	University of the Aegean, Greece
Yahya Slimani	University of Manouba, Tunisia
Dirk Staehle	HTWG Konstanz, Germany
Burkhard Stiller	University of Zurich, Switzerland
Jean Thiriet	GIPSA lab, France
Elias Tragos	Institute of Computer Science, FORTH, Greece
Alicia Triviño	University of Malaga, Spain
Ming-Fong Tsai	Feng Chia University, Taiwan
Angeliki Tsioliaridou	Foundation for Research and Technology, Greece
Hans van den Berg	TNO, The Netherlands
Rob van der Mei	Centrum voor Wiskunde en Informatica, The Netherlands
Wei Wei	Xi'an University of Technology, China
Miki Yamamoto	Kansai University, Japan

Organizers

General Chair

Mari Carmen Aguayo-Torres	Spain

General Co-chairs

Abdelhamid Mellouk	France
Gerardo Gómez	Spain

TPC Chair

Javier Poncela	Spain

Proceedings Chair

Gerardo Gómez	Spain

Asia/Pacific Liaison Co-chairs

Nadeem Javaid	Pakistan
Lei Shu	China

America Liaison Chair

Eduardo Cerqueira	Brazil

Europe Liaison Chair

Periklis Chatzimisios	Greece

Middle East/Africa Liaison Co-chairs

Samira Moussaoui	Algeria
Nidal Nasser	Kingdom of Saudi Arabia

Web and Publicity Chair

Gerardo Gómez	Spain

Local Organizing Co-chairs

Javier Poncela	Spain
Gerardo Gómez	Spain

Steering Committee

Torsten Braun	Switzerland
Vassilios Tsaoussidis	Greece
Peter Langendörfer	Germany
Geert Heijenk	The Netherlands

Yevgeni Koucheryavy	Finland
Otto Carle	Germany
Ibrahim Matta	USA

Sponsors

Universidad de Málaga (www.uma.es)

Escuela Técnica superior de Ingeniería de Telecomunicación (www.etsit.uma.es)

Departamento de Ingeniería de Comunicaciones (www.ic.uma.es)

International Federation for Information Processing (www.ifip.org)

International Federation for Information Processing Law Group

Keynote Speakers

5G for People and Things – Expanding the Human Possibilities of Technology

Preben Mogensen

Aalborg University, Denmark

The commercial launch of the forthcoming fifth-generation (5G) mobile communication system is expected to start from 2020. 5G has three key drivers: to provide perception of unlimited access to services in the cloud; to be ultrafast responsive for real-time remote and automation control; and to give reliable and secure connectivity to an enormous number of low-power and low-cost devices (Internet of Things, IoT). Some of the key radio technologies to reach these 5G targets are to move up in frequency bands so as to have access to more spectrum, to densify the network by deploying ultra-dense small cells, and to enhance the transmission efficiency by MIMO and advanced transceivers. Finally, the overall 5G network architecture will be programmable and software driven. This presentation will discuss Nokia's view on 5G.

Efficient Networking in Millimeter Wave-Bands

Joerg Widmer

Institute IMDEA Networks, Madrid, Spain

State-of-the-art wireless communication already operates close to Shannon capacity and one of the most promising options to further increase data rates is to increase the communication bandwidth. Very high bandwidth channels are only available in the extremely high frequency part of the radio spectrum, the millimeter wave-band (mm-wave). Upcoming communication technologies, such as IEEE 802.11ad, are already starting to exploit this part of the radio spectrum to achieve data rates of several gigabits per second. However, communication at such high frequencies also suffers from high attenuation and signal absorption, often restricting communication to line-of-sight (LOS) scenarios and requiring the use of highly directional antennas. This in turn requires a radical rethinking of wireless network design. On the one hand, such channels experience little interference, allowing for a high degree of spatial reuse and potentially simpler MAC and interference management mechanisms. On the other hand, such an environment is extremely dynamic and channels may appear and disappear over very short time intervals, in particular for mobile devices. This talk will highlight some of the challenges of and possible approaches for networking in the mm-wave band.

Contents

Network Architecture and Applications

Next Generation Services

Resource Management

Wireless and Wired Networks

Wireless Technologies

Downlink Packet Scheduling Algorithm Using Tabu Method in LTE Systems

Radhia Khdhir[1], Kais Mnif[1,2(⊠)], and Lotfi Kammoun[1,2]

[1] LETI Laboratory ENIS, University of Sfax, Sfax, Tunisia
{rkhdhir,kais.mnif,lotfikamoun2}@gmail.com
[2] LETI Laboratory ENET'COM, University of Sfax, Sfax, Tunisia

Abstract. This paper addressed the problem of packet scheduling (PS) on the 3GPP Long Term Evolution (LTE) downlink (DL). The main contribution of this work was to propose a new scheduling and resource allocation scheme that deals with QoS requirements. The objectives of this proposed scheduler are to maximize the system's sum throughput, to allow a fair distribution of available RBs and to handle GBR and NGBR traffic in LTE downlink systems. The performance of the proposed approach was compared with previous resources allocation and scheduling algorithms such as Best-CQI, RR, and QoE downlink schedulers. Simulation results show that it is possible to achieve a considerable gain in both system's throughput and fairness.

Keywords: Scheduling · LTE · Downlink · Throughput · QoS

1 Introduction

The Orthogonal Frequency Division Multiple Access (OFDMA) and Single Carrier Frequency Division Multiple Accesses (SC-FDMA) are techniques used for radio transmission and reception in LTE respectively for the Downlink and Uplink. The LTE system is expected to provide peak data rates in the order of 50 Mbit/s in Uplink (UL) with 20 MHz spectrum allocation and 100 Mbps in Downlink (DL), [1]. In LTE, the transmissions Downlink (DL) and uplink (UL) are organized through 10 ms time frames. Two frame types are supported: the first type is applicable for Frequency-Division Duplexing (FDD) whereas the second is applicable for Time-Division Duplexing (TDD). The structure of frame type 1 is illustrated in Fig. 1. Each time frame (10 ms) is divided into 10 sub-frames equal to the duration of 1 ms called Transmission Time Interval (TTI). In FDD, Uplink and Downlink transmissions are separated in the frequency area [2]. The structure of frame type 2 is illustrated in Fig. 2. Each frame (10 ms) is divided into two sub-frames of 5 ms. Each sub-frame contains a special sub-frame and 4 other sub-frames. The duration of the special sub-frame is 1 ms and contains three fields of DwPTS (Downlink Pilot Time Slot), GP (Gurand Period) and UpPTS (Uplink Pilot Time Slot).

In the frame type 2, there are 7 different patterns of uplink-downlink switching, termed uplink-downlink configurations 0 through 6. In LTE Downlink (DL), the total bandwidth is divided into multiple sub-bandwidths. These are regrouped in PRBs (Physical Resources Block). A PRB is defined by a couple frequency and time

© Springer International Publishing Switzerland 2015
M.C. Aguayo-Torres et al. (Eds.): WWIC 2015, LNCS 9071, pp. 3–17, 2015.
DOI: 10.1007/978-3-319-22572-2_1

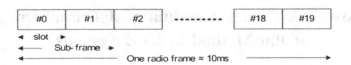

Fig. 1. Frame structure type 1 [2]

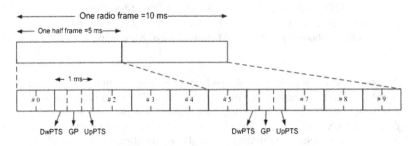

Fig. 2. Frame structure type 2 [2]

domains. In fact, a PRB is 0.5 ms in length (one slot in the time domain) and contains a contiguous set of 12 subcarriers (180 kHz in the frequency domain) from each OFDM symbol, as shown in Fig. 3. Therefore, this PRB is the basic transmission unit of a user's data in both uplink and downlink. The number of PRB's in a frequency domain is between 6 and 110 [3]. The LTE standard defines nine Qualities of service class identifiers (QCI), four GBR (Guaranteed Bit Rate) and five non-GBR [4], while providing a Quality of Service (QoS) for multiple types of traffic.

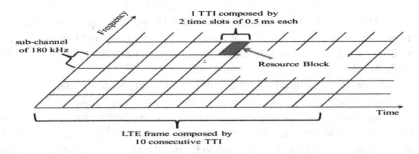

Fig. 3. Downlink resource grid [13]

In the LTE standard, there are no defined specific scheduling algorithm nor allocation algorithm. Consequently, an LTE scheduling and allocation algorithm has been discussed by many researchers from both academic and industrial fields. An LTE downlink scheduler selects a set of UEs to be scheduled in the following TTI based on their QoS requirements and many other conditions. In this work, the main contribution was to propose a new scheduling scheme for OFDMA system, by considering GBR and non-GBR traffic, the maximization throughput and the user fairness into consideration.

This paper is organized as follows: Sect. 2 presented the review of existing downlink scheduling algorithms in OFDMA. The system and our scheduling algorithm were introduced in Sect. 3. The simulation results and discussions were detailed in Sect. 4. We finally drew the conclusion of our work in Sect. 5.

2 Related Work

LTE downlink scheduling algorithms have been discussed by many authors. From the literature overview, in the Best Quality Indication (BCQI) scheduling the user who has the best channel quality gets served. But, the UEs that suffer from bad channel conditions will never be served by this scheduler [5]. So, UEs that are far away from eNodeB never get the resources. Therefore, the BCQI achieve better throughput results but it is poor in terms of fairness. Authors in [6], relied on an opportunistic approach to allocate the radio resources. Mushtaq's focused on the Mean Opinion Score MOS, average throughput, and channel condition for GBR and non-GBR traffic to calculate the UEs priorities. To evaluate the priorities of the UEs, authors relied on the Quality of Experience (QoE) metrics. The authors proposed in [7] two scheduling algorithms based in MIMO-FDPS (Multiple Input Multiple Output – Frequency Domain Packet Scheduling) problem. The main motivation of their work cannot provide QoS satisfaction for different users. In [8], the authors proposed a new scheduling algorithm namely the Quality-aware DRX (Q-DRX) scheme. The objective of this proposed algorithm is not only to improve the QoS but also to save the UE's power. Q-DRX is evaluated in terms of Throughput Fairness Index, System Throughput, Packet Loss Rate and Packet Delay. The performance of the Q-DRX scheme is better than other scheduling algorithms such as RR, BCQI and PF. Lin and Yue in [9], proposed a novel algorithm for the OFDMA system namely Channel-Adapted and Buffer-Aware (CABA). The CABA algorithm, which is based on the QoS for Real Time and Non-Real Time services to schedule the UE's. In contrast, using the CABA algorithm, the packet loss rate can increase because this scheduler does not consider the packet delays. In the work referenced by [10], a new packet scheduling scheme was presented. In this scheme, the authors combined both of the time domain and frequency domain scheduling. The aim of this algorithm is to maximize the throughput guaranteeing the minimum delay packet for each UE. The limit of this proposed scheme does not base on the channel condition allowing the RB's to UE's. In [11], a scheduling method is proposed. This method based on optimal DRX parameters guaranteeing the delay and power saving constraints, but does not rely on any other parameters like QoS, fairness, throughput etc. Also this proposed method is applied with two users only. The following table gives a summary of the mentioned algorithms.

Ref	Strengths	Limitations
[5]	The Best Quality Indication (BCQI) scheduling is proposed. This scheduler served the UE's which have the best channel quality	Does not consider different levels of fairness: the UE's that suffer from bad channel conditions will never be served by this scheduler

(Continued)

(Continued)

Ref	Strengths	Limitations
[6]	Authors proposed a new downlink scheduling algorithm. This algorithm considers many conditions Mean Opinion Score MOS, average throughput, channel condition, and Guaranteed Bit Rate (GBR) non-GBR traffic to calculate the priorities of UEs	None
[7]	Two scheduling algorithms based in MIMO-FDPS (Multiple Input Multiple Output–Frequency Domain Packet Scheduling) problem are proposed	Does not consider the service differentiation
[8]	The authors proposed a new scheduling algorithm namely the Q-DRX scheme. The objective of this proposed algorithm is to improve QoS and power. Q-DRX is evaluated in terms of Throughput Fairness Index, System Throughput, Packet Loss Rate and Packet Delay	None
[9]	Proposed a novel algorithm for the OFDMA system CABA. The CABA based on the QoS for Real Time and Non-Real Time services to schedule the UE's	Does not consider the packet delays. So the packet loss rate can increase
[10]	Presented a new packet scheduling scheme. The aim of this algorithm is to maximize the throughput guaranteeing the minimum delay packet for each UE	Does not rely on the channel condition to assign the RB's to UE's
[11]	A scheduling method is proposed. This method based on optimal DRX parameters guaranteeing the delay and power saving constraints	Does not rely on any other parameters like QoS, fairness, throughput. This method is simulated with only two UE's

To sum up, The objectives of downlink schedulers are to be able to share the total system bandwidth fairly according to the QoS requested by each user, to minimize the power consumption while ensuring feasible algorithm complexity and system scalability and maximizing the throughput with respect to the QoS.

3   System Model and Proposed Scheduling Algorithm

3.1   System Model

In LTE, the evolved NodeB (eNodeB) is the entity in charge of performing the resource allocation and the Packet Scheduling task. The PS is considered the most important step of RRM (Radio Resource Management) feasible per eNodeB [12]. LTE PS comprises time-domain (TD) and frequency domain (FD) scheduling algorithms. The TD scheduler selects a set of UEs requests to be served in the next TTI based on their QoS requirements. The selected set of UEs requests is passed to the FD scheduler that determines the RBs that should be allowed to them relying on the channel quality. The scheduling algorithm of our system is shown in Fig. 4.

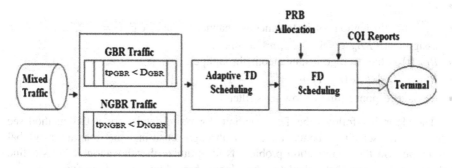

Fig. 4. DPSA-Tabu system model

As shown in Fig. 4, the packets coming in mixed traffic will be classified into two classes: a GBR class and NGBR class. So, each type of packet will be delivered in an independent queues: GBR queue and NGBR queue. These two queues will be served on the basis of opt-tabu algorithm [14] (see Sect. 3.2.1). We define t_{pGBR} the GBR packet delay and D_{GBR} is the delay budget which is the upper delay bound of the GBR traffic. Therefore, each packet delay of a GBR type must not exceed this delay budget. Same reasoning for NGBR class: t_{pNGBR} is the NGBR packet delay and D_{NGBR} is the delay budget which is the upper delay bound of the NGBR traffic.

Let us consider a cellular network where downlink OFDMA system bandwidth is divided into m RBs, one eNodeB and n active UEs. In this research, we consider an infinitely backlogged model in which there is always data available for the service for each UE. The eNodeB can allocate m RBs to a set of n UEs. Each time slot, multiple RBs can be assigned to a single UE. In other words, each PRB however can be assigned to one user at most.

3.2 Proposed Scheduling Algorithm

In this subsection, we first briefly explained the concept of opt-tabu algorithm referenced in [14]. Then, we presented the downlink packet scheduling algorithm using the Tabu method based on the opt-tabu criterion. This novel scheduling algorithm for downlink LTE system, namely **DPSA-Tabu** (Downlink Packet Scheduling Algorithm) using the Tabu method. The performance of this proposed algorithm was presented in Sect. 4.

3.2.1   Opt-Tabu Scheduler [14]

The scheduler receives the matrix M as input, with $[n \times m]$ as dimensions, where n is the number of users (UEs) and m is the number of PRBs. The matrix values are calculated according to the "Proportional fair scheduling" metric (PF) [15]. For each user, we calculate the amount of $M_{i,c}$. where:

- $M_{i,c} = \frac{r_{UE_i}^{PRB_c}}{R_{UE_i}(t)}$.
- $r_{UE_i}^{PRB_c}$ the throughput of instantaneous channel for user UE_i ($i = 1, 2, ..., n$) if we assign it a PRB_c ($i = 1, 2, ..., m$) at time t.
- $R_{UE_i}(t)$ is the average instantaneous throughput.
- $R_{UE_i}(t) = \frac{1}{N_T} R_{UE_i}(t-1) + \frac{1}{N_T} r_{UE_i}^{PRB_c}(t-1)$.
- N_T as a response time of low-pass filter.

The algorithm follows the Tabu method (for more details about this method see [16, 17]) to search a better allocation through ensuring the maximum global throughput. So the optimization problem is to optimize the allocation s. Let's define $f(s)$ as the function that calculates the global throughput at each iteration or each assignment between UE_i and PRB_c. so:

$$f(s) = \sum_{i=1}^{n} \sum_{c=1}^{m} M_{i,c}, \text{ for } (i = c)$$

Let's define:

- s is the current solution (current allocation),
- s^* is the best-known solution (best allocation),
- $N(s)$ is the possible permutations (between two UEs),
- T is the Tabu list (tabu memory),
- $f(s)$ is the function which calculates the throughput system.

The steps of the algorithm are as follows:

Step 1:   Assign PRBs to UEs at random: $UE_1 \leftarrow PRB_1$; $UE_2 \leftarrow PRB_2$... $UE_n \leftarrow PRB_m$ and calculate the matrix values $M_{i,c} = \frac{r_{UE_i}^{PRB_c}}{R_{UE_i}(t)}$ for each PRB_c.

Step 2:   Save the allocation (in step 1) and calculate the global system throughput f (s) (in this paper, we define the global system (uplink) throughput as the sum of all UE's instantaneous throughput in the uplink divided by the average instantaneous throughput). So we compute the sum of the diagonal matrix M to calculate the global system throughput. We chose the diagonal of the matrix M because one resource block can be assigned to one UE in each slot.

Step 3:   Follow the Tabu method in order to improve the allocation carried out in Step 1: swap the rows of matrix M (for example, Assign PRB$_1$ to user UE$_2$ and PRB2 to user UE1opposite to the initial case (step 1)). Then, calculate f (s) for this allocation.

Step 4:   After the comparison with the preceding allocation (allocation1 in step 1) and current allocation (allocation 2 in step 3), if allocation 2 is better than allocation1 (i.e. $(f(s) > f^*)$ then we consider the optimal allocation (s^*) our current solution and save the permutation in the subset N(s). Else we consider the optimal solution (*s**) the preceding allocation and save the permutation in the T Tabu memory. This Tabu memory contains the achieved permutations which have not improved the previous allocations. So it is useless to revisit this configuration.

Step 5: Repeat step 3 and step 4 until the end of the number of users n by searching the best global system throughput f^*.

Step 6: Find the best allocation (*s**) which corresponds to f^* (the maximum calculated throughput).

Step 7: Apply s^* allocation (the optimal allocation) which corresponds to f^*).

Step 8: Repeat Step 2 up to Step 7 until all PRBs are allocated.

3.2.2 The Downlink Packet Scheduling Algorithm Using the Tabu Method (DPSA-Tabu)

The objective of our work is to propose and model a novel downlink scheduling algorithm not only by keeping a high system throughput but also guaranteeing the QoS constraints for all UE's (Fig. 5).

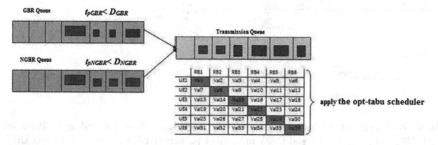

Fig. 5. An illustration of downlink transmissions considering 6 RBs and 6 UEs including GBR packets and NGBR packets

As mentioned in Sect. 3.1, the packets coming in mixed traffic are then classified into two classes: a GBR and NGBR class. These two queues will be served on the basis of opt-tabu [14]. We define t_{pGBR} the delay of packet p of GBR traffic and D_{GBR} is the delay budget which is the upper delay bound of GBR traffic. Therefore, each packet delay of a GBR type must not exceed this delay budget $t_{pGBR} < D_{GBR}$. Therefore, if this condition is not respected the packet will be removed from the GBR queue.

The same reasoning is applied for the NGBR class: t_{pNGBR} is the delay of packet p of NGBR traffic and D_{NGBR} is the delay budget which is the upper delay bound of the NGBR traffic $t_{pNGBR} < D_{NGBR}$. (i.e.: $D_{GBR} < D_{NGBR}$). Here, we define $leng_{GBR}$ the length of GBR queue and ρ_{GBR} the threshold size of the GBR queue. For the GBR packets buffered in a GBR queue, they are delivered into every slot. For the NGBR packets buffered in the NGBR queue, they are delivered whenever the condition ($leng_{GBR} < \rho_{GBR}$). Then schedule the GBR and the NGBR packets admitted to be delivered based on the opt-tabu criterion.

The steps of the algorithm are as follows:

Step 1: Deliver GBR packets buffered in GBR queue if $t_{pGBR} < D_{GBR}$ in the current scheduling s.

Step 2: Deliver NGBR packets buffered in NGBR queue if $t_{pNGBR} < D_{NGBR}$ and $leng_{GBR} < \rho_{GBR}$ in iteration s + 1.

Step 3: Apply the opt-tabu algorithm with UEs which have the admitted packets to deliver (in steps 1 and 2).

Step 4: Drop the GBR traffic if their delay constraint is violated with respect D_{GBR}. Drop the NGBR traffic if their delay constraint is violated with respect D_{NGBR}.

Step 5: Repeat step 1 up to step 4 until all PRBs are allocated or the two GBR and NGBR queues are empty.

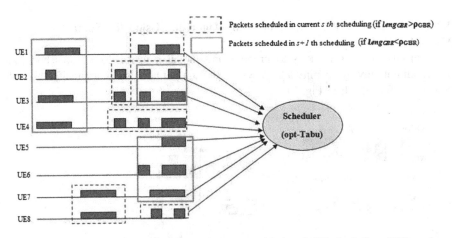

Fig. 6. An illustration of downlink transmissions considering 8 UEs including GBR packets (UE1, UE2, UE3, UE4, UE7 and UE8) and NGBR packets (UE2, UE3, UE5, UE6 and UE7)

Figure 6 shows an example of a transmission scenario for our proposed algorithm considering the packets of type GBR and NGBR traffic and 8 UEs.

Here we suppose two cases:

Case 1: In the current s scheduling, Assume that $leng_{GBR} > \rho_{GBR}$. Thus, the users have GBR packets (UE1, UE2, UE3, UE4, UE7 and UE8) can only deliver their packets in the current iteration s by our definition.

Case 2: In s + 1 iteration, Assume that $leng_{GBR} > \rho_{GBR}$. Thus, the users have GBR packets (UE1, UE2, UE3, UE4, UE7 and UE8) and NGBR packets (UE2, UE3, UE5, UE6 and UE7) can deliver their packets in s + 1 scheduling by our definition.

The prediction of the fluctuation of the traffic is plotted in Fig. 7. So, we can firstly calculate the steady state probability of the GBR and NGBR queue length and we can determine the $leng_{GBR}$ (length of GBR traffic queue). Thus, make the scheduling decision: **case 1** and **case 2**.

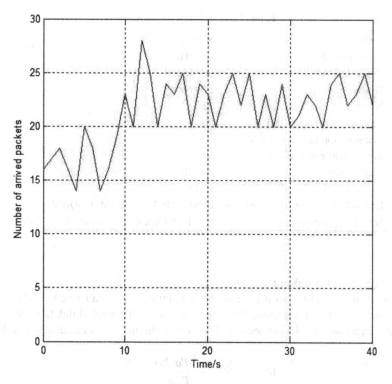

Fig. 7. Number of arrived packets

4 Simulation Results and Discussions

In this section we presented the simulation results obtained by applying the algorithms explained in Sect. 3.

4.1 Simulation Parameters

In order to view the performance of the proposed scheduler (DPSA-Tabu) we use traces generated in 3GPP deployment evaluation [18]. The configuration parameters used in this simulation are shown in Table 1.

4.2 Simulation Results

In this subsection, we presented the results obtained from the simulation that were achieved on the scheduler DPSA-Tabu. The conducted simulation was designed to analyze the following aspects of the system performance under different scenarios.

Table 1. Simulation parameters

Parameter	Setting
System bandwidth	10 MHz
Type of system	Single cell
Subcarrier spacing	15 kHz
Number of subcarriers per PRBs	12
Number of available PRB	50
Transmission time interval(TTI)	1 ms
Total number of used subcarriers	600
Carrier frequency	2.5 GHz
Frame duration	10 ms
Link adaptation ACM Modulation	BPSK, QPSK, 16-QAM, 64-QAM
Scheduling algorithms	RR, Best CQI, QoE scheme, DPSA-Tabu

4.2.1 System Throughput

The system throughput is measured as the amount of user data carried by the system (total number of bits transmitted from the UEs) over the total simulation time. It is generally expressed in bits per second. The system throughput is calculated as follows:

$$th_{sys} = \frac{\sum_{i=0}^{nb\_pck} Packet\_size_i}{T_{sim}}$$

Where $Packet\_size_i$ the size of packet i in Mbit, nb_pck is the number of packets transmitted during the simulation and T_{sim} is the simulation time measured in seconds.

The average system throughput of RR, Best CQI, QoE scheme and DPSA-Tabu algorithms versus a number of UEs is shown in Fig. 8. We can conclude that DPSA-Tabu provides the highest throughput. This is explained by our proposed scheme (DPSA-Tabu) that allocates the RBs to UEs with the best channel conditions and because it relies on the opt-tabu criterion to schedule the packets: the opt-Tabu considers the first objective is to maximize the total system throughput [14]. We can classify DPSA-Tabu scheme among the QoS-aware schemes. This category of algorithms distinguishes between different UEs and assigns less RBs to low priority applications (in this case less resource for the packets of type NGBR Traffic). In contrast, the QoS-aware algorithms give more resource for the best priority applications (in this case the packets of type GBR traffic) [19].

The result shows that the system throughput of the Best CQI algorithm is better compared to the QoE and RR, because this algorithm selects only the UEs which have the best channel conditions.

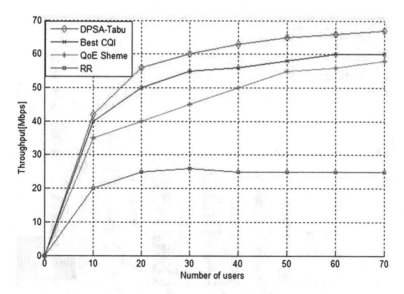

Fig. 8. System throughput

4.2.2 Packet Loss Rate (PLR)

The Packet Loss Rate is the ratio of the number of packets lost to the number of packets sent:

$$\frac{\textit{Number of packets lost}}{\textit{Number of packets sent}}$$

The Packet Loss Rate is shown in Fig. 9. The performance of RR scheduler in terms of packet loss rate is a better than the other downlink scheduling algorithms. This is normal because the RR assigns RBs cyclically. Thus, each UE has the opportunity to get radio resources.

The DPSA-Tabu is in the second position. This is explained by the fact that if a packet delay exceeds the delay threshold (D_{GBR} and D_{NGBR}) then it is classified to be the lost packet. Our proposed scheme is better than QoE and Best CQI schemes: the Best CQI BCQI has lowest performance. Because it allocates the RBs to UEs with the best channel conditions, while the packets of other UEs get lost due to insufficient resources.

4.2.3 Fairness Index

The fairness of the approaches is evaluated by the Jain's fairness index [20]. In our context, fairness index can be calculated as:

$$\mathbf{F}(\mathbf{res}_1, \mathbf{res}_2, \ldots \mathbf{res}_n) = \frac{\left(\sum_{j=1}^{n} \mathbf{res}_j\right)^2}{n \times \sum_{j=1}^{n} (\mathbf{res}_j)^2}$$

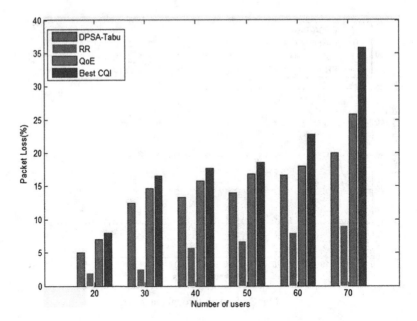

Fig. 9. Packet Loss Rate

Where n the total number of UEs and res_j is the number of resources assign to UE j. Jain's fairness index returns a value between 0 and 1, 1 represents the highest fairness in the system.

Figure 10 shows the results of fairness for the schedulers RR, Best CQI, QoE and DPSA-Tabu. The maximum Jain's fairness index is obtained by an RR scheduler. This is normal because the RR assigns RBs cyclically so that the same throughput is guaranteed for all UEs. The simulation results show that DPSA-Tabu attained

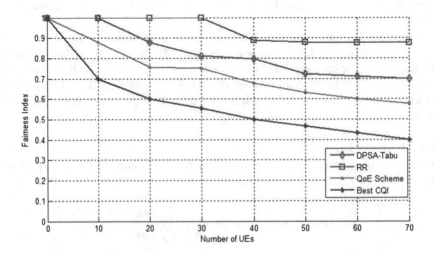

Fig. 10. Fairness index

interesting results compared to RR scheme. The QoE Scheme is in third position: it tries to increase the user perception (MOS) while considering the throughput requirement of RT users.

The Best CQI has a low fairness index compared to RR, QoE and DPSA-Tabu because the UEs that will receive resources are those with the best channel conditions.

4.2.4   Served Users

Figure 11 shows the served users by the DPSA-Tabu scheduler. It is clearly observed that this proposed scheduler serves an interesting number of UEs among the total number: in each TTI, the DPSA-Tabu serves most of GBR packets and gives them all their requirements.

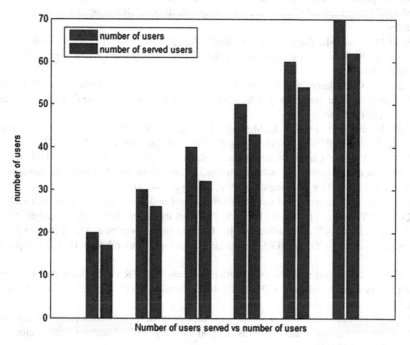

Fig. 11. Served users by DPSA-Tabu

5   Conclusion

In this paper, we proposed a novel scheduling algorithm named DPSA-Tabu. The DPSA-Tabu aims to maximize the system's sum throughput, to allow a fair distribution of available RBs and to handle GBR and NGBR traffic in LTE downlink systems. The performance of this algorithm is evaluated, considering LTE configuration parameters. The System performance was evaluated using simulations. The Simulation results prove that the DPSA-Tabu allows a better distribution of available RBs between the UEs while at the same time keeping the system's capacity utilization as good as possible. As a future work, we propose to further focus on evaluating QoS parameters for multimedia traffic and handle this algorithm in an LTE-A environment.

References

1. LTE; Evolved Universal Terrestrial Radio Access Access (E-UTRA); LTE physical layer; General description (3GPP TS 36.201 version 11.1.0 Release 11), February 2013
2. 3GPP. E-UTRA and E-UTRAN overall description, Stage 2, TS 36.300 V8.10.0, (2009)
3. 3GPP. Evolved Universal Terrestrial Radio Access (E-UTRA): Physical Channels and Modulation TS 136 211 V11.5.0, January 2014
4. LTE; Evolved Universal Terrestrial Radio Access (E-UTRA) and Evolved Universal Terrestrial Radio Access Network (E-UTRAN); Overall description; Stage 2 3GPP TS 36.300 version 11.7.0 Release 11, September 2013
5. Ramli, H.A.M., Basukala, R., Sandrasegaran, K., Patachaianand, R.: Performance of well known packet scheduling algorithms in the downlink 3GPP LTE system. In: IEEE 9th Malaysia International Conference on Communications (MICC), pp. 815–820, December 2009
6. Sajid Mushtaq, M., Augustin, B., Mellouk, A.: QoE-based LTE downlink Scheduler for VoIP. In: Wirless Communications and Networking Conference (WCNC), pp. 2190–2195. IEEE (2014)
7. Lee, S., Choudhury, S., Khoshnevis, A., Xu, S., Lu, S.: Downlink MIMO with frequency-domain packet scheduling for 3GPP LTE. In: INFOCOM 2009, pp. 1269–1277. IEEE (2009)
8. Sajid Mushtaq, M., Fowler, S., Mellouk, A., Augustin, B.: QoE/QoS-aware LTE downlink scheduler for VoIP with power saving. J. Netw. Comput. Appl. 51, 29–46 (2014)
9. Lin, Y., Yue G.: Channel-adapted and buffer-aware packet scheduling in LTE wireless communication system. In: 4th International Conference on Wireless Communications, Networking and Mobile Computing (WiCOM), pp. 1–4, October 2008
10. Delgado, O., Jaumard, B.: Joint admission control and resource allocation with GoS and QoS in LTE uplink. In: IEEE GLOBECOM Workshops, pp. 829–933, December 2010
11. Jha, S.C., Koç, A.T., Vannithamby, R.: Optimization of optimization of mobile internet applications over LTE. In: IEEE Vehicular Technology Conference (VTC Fall), September 2012
12. LTE; Evolved Universal Terrestrial Radio Access (E-UTRA); Medium Access Control (MAC) protocol specification (3GPP TS 36.321 version 9.3.0 Release 9), ETSI TS136 321 (2010)
13. Capozzi, F., Piro, G., Grieco, L.A., Boggia, G., Camarda, P.: Downlink packet scheduling in LTE cellular networks: key design issues and a survey. IEEE Commun. Surv. Tutorials 15 (2), 678–700 (2013)
14. Khdhir, R., Mnif, K., Kamoun, L., Nuaymi, L.: New scheduling algorithm for Uplink LTE System. In: International Symposium on Network Computing (ISNCC) (2014)
15. Suk-Bok, L., Pefkianakis, L, Meyersonand, A, Xu, S., Songwu, L.: Proportional fair frequency-domain packet scheduling for 3gpp LTE. In: INFOCOM, pp. 2611–2615. IEEE (2009)
16. Laguna, M., Barnes, J., Glover, F.: Intelligent scheduling with tabu search: An application to jobs with linear delay penalties and sequence dependent setup costs and times. J. Appl. Intell. 3, 159–172 (1993)
17. Pilegaard Hansen, M.: Tabu search for multiobjective optimization: Mots. In: MCDM 1997, Cape Town, pp. 6–10, January 1997
18. Technical specification group radio access networks – Deployment aspects. 3GPP TR 25.943

19. Haidar, S., El-Hajj, W., Tohme, K.: A QoS-aware uplink scheduling paradigm for LTE network. In: International Conference on Advanced Information Networking and Applications, pp. 1097–1104. IEEE (2013)
20. Jain, R., Chiu, D.M., Hawe, W.: A Quantitative Measure of Fairness and Discrimination for Resource Allocation in Shared Systems, Technical report TR-301, DEC Research Report (1984)

Online Charging Based on Machine Context for M2M Communication in LTE

Ranko Maric, Tomislav Grgic$^{(\boxtimes)}$, Maja Matijasevic, and Ignac Lovrek

University of Zagreb, Faculty of Electrical Engineering and Computing,
Unska 3, 10000 Zagreb, Croatia
{ranko.maric,tomislav.grgic,maja.matijasevic,ignac.lovrek}@fer.hr
http://www.fer.unizg.hr

Abstract. Efficient management of scarce access network resources for growing volume of Machine-to-Machine (M2M) communications play an important role in a Long Term Evolution (LTE) network. Understanding the communication requirements of machine-to-machine (M2M) services, and linking them to technical, as well as economic aspects, is a crucial step towards "smarter" charging of such services. We discuss the capabilities of M2M services to postpone their communication in LTE's core network, called the Evolved Packet Core (EPC), to avoid times when usage of network resources would be expensive (e.g., while the network is congested). We introduce a context of a group of machines, which describes the postponement capabilities of M2M communication, which is used as an input to the online charging process. We illustrate the proposed approach and its benefits using a smart home M2M service as an example.

1 Introduction

The range of potential applications for machine-to-machine (M2M) communications is huge – from wireless sensors and phones to emerging smart infrastructures for transport, utilities, health, and smart cities. The main elements of M2M communication include a set of "(M)achines", a wireless network, and an M2M application entity (AE), typically a remote server, where all the data gathered by the machine are stored and processed. The amount of data globally transmitted between the machines and respective AEs is steadily increasing. By the year 2018, global mobile M2M traffic is expected to reach 900 TB per month (compared to 50 TB per month in 2013) [2]. With other mobile traffic also growing fast, at an estimated annual rate of 61 %, mobile network operators (MNOs) will continue to struggle to use (and to monetize as well) the available capacity as efficiently as possible. This includes two parallel and interrelated goals: first, to alleviate peak network traffic during "rush hours", and second, to keep their customers happy by providing an adequate quality of service (QoS) to M2M users and M2M service providers, even if/when the network is congested.

For M2M services, such as smart metering or home energy consumption management, understanding the communication requirements, and linking them to

© Springer International Publishing Switzerland 2015
M.C. Aguayo-Torres et al. (Eds.): WWIC 2015, LNCS 9071, pp. 18–31, 2015.
DOI: 10.1007/978-3-319-22572-2_2

technical, as well as economic aspects, is a must. One mechanism that does that is based on dynamic congestion-based pricing plans, meaning that the network traffic sent through the mobile network while the network is congested is charged at a higher rate [9,18]. Congestion-based pricing plans are particularly suitable for M2M services (or classes of services) that have deterministic or foreseeable communication requirements [19]. What the current 3GPP online charging system (OCS), which is responsible for real-time cost calculation and service authorization, does not take into account (by design) are the communication requirements and the contextual situation of M2M services that are being charged [13], nor do the OCS implements the mechanisms for "smarter" authorization of services given their context.

In this paper, we aim to explore the idea of online charging based on machine context for M2M communications in LTE Evolved Packet Core (EPC) network, and probe further by proposing a (very preliminary) specification for an application-specific context of a (set of) machine(s) involved in M2M service provisioning. For example, we envision that smart meters that periodically measure some non-critical environmental parameters, and send their readings to an AE regardless of network conditions (high/low tariff), could be "instructed" by the M2M application to postpone sending their readings to a time when the network is no longer congested (at low tariff). In this scenario, the desired outcome for an MNO would be to reduce the peak network load during critical times (with M2M service providers tending to minimize own cost and avoid sending data at high tariff, given that choice), as well as to better utilize its own scarce resources while accommodating the needs of M2M service providers (and end-users). As opposed to existing scheduling schemes in LTE that manage network resources at physical and data link layers [7,14], in our approach the application decides whether to postpone the communication or not.

While this high-level concept is quite clear, there are many open issues that are not covered by related work, nor emerging standards (specifically, the 3GPP Machine-Type Communications [1] and the recent oneM2M Candidate Release, August 2014 [3,4]). The M2M service context proposed in this paper is a possible first step. It refers to a group of machines used jointly for a certain purpose (i.e., M2M service), wherein the communication requirements and context of each machine in the group (e.g., above-mentioned postponement capability) affect the context of the whole group. The online charging system considers the context of a group, and determines whether to authorize the communication or not for each machine in the group. A context monitoring mechanism is also introduced, which notifies the charging process on M2M communication postponement capabilities in a given point of time.

The rest of the paper is structured as follows. Section 2 summarizes the related work, and Sect. 3 presents the communication requirements of M2M services. Section 4 introduces the idea of M2M service context and describes its use in online charging. Section 5 presents an example, and Sect. 6 concludes the paper.

2 Related Work

A large-scale measurement and characterization of cellular M2M traffic [19] shows that the M2M traffic exhibits diurnal patterns in which M2M traffic peaks correspond to working hours (and thus to intensive smartphone usage), and that the machines are more likely to generate synchronized traffic resulting in bursty aggregate traffic volumes. To alleviate traffic peaks, many M2M scheduling mechanisms have been proposed in the physical layer, such as, a protocol extension of the Random Access Procedure in LTE [8], Physical Resource Block-based scheduling framework [10], or a scattering-based load balancing technique [5]. Although these solutions improve the performance of an LTE access network in cases of M2M communication during congestion times, and may reduce the price of the network resources used, they do not consider a broader context in which the M2M communication takes place. In our approach, however, we consider the context of the respective M2M communications, and represent it as a dynamically changing set of QoS requirements. For the purposes of this work, we use the QoS-based classification of machines that has been proposed in [16].

A key benefit of our approach, compared to the approaches focused only on the physical layer in LTE, is twofold. First, the postponement time of the M2M communication is not limited by the technical constraints of the physical layer in LTE, and second, the goal of postponement (in general case) may be not only to alleviate traffic peaks, but also to achieve more complex application-level goals (e.g., to allow the machines to communicate only during the cheapest daily tariff). Existing literature already offers solutions that partially consider M2M application requirements in charging (e.g., an auction-based traffic management scheme [15], or the Smart Data Pricing approach [18]), but they require an additional software to be installed on the machines (which our approach does not).

This work utilizes the well-known concept of congestion-based pricing [9,18], which enables charging of network resources by using a higher tariff when the network is congested, and by using a normal tariff otherwise. An example is the Network Load Based Pricing Scheme [17] in LTE, in which network congestion is determined by a threshold parameter, expressed as a certain percentage of the maximum network load. Although congestion-based pricing schemes have shown to help alleviate peaks in network traffic, they also must be followed with charging mechanisms that would (for the benefit of the user) in some cases reject new connections in congestion times to save users' budget. An example of such mechanism is proposed in the charging context model, which we proposed in our previous work [11,12]. The model of charging context is in this work further extended to encompass the specific requirements of an M2M communication (e.g., a discussion on which information encompasses the charging context in case of M2M communication).

To summarize, this work fills the gaps which are missing in the related work: it relates each machine with a maximum postponement time that matches the machine's communication context; it manages the network congestion by postponing the traffic generated by the machines (when possible, and if economically justified), without the need to install any additional software on the machines;

and it combines the characteristics of the known congestion based pricing schemes with the M2M communication characteristics, which ultimately enables "smarter" online charging of M2M services.

3   M2M Communication Requirements

For the purposes of this paper, the term *M2M communication* refers to a data transmission that takes place between a respective machine and an M2M Application Entity (AE), which represents an entity (usually a remote server) where all the data gathered by the machine are stored and processed.

3.1   Description of Communication Requirements of Machines

We adopt a QoS-based classification of communication requirements of machines, initially proposed in [16]. The parameters used for classification are the following:

- A requirement for *real-time communication*, which denotes whether an M2M communication should be carried out in real time or it may be postponed;
- A requirement for *accuracy*, which denotes the tolerance for maximum packet loss rate in the M2M communication observed; and,
- A requirement for *priority*, which marks how packets belonging to the M2M communication should be handled in MNO nodes in periods of network congestion.

A combination of those parameters determines communication requirements of a machine at a certain point of time. Based on those parameters, communication requirements of machines are categorized into four classes (Table 1): *Mobile Streaming*, *Smart Metering*, *Regular Monitoring*, and *Emergency Alerting*, as described next.

Mobile Streaming class communication requirements require low packet delay, have high demand for priority, and have low requirement for accuracy. Typical machines that have such communication requirements are audio and/or video streaming devices (e.g., surveillance cameras). They usually consume most of the bandwidth for data transmission, compared to other types of machines. For example, data transmission of a high definition video stream would require up to several Mbits per second data rate. Smart Metering class communication requirements have high demand for accuracy, and have low requirements in terms of real-time communication and priority. High demand for accuracy is needed as any data transmission errors could result in delivering incorrect data to the AE. Typical machines that have such communication requirements include smart metering machines (e.g., for electricity, for water, or for gas). Most smart metering machines communicate on an on-demand basis. Data does not need to be sent immediately upon request, although the metered value may be associated with a fixed timestamp and stored locally in the machine, waiting to be sent. Therefore, fairly large delays in data transmission can be tolerated.

Regular Monitoring class communication requirements have low demands for all the observed parameters. Machines with such communication requirements are usually used for remote control, as well as for monitoring and automation of remote processes. Such machines usually send/receive very small amounts of data, such as, short control and signaling messages. The data may be transmitted either periodically or on demand. Since the transmitted data is usually several tens of bytes in size, loss rate of one in thousand packets is tolerable. Finally, in this class, the M2M communication may be executed in near real-time. Emergency Alerting class communication requirements have high demands for all the observed parameters. Machines with such communication requirements are used for detection of and alerting in emergency situations (security cameras, gas leaking sensors, etc.). Therefore, these machines may generate varying amounts of data (e.g. alarm device would typically send short signaling messages, while a security camera would typically transmit a continuous video signal). Priority of such communication is high, as data needs to be transmitted within a shortest possible time frame, and this has to be done as accurately as possible.

Table 1. Classes of communication requirements of machines

	Mobile streaming	Smart metering	Regular monitoring	Emergency alerting
Real-time communication	High	Low	Low	High
Accuracy	Low	High	Low	High
Priority	High	Low	Low	High

To summarize, it should be noted that any given machine may have different communication requirements in different contexts. For example, a gas meter would have *Smart Metering* communication requirement if the consumption of gas is within a predefined "normal" range, but it may switch to *Emergency Alerting* if the gas consumption exceeds a certain value.

3.2 Discussion on M2M Communication Postponement Capabilities

In general, a potential capability to postpone M2M communication depends on the technical, economic, and contextual constraints (Fig. 1). Technical constraints are determined by a machine's capability to locally save the data to be transmitted, that is, while the M2M communication is delayed. We state t_t as a maximum time the data may be stored in the machine's local memory. For example, t_t for a video camera would be determined by buffer size, and that of a metering machine by its memory size, both referring to the maximum recording time that can be stored on a machine. Economic constraints relate to the question of whether it would pay off (either to an MNO or to a person/entity who pays for the M2M communication) to postpone the M2M communication.

It is expressed as t_e, which is a maximum time an M2M communication may be postponed given the economic constraints. For example, if the M2M communication is to be initiated while the network is congested, meaning at a higher price per bit (in congestion based tariff model), it could be estimated that postponing the M2M communication (until the congestion is over) by a certain time interval would be economically justified. Contextual constraint is determined by the very communication requirements of the machine observed, in a given situation. It is expressed as t_c, which is a maximum time to postpone the M2M communication given the machine's current communication requirements. For example, a surveillance camera in a smart home would normally have *Mobile Streaming* communication requirements, which would allow fairly large delays, but if there is an emergency situation at home (e.g., a fire), the camera would switch to *Emergency Alerting* communication requirements, which would require the lowest delay possible.

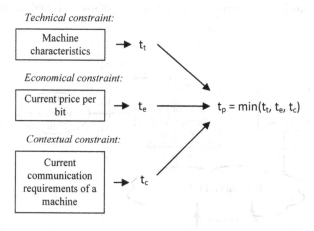

Fig. 1. Technical, economic, and contextual constraints of M2M communication

In general, each machine may be associated with its own t_t, t_e, and t_c parameters, while t_e and t_c may dynamically change while the machine is in use (t_t is in this model considered as a constant for each machine). At the observed point of time, a maximum time to postpone an M2M communication t_p is the minimum value of the t_t, t_e, and t_p current values, $min(t_t, t_e, t_c)$ (Fig. 1). This may result in dynamic changes of the t_p parameter for each machine as well, which would result in different delays (or no delay at all) to be used to postpone the machine's M2M communication at different points of time.

The next step is to determine a relation between the online charging process and the "smart" communication postponement. We elaborate on this issue in the next section.

4 A Model of an M2M Service Context for Online Charging

The term "M2M Service" is used to describe an application logic for providing a certain service to a user, by using a group of machines $m_1, m_2, ..., m_p$ and an AE. Machines use MNO's access network to connect to the AE through the EPC (assuming that the AE is situated outside of the MNO's domain), as shown in Fig. 2. The observed M2M communications are established between each machine and the AE. Next, the MNO runs an M2M Server which is responsible for monitoring the M2M Service Context and for coordinating processes of online charging with the OCS, as described later. AE communicates with the M2M Server by using an Application Programming Interface (API), while other functions communicate by using standard Diameter-based reference points (Gy, Ro, and Mc). This functional architecture is in accordance with the standard oneM2M architecture [3, 4]. M2M server in this case would stand as an M2M Common Service in a standard architecture, having the operator-controlled communication model [1].

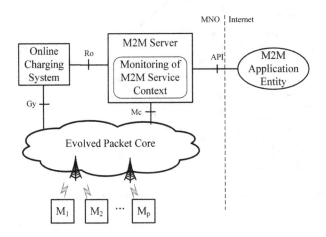

Fig. 2. A reference architecture for M2M service context model

4.1 Specification of M2M Service Context

The M2M Service Context refers to the capabilities of machines to postpone the respective M2M communications, given the contextual constraints explained earlier. In general, t_c of each machine may dynamically change due to the changes in communication requirements of other machines. Therefore, we represent the M2M Service Context as a Moore Finite-State-Machine (FSM), where each FSM-state represents an unique combination of communication requirements of machines, and hence represents a unique set of machines' t_c values. A transition between two states is triggered by a change of communication requirements of one or more machines. The formal notation of the FSM, used to model the M2M Service Context, is given next:

- M: $\{m_1, m_2, \ldots, m_p\}$ – a group of p machines;
- S: $\{s_1, s_2, \ldots, s_n\}$ – a finite set of n FSM-states, where s_1 is the initial FSM-state;
- Σ: $\{\sigma_{kl}\}, k \in [1, 2, \ldots, x], l \in [1, 2, \ldots, p]$ – input alphabet, where each letter represents one communication requirement of one machine;
- x – a number of communication requirements of each machine;
- T: $S \times \Sigma \to S$ – a transition function, which switches to the next FSM-state given the previous FSM-state and the input letter;
- Λ: $\{t_{cij}\}, i \in [1, 2, \ldots, n], j \in [1, 2, \ldots, p]$ – output alphabet, where each letter represents current t_c of each machine; and,
- G: $S \to \Lambda$ – a group of output functions that map FSM-states to outputs as follows:

$$g_1 : s_1 \to \{t_{c11}, t_{c12}, \ldots, t_{c1p}\} - \text{output function for } s_1;$$

$$\vdots$$

$$g_n : s_n \to \{t_{cn1}, t_{cn2}, \ldots, t_{cnp}\} - \text{output function for } s_n.$$

As each machine establishes an M2M communication with the AE regardless of other machines, each machine will be charged by using a separate online charging process. However, the proposed model of M2M Service Context allows t_c for each machine to be determined based on the current FSM-state (and thus based on the communication requirements of other machines).

4.2   Using M2M Service Context in Online Charging

The OCS could use the M2M Service Context to decide whether to authorize an M2M communication or not (e.g., the OCS might reject M2M communication if current communication requirement of a machine would allow postponement, and if price per bit is currently above the acceptable level from the perspective of a user of the M2M service). To do so, M2M Service Context has to be monitored while the M2M Service is in use (and while the respective M2M communications are being charged). We consider the monitoring process of M2M Service Context to run at the M2M Server (Fig. 2). (The monitoring process for context-based charging has been introduced as a concept in our past works as a part of the context-based charging model. For further information, an interested reader is referred to [11, 13].) The monitoring process is responsible for the following:

- Maintaining the current FSM-state of a group of machines;
- Changing to a new state if communication requirements of at least one machine in the group have changed; and,
- Informing the online charging process (upon request) whether to authorize an M2M communication or not.

Based on the current communications requirements of machines and on the analysis of the data that the machines send, the M2M AE maintains and regularly updates the M2M Service Context and the t_t values for each machine. The MNO's M2M Server is updated by the M2M AE in real time with t_t parameters and any changes in the M2M Service Context.

Two key interaction scenarios between the respective entities are shown in Figs. 3 and 4. Figure 3 shows a situation in which a machine requests an M2M communication from a relevant Service Provisioning Function (SPF) in EPC (1), and the M2M communication is granted on request (7). The M2M communication request (1) triggers the SPF to request authorization of the M2M communication (2). This would next trigger the OCS to indicate to the M2M Server the current value of t_e (if such value is available or may be determined at the OCS), and to request the M2M communication postponement (3). The monitoring process at the M2M Server determines that no postponement is needed or possible (based on t_p calculation, Fig. 1) (4, 5). Following this, the OCS authorizes the communication (6, 7).

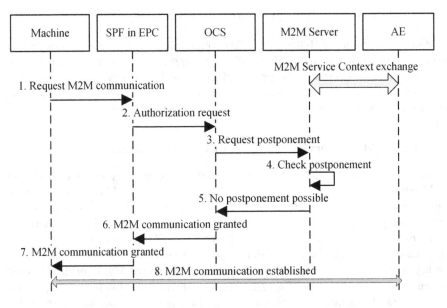

Fig. 3. Interaction between entities in case the requested M2M communication is not postponed

Figure 4 shows a situation in which a machine requests an M2M communication (1), which is followed by authorization requests that are performed in the same way as in the previous case (2, 3), but the M2M communication is denied (6, 7) based on a postponement decision at the M2M Server (3–5). After the M2M communication is denied, the monitoring process sends the current t_p value to the machine (8). This value is used to initiate a timer at the machine.

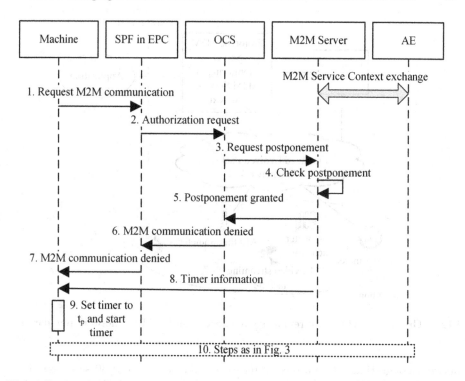

Fig. 4. Interaction between entities in case the requested M2M communication is postponed

Once the timer expires, the machine would attempt to establish the M2M communication again, which results in granting the M2M communication (assuming that the reason for the delay is no longer there).

5 Example: M2M Service for Smart Home

We illustrate the proposed model using a smart home heating M2M service as an example. A user has subscribed to a "smart home" M2M service, which allows the service provider to remotely control and operate the central heating equipment installed in the user's home. The following machines are considered (Fig. 5): (1) a gas meter, since in this example gas is used for heating; (2) a heater actuator, which is used to remotely turn the heater on and off; (3) a video streaming machine, which is used for home security video surveillance (of, e.g., home entrance); and (4) a thermometer, which measures current temperature in the home. All the above machines are remotely operated by an AE located in the Internet. All the machines have Internet access enabled over an LTE EPC network, which charges the M2M service provider for the traffic generated by each machine, by using a congestion-based tariff model. (In our initial laboratory prototype we use emulated sensors and emulated EPC network with periods of

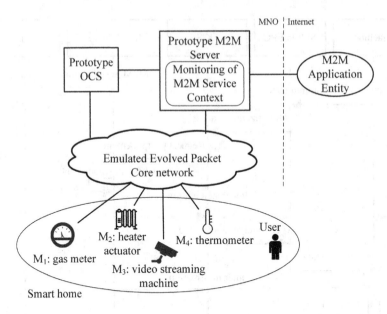

Fig. 5. Group of machines for remote surveillance in an LTE EPC network (emulation)

network congestion set to 5-second intervals that occur every 30 seconds). The "smart home" M2M service maintains a set temperature in the home, but is also designed to recognize potentially dangerous situations, like gas leak (or, gas flow above acceptable level, which would, for example, trigger the M2M service to shut down the heater).

In the above scenario, it is of interest of the M2M service provider to pay as little as possible for the M2M communication, which occurs between the machines and the AE. Therefore, the M2M communications should be postponed during network congestion when possible. To do so, the M2M service utilizes the M2M Service Context. The M2M Service Context encompasses three FSM-states (s_1, s_2, and s_3), as depicted in Fig. 6. Each FSM-state represents one combination of communication requirements of the group of machines. FSM-states s_2 and s_1 distinguish between the situations in which the user is at home or he/she is not, respectively, but in both cases gas readings are normal. (The M2M Service may ascertain user's absence by, e.g., analyzing the readings from the video streaming machine). FSM-state s_3 describes a situation in which the gas reading is above a normal level. In each FSM-state, each machine is associated with a t_{cij} value, where i represents the state and j represents the machine. For example, thermometer readings may be postponed for 30 min if the user is absent, for 1 min if the user is at home, or the reading could not be postponed at all in s_3 (gas leak – immediate response is required). (It should be noted that the t_c values in this example are for illustration purposes only.) A transition from s_1 to s_2 (and vice versa) is triggered by a change in communication requirements of M_3 (i.e., the M2M service concludes the user has come home, and increases

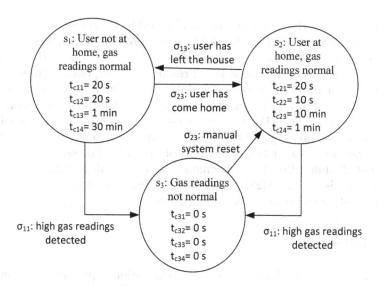

Fig. 6. M2M Service Context of the group of machines: states and transitions

M_3's t_c value from 1 min to 10 min due to the fact that there are less demands for real-time surveillance when the user is at home). Similarly, transitions from s_1 to s_3 and from s_2 to s_3 are triggered by a change in communication requirements of M_1. In this example, transition from s_3 to s_2 is triggered by a manual system reset, e.g., by a gas technician after fixing the gas system. (Transition from s_3 to s_1 is not allowed for the sake of safety - potential gas leakage must be inspected on-site by a technician, which is possible only if the user is at home.)

Our setup includes a prototype SPF in EPC, which is responsible for policy-based resource management and charging, a prototype OCS, which performs online charging, and a prototype M2M server, which monitors the M2M Service Context. The emulated machines are implemented in Java, and they are integrated with Policy Control 2.0, a software that emulates policy-based resource reservation mechanisms in LTE and provides a prototype functionality of the OCS and the M2M Server. Policy Control 2.0 has already been used in our previous works [11,13].

In our demonstration scenario we control the M2M communication of machines from the M2M Server, by granting the M2M communication or postponing it, based on the calculation of the t_p value given the current FSM-state and the t_e (technical constraints of machines were not considered in the demonstration). We use signaling scenarios presented in Figs. 3 and 4. In the cases when the communication is requested when network resources are expensive, the communication is postponed and attempted later (after the congestion is over or when t_p expires).

The demonstration shows the key benefit of utilizing the M2M Service Context in online charging: the decision whether to allow the communication or to postpone it, is made based on both the communication requirements of the group of machines, and on the economic constraint posed by the congestion-based tariff scheme. Therefore, it is left to the M2M Service provider to decide which M2M communication could be postponed and in which contextual situations it could be done, and in times when the network resources are expensive. Moreover, the machines do not have to use the same sink to establish a communication with the M2M AE, nor does their relative geographical locations compromise the ability to maintain the M2M Service Context of the entire group of machines. Finally, the model provides the M2M AE with an ability to generate and change the M2M Service Context based on the application-level decisions of the M2M service, but the full utilization of the model can only be done within the MNO's network (that is, at the M2M Server), where economical constraint is added up to the postponement decision making process.

6 Conclusion

Any given machine may have different communication requirements in different contextual situations. Such situations mostly depend on the application logic of an M2M Service, which would in some cases tolerate postponing a certain M2M communication. By combining the contextual constraint with other relevant constraints of M2M communication (that is, technical and economic), we used a resource authorization capability of an online charging system to "smartly" manage M2M communications in cases when postponement would pay off for both the MNO and the M2M service user. The M2M service management has been realized on a group of machines by monitoring the M2M Service Context (which is represented as a FSM), where each FSM-state reflects a unique combination of postponement capabilities of the machines in the group.

A next step in our research will be to design a simulation model based on the M2M service context, in order to evaluate model performance. We plan to utilize one of the existing M2M context management platforms (e.g., [6]) in the standard M2M architecture [1], and compare the performance of our approach with the related work [15,18].

Acknowledgment. The research leading to these results has received funding from the project "Information and communication technology for generic and energy-efficient communication solutions with application in e-/m health (ICTGEN)" co-financed by the European Union from the European Regional Development Fund.

References

1. 3GPP 22.368: Service requirements for Machine-Type Communications (MTC) (2014)
2. Cisco visual networking index: Global mobile data traffic forecast update, pp. 2013–2018, February 2014
3. oneM2M TS 0001: oneM2M functional architecture (2015)
4. oneM2M TS 0002: oneM2M requirements (2015)

5. Chang, C.W., Chen, J.C., Chen, C., Jan, R.H.: Scattering random-access intensity in LTE Machine-to-Machine (M2M) communications. In: IEEE Globecom Workshops, pp. 4729–4734, December 2013

6. Chihani, B., Bertin, E., Crespi, N.: Enhancing M2M communication with cloud-based context management. In: 6th International Conference on Next Generation Mobile Applications, Services and Technologies (NGMAST), pp. 36–41, September 2012

7. Ghavimi, F., Chen, H.H.: M2M communications in 3GPP LTE/LTE-A networks: Architectures, service requirements, challenges and applications. IEEE Communications Surveys Tutorials to appear (2014)

8. Giluka, M., Prasannakumar, A., Rajoria, N., Tamma, B.: Adaptive RACH congestion management to support M2M communication in 4G LTE networks. In: IEEE International Conference on Advanced Networks and Telecommuncations Systems (ANTS), pp. 1–6, December 2013

9. Gizelis, C., Vergados, D.: A survey of pricing schemes in wireless networks. IEEE Commun. Surv. Tutorials 13(1), 126–145 (2011)

10. Gotsis, A., Lioumpas, A., Alexiou, A.: M2M scheduling over LTE: Challenges and new perspectives. IEEE Veh. Technol. Mag. 7(3), 34–39 (2012)

11. Grgic, T.: Online Charging for Services in Communication Network based on User-related Context. Ph.D. thesis, University of Zagreb, Faculty of Electrical Engineering and Computing, April 2013

12. Grgic, T., Matijasevic, M.: 'Smarter' online charging for over-the-top services by introducing user context. In: Proceedings of 5th Joint IFIP Wireless and Mobile Networking Conference, pp. 81–87, September 2012

13. Grgic, T., Matijasevic, M.: An overview of online charging in 3GPP networks: New ways of utilizing user, network, and service-related information. Int. J. Netw. Manage. 23, 81–100 (2013)

14. Lien, S.Y., Chen, K.C., Lin, Y.: Toward ubiquitous massive accesses in 3GPP machine-to-machine communications. IEEE Commun. Mag. 49(4), 66–74 (2011)

15. Lin, G.Y., Wei, H.Y.: A multi-period resource auction scheme for machine-to-machine communications. In: IEEE International Conference on Communication Systems (ICCS), pp. 177–181, November 2014

16. Liu, R., Wu, W., Zhu, H., Yang, D.: M2M-oriented QoS categorization in cellular network. In: 7th International Conference on Wireless Communications, Networking and Mobile Computing (WiCOM), pp. 1–5, September 2011

17. Mir, U., Nuaymi, L.: LTE pricing strategies. In: 77th IEEE Vehicular Technology Conference, pp. 1–6, June 2013

18. Sen, S., Joe-Wong, C., Ha, S., Chiang, M.: Smart data pricing (SDP): Economic solutions to network congestion. In: Haddadi, H., Bonaventure, O. (eds.) Recent Advances in Networking, vol. 1, pp. 221–274 (2013)

19. Shafiq, M., Ji, L., Liu, A., Pang, J., Wang, J.: Large-scale measurement and characterization of cellular Machine-to-Machine traffic. IEEE/ACM Trans. Network. 21(6), 1960–1973 (2013)

Cloud Computing-Based Message Dissemination Protocol for Vehicular Ad Hoc Networks

Salim Bitam[1](✉) and Abdelhamid Mellouk[2]

[1] LESIA Laboratory, Department of Computer Science,
University of Biskra, Biskra, Algeria
salim.bitam@laposte.net
[2] Image, Signal and Intelligent Systems Laboratory-LISSI,
Department of Networks and Telecoms, IUT C/V,
University of Paris-Est, Créteil, France
mellouk@u-pec.fr

Abstract. A Vehicular Ad Hoc Network (VANET) is a rapidly evolving field with growing 5th generation mobile networks and peer-to-peer services to deliver both safety and traffic benefits. However, message transmission in VANET suffers from several disadvantages such as the frequent intermittent connectivity because of high velocity of VANET vehicles and to their limited capacity in terms of bandwidth. To ensure reliable connectivity, we propose in this paper, a new message dissemination protocol for VANET based on cloud computing, called Cloud computing-based message Dissemination protocol for VANET (ClouDiV). Considered as a geographic protocol, ClouDiV provides an adaptive dissemination of safety and non-safety messages through a cloud computing architecture. Simulation results taken with ns-2 in realist urban settings showed that ClouDiV improves the connectivity performances criteria in spite of network size.

1 Introduction

Advances in wireless communication technologies have increasingly interested in smart vehicles equipped with communication capabilities, processing and computing devices, sensors, aiming to improve road safety (collision avoidance, driver assistance, emergency management, etc.) and to satisfy computational services requested by passengers with certain level of reliability, scalability, efficiency, and security. To support these challenges, several vehicular technology companies have provided many innovative vehicle services to the customers through a special kind of wireless mobile networks named Vehicular Ad-hoc Network (VANET). A VANET consists of a set of mobile nodes (i.e. Vehicles) and fixed nodes known as Roadside Units (RSUs). The two main functionalities of a VANET is to support communication between vehicles through Inter-Vehicle Communication (IVC) and between vehicles and RSUs through Vehicle-to-Roadside Communication (VRC), often using Global Positioning System (GPS) integrated into vehicles to facilitate location-based services [1].

© Springer International Publishing Switzerland 2015
M.C. Aguayo-Torres et al. (Eds.): WWIC 2015, LNCS 9071, pp. 32–45, 2015.
DOI: 10.1007/978-3-319-22572-2_3

Some of the important properties of VANET that affects communications is the high speed of the vehicles, limited computational capacities of onboard computers, area restrictions (such as buildings, tunnels, etc.), high congestion of channel due to the high density of vehicles in some roadways. Therefore, these properties lead to a network with intermittent transmissions, topology change, frequent fragmentation, and small effective diameter that make message dissemination a challenging task in this kind of networks [2].

To deal with this accidental connectivity, we propose in this study a new message dissemination protocol for VANET called Cloud computing-based message Dissemination protocol for VANET (ClouDiV). To the best of our knowledge, there is no cloud computing-based protocol which has been proposed for message dissemination in VANET, despite the few attempts at integrating cloud computing with vehicular networks. ClouDiV put the advantages of cloud computing available to forward data packets between VANET nodes in an efficient way, which improve safety and non-safety message transmissions according to various dissemination metrics. Also, digital requests of car drivers and passengers could be satisfied by the various cloud computing services such as processing, storage, and bandwidth.

Cloud computing is a new computing model consisted of a pool of physical compute resources such as processor, memory, and network bandwidth, potentially distributed physically across big servers known as data centers. The data centers can be organized on demand into a dynamic logical entity that can grow or shrink over time, to satisfy computational requests of end users including performance, reliability, cost, and security, usually through the Internet against a leased resource fee [3]. We note that the various vehicular devices such as onboard computers, passenger smartphones and, personal digital assistants could be considered as mobile data centers helping to provide more cloud services [4].

So that the transmission receives benefits from the Cloud, ClouDiV proposes that all available cloud resources namely, bandwidth of different end users (i.e. car drivers, passengers, traffic authorities, etc.) contribute to disseminate messages between VANET nodes. Mainly, ClouDiV is considered as a geographic protocol that disseminates messages through an adaptive connectivity process based on data centers of the cloud. Moreover, this protocol uses a particular kind of packet transmission known as stochastic broadcasting [5] when it launches the route discovery phase, which is in hybrid mode (proactive and reactive route discovery) as described below.

In order to validate this proposal, a set of ClouDiV simulation experiments are carried out in ns-2 [6] extended to the cloud computing infrastructure by the framework greencloud [7]. These experiments are compared with a reliable inter-vehicular routing protocol for vehicular ad hoc networks (RIVER) [8] in terms of average end-to-end delay, packet delivery ratio, and routing overhead.

The rest of this paper is organized as follows. In Sect. 2, we present an overview of the vehicular cloud computing. Section 3 reviews and discusses the existing studies in which the cloud computing has been applied to disseminate messages in vehicular networks. Section 4 describes the proposed protocol, followed by Sect. 5 that demonstrates the simulation study and depicts the results obtained by our solution, and compared to those reached by RIVER protocol. Finally, Sect. 6 concludes and outlines some future research directions.

2   Cloud Computing for VANET: Definition and Architecture

As introduced in [9], Cloud Computing for VANET (VANET-Cloud model) is defined as a new cloud computing infrastructure, consisted of an important number of computing nodes including stationary data centers, as well as a set of mobile computing devices installed onboard of vehicles such as onboard computers, passenger PDAs, onboard computers of traffic authorities, and so on. VANET-Cloud takes advantage of cloud computing resources and services to better serve VANET users (i.e. drivers and passengers) in terms of providing digital resources such as processing, storage, bandwidth, with very low cost.

As shown in Fig. 1, the VANET-Cloud model is formed by two sub-models: the permanent (stationary) cloud sub-model consisting of data centers, and the temporary (mobile) cloud sub-model that is composed of vehicles computing resources. On the one side, the permanent VANET-Cloud takes advantages of the conventional cloud and makes them available to VANET entities such as vehicles and RSUs. On the other side, the temporary VANET-Cloud renders the computing resources of VANETs such as onboard computers, passenger devices, and transportation servers, possible to a client against a rent price.

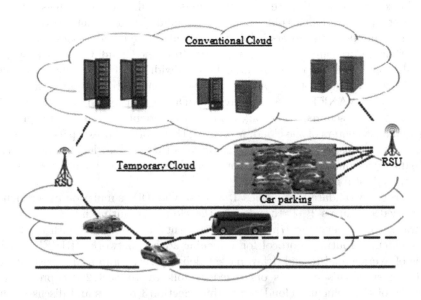

Fig. 1. VANET-cloud architecture

3   Related Work

Nowadays, some recent research works have proposed the use of the cloud computing to tackle with vehicular network issues.

Among these studies, we can cite a new routing scheme called VehiCloud [10], which is established to deal with unreliable inter-vehicle communications and to extend the restricted computational capabilities of vehicle devices using a cloud computing architecture. To ensure routing service, VehiCloud models the highly dynamic network topology as a time-space link graph taking into account a time dimension, lacked in a conventional network connectivity graph. This scheme proposed that each vehicle predicts its future locations by generating way point messages, which describe the trajectory of the vehicle's movement. These way point messages are collected by a decision module established on a cloud infrastructure that is responsible for making routing decisions for inter-vehicle communication. More specifically, this cloud-based module selects paths in terms of message delivery ratio by respecting the constraints of end-to-end delay and communication cost. We can suggest that further routing improvements could be brought if VehiCloud takes advantages of conventional cloud capabilities.

In [11], another issue has been addressed and solved by making use of the cloud computing infrastructure which is the seamless access to the Internet. To achieve this, a cloud-supported gateway model, named Gateway-as-a-Service (GaaS) was proposed to provide efficient gateway connectivity and to enhance the usage experience of Internet for vehicular networks. GaaS proposed that a specialized cloud servers are conceived to ensure the gateway functions including gateway registration, discovery, selection, dispatching, and handoff. Despite, this global functionality, GaaS focuses primarily on the Internet connection, and did not consider digital resources of vehicles.

The vehicular network literature mentions another vehicular cloud-based scheme called Vehicular Cloud (VC) model [12]. Defined as a new mobile cloud computing model, VC is formed by the aggregation of underutilized vehicles' computing resources such as processing, storage, sensors, Internet connectivity, which can be available to drivers or rented out over the Internet to different customers. A simulation study of VC has shown that increasing network density leads to a lower delay on the transmission. However, VC didn't take into consideration the effect of storage and its structure can be extended to take advantage of stationary cloud capabilities.

In [13], three major cloud entities were proposed: Vehicular Cloud (VC), Vehicles using Cloud (VuC), and Hybrid Cloud (HC). In this research activity, VC is divided into two scenarios: the former is a static cloud referring to stationary vehicles and providing cloud services, and the latter is a dynamic cloud, which is set up on demand in an ad hoc manner. Moreover, VuC allows the vehicular network to connect to the cloud through the RSUs, whereas, the HC is the combination of VC and VuC. It is worth mentioning that this proposal requires that the vehicle computing resources didn't belong to VC only if these vehicles are in a stationary state.

To deal with the human security issues of car drivers, authors of [14] proposed another cloud model called vehicular cloud (abbreviated V-Cloud). The architecture of V-cloud is a set of three vehicular network layers including in-car Vehicular Cyber-Physical System (VCPS) of sensors, Vehicle-to-Vehicle network (V2V), and Vehicle-to-Infrastructure network (V2I) layer. VCPS sensors are responsible for ensuring driver security by incorporating context awareness, healthcare monitoring and mood detection of the vehicle driver while driving. The authors concluded that V-Cloud can offer real-time services, aiming to improve drivers safety and comfort degree especially, in circumstance when driver is not healthy and comfortable enough to drive. In order to get quick responses to these critical cases, V-cloud could be expanded to take advantage of the computing devices installed onboard of vehicles.

A pure Cloud formed by vehicle computing components has been proposed in [15]. It is a new service concept known as Sensor as a Service (SenaaS) that put the components of vehicle communication platforms (VCPs) (such as sensors and computing devices) available to third-party vehicle monitoring applications. Despite the successful development of a SenaaS prototype over a VCP that supports real-time intelligent truck monitoring services on about one thousand tank trucks for fuel distribution, this study can offer more interesting results in the case of considering computing power of traditional cloud computing.

A new approach that exploits the use of a RSU as a cloud servers, was proposed in [3]. The authors proposed that a RSU can act as a cloud directory that stores information about the available computing resources of vehicles (e.g., bandwidth, storage capacity) in its transmission range. This scheme suggested that every RSU will share with its neighbor RSUs, the computing information of its vehicles, so that the operation area of the proposed cloud will be increased.

To provide safety and non-safety services in vehicular applications, Vehicular Cloud for Roadside scenario (VCR) was proposed in [16]. VCR offers these services through public and private vehicular clouds. The public vehicular cloud is a part of RSU, where the private one is formed by OnBoard Units (OBUs) of vehicles. To deploy VCR, the authors proposed that Google App Engine Cloud environment may be accessed as public services. Also, Java-based Universal Description, Discovery, and Integration (JUDDI) private registry was considered as the private vehicular cloud. VCR proposed that each vehicle sets up one JUDDI private registry to communicate with each other, so that the interoperability issue produced by different OBU systems (e.g., DSRC, Wi-Fi, WAVE, WiMaX, CALM) is solved. We note that VCR could be improved by allowing direct transmission between vehicles and traditional cloud servers.

4   Description of ClouDiV: Our Proposal

ClouDiV is a message dissemination protocol proposed for vehicular networks, based on a cloud computing architecture. ClouDiV combines the use a fixed cloud computing infrastructure (i.e. data centers) and a flexible cloud structure based on onboard computers of vehicles. Therefore, the computing powers of both permanent and temporary vehicular cloud structures can be available in benefit of various consumers by offering much higher bandwidth compared to message dissemination schemes based on pure vehicular network infrastructures.

In this proposal, we assume that the vehicular network is formed by different VANET nodes (i.e. vehicles and RSUs), as well as the various cloud servers (i.e. data centers) located in the traffic environment. ClouDiV is considered as a hybrid message dissemination protocol, where a proactive approach is suggested to be applied by each data center in order to discover fresh and updated routes toward each node in the network. Furthermore, a reactive approach is defined to be performed by each vehicle aiming to find the nearest data center as an intermediate node, which could quickly provide a fresh route toward the desired destination. In the following subsections, ClouDiV is explained, starting with the used routing tables, then the various ClouDiV phases are presented.

4.1 ClouDiV Routing Tables

Due to the distinction between used nodes in this dissemination approach (i.e. data centers and VANET nodes) in terms of functions, computing power, storage space, transmission bandwidth, we propose the use of two different types of routing tables: data center routing table and VANET node routing table. Each type implies the use of a particular kind of a routing process, as explained below.

4.1.1 Data Center Routing Table:

Owning to the stationary nature of the data center and its huge capacities of processing and storage, as well as its very large transmission range, we propose that each data center is equipped of a routing table consisted of a set of entries. Each entry is devoted to one destination node in the network, in which the entire route (from this data center to the destination) is saved. Moreover, various transmission parameters such as the average end-to-end delay and the average bandwidth are also memorized.

The data center performs periodically a proactive route discovery in order to update its routing table. Therefore, any future use of the saved routes does not be affected by an additional delay, caused by launching a new route discovery. Figure 2 shows an example of a vehicular network with two data centers, where routing table of data center DC1 is presented in Fig. 2a.

4.1.2 VANET Node Routing Table:

Each VANET node possesses its own routing table, which is consisted of a set of entries, each entry is dedicated to one destination (if requested) that can be a data center or a regular VANET node. More specifically, each entry contains the destination identifier and the identifier of next hop node toward the destination. The idea of saving the next hop instead of saving the entire route is to reduce the memory space of this routing table, since these nodes (onboard computers) possess limited computing resources. Also, each routing table entry includes the link delay and bandwidth information, a hop count field indicating the number

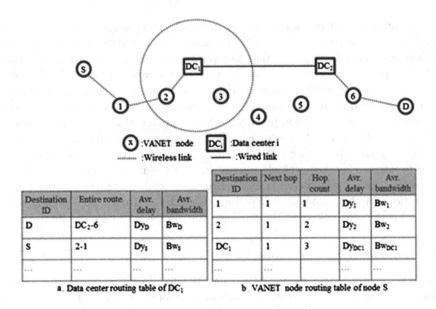

a. Data center routing table of DC₁   b. VANET node routing table of node S

Fig. 2. Data center and VANET node routing tables

of hops to reach the destination, which could be used to choose the shortest path if there is more than one path to the same destination. The routing table of node S is presented in Fig. 2b.

4.2 ClouDiV Message Dissemination Phases

4.2.1 Beaconing Phase

This phase aims to ensure an update of routing tables using beacon packets, transmitted periodically. As a result, active links between each VANET node and each data center are updated, by refreshing different transmission parameters such as the available bandwidth and the measured end-to-end delay. Also, routing information between VANET nodes is also saved and updated in order to perform a conventional routing (i.e. without the help of the cloud computing infrastructure) in the case of lacking data centers. We note that a link is marked as invalid in a routing table if a node does not get information from the nodes neighbor for a specified amount of time. Thus, the other nodes are informed of this unavailable link using an error packet.

4.2.2 Route Discovery Phase

When one node desires to disseminate messages to a destination, it first checks whether the route is present in its routing table, then the source node starts disseminating data packets, otherwise data packets are buffered until a valid route is discovered. To discover a route, two complementary processes are applied: a proactive routing and a reactive routing. The source node starts with a reactive

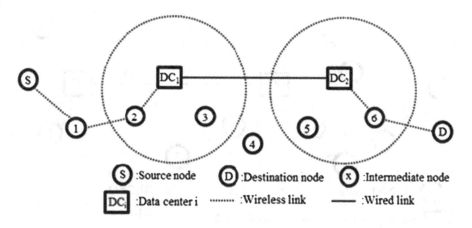

Fig. 3. ClouDiV routing processes

(on-demand) routing in order to find a data center. As shown in the example presented in Fig. 3, the source node S starts a reactive routing when it decides to disseminate messages to node D. Accordingly, path (S-1-2-DC1) is discovered. Afterwards, the data center DC1 uses the path (DC1-DC2-6-D) to reach the final destination D, which is discovered after performing a previous proactive routing.

a. ClouDiV Proactive Routing: This process is performed by each data center in the network aiming to find all routes from this data center toward every node in the network (supposed as a prospective future destination). Therefore, these routes can be used by any node in order to transmit data toward a destination via this data center. To achieve this, the data center generates a particular control packet called Routing Information REQuest (RI-REQ) aiming to gather different routing information concerning all nodes in the network, including the active links, next-hop node toward a destination, position and velocity of a node.

A RI-REQ is broadcasted periodically to the neighbor nodes of data center then, the neighbor node forwards this RI-REQ to its neighbors, except for neighbors which are data centers expected to conduct their own proactive routing process separately. Each node receives a RI-REQ, generates a new control packet named Routing Information REPly (RI-REP) containing the requested routing information, which is forwarded to the original data center (i.e. the sender) through the reverse route. In its turn, the data center refreshes its routing table entries with the received information hence the updated routes are ready to be used to disseminate messages toward any destination.

In Fig. 4, DC1 generates and broadcasts periodically a RI-REQ to its immediate neighbor nodes (i.e. nodes 3, 6, and DC2) then, each node rebroadcasts the same RI-REQ to its neighbors, except to DC2 that launches its own proactive routing separately. When a node received a RI-REQ, it generates a RI-REP and sends out it to DC1 to communicate its refreshed routing information such as the active links, nodes ID toward a destination, next-hop node toward this

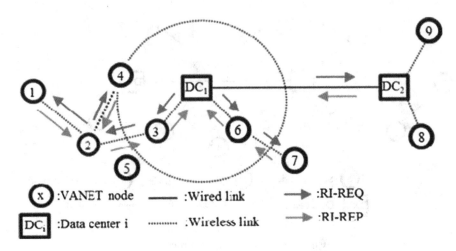

Fig. 4. ClouDiV proactive routing process

destination, the position and velocity of this node. After receiving all RI-REPs, DC1 updates its routing table and constructs entire routes toward various destinations. For example, to reach node 8, DC1 sends out data packets through the route (DC1-DC2-8).

b. ClouDiV Reactive Routing: To disseminate messages to a destination node, a Route REQuest packet (RREQ) is generated by the source node only if needed (on-demand). This RREQ is launched and broadcasted stochastically to the immediate neighbors of the source node in order to find a data center which knows the destination path. Stochastic broadcasting means that the RREQ is transmitted to a limited percentage of neighbor nodes that is enough to find a data center that knows the destination. This kind of broadcasting is applied to reduce the routing overhead caused by the control packet flooding [6].

The RREQ packet is identified by an identifier (ID) and includes the source node ID, the destination ID, and the maximum lifespan of the route request. Also, this packet records a hop count initialized with zero value and incremented while encountering an intermediate node until discovering the data center. Every encountered intermediate node checks also, if it has already received this RREQ packet (using the RREQ ID), if so, the RREQ will be dropped otherwise, this intermediate node records the RREQ ID and the source node ID in the appropriate routing table entry. Afterwards, the intermediate node checks the existence of a route toward a data center in its routing table. If it is not the case, the current node rebroadcasts the RREQ packet in the same manner such as the source node. However, if a route to a data center occurs in a routing table, the intermediate node generates a Route rePly packet (RREP) which will be forwarded to the source node along the same path in reverse.

Likewise, RREP packet records the next hop node at the routing table of each visited node to indicate its sender until reaching the source node. Consequently,

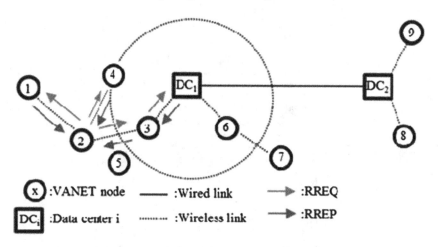

Fig. 5. ClouDiV reactive routing process

the source node can start disseminating data packets to the discovered data center through the next hop node found by ClouDiV reactive routing process. After that, the data center sends out these data packets to the final destination using the entire route found by ClouDiV proactive routing process.

Figure 5 shows a reactive routing process executed by node 2 that wants to disseminate data packets to node 8. First, node 2 generates and broadcasts a RREQ packet to its immediate neighbor nodes using a stochastic broadcasting. Here, we assume that only 3/4 of these neighbors receive the RREQ packet (i.e. nodes 1, 3, and 4) to perform a stochastic broadcasting. In its turn, each neighbor that received the RREQ and did not know the route to a data center, rebroadcasts this same RREQ packet to its neighbors, until reaching the first data center like DC1 in this example.

After reaching DC1, this data center generates a RREP and sends it out to node 2 along the reverse route. Hence, node 2 is informed that it could disseminate its data packets to node 3 as next hop node then, the node 3 can transmit data packets to DC1. After receiving data packets, DC1 can forward them to node 8 using the route (DC1-DC2-8) found by its last proactive routing process.

5   Performance Evaluation

To evaluate the performance of ClouDiV protocol, a set of simulations on urban scenarios have been conducted on the network simulator ns-2 [6], extended to the cloud computing infrastructure by the framework greencloud [7].

5.1   Mobility Model and Parameter Settings

To cope with the reality aspect of this simulation, we have developed a mobility pattern representing the downtown of Biskra city in Algeria with a surface area

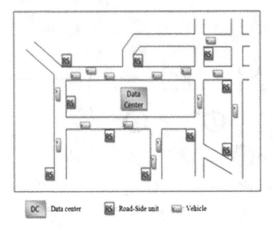

Fig. 6. Map of mobility scenario of the downtown of Biskra city

of 1500 × 1500 square meters, as presented in Fig. 6. In the studied network, two scenarios of 50 and 75 mobile nodes (vehicles) moving with a speed chosen randomly between 1 and 20 m/s are considered, as two different vehicular network densities. For each scenario, 10 RSUs distributed uniformly, as well as 1 data center located at the center of the studied area, with a transmission range of 1000 m and a transmission power of 16 dBm are introduced. The data center is based on a three-layer network with 1 switch in the core network, 2 switches in the aggregation network, and 3 switches in the access network. Moreover, 18 servers are physically attached to the access network with 1 Gigabyte/s of bandwidth.

According to IEEE 802.11p standard (Wireless Access in Vehicular Environments -WAVE-) proposed specifically for VANETs, these scenarios were simulated during 500 seconds, with the TwoRayGround propagation model. We have used the Transmission Control Protocol (TCP) as a transport layer protocol where a packet has a size of 1000 bytes. The number of bytes transmitted per second is fixed to 0.01 Mbytes. In this study, we have considered the File Transfer Protocol (FTP) as an application layer model with 25 vehicles act as source nodes whereas, the remaining vehicles constitute the destinations.

5.2   Significant Results and Discussion

In order to measure the quality of message dissemination in a vehicular network, ClouDiV is evaluated following the traffic safety metrics: the average end-to-end delay, the Packet Delivery Ratio (PDR), and the Normalized Overhead Load (NOL). These metrics are explained in [17]. We have compared the performance of our proposed with the Reliable Inter-VEhicular Routing (RIVER) protocol proposed for VANETs. Simulation results are depicted in Figs. 7, 8 and 9.

As shown in Fig. 7, ClouDiV disseminates data packets with a decreased end-to-end delay. It is due to the time saved by the proactive routing process

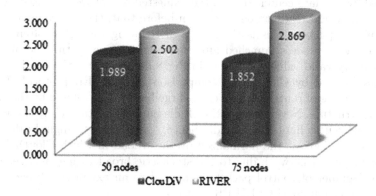

Fig. 7. Average end-to-end delay (seconds)

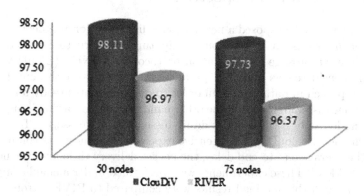

Fig. 8. Packet delivery ratio

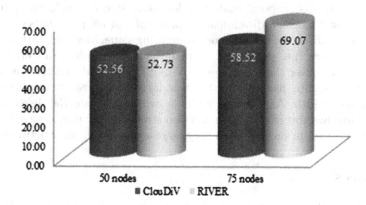

Fig. 9. Normlized overhead load

performed by the data center. In fact, the requested routes are still discovered by the data center and ready to be used, even before that, the source node desires to disseminate packets, this is the reason of reducing the delay, often caused by the discovery process launched after requesting a new path. The observed packet delivery ratio values presented in Fig. 8 demonstrates the good delivery of packets ensured by ClouDiV in comparison with RIVER protocol. This is because of the use of routes with an extra large bandwidth, offered by the cloud-based infrastructure. Nevertheless, RIVER disseminates data packets through an ordinary path with a limited bandwidth hence, several packets might be dropped. Figure 9 gives a look at the normalized overhead load in which ClouDiV leads to a non congested network due to the stochastic broadcasting that generates a reduced number of control packets compared to an exhaustive broadcasting process such as employed by RIVER protocol.

6   Conclusion and Perspectives

In this study, we have proposed a new message dissemination protocol for vehicular ad-hoc networks based on cloud computing infrastructure, called Cloud computing-based message Dissemination protocol for VANET (ClouDiV). This protocol is considered as a hybrid protocol that applies on the one hand, a proactive approach in data centers in order to discover routes ready for use in a future message dissemination. On the other hand, a reactive routing is applied by the other nodes, only if these nodes desire disseminating messages. To evaluate the performance of ClouDiV, an extensive experimental study was conducted in terms of the average end-to-end delay, the packet delivery ratio and, the normalized overhead load. These experiments were performed under a cloud computing infrastructure and the obtained results were compared to RIVER protocol proposed for vehicular networks.

We conclude that this study indicates clearly that ClouDiV provides a reduced end-to-end delay and, an increased packet delivery ratio. Moreover, message dissemination with this proposal leads to a less congested network. We note that this Cloud-based message dissemination protocol can offer a number of desirable features such as the use of more computing capacities and various cloud computing services (i.e. processing, storage, bandwidth, platforms etc.). Also, vehicles use less power than with a pure VANET, since data centers are widely used to forward data packets due to their larger coverage area and to their important bandwidth. As a future work, we will investigate the dissemination issue of a large amount of data such as video streaming for providing safety and non-safety services, in particular on very large scalable vehicular networks.

References

1. Zeadally, S., Hunt, R., Chen, Y.S., Irwin, A., Hassan, A.: Vehicular Ad Hoc networks (VANETS): status, results, and challenges. Telecommuni. Syst. 50(4), 217–241 (2012)

2. Schoch, E., Kargl, F., Weber, M., Leinmuller, T.: Communication patterns in vanets. IEEE Communi. Mag. **46**, 119–125 (2008)
3. Mershad, K., Artail, H.: Finding a STAR in a vehicular cloud. IEEE Intell. Transport. Syst. Mag. **5**(2), 55–68 (2013)
4. Bitam, S., Mellouk, A., Zeadally, S.: VANET-Cloud: a generic cloud computing model for vehicular ad-hoc networks. IEEE Wirel. Commun. Mag. **22**, 96–102 (2015)
5. Bitam, S., Mellouk, A.: QoS swarm bee routing protocol for vehicular ad hoc networks. In: IEEE ICC, Kyoto, Japan, pp. 1–5 (2011)
6. Network simulator, ns-2. Available: http://www.isi.edu/nsnam/ns/
7. Greencloud, Available: http://greencloud.gforge.uni.lu/
8. Bernsen, J., Manivannan, D.: RIVER: a reliable inter-vehicular routing protocol for vehicular ad hoc networks. Comput. Netw. **56**(17), 3795–3807 (2012)
9. Bitam, S., Mellouk, A., Zeadally, S.: VANET-cloud: a generic cloud computing model for vehicular Ad Hoc networks. IEEE Wirel. Commun. **22**(1), 96–102 (2015)
10. Qin, Y., Huang, D., Zhang, X.: Vehicloud: Cloud computing facilitating routing in vehicular networks. In: 11th IEEE International Conference on In Trust, Security and Privacy in Computing and Communications (TrustCom), pp. 1438–1445 (2012)
11. Lin, T.W., Shen, J.M., Weng, H.C.: Cloud-supported seamless Internet access in intelligent transportation systems. Wirel. Pers. Commun. **72**(4), 2081–2106 (2013)
12. Olariu, S., Hristov, T., Yan, G.: The next paradigm shift: from vehicular networks to vehicular clouds. In: Developments in Mobile Ad Hoc Networking: the Cutting Edge Directions. Wiley, New York (2012)
13. Hussain, R., Son, J., Eun, H., Kim, S., Oh, H.: Rethinking vehicular communications: merging VANET with cloud computing. In: 4th IEEE Cloud Computing, pp. 606–609 (2012)
14. Abid, H., Phuong, L.T.T., Wang, J., Lee, S., Qaisar, S.: V-Cloud: vehicular cyber-physical systems and cloud computing. In: 4th International Symposium on Applied Sciences in Biomedical and Communication Technologies (2011)
15. Zingirian, N., Valenti, C.: Sensor clouds for Intelligent Truck Monitoring. In: IEEE Intelligent Vehicles Symposium, pp. 999–1004 (2012)
16. Baby, D., Sabareesh, R.D., Saravanaguru, R.A.K., Thangavelu, A.: VCR: vehicular cloud for road side scenarios. Adv. Comput. Inform. Technol. **178**, 541–552 (2013)
17. Bitam, S., Mellouk, A.: Routing for vehicular Ad Hoc networks. In: Bio-Inspired Routing Protocols for Vehicular Ad Hoc Networks, pp. 29–50. Wiley (2014)

PerformLTE: A Testbed for LTE Testing in the Future Internet

Almudena Díaz-Zayas[✉], Cesar A. García-Pérez, Álvaro M. Recio-Pérez, and Pedro Merino-Gómez

Universidad de Málaga, Andalucía Tech Ampliación Campus Teatinos, 29071 Málaga, España
{almudiaz,garciacesaraugusto,amrecio,pedro}@lcc.uma.es
http://www.morse.uma.es

Abstract. The flat architecture adopted in LTE increases the scalability of the network in order to accommodate large volumes of user traffic, reduces packet latency and the cost per byte. At the same time the enhanced Node B (eNB) has increased its complexity which have implied the appearance of new challenges in the field of experimental performance tests [1]. To cope with these challenges, access to a real and controlled experimentation environment is needed. Nevertheless, the high cost of laboratory equipment makes it difficult to carry out realistic experiments for most research teams, whose work usually rely on simulations. A combination of highly configurable equipment and software tools accessed remotely seems to be the best solution to improve research activities around LTE technologies and beyond. PerformLTE testbed provides a controlled environment where LTE end-to-end IP communication, including radio impairments and network perturbations, and complex network setups can be reproduced.

Keywords: Testbed · LTE · QoS · Future internet · 5G

1 Introduction

According to Cisco [4], "the global mobile data traffic grew 69 percent in 2014, reaching nearly thirty times the size of the entire global Internet in 2000". It is also expected that "by the end of 2014, the number of mobile-connected devices will exceed the number of people on Earth and by 2019 there will be nearly 1.5 mobile devices per capita". Meanwhile mobile users continue to demand a high quality of service every day and at all locations. To ensure that users are satisfied when accessing services, very expensive tools and hardware are required. In this global economic context, it is difficult for researchers, application developers and service providers to obtain these tools. Network operators usually have access to different levels of information regarding the performance of their networks, which are known as Key Performance Indicators (KPI), but this information may not be enough to evaluate how the network's internal variables are related to

© Springer International Publishing Switzerland 2015
M.C. Aguayo-Torres et al. (Eds.): WWIC 2015, LNCS 9071, pp. 46–59, 2015.
DOI: 10.1007/978-3-319-22572-2_4

the actual user experience. To overcome these limitations, we have developed an experimentation platform that enables advanced research studies over LTE. This platform provides access to very complex configurations of the radio access, basic channel emulations based on 3GPP reference channel profiles and measurements which cover most of the layers of the radio access and user application protocols.

FIRE is an European initiative which aims to create an open research environment to facilitate strategic research and development on new Internet concepts providing an instrument to carry out large-scale experimentation on new paradigms. PerformLTE is one of the facilities of the FIRE ecosystem. It is part of the Fed4FIRE [2] initiative, which aims to federate open, reliable and accessible platforms for the research communities and FLEX, an initiative towards the provision of 4G and 5G experimental facilities.

The paper is organized as follows. In Sect. 2 we provide a detailed description of the functionalities provided by the testbed and the different scenarios offered. Section 3 introduces our approach to position the testbeds towards 5G. Finally Sect. 4 summarize the contributions of the testbed in the field of LTE experimentation.

2   PerformLTE: A Testbed for Mobile Experimentation in the Future Internet

2.1   PerformLTE Methodology

PerformLTE methodology follows an holistic approach, combining different type of equipments, LTE radio access equipments, Evolved Nodes B (eNBs), User Equipments (UEs), both commercial and engineered to provide measurements, and an Evolved Packet Core (EPC) emulation system. All these elements can be combined and experimentation can be performed in all the components of an LTE network. In general terms, LTE connectivity is provided through three different solutions, each one with a focus on a different research aspect, moving between emulation and real-world environments. Three main scenarios can be differentiated based on the radio access type:

- Scenarios based on conformance testing equipment that provides a full LTE end-to-end emulation, including channel emulation with different fading profiles and operation in all the standardized LTE bands, both FDD and TDD. This equipment allows the configuration of multiple levels of the LTE Radio Access Network (RAN) stack, so researches can study the effect of different parameters as well as the motorization of the full network.
- Scenarios based on commercial off-the-shelf eNBs. These scenarios provide functionality close to the one provided by operators. Configuration is based on OAM interfaces, some proprietary, some other based on standards like TR.069. Researchers can test the policies that operators are able to setup and can provided very complex configurations of the EPC network.
- Scenarios based on commercial LTE networks, in which the testbed offers applications and tools to extract information from the state of the network and correlate it with performance indicators from IP and application levels.

Furthermore, the testbed integrates some standard experimentation tools, like OMF and OML [3]. These experimentation interfaces enables the orchestration and configuration of the elements of an experiment using a standard description (OEDL), that provides a flexible and programmatic way of executing experiments and collecting results, and is under integration to provide resource reservation via the Fed4FIRE portal.

All these scenarios can be used with instrumented Android phones that provide information of the network extracted from the UE side, as well as capture incoming and outgoing IP traffic, that can be later used with post-processing tools to correlate KPIs from different layers of the stack, including QoE measurements based on subjective perception estimation. Additionally, a power analyzer can be connected to the UEs in order to obtain also information about energy consumption which remains one of the most important challenges of future mobile communication. The different radio access types can be used incrementally in an experiment, moving from laboratory to real life. Figure 1 depicts some of the possible usages of the testbed.

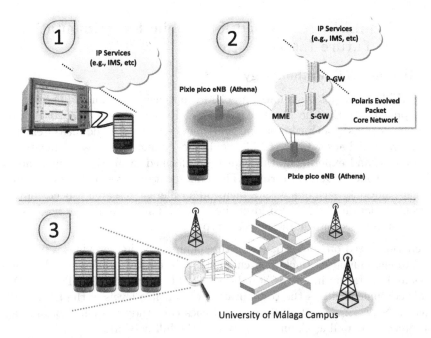

Fig. 1. PerformLTE testbed

The configurations offered by the testbed cover a broad spectrum of experiments, from applications and services to innovative network solutions. For example, developers could take advantage of the eNB emulator to test their applications under controlled radio propagation scenarios. Researchers interested in radio resource management could access the information retrieved from real mobile devices to see how different radio access configurations affect the performance of mobile applications running on mobile devices.

Currently, the performance metrics collected by the PerformLTE testbed are oriented to radio, IP communications, QoS and QoE, EPC, and battery consumption. Additionally, the testbed is capable of providing traces from most of the involved signaling procedures and statistics of network procedures. All these measurements are post-processed and correlated in order to obtain a fully detailed picture to characterize the performance of mobile applications and services in a specific context.

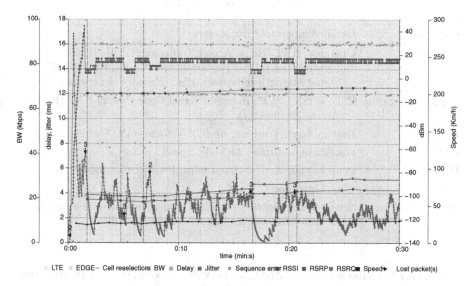

Fig. 2. RTP session monitoring results from a commercial LTE deployment.

2.2 Instrumented Mobile Devices

Since 2004, the UMA has worked on the development of monitoring tools for smartphones [6–8]. We started our proprietary development with SymPA tool for the Symbian platform and have continued with TestelDroid, an Android-based tool for monitoring communications performance and radio issues [9]. These tools have been used to analyze the performance of video streaming [10], VoIP services and also energy consumption [11]. These tools collect not only simple metrics such as throughput, but also radio parameters such as received signal strength, radio access technology in use, current IP traffic and much more to obtain a fully detailed picture to characterize the scenario where the results have been obtained. Table 1 provides a summary of the main functionalities provided by TestelDroid. Collected data can be logged using highly analyzable plain text files (except for traffic capture, stored in PCAP format). The objective of these tools is to take advantage of the engineering features provided by current commercial smartphones for the development of software tools which enable us to capture the QoS (Quality of Service) perceived by final users of mobile services and its correlation with the internal performance and configuration of networks and devices. At this point, we would like to remark on the importance of capturing, in a standard format, the traffic in a mobile phone. This capture can be used by experimenters to analyze the traffic in more detail and use their own tools and methodologies.

Table 1. TestelDroid capabilities

Capabilities	Detailed monitored parameters
Network	Operator, RAT (Radio Access Technology), CID (Cell Identification), LAC (Location Area Code), RSSI (Radio Signal Strength Indicator), PSC (Primary Scrambling Code)
Neighbouring cells	PSC, RSSI, RSCP (Received Signal Code Power) RAT (Radio Access Technology)
Battery	Battery level, Temperature (C), Voltage (mV) Current (mA)
GPS	Longitude, Latitude, Altitude, Speed
IP traffic	Pcap format, Arrival timestamps, Promiscuous mode
Connectivity test	Ping, Open ports
Active traffic test	Server-Client mobile-to-mobile, Transfer of auto-generated file, Bit rate monitoring, Average transfer speed

So as a key element of our testbed, we provide a pool of devices running our passive monitoring software tool called TestelDroid. Passive monitoring tools represent a scalable alternative for general purpose analysis of mobile applications' performance. Different aspects may be studied together using the passive approach including communication performance, memory usage and battery consumption among others. These monitoring tools complement and enhance network self-optimization procedures extending the observation points to additional protocol layers and to the user device and applications perspective. The instrumented mobile devices can be used by service providers and mobile developers to deploy their latest services, applications, protocols or any other aspect susceptible to modification in Android smartphones, and to test their performance over LTE mobile networks.

2.3   LTE Radio Access

For LTE radio access we provide three experimentation scenarios, each one with a different profile moving between emulation and the real-world. These scenarios are described in the following subsections.

Emulated Radio Access. The team at UMA has experience in the development of LTE signaling software for commercial eNB emulators. We have collaborated with companies such as AT4 Wireless (one of the major mobile certification laboratories), Keysight Technologies (formerly Agilent, one of the most relevant providers of testing equipments) and Alcatel Lucent. In this context, the UMA team has modified an eNB emulator, the T2010A from Agilent Technologies (formerly E2010 from AT4Wireless), to enable its use as an experimentation platform [13] to which commercial smartphones can be connected. The result is

Table 2. eNB emulator: summary of configurable features

Capabilities	Summary of configurable features
Cell configuration	Duplex mode, Frequency band, DL EARFCN, UL EARFCN, UL bandwidth, DL bandwidth, Cell id, TDD Frame Conf., Special Subframe Conf., Cell power, Simulated path loss, MCC and MNC
Reference measurement channels	Downlink transmission mode, for each Subframe and downlink codeword is possible to configure the MCS, the number of RB and the RB Offset for uplink and downlink
HARQ	Maximum HARQ transmissions in uplink and downlink, TDD feedback mode and the redundancy version list
Measurements	Enable/Disable CQI/PMI/RI reporting, CQI/PMI Feedback Type, CQI/PMI and RI Report Configuration Indexes, Enable/disable RSRP/RSRQ Measurements Configuration, Filter Coefficient for RSRP and RSRQ, Periodic Measurement Report Interval
Advanced L1 configuration	Number of PDCCH symbols, Common search space aggregation level, UE-Specific search aggregation level, PHICH duration, PHICH resources, PRACH configuration and root sequence indexes, PRACH frequency offset, Enable/Disable group hopping and sequence hopping and cyclic shift configuration
Advanced L2 configuration	C-RNTI, Number of RACH preambles, Initial received target power, Power ramping step, Contention resolution timer, Scheduling request value, PUCCH request configuration, DSR transmission max
RRC/NAS	Several RRC timers (T300, T301, T310, T311, N310, N311) access point name, IP version, IP address and radio link failure detection
Security	Enable/Disable security, Integrity algorithm, Ciphering algorithm and Authentication type
Channel emulation	Fading channel emulation (Several profiles defined by the 3GPP: EPA5, EVA5, EVA70, ETU70, ETU300 and HST), Noise generation

an experimental environment where radio access conditions can be fully configured and the effect of these configurations at the application level on the UE can
be measured using our monitoring software, TestelDroid. Some of the parameters which are configurable through the emulator are described in Table 2 and
Table 3 lists some of the measurements that can be obtained.

The T2010A, is a generic platform used not only in conformance RF and
signaling testing but also for design verification. In addition to these features, it
also integrates channel emulation and digital generation of impairments such as
AWGN, which is a critical feature for achieving high accuracy when setting SNR
conditions. Standard multipath fading profiles defined by 3GPP are supported
to emulate reference propagation conditions. MIMO is a key feature in LTE, as
it is one of the foundations of the technology's high rates and spectral efficiency.
The T2010A provides up to 4 × 2 integrated MIMO features, thus increasing
the range of test possibilities with interesting network configurations.

This radio access scenario provides an experimental environment where experiment conditions and results can be repeated and reproduced. The scenario is
limited to one device connected to one emulator. For large scale experimentation,
we recommend scenario 2 described in the following section.

Table 3. Measurements in the emulation system

Application level	Goodput, jitter, MOS, PESQ, delays
Transmitter measurements	Total output power, occupied bandwidth, CCDF, EVM versus symbol, EVM versus carrier, EVM constellation, spectral flatness
Receiver measurements	HARQ statistics, CQI, Throughput, BLER per channel
Traces and messages	Subframes, RRC Messages, NAS messages

As an example of the type of results we can obtain in this scenario, Fig. 3
shows the relation between the PDCCH (Physical Downlink Control Channel)
& PDSCH (Physical Downlink Shared Channel) BLER (Block Error Rate) and
the IP packet losses. It can be appreciated that the relation is not strictly linear
because of the randomness associated with AWGN and fading impairments,
resulting in bursty behaviors. This relationship is also governed by the operation
of HARQ, as the incremental redundancy increases the probability of correct
reception with each retransmission. An RLC SDU containing an IP packet is
lost only after the maximum number of unsuccessful retransmissions has been
reached; in this case there were three retransmission configured.

A Proprietary LTE Deployment. The testbed is also composed by two
commercial LTE pico-cells and a commercial EPC. This deployment with real
antennas provides a more realistic environment still under the control of the

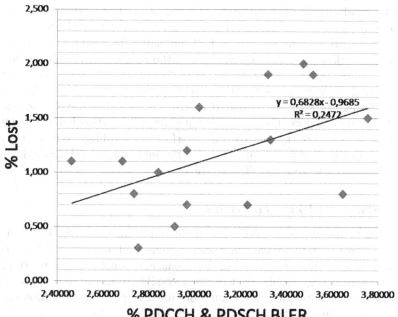

Fig. 3. Cross-layer correlations of the monitoring results

Table 4. Summary of configurable parameters in a commercial pico-cell

Capabilities	Configurable parameters in a commercial pico-cell
Air interface	DL and UL bandwidth, Number of antennas, DL and UL EARFCN, HARQ configuration, RLC and PDCP buffers and timers configuration, UM and AM parameters, Ciphering and security configuration
Radio resource management	Radio admission control, DL and UL minimum bit rate, VoIP consumption, etc., Transmit power and power control, Downlink and uplink scheduler, maximum number of transmissions, maximum HARQ timer, etc., Semi-static scheduling parameters
Connection management	Access barring parameters, cell parameters, cell ID, PLMN, etc., RRC timers, reestablishment timer, connection timer, etc
Mobility	Maximum transmission power that the UE might use in uplink, Minimum required reception level, cell reselection parameters, S1 and X2 handover parameters, Measurements configuration
Transport	QoS configuration

experimenter. The eNBs can be configured via proprietary interfaces, and there are ongoing efforts on the automation the configuration of new nodes based on OAM standards. Table 4 summarizes some of the key features that can be configured in the pico-cell. Moreover, pico-cell logging files will be accessible.

This nodes are integrated with an EPC emulator that can be used to define multiple network setups. For instance using the emulators, roaming scenarios can be executed by the definition of two different PLMNs each one with its corresponding LTE deployment. Furthermore these emulators provides carrier grade performance, we have measured 60 Mbits/s using a band 7 base station with 10MHz and supports the configuration of negative testing behaviors. Other interesting features are the provision of interfaces to establish dedicated bearer creation properties and in the latest version the inclusion of an IMS deployment which will be used to test VoLTE scenarios.

2.4 Commercial LTE Deployments

In addition to the emulated eNBs and the commercial pico-cells, PerformLTE provides a pool of instrumented smartphones connected to national LTE deployments available in Málaga (Spain). In this scenario it is not possible to configure LTE radio access, only mobile devices are accessible to install new applications or modify the software. However results obtained in previous scenarios can be matched with results obtained in commercial LTE networks.

2.5 Power Consumption Measurements in Mobile Devices

To carry out the analysis on battery life characterization, a key factor in mobile devices, we have a power analyzer provided by Keysight Technologies. This device can act as a 2-quadrant DC voltage source capable of generating arbitrary waveforms and/or an oscilloscope with data capturing capabilities. As a source, it can provide up to 20 V, up to ± 3 A. Power rating is 20 W. As a measurement tool, it is capable of measuring values down to nA and µV at a rate of 5.12 µs/sample for one parameter. Our equipment features advanced source modes, including a battery emulator mode and a battery charger mode. The former imitates the effects of charging or discharging the battery, including a programmable output resistance from $-40\,m\Omega$ to $+1\Omega$, while the latter emulates the behavior of a battery charger, which cannot sink current. In addition, the source mode also provides an arbitrary waveform generator to create custom waveforms. Table 5 shows the adjustable parameters in source mode. It is possible to store measurement data for up to 99,999 hours using the data logger function. Data can be exported to a file, which can be analyzed and graphed later.

2.6 Post-processing and Reporting Tools

In addition, the testbed incorporates post-processing tools to further analyze and correlate the data collected. The toolchain allows the inspection of the IP

Table 5. Source function capabilities

Capabilities	Description
Emulated modes	2 Quadrant power supply; Unipolar power supply; Battery emulator; Battery charger; Constant current load; Constant voltage load
Parameters	Voltage; current
Additional features	Arbitrary waveform generator; Current limit; Voltage limit; Resistance; Over voltage protection; Over current protection; Oscillation protection

traffic both at source and destination, to obtain typical communication statistics such as packet loss rate, throughput, inter packet arrival, end to end delay and jitter. Figure 2 is an example of the type of result that can be reported in this scenario. The figure has been obtained using the post-processing tool chain. Figure 2 is a vector graphic generated using the files containing the temporal evolution of the IP traffic and radio parameters collected by TestelDroid. In the legend below it, we find the color code and on both sides a number of vertical axis are used for different magnitudes. In the background, different colors are used to illustrate which Radio Access Technology (RAT) is being used at a certain point in time. Cell changes would have been indicated by a vertical dashed line. The instantaneous bandwidth is represented with a green dotted line, with each dot representing the throughput calculated when receiving a new data packet averaging over the last second. Although the line is shown as continuous for the sake of clarity, only the dots indicate actual reception of packets. The inter-packet delay represented with orange dots, which represent the time elapsed between the receptions of consecutive data packets. This magnitude is extremely valuable for identifying service interruptions and delay quantification effects in the network and codecs. An inter-packet delay of 0 indicates that two packets have been received together at the IP level, and the concentration of points suggests the technology is the codec frame timing. The jitter (in red) is an indication of the delay variation. Packets received at a constant rate would have a low jitter, whereas connectivity gaps or highly varying delays would result in a high jitter. A burst of lost packets is marked with a black arrow and a number, indicating the amount of packets that have not been received. Packets received out of sequence would be marked with yellow points. A blue line represents the Received Signal Strength indicator (RSSI), which is a measurement of the total signal power received by the mobile phone in its reception bandwidth.

3   PerformLTE Towards 5G

3.1   5G Challenges and Trends

The 5G Infrastructure Public Private Partnership has defined some of the challenges that will have to face future 5G communication: 1000 times higher wireless capability, 90 % of energy savings per service provided, reducing service creation time, facilitating dense deployments, reducing downtime to a "zero perceived" and so on. These high level requirements are produced to enable new incoming services and products, that will push to the limits the performance and capacity of future networks and will be provided by improvements in all the elements of the network, from the appearance of new radio access technologies to new designs of the core and transport networks. NGMN [5] provides an excellent overview on future applications related with their expected user experience KPIs, as well as some of the current trends to support these new scenarios.

5G will provide heterogeneous access to the radio access technologies, combining them to improve reliability, performance and availability of connections. There are research groups working on the provision of new waveforms and it is clear the mmWave spectrum will be exploited [12]. Massive MIMO is another important trend being explored.

Other trends on the radio access which are already coming in future 3GPP specifications are control/data plane separation, also referred as dual connectivity. In these scenarios, the control plane is transported over a different carrier, even from a different technology that the data plane. This is particularly interesting, as it allows to combine macro cells to provide the control plane with small cells that will provide better performance figures on the data plane. This type of architecture will improve also handover time. Along these lines, there is the so called network densification, which is essential to guarantee availability and to improve performance on the network. Carrier aggregation, already standardized in LTE Release 10, is very interesting to increase throughput figures. The concept is now being extended to provide aggregation using unlicensed bands where more spectrum might be available.

The core network will also suffer major changes. There are some trends to simplify its architecture and reduce the signaling overhead. Some trends also cover the deployment of core network functionality inside the nodes to drastically reduce latencies and even the forwarding of traffic from one node to another when communication peers are connected to geographically close nodes. NFV and SDN are also very important concepts as they will provide the required network flexibility, in order to integrate and deploy new services or radio access nodes. The functions of the networks will be distributed and accessed from the best location to reduce delays. Operation and management will also has to be improved. The flexibility and densification of the network will demand the improvement of SON techniques as well as of the simplification and standardization of OAM interfaces. To reduce CAPEX and OPEX infrastructure sharing techniques are being developed, tools to integrate third parties deployment are also on the way. Virtualization of the full is a key concept to target this objectives.

3.2 Future Work: PerformLTE Evolution

PerformLTE is evolving to enable 5G experimentation for the future Internet. Figure 4 depicts the target architecture of PerformLTE. As represented, UMA

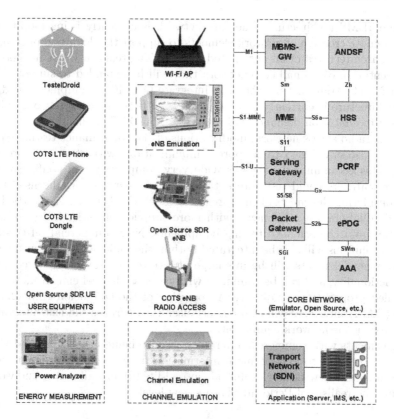

Fig. 4. PerformLTE evolution

expect to operate a very dynamic testbed where different types of solutions could be deployed and combined easily.

The research roadmap for PerformLTE covers improvements in all the aspects of the testbed, our goal being to support experimentation and research on future wireless technologies and to contribute to the materialization of future 5G standards. In the next cycle of functionality, PerformLTE will strengthen its current research methodology, broadening the spectrum of scenarios to enable advanced applied research in real-life conditions.

PerformLTE will evolve in the field of SDR (Software Defined Radio) and open source protocol stacks that could provide flexible use of spectrum, established as requirement for 5G networks, and enabling researchers to modify to the communication stack, that will potentially boost reliability, quality and interoperability at the same time speeds up 5G development. One of the platforms that is being explored is OpenAirInterface, an open source solution that implements the stack of user equipment, base stations and core network.

Extensions of the core network to evolve toward Release 12 are also foreseen. The testbed will include support for non 3GPP radio access technologies, in particular Wi-Fi handover is envisioned, and support for broadcast services based on the eMBMS architecture. The core network is currently being modified to enable remote creation of network elements to support the definition of complex network architectures in an automated fashion. The team in UMA has also an implementation of a small core network that will be extended to support NFV and SDN. The transport network will integrate OpenFlow equipments and the IMS architecture is currently being deployed. APIs to the core network will be provided to enable on demand QoS reservation by OTT applications.

In the radio access network, modifications of the conformance testing equipment are also envisioned to support communications with standard core networks. This communication will provide very complex system configurations, where researchers could test core network improvements in any licensed band even considering the effects of the wireless channel. Furthermore the testbed has reached collaboration agreements with more suppliers in order integrate more emulation and conformance testing equipments. New commercial off-the-shelf (COTS) solutions will also be integrated both in the radio access and in the user side, this new elements will be in charge of introducing standardized commercial functionality, and can be combined with wireless channel emulators to have controlled propagation conditions. Automation of the Operacion And Maintenance (OAM) interfaces will also be very useful, as permits the fast integration of heterogeneous network equipment.

Agreements with commercial operators are also being negotiated, and UMA expects to be able to extract more information from commercial deployments and even to test new network solutions in real-life urban radio access networks, boosting the realism of PerformLTE to a new level.

4   Conclusion

This paper introduces PerformLTE, an LTE testbed which enables the deployment and execution of complex LTE experiments in three different ways. As a first option, the experimenter can use the most controlled and configurable platform, a complete proprietary LTE network build on top of the LTE testing equipment employed by certification laboratories. Once the configurations have been evaluated in this scenario, the same experiment or new experiments can be validated with real eNBs deployed in a proprietary LTE network integrated by commercial pico-cells and an EPC. In the last scenario, PerformLTE allows the remote evaluation of the experiments providing access to off-the-shelf devices connected to LTE commercial networks deployed in Malaga. The mobile devices used in the three scenarios are Android phones which are instrumented to monitor radio and IP traffic parameters. The usage of commercial devices is a key factor in testing real applications, monitoring radio parameters and measuring application's performance and QoS as perceived by final users. In addition, we provide post-processing tools to further analysis and correlate the data collected. The tool chain allows the inspection of the IP traffic both at source and destination to obtain typical communication statistics such as packet loss rate, throughput, inter packet arrival, end-to-end delay and jitter. Combining this information with information provided by the eNB emulator, pico-cells and EPC we can obtain very useful cross layer information and correlations. PerformLTE also incorporates a DC Power Analyzer to cope with the challenge of optimizing battery life. The development of better batteries still presents significant challenges and the deployment of energy saving mechanisms across the range of devices, technologies and services becomes highly relevant when trying to increase mobile devices' autonomy and their intensive usage.

Acknowledgement. This work has been funded by the Government of Andalusia under grant P11-TIC-7659, by the Spanish Ministry of Economy and Competitiveness under project TIN2012-35669 and European Regional Development Fund (EDRF) from the European Commission. This work was carried out with the support of the Fed4FIRE-project (Federation for FIRE), an Integrated project receiving funding from the European Union's Seventh Framework Programme for research, technological development and demonstration under grant agreement no 318389.

References

1. Rumney, M. (ed.): LTE and the Evolution to 4G: Design and Measurement Challenges. Agilent Technologies, USA (2009)
2. Fed4FIRE project official web site. http://www.fed4fire.eu/
3. Rakotoarivelo, T., Ott, M., Jourjon, G., Seskar, I.: OMF: a control and management framework for networking testbeds. ACM SIGOPS Operating Syst. Rev. **43**(4), 54–59 (2010)
4. Cisco: Visual Networking Index: Global Mobile Data Traffic Forecast Update, 2014–2019, Cisco, Technical report (2015)
5. Next Generation Mobile Networks (NGMN), 5G White Paper, Technical report (2015)
6. Diaz, A., Merino, P., Gil, A., Munoz, J.: x-AppMonitor μAgent: a tool for QoS measurements in cellular networks. In: 3rd International Symposium on Wireless Communication Systems, ISWCS 2006, pp. 343–347, 6–8 September 2006
7. Díaz, A., Merino, P., Rivas, F.J.: Mobile application profiling for connected smartphones. IEEE Pervasive Comput. **9**(1), 54–61 (2010)
8. Rivas, F.J., Díaz, A., Merino, P.: Characterizing traffic performance in cellular networks. IEEE Internet Comput. **18**(1), 12–19 (2014)
9. Álvarez, A., Díaz, A., Merino, P., Rivas, F.J.: Field measurements of mobile services with android smartphones. In: Consumer Communications and Networking Conference (CCNC), 2012, pp. 105–109. IEEE, 14–17 January 2012
10. Díaz, A., Merino, P., Rivas, F.J.: QoS analysis of video streaming service in live cellular networks. Comput. Commun. Elsevier **33**(3), 322–335 (2010)
11. Díaz, A., Merino, P.: A testbed for energy profile characterization of IP services in smartphones over live networks. ACM Springer Mobile Networks and Applications (MONET) **15**(3), 330–343 (2010)
12. Andrews, J.G., Buzzi, S., Choi, W., Hanly, S.V., Lozano, A., Soong, A.C.K., Zhang, J.C.: What Will 5G Be? IEEE J. Sel. Areas Commun. **32**(6), 1065–1082 (2014)
13. Díaz, A., Merino, P., Rivas, F.J.: Test environment for QoS testing of VoIP over LTE. In: Network Operations and Management Symposium (NOMS), pp. 780–794, 2012. IEEE, 16–20 April 2012

Analysis of CQI Traces from LTE MIMO Deployments and Impact on Classical Schedulers

Jose Oscar Fajardo$^{(\boxtimes)}$, Ianire Taboada, and Fidel Liberal

ETSI Bilbao, University of the Basque Country (UPV/EHU),
Alameda Urquijo s/n, 48013 Bilbao, Spain
{joseoscar.fajardo,ianire.taboada,fidel.liberal}@ehu.es

Abstract. This paper deals with the classical problem of radio resource management in LTE MIMO, with special focus to the specific radio channel characteristics in commercial LTE networks. First, we provide some conclusions about the Channel Quality Information traces obtained through field testing. From this analysis, we perform a series of experiments by means of an LTE emulator in order to evaluate the accuracy of different fading models used in the 3GPP. As a first outcome of the paper, we infer several fine-grain channel characteristics useful to feed further research work in the area of LTE MIMO. As a second contribution of the paper, we analyze the performance of classical schedulers (i.e., Round Robin, Best CQI and Proportional Fair) under the obtained LTE MIMO channel conditions. Specifically, we analyze the impact of the channel feedback reporting rate in scenarios with multiple greedy sources.

Keywords: LTE MIMO traces · Live testing · Radio resource scheduling · CQI reporting rate

1 Introduction

Nowadays, Long Term Evolution (LTE) technology has widespread support through all the continents. According to the Global mobile Suppliers Association (GSA), as for January 2015 there are 360 commercial LTE networks deployed in 124 countries [1]. From the five different LTE device categories defined in 3GPP TS 36.306 (until Release 9) [2], actual deployments only support up to Category 4. This feature implies a peak downlink bitrate in LTE networks of 75 Mbps when single-input single-output (SISO) is used, and 150 Mbps in multiple-input and multiple-output (MIMO) transmission mode. Additionally, 49 of these networks support LTE-Advanced (LTE-A) (3GPP Release 10 and on) with Carrier Aggregation (CA) and peak data rates of 300 Mbps for MIMO-enabled Category 6 devices.

Jointly with these worldwide deployments, there is an increasing interest from the research community to study the performance of different proposals (e.g., channel-aware schedulers, channel-aware application servers, etc.) in real-world conditions (e.g., [3]). Although well-known LTE simulators [4–6] have been

© Springer International Publishing Switzerland 2015
M.C. Aguayo-Torres et al. (Eds.): WWIC 2015, LNCS 9071, pp. 60–73, 2015.
DOI: 10.1007/978-3-319-22572-2_5

widely used in the past years, it is important to analyze and characterize the real-world radio performance in different conditions and mobility patterns.

The quality of the radio channel may be estimated through a series of radio parameters, i.e.: Received Signal Strength Indicator (RSSI), Reference Signal Received Power (RSRP), Reference Signal Receive Quality (RSRQ) and Signal-to-Noise Ratio (SNR). Most of these radio parameters can be monitored in regular LTE smartphones though dedicated software (e,g, [7]). Beyond all these power-related measurements, the key parameter to determine the performance of User Equipments (UE) in LTE is the Channel Quality Information (CQI). This parameter determines the coding efficiency [8] supported to meet the target Block Error Rate (BLER) of 10 %. Under good radio channel conditions, the CQI value reported by the UE to the E-UTRAN Node B (eNodeB) would be high, resulting in a high Modulation and Coding Scheme (MCS) index and better radio efficiency.

UEs may be requested to report CQI values in a periodic basis and to send aperiodic CQI reports upon request by the eNodeB. Reported CQI values can be configured to a unique value for the whole bandwidth (wideband CQI) or different CQI values for determined frequencies (sub-band CQI). In addition to CQIs, UEs are requested to report the Rank Indicator (RI) parameter in MIMO transmissions. This parameter is critical to understand if UEs estimate that two spatially multiplexed layers shall be used (RI = 2) or if it is better to receive the same information from different antennas (RI = 1). When reported periodically, the CQI Reporting Rate (CRR) determines the frequency for sending quality feedbacks in the uplink [9]. The frequency for reporting RI values is usually configured as a multiple of CRR value.

Unfortunately, CQI values cannot be generally accessed though commercial LTE devices and UEs specifically enabled for drive testing are required. Few studies provide detailed information concerning CQI values. In [10], authors illustrate the temporal evolution of CQI values in stationary and mobility conditions in one LTE network with 10 MHz of bandwidth. However, no information is provided about the RI value and consequently the specific MIMO mode at each moment is unknown. In [11], an almost linear relationship between CQI and RSRP values is depicted. However, these experiments are performed in an experimental testbed and not in real-world commercial LTE networks. Additionally, the experiments are based on SISO transmissions and the applied fading channels are not detailed.

Most of LTE performance studies are based on other radio parameters. Generally speaking, measured SNR is used to estimate the expected BLER in different coding schemes, and thus to generate the most accurate CQI value for the current conditions. However, this relationship may be complex in MIMO scenarios [12] and its actual implementation is up to device vendors. Thus, SNR values are not always an accurate estimator of the reported channel quality and CQI traces are generally preferred to analyze the experienced performance. As shown in [10], the relationship between SNR and CQI at different antennas depends on the experienced channel variability at each antenna. Additionally, SNR values are not always accessible from LTE devices. In [13], authors propose a method to estimate SNR values from RSRP and RSSI measurements. Finally, some other authors try to analyze the experienced performance and its root causes by profiling application-level data [14–16].

In summary, it is evidenced that analyzing and characterizing the behavior of CQI values in modern LTE networks is a very challenging but appealing problem. This paper is intended to provide some evidence about the expected radio channel characteristics, focusing on the downlink of LTE MIMO transmissions. In Sect. 2, beyond providing raw CQI traces, we identify several specific effects and limitations that we found when performing drive tests, and we discuss the main causes of these issues. Additionally, in Sect. 3 we show a basic performance study concerning classical radio resource schedulers under the identified propagation conditions. Finally, Sect. 4 provides the conclusions to the paper.

2   Characterizing LTE MIMO Channels

This section deals with the first objective of the paper, namely the characterization of downlink radio channels in deployed LTE MIMO networks. As explained before, instead of using radio parameters such as RSSI, RSRP, RSRQ or SNR, we analyze the behavior of CQI traces obtained from real-world measurements in commercial networks. Regular LTE devices do not provide these CQI values to drive test tools, and thus specialized equipment must be used to gather CQI traces from outside the operator. As we will discuss in this section, mapping lower level radio parameters (even SNR values) to CQI is not always a direct relationship. First, specific mapping schemes are open to vendors' implementations. Second, the values for radio parameters that can be gathered by different drive test tools only provide limited information in LTE MIMO scenarios.

As a result, we make use of a specialized drive test toolset that allows us to gather CQI values and analyze their relationship to other parameters. However, even this kind of specialized equipment imposes a series of limitations to the collected CQI traces that need to be studied and addressed.

As a step forward, we use an LTE emulator to run a series of experiments taking into account different LTE Test Points used by the 3GPP in TS 37.901 [17]. This way, we are able to compare the coarse-grain characteristics of the drive test traces with the experimental traces, and to detect some behavioral patterns. Finally, we infer a series of fine-grain characteristics that could be used to derive CQI models useful for realistic LTE MIMO simulations.

2.1   Coarse-Grain CQI Traces Through Field Testing

At an initial step, drive tests were performed to gather the performance experienced by UEs in different live LTE networks. Test data were gathered in different mobility patterns and different cities in the North of Spain, using commercial cells deployed in the 2.6 GHz band (LTE Band 7) with 20 MHz of bandwidth.

The test equipment consisted of a laptop connected to LTE with a Samsung GT-B3730 USB dongle and running ASCOM TEMS Investigation as drive test tool. This USB dongle is an LTE Category 3 device, which imposes a series of constraints in the measurements.

First, Category 3 devices are capable of operating in SISO and MIMO with a maximum of two layers for spatial multiplexing in the downlink [2]. Since October 2014, several deployments in Spain support LTE-A with Carrier Aggregation of 40 MHz, by mixing downlink transmissions from 1.8 GHz and 2.6 GHz bands. However, Category 6 or higher devices are required to support CA and therefore the downlink bandwidth is limited to 20 MHz with Category 3 devices.

Secondly, Category 3 devices are limited to support up to 75 Mbps in the downlink with one layer, and 100 Mbps with two spatial layers in MIMO. This limitation imposes a restriction in the MCS value that can be assigned to an UE in MIMO (MCS of 23 for 20 MHz cells). Category 4 devices do not impose this limitation, and therefore 150 Mbps could be achieved in downlink. However, this effect does not impact generation and reporting of CQI values since the limitation is applied in the eNodeB.

In addition to UE capacities, the configuration of the deployed LTE networks has an impact on the experienced results. As an example, Fig. 1 illustrates an excerpt of 260 s from a drive test trace obtained from TEMS Investigation.

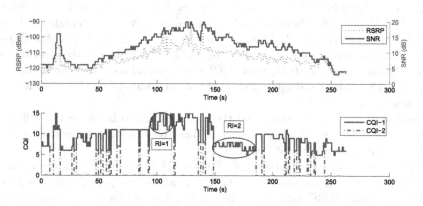

Fig. 1. Example trace from field testing in LTE MIMO.

In the first subplot, we show RSRP and SNR values reported by the device. Ideally, SNR is used to calculate CQI values in the two available antennas, although the actual mapping is open to device manufacturers. As can be observed, UE's mobility implies high variability and wide range of SNR values.

In the second subplot, we show the collected CQI values reported by the two antennas. First, it must be noted that reported SNR values are aggregated for the two antennas, being difficult to infer the contribution of each antenna and the expected individual CQI values. Second, it can be observed that the second CQI value is either zero or the same as the first CQI value.

This effect must be understood by taking into account the Transmission Mode of the LTE cell [8]. The monitored networks are mainly based on Transmission Mode 3, which allows one of the following transmission schemes at each moment:

- Transmit Diversity or Space Frequency Block Codes (SFBC). In this MIMO scheme, the eNodeB transmits the same information through two antennas. CQI values reported by UEs are associated to the best channel condition from the two antennas and RI values are set to one.
- Large delay CDD or Open Loop Spatial Multiplexing (OLSM). In this MIMO scheme, the eNodeB transmits different information through two antennas and higher bitrates can be achieved. CQI values reported by UEs are associated to the best condition achievable at the two antennas simultaneously, which is the worst of the two channel conditions. Reported RI values are set to two in this case.

As a result, based on the radio performance experienced by two different reception antennas, the MIMO scheme varies along time as illustrated in Fig. 1. UEs are in charge of generating both CQI values and estimating the most beneficial transmission scheme that maximizes the downlink bitrate. From that estimation, UEs report a single CQI value together with the preferred RI.

The main implication of this effect is the complexity to characterize the behavior of CQI values directly from CQI traces. Since different fading conditions may affect to different antennas, similar SNR values may result on higher or lower CQI-1 values if SFBC or OLSM is preferred. Thus, it must be noted that CQI-1 and CQI-2 values reported by the drive test tool are not directly those estimated for the two antennas. Instead, those CQI traces would include some periods of individual CQI values and some periods of the maximum CQI achievable at both antennas at the same time.

As a step forward, we processed the captured traces isolating the different transmission schemes. Figure 2 illustrates these results for a series of traces in similar mobility conditions at 20 km/h.

The left plot in Fig. 2 illustrates the Empirical Cumulative Distribution Function (ECDF) of CQI values. As can be observed, OLSM periods provide lower CQI values than SFBC periods. Although this fact is observed in most of the performed drive tests, several scenarios provide high CQI values also for OLSM, when both antennas experience good channel conditions at the same time.

In order to provide some further evidence of the different characteristics experienced by CQI in both transmission schemes, the right plot in Fig. 2 shows the ECDF of monitored CQI burstlengths. In this paper, CQI burstlengths are considered as periods of time with non-variable CQI value. At this time scale, CQI values seem to be less variable for OLSM periods than SFBC periods although for both of them maximum burstlengths are around 15 s.

Figure 2 also provides evidence of another limitation of the drive test toolset concerning the granularity of the samples. As can be observed, CQI burstlengths start with a lower value of 1 s and this fact is not caused by either the network configuration or the drive test software.

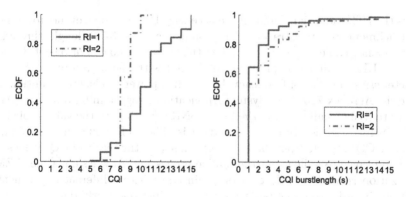

Fig. 2. Different characteristics of CQI traces in SFBC (RI = 1) and OLSM (RI = 2) periods.

Monitored LTE networks are configured to operate with Transmission Mode 3, requesting UEs to send wideband CQI reports every 5 ms and RI feedbacks every 80 ms. The former value determines the granularity of CQI measurements at the eNodeB, while the latter value limits the frequency for switching between transmission schemes. Likewise, the drive test software is configured to gather test data every 200 ms from the UE. Therefore, the limitation seems to be related to the granularity used by the LTE device to report radio parameters to the drive test software. In this sense, it is not clear how these values are generated from the whole set of values in the last period.

In summary, we state that specialized drive test tools, as used in this paper, provide significant information to understand the experienced performance of radio channels in LTE MIMO through the analysis of CQI values. However, in order to characterize its temporal evolution, we must identify the transmission scheme at each moment. Additionally, although useful for coarse-grain estimations, the granularity of CQI traces is too low and invalidates the results to generate fine-grain CQI traces aimed to feed further LTE simulation studies.

2.2 Fine-Grain CQI Traces Through LTE Emulation

Taking into account the previous conclusions, we performed a series of experiments in order to understand the possible behavior of CQI traces at sub-second scope. The most accurate methodology would involve accessing real-world traces from deployed commercial eNodeB equipments, which is problematic due to accessibility/privacy and performance issues. Even in that case, the trace granularity would be limited to the CRR value configured at the mobile network operator, i.e. 5 ms in the monitored networks.

Therefore, this paper addresses the problem from an alternative methodology, which is illustrated in Fig. 3. We used the Aeroflex 7100 LTE emulator to gather finer-grain radio measurements, which provides CQI samples up to the practical limit of 2ms in CRR. This emulator performs the role of the eNodeB, since it creates the LTE radio signal and all the necessary LTE protocol events to support the attachment and registration of the Samsung GT-B3730 dongle through a radiofrequency cable. In order to emulate the overall radio conditions of the field tests, the LTE emulator is properly configured with the monitored LTE radio characteristics in terms of frequency, bandwidth, power levels, etc. Additionally, we use the Aeroflex 7100 Test System Application Programming Interface (API) in order to dynamically modify the target SNR according to the values collected by TEMS Investigation in a per second basis. The LTE emulator is configured to request CQI reports from the UE every 2 ms, and the received CQI values are logged and saved to a file for further offline processing. At the same time, TEMS Investigation is used to collect coarse-grain statistics in different experimental conditions in order to check reported values against real-world data.

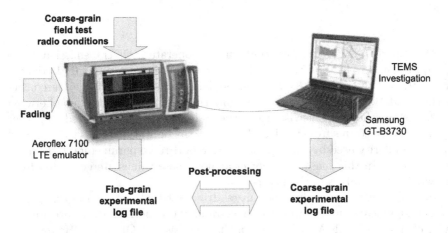

Fig. 3. Testbed for realistic LTE experiments.

In order to test different fading conditions, each experiment adds to the generated LTE signal a different fading pattern. According to 3GPP TR 37.901 Test Points for LTE, three different Extended Vehicular A (EVA) propagation conditions have been tested:

- EVA5: EVA occurs frequently in deployments.
- EVA70: Adds EVA70, high SNR coverage which is common in low frequency (<1 GHz) band networks.
- EVA200: Covers high Doppler, high SNR scenario which is common in high frequency (≥1 GHz) band networks.

Figure 4 illustrates obtained experimental coarse-grain results in terms of CQI ECDF (upper plot) and CQI burstlength ECDF (lower plot) as reported by TEMS Investigation. This figure also includes the statistical properties of the selected field test CQI traces, separated between OLSM and SFBC periods.

As expected, none of the propagation conditions perfectly matches any of the real-world traces. However, we can observe specific trends as follows:

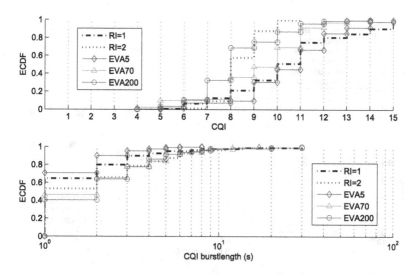

Fig. 4. Experimental traces vs. 3GPP LTE Test Points.

- CQI traces in MIMO Transmit Diversity periods are closer to EVA5 fading condition in both CQI and CQI burstlength first order statistics.
- CQI traces in MIMO OLSM periods are closer to EVA70 and EVA200 fading conditions in both statistics.

We may interpret these results considering the LTE Transmission Mode 3 and possible switching between the two alternative transmission schemes. As explained before, SFBC is used when one of the antennas experiences a significant better channel condition compared to the other antenna. In this case, it seems that the best antenna follows a less severe fading condition such as EVA5. OLSM is used when the estimated bitrate using two layers in the worst radio condition achieves a higher bitrate than a unique layer through the best antenna. Therefore, OLSM CQI traces are associated to the more severe fading condition of the two antennas. Although high CQI values have been monitored in OLSM, most of the field test experiments provide lower CQI values and are therefore associated to more severe fading conditions.

In order to infer the possible behavior of CQI at sub-second level, we use the experimental CQI traces reported by the Samsung GT-B3730 and captured at the LTE emulator. Figure 5 illustrates the results of the actual CQI traces at 2 ms of reporting period.

In the upper plot, we confirm that aggregated CQI values reported by TEMS and actual CQI values reported by UE to the eNodeB follow similar statistics. However, CQI values over time are much more variable than coarse-grain reports. In the lower plot, we illustrate the ECDF of CQI burstlengths and we confirm that burstlengths beyond 200 ms are hardly probable in any scenario.

Additionally, we observe that EVA5 fading channels exhibit higher burstlengths than the other two fading conditions. This feature may be

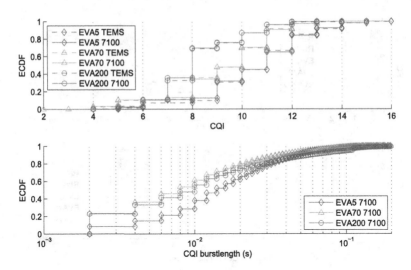

Fig. 5. Burstlength of CQI traces at LTE frame level.

benefitial to avoid low-level retransmissions due to fast channel variability, and can be exploited by channel-aware scheduling strategies to optimize the performance of the cell.

3   Impact on Classical Scheduling Strategies

In order to evaluate the impact of the obtained channel characteristics, this section presents the results of a simple exercise concerning the introduction of experimental CQI traces into the analysis of LTE eNodeB scheduling strategies.

We analyze the performance of well-known scheduling algorithms (Round Robin, Best CQI and Proportional Fair) under the obtained LTE MIMO channel conditions. Specifically, we focus on the impact of CRR in a controlled simulation-driven LTE scenario due to the significance of CQI feedback granularity in variable radio channels.

3.1   Simulation Methodology

In order to introduce the required experimental CQI values in the simulations, we implemented a basic LTE simulation environment in MATLAB, where obtained LTE MIMO CQI traces are configured as input vectors for the event-driven simulation. The main features considered in the simulation code are the effect of different multi-user scheduling strategies and the effect of retransmissions due to inaccurate channel estimations associated to CRR and CQI delay values.

Table 1 summarizes the main simulation parameters.

As typical in current LTE networks, we use scheduling decisions and transmission slots of 1 ms. Considering an LTE cell of 20 MHz, the scheduler needs to

Table 1. Simulation parameters.

Parameter	Value
Transmission Time Interval (TTI)	1 ms
Number of Resource Blocks (RB)	100
LTE transmission mode	MIMO OLSM
Scheduling algorithms	BC, RR, PF
CQI reporting rate	2, 5, 10, 20, 40, 80, 160 ms
CQI delay	3 ms
Number of UEs	20 UEs, in two classes
Channel model	EVA5, EVA200
Traffic model	Greedy sources
Simulation length	1000 s

determine how to assign a total of 100 Resource Blocks (RB) among the different users at each transmission slot.

The scheduling policies used in our experiments are:

- Round Robin (RR): With this discipline, the RBs are fairly shared among users.
- Best CQI (BC): This policy assigns RBs fairly among the users with the estimated highest instantaneous CQI.
- Proportional Fair (PF): This discipline consists in assigning RBs fairly among the users with the highest ratio of the estimated current transmission rate and the current averaged throughput for a window of 100 ms (without taking into account retransmitted bits).

Once the scheduler decides the number of assigned RBs per user, the eNodeB determines the MCS and the Transport Block Size (TBS) for each user according to [8] (Table 7.1.7.2.2-1 employed for MIMO). Both MCS and TBS values depend on the reported CQI value and the number of assigned RBs.

Aimed at analyzing the impact of the CRR in classical schedulers, we consider CRR values employed in commercial LTE networks [17]: 2, 5, 10, 20, 40, 80, 160 (in ms). Moreover, we assume a CQI delay of 3 ms caused by the CQI measurement at the UE side, the CQI feedback transmission and the CQI processing at the eNodeB [18]. This way, the resource allocation algorithms use partial channel quality information. If the available CQI estimation in the scheduler is higher than the actual CQI at the UE, we force a retransmission in the following Transmission Time Interval.

We have carried out simulations of 1000 s length. We consider 20 greedy traffic sources in the cell, each traffic source corresponding to a mobile user. We consider two classes of users in reference to the channel characteristics: 10 users follow the obtained EVA5 CQI model and 10 users follow EVA200. Concerning these two channel models, we shall note that EVA5 provides lower CQI variability and higher CQI values.

3.2   Analysis of Results

We focus on the study of the achievable aggregated cell throughput as a measure to evaluate the performance of the different scheduling strategies under the described LTE channel characteristics and CRR configurations.

First, we analyze the results for the aggregate values taking into account the two considered classes of users.

Left-graph in Fig. 6 shows the results for the effective throughput, which refers to correctly transmitted data (without taking into account retransmissions). Right-graph of Fig. 6 illustrates the total amount of traffic used in the cell for retransmissions due to inaccurate channel estimations at the eNodeB.

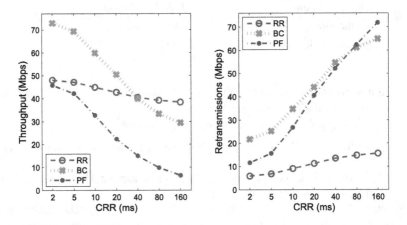

Fig. 6. Effective throughput (left) and wasted throughput caused by retransmissions (right).

As can be observed, channel-aware disciplines exhibit severe degradations as CRR increases, while RR shows a more stable performance. Furthermore, it is clear that channel-aware policies cause more retransmissions than RR; with a notable increase with the CRR value.

This effect is mainly associated to the inherent behavior of the analyzed schedulers. Channel-aware schedulers prioritize the transmission of traffic associated to users with high CQI values. However, those channel states exhibit more variability and the probability to transit to channel states with lower CQI is high. As a result, the eNodeB would overestimate the transmission capacity for those users leading to higher error probability in the transmissions. In the case of RR, users are selected regardless their channel condition. As cited before, users with lower CQI values are associated to less variable channel states, thus leading to lower transmission capacity but lower error probability.

As a result, the overall performance of BC provides higher bitrates in the lower CRR values (up to CRR = 20 ms) and exhibits more severe degradations for higher CRR values where the probability of inaccurate CQI estimations increase.

Beyond aggregate cell performance values, Fig. 7 illustrates the throughput results of the two classes of users; the left-graph belongs to users in better channel conditions (EVA5) and right-graph belongs to users in worse channel conditions (EVA200). EVA5 results in higher CQI values and less CQI variability compared to the EVA200 channel model. In the left-graph, we can see the prominent improvement of BC for the class of users in good channel conditions, while users in bad channel conditions are penalized. In these conditions, RR behaves as the fairest scheduler and the most reliable against high CRR values.

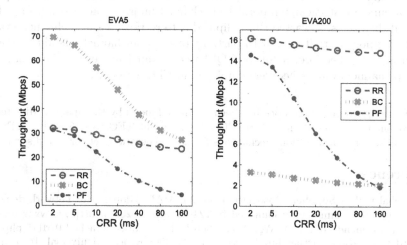

Fig. 7. Per-class effective throughput.

4 Conclusions

The main contribution of this work is the characterization of downlink radio channels in deployed LTE MIMO by means of CQI traces obtained from real-world measurements in commercial networks. We state that, although specialized drive test tools provide useful information to understand the achieved performance of LTE MIMO channels, the granularity of CQI traces is not enough for characterize its temporal evolution. For that purpose, we achieve to obtain CQI samples each 2 ms by means of Aeroflex 7100 LTE emulator for different fading conditions. We conclude that CQI traces in MIMO Transmit Diversity are closer to less severe fading conditions (such as EVA5), and that OLSM CQI traces are associated to more severe fading conditions (such as EVA70 and EVA200).

Although this is not an intrinsic feature to the different MIMO transmission modes, it has to do with the fact that MIMO OLSM uses the lower of the different CQI values. In the scenarios analyzed in this paper, it is hardly probable that all the antennas are in good channel conditions. Anyway, the results obtained in this paper do not preclude the possibility of experiencing high CQI values in MIMO OLSM in other scenarios.

Furthermore, we briefly depict the performance of classical schedulers under the obtained LTE MIMO CQI traces for different channel quality reporting periods. We consider a simulation scenario with two classes of users that differ in channel characteristics, EVA5 (good conditions) and EVA200 (bad conditions), driven in both cases by the coarse-grain SNR values. As main conclusion, we state that for CRR values lower than 20 ms BC exhibits the best performance in terms of throughput, even though it causes a notable number of retransmissions.

As future work, we identify two main areas for study. First, obtained CQI traces could be used to derive a parametrized LTE channel model that provides accurate statistical/temporal LTE channel information. Second, in order to avoid the excessive wasted throughput due to retransmissions, channel-aware scheduling policies that cope with partially observable channels should be studied/proposed. Therefore, a future CQI-based channel model will be useful to feed up channel-aware schedulers employed in LTE networks.

Acknowledgement. This work has been partially funded by the Spanish Ministerio de Economia y Competitividad (MINECO) under grant TEC2013-46766-R: QoEverage - QoE-aware optimization mechanisms for next generation networks and services.

References

1. Global mobile Suppliers Association (GSA): MAP: Global LTE network deployments, 360 commercially launched in 124 countries (2015). http://www.gsacom.com/downloads/pdf/LTE_World_map_360_LTE_networks_launched_070115.php4
2. 3rd Generation Partnership Project.: TS 36.306: Evolved Universal Terrestrial Radio Access (E-UTRA); User Equipment (UE) radio access capabilities. (Release 12) (2014). http://www.3gpp.org/DynaReport/36306.htm
3. Rivas, F.J., Daz, A., Merino, P.: Obtaining more realistic cross-layer QoS measurements: a VoIP over LTE use case. J. Comput. Network. Commun. **2013**, 10 (2013). Article ID 405858
4. Mehlfuhrer, C., Ikuno, J.C., Simko, M., Schwarz, S., Wrulich, M., Rupp, M.: The Vienna LTE simulators-Enabling reproducibility in wireless communications research. EURASIP J. Adv. Sig. Proc. **2011**, 29 (2011)
5. Piro, G., Grieco, L.A., Boggia, G., Capozzi, F., Camarda, P.: Simulating LTE cellular systems: an open source framework. IEEE Trans. Veh. Technol. **60**(2), 498–513 (2011)
6. Piro, G., Baldo, N., Miozzo, M.: An LTE module for the ns-3 network simulator. In: Proceedings of the 4th International ICST Conference on Simulation Tools and Techniques (SIMUTools 2011), pp. 415–422 (2011)
7. Alvarez, A., Diaz, A., Merino, P., Rivas, F.J.: Field measurements of mobile services with Android smartphones. In: Proceedings of 2012 IEEE Consumer Communications and Networking Conference (CCNC) (2012)
8. 3rd Generation Partnership Project.: TS. 36.213: Evolved Universal Terrestrial Radio Access (E-UTRA); Physical layer procedures (Release 12) (2014). http://www.3gpp.org/dynareport/36213.htm
9. Basukala, R., Ramli, H.A.M., Sandrasegaran, K., Chen, L.: Impact of CQI feedback rate/delay on scheduling video streaming services in LTE downlink. In: Proceedings of 2010 12th IEEE International Conference on Communication Technology (ICCT) (2010)

10. Sevindik, V., Wang, J., Bayat, O., Sevindik, V., Weitzen, J.: Performance evaluation of a real long term evolution (LTE) network. In: Proceedings of 2012 IEEE 37th Conference on Local Computer Networks Workshops (LCN Workshops) (2012)
11. Slanina, M., Klozar, L., Hanus, S.: Practical measurement of data throughput in LTE network depending on physical layer parameters. In: Proceedings of 2014 24th International Conference Radioelektronika (RADIOELEKTRONIKA) (2014)
12. Ikuno, J.C., Pendl, S., Simko, M., Rupp, M.: Accurate SINR estimation model for system level simulation of LTE networks. In: Proceedings of 2012 IEEE International Conference on Communications (ICC) (2012)
13. Landre, J.B., Rawas, Z.E., Visoz, R.: LTE performance assessment Prediction versus field measurements. In: Proceedings of 2013 IEEE 24th International Symposium on Personal Indoor and Mobile Radio Communications (PIMRC) (2013)
14. Laner, M., Svoboda, P., Romirer-Maierhofer, P., Nikaein, N., Ricciato, F., Rupp, M.: A comparison between one-way delays in operating HSPA and LTE networks. In: Proceedings of 2012 10th International Symposium on Modeling and Optimization in Mobile, Ad Hoc and Wireless Networks (WiOpt) (2012)
15. Bayer, J., Belschner, J., Chen, J., Klein, O., Linz, R., Muller, J., Xiang, Y., Zhao, X.: Performance measurement results obtained in a heterogeneous LTE field trial network. In: Proceedings of 2013 IEEE 77th Vehicular Technology Conference (VTC Spring) (2013)
16. Becker, N., Rizk, A., Fidler, M.: A measurement study on the application-level performance of LTE. In: Proceedings of 2014 IFIP Networking Conference (2014)
17. 3rd Generation Partnership Project.: TR. 37.901: Technical Specification Group Radio Access Network; User Equipment (UE) application layer data throughput performance (Release 11) (2014). http://www.3gpp.org/DynaReport/37901.htm
18. Dai, H., et al.: The evaluation of CQI delay compensation schemes based on jakes model and ITU scenarios. In: Proceedings of 2012 IEEE Vehicular Technology Conference (VTC Fall) (2012)

Network Mobility and Mobility Management

A Survey on Wireless Sensors Networks Security Based on a Layered Approach

Raul A. Fuentes-Samaniego[1], Ana Rosa Cavalli[1], Juan A. Nolazco-Flores[2], and Javier Baliosian[3]([✉])

[1] Telecom SudParis, Evry, France
{fuentess,ana.cavalli}@telecom-sudparis.eu
[2] ITESM Tec de Monterrey, Monterrey, Mexico
jnolazco@itesm.mx
[3] Universidad de la Republica, Montevideo, Uruguay
baliosian@fing.edu.uy

Abstract. The Internet of Things (IoT) is one of the most novel networking paradigms and there are yet too many technologies defining themselves as IoT complicating the scenario for developing a fully IoT environment. The situation becomes even harder when security and privacy are considered. In this paper, we present a survey on the security aspects of an IoT conformed by wireless sensors communicating through the IEEE 802.15.4 standard. This survey follows a revision of the state of art in a layer-by-layer systematic analysis.

Keywords: IoT · WSN · 6LoWPAN · CoAP · 802.15.4

1 Introduction

The Internet of Things (IoT) is "a world-wide network of interconnected objects uniquely addressable, based on standard communication protocols" [1]. The IoT is composed by "interconnected objects", which usually have a wireless network device as a medium of communication, the objects (or things) include a great variety of technologies for an equally diverse list of objectives. Additionally, the IoT needs a "standard communication protocol" to be able to connect the different types of nodes. The different types of nodes are a "world-wide network" as it can be composed of hundreds of nodes conforming one or more networks throughout the world. It is required to consider the three aspects mentioned above at the same time to be able to develop applications for the IoT [2]. Aside from them, the legal implications of the data collected from the objects and the security concerns that have to be handled by the applications are necessary to be considered. The sum of the five previous aspects for the development of an IoT application is referred in this work as a fully IoT environment as shown in the Fig. 1.

The IoT can be composed by a great variety of objects, with different origins, using different schemes for their identification and for handling information, examples are the Radio-Frequency IDentification (RFID) tags, sensors, actuators, mobile phones, between others. Applications under IoT are varied such

© Springer International Publishing Switzerland 2015
M.C. Aguayo-Torres et al. (Eds.): WWIC 2015, LNCS 9071, pp. 77–93, 2015.
DOI: 10.1007/978-3-319-22572-2_6

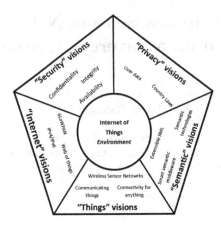

Fig. 1. "Internet of Things" paradigm as a result of the convergence of different visions.

as smart homes, smart cities, traffic congestion monitoring, waste management. Given its ubiquity, very sensible and personal information may travel across this network, security and privacy in the IoT are of paramount importance. Still, many IoT devices have shown to have vulnerabilities that are easy to exploit [3]. Even more, standards widely used by IoT implementations, such as Wireless Sensor Network (WSN) and RFID, were not designed with security in mind [4–6].

The survey has as objective to produce a review of the state of the art regarding to the IoT, taking as a platform the WSN whose sensors works with the IEEE 802.15.4 standard. The Sects. 2 to 4 reviews the state of art respect to the OSI layered model. Specifically the Sect. 2 is a review of the two lowest layers: Physical and Data-link layers which correspond to the IEEE 802.15.4 standard. The Sect. 3 is dedicated to the Network layer, which is focused on IPv6 and its constrained version for WSN networks. The Sect. 4 is the review of the upper layers, and finally in the Sect. 5 the conclusions are presented.

2   Physical and Data-Link Layers

The work on the lower layers of sensor networks has been centered around their performance issues. However, as they started to be an important part of the IoT, their security issues have gained in importance. To bound the scope of this work, when reviewing the work made for the low network layers, this survey focus on the IEEE 802.15.4-2006 standard due to its ubiquity and its good control of unreliable transmissions, latency and freshness of the messages, as well as by its MAC layer security mechanism with Advanced Encryption Standard (AES) 128-bits, and its native support for IPv6.

2.1   PHY Layer

Vulnerability Analysis. The main vulnerabilities that any WSN node can face at the PHY layer are [7]: (i) Conflicts due to the nature of the wireless communication allows jam situations to happen, where two or more nodes begin to transmit provoking the overlapping of their signals. (ii) The exhaustion of the limited power supply of the nodes. Too many transmissions can lead to a faster exhaustion. The traffic can be originated by malicious attackers or by the hot-spot problem as shown in the Fig. 2. (iii) The tampering of the sensor brings the risk of subtracting information or hardware that is vital for its correct operation or even acquiring control over it. (iv) A shutdown of one or more nodes, for any given reason, can cause a loss of redundancy, bringing up the risk to lose the connectivity on different parts of the WSN topology.

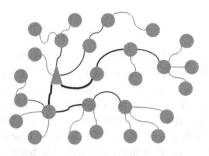

Fig. 2. Hot-spot dilemma: Certain nodes will carry the messages to others nodes, thus, transmitting more often and spending faster their power supply [8].

Threat Analysis. The following are some examples of threats at the PHY layer: (i) Bit errors caused by devices that flood the same area of sensors and with signals transmitted on the 2.4 GHz channel (jamming). If the nodes try to retransmit while are in a JAM situation they can exhaust their power supply prematurely. (ii) Physical damage or stealing of sensors and sink nodes: the keys in the memory of the nodes could be subtracted, as well as the data collected in them. (iii) The read of the wireless data (Sniffing) with the risk of the credentials stealing or private information acquiring.

2.2   MAC Layer

Vulnerabilities Analysis. The main vulnerabilities that any WSN node can face at the MAC layer are: (i) An unreliable transfer since the upper protocols are connectionless, the risk of having a higher channel error rate exist; thus forcing the allocation of resources to error handling in this layer. (ii) Unauthorized nodes joining to the WSN network. (iii) Latency in the multi-hop routing, the network congestion and the node processing can lead to a greater latency in the network, thus making it difficult to achieve synchronization among sensors [6]. (iv) The collision of messages due to a bad control of the message flow or an excess of nodes for the control to be executed successfully. (v) The exhaustion of the medium due to continuous transmission, with the risk of depleting the power supply of the sensors.

Threat Analysis. Following is a list of the possible threats on this layer, mainly the DoS attacks. (i) Bits errors by denial of services (DoS) attacks. Under a DoS persistent attack, the sensor's authentication could fail leaving them isolated. Additionally, the DoS will reduce the bandwidth for all the nodes. (ii) Read wireless packets (Sniffing): Malicious nodes could be able to steal credentials for the AES mechanism on this layer. (iii) Impersonate other WSN nodes as the sink nodes, for taking partial or total control over the network. The communication can be compromised as the nodes could get and process traffic that should not be getting.

2.3   Discussion

The risks associated with the Data-Link layer such as collisions, exhaustion and the uneven access to the medium can be mitigated by the use of encryption on the MAC layer because it is able to separate unauthorized nodes from the network. For tampering attacks, the selection of sensor hardware and how they are placed define their resistance against those attacks. However, this selection may probably cause a higher sensors cost. The importance of the data which is held or forwarded by the sensors must help to decide between price and security.

The most obvious alternative to prolong the network lifetime is placing a higher capacity battery on key nodes. However, the work in [8] proposed mobile sink nodes for reducing the hot-spot risk, and it concluded that using a path-constrained mobile sink may improve the network lifetime. However, it is not always possible to create mobile sink points. In the case they are used, their velocity has to be carefully considered, the work in [9] shows that the IEEE 802.15.4 standard is not able to maintain a node's connectivity for fast moving nodes.

It is possible to defend the network against jamming using various forms of spread-spectrum or frequency hopping communication. However, those mechanisms require more complex hardware and permanent power supply, the low-cost and low-power sensors are quite limited in this aspect [7,10]. Still, the same work concluded than a well designed antenna polarization can properly handle some jamming attacks. The work in [11] also suggests a series of measures to control jamming attacks: (i) Detection techniques: deploying elements for discovering instantly a jamming attack. (ii) Proactive countermeasures: software measures, such as changing the MAC protocol for adding FHSS. Some of the techniques are compatible with the IEEE 802.15.4 standard. (iii) Reactive countermeasures: enable reactions only when a jamming attack is detected, many techniques are compatible with the IEEE 802.15.4 standard. (iv) Mobile Agent-based solution: Special mobile-agents are defined and used as autonomous programs with the ability to move from host to host, in this case for finding new paths free of jamming attacks.

The passive and active protection can handle the risk of tampering [6,10]. The passive mechanisms are those who do not need additional power and include technologies that protect a circuit from being detected. Examples are the protective coatings and the tamper seals. The active defenses are related to special hardware circuits to prevent sensitive data from being exposed. Due to the cost of the active defenses, it will hardly be seen in the sensors [10].

The suggestions in [6] related to hardware choices can have an impact against the tampering attacks, for instance: (i) periodical checking of the location for detecting any tampered sensor. (ii) Acquiring hardware capable of self-termination. This can be very useful for avoiding any risk of shared keys or data, falling into the wrong hands. (iii) Low-cost protection countermeasures as a randomized clock signal, randomized multi-threading, robust low-frequency sensor which kills the processor at the first tamper try, restricted program counter and top-layer sensor meshes for being an annoyance to micro-probing attackers.

The authentication mechanism can begin on the Data-Link layer, the greatest benefit is that, almost everything inside the IoT environment will be hidden from passive observers (sniffing) as the MAC layer has Advanced Encryption Standard (AES) 128-bits. Some platforms as ZigBee already implement a system based in PANA for authentication, meanwhile open-source, such as Contik, offers a similar alternative.

3   Network: IPv6 and Routing Protocol

With the IEEE 802.15.4-2006 standard, the nodes inside of the WSN subnetwork use the 6LoWPAN protocol meanwhile the other nodes use the IPv6 protocol. Before handling the analysis of the vulnerabilities and threats, we will first focus on two areas related to the adaptation of IPv6 to WSN: the techniques for the compression of IPv6 with its secondary protocols. And, the types of communication between nodes that are inside the IoT environment.

3.1   6LowPAN

The 6LowPAN specifications are defined in [12,13]. The UDP header, the IPv6 protocol, the ICMPv6 sub-protocol and the Neighbor Discovery protocol, which is part of ICMPv6, are severely modified for adapting them to an environment where multicast is not desired and the size of the messages must be small.

The IPv6 header is strongly modified to compress it from 40 bytes to 3 bytes using the Header Compression technique (HC1) [14]. *Because the version field is removed, it is mandatory to use only 6LowPAN inside of the WSN subnetwork.* If only one address is used, the header will have a length of 40 bits (5 bytes) otherwise will be of 48 bits (6 bytes). The Fig. 3 shows a 6LoWPAN header. The terms 6LoWPAN subnetwork and WSN subnetwork are interchangeable in this work.

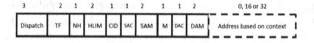

Fig. 3. A general overview of the 6LoWPAN header.

A new IPv6 header is defined as *RH4 routing header* [15] used by the routing protocol defined in [16] called IPv6 Routing Protocol for Low-Power and Lossy Networks (RPL). The RPL is an addresses-based mechanism instead of location-based.

Neighbor Discovery Protocol. The ICMPv6 sub-protocol Neighbor Discovery (ND) is a key element of IPv6. It allows the nodes to perform an auto-configuration without the need of a third service as DHCP. The standard ND uses the stateless auto-configuration (SLAAC) and the stateful configuration which is equivalent to the normal configuration on IPv4. The ND protocol for 6LoWPAN was redesigned in [13] deprecating some elements stated in [12]: The Duplicate Address Detection (DAD) messages are reduced to a minimum, the multicast is taken away, and special messages for nodes on duty sleep are introduced to ND. Additionally, the order of messages sent is changed giving priority only to RA ones.

Routing Protocol for Low-Power and Lossy Networks (RPL). The RPL routing protocol is used to route messages between nodes on a mesh topology or star topology. The work in [17] concluded that RPL is able to deliver messages on multipoint-to-sink and sink-to-multipoint, including point-to-point but is not optimal for the last, due to the RPL nature. The routing protocol is defined in [16] and is stated that RPL can work in "unsecured", "pre-installed" and "authenticated" mode for authentication purposes. The first mode consists of RPL messages without any security mechanism. On the second mode, the nodes have pre-installed keys for RPL. And finally, in the third mode the nodes use pre-installed keys to request to a third authority server for a new key.

The RPL protocol has been designed for 6LoWPAN and was released in March 2012. Therefore, RPL needs to have more experiments to measure the actual performance of ZigBee IP or Contiki in real environments. As well, more security analyses must be realized, particularly, how it reacts to malicious or malfunctioning nodes, and against wormhole attacks [10].

3.2 Type of Communication

The most important types of communication between the IoT environment entities are: (i) Sensor-Sensor & Sensor-Sink: It will carry data and commands for the sensor. Sink and sensors will pass the information as shown on the Fig. 4a. (ii) Sensor & Border router: The translation from the IEEE 802.15.4 subnetwork with 6LoWPAN to another subnetwork, as Ethernet with IPv6, is made with a special gateway as shown in the Fig. 4b.

Vulnerabilities Analysis. All the well-known risks of vulnerabilities on IP networks still apply, however, 6LowPAN bring new challenges and risks that can be exploited. More work is needed for developing a well-defined list of risks for 6LoWPAN. Yet, the following risks are identified:

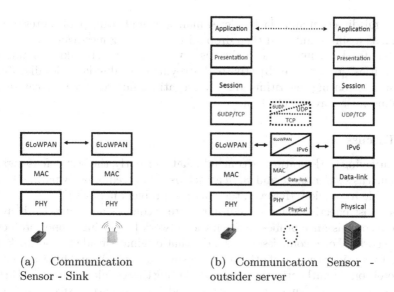

Fig. 4. Type of communication based in layers.

- The nodes answer to fake ND messages, adding extra scopes to their configuration.
- Malicious nodes transmitting poisoning messages against the RPL protocol.
- Malicious nodes trying to pass by other nodes, by example the ZigBee IP coordinator.
- Heavy reconnaissance scans on the 6LoWPAN network can lead to deplete the power supply as they force the sensors to transmit more often.
- The hot-spot problem could still be traced on this layer.
- WSN nodes using IPv6, IPv4 or other type of network layer protocol instead of 6LoWPAN, as this can provoke unexpected behaviors.

The SLAAC configuration in the nodes generates a specific weak point for the 6LoWPAN nodes: *The sensors are very weak against reconnaissance attacks.* Of the 64 bits space, only 16 will be used, and always on the lowest part. Once the node generates a valid address, it will never use another one. Therefore, a reconnaissance attack on the WNS subnetwork would be trivial.

Our Threat Analysis. The following list enumerated a series of DoS attacks that can afflict any type of WSN, with respect of to the network layer [10]:

- DoS neglect and greed: When a malicious node is giving false information to other nodes, trying to trick them to route all the messages to it, as spoofing a sink point, and then just drop the messages or reduces their priority values of the fields if any.
- DoS homing or hot-spot problem: It is possible to localize specific nodes inside of the WSN subnetwork. In other WSN protocols, this can lead to geo-localization as well.

– DoS misdirection and black hole: A malicious node can spoof routes or even pass as a sink point, and then drop all the incoming messages.
– Sybil attacks: defined as a "malicious device illegitimately taking on multiple identities" [6] with the objective of destroying the redundancy for distributed systems, routing algorithm, data aggregation, fair resource allocation and foiling misbehavior detection.

3.3 Discussion

After surveying the literature we conclude that, currently, the best defense against a DoS such as *sybil, neglect,* and *greed* attacks is having redundancy paths [10] that RPL is able to provide. However, the hot-spot problem persists [8].

The most effective defense against remote reconnaissance attacks, is avoiding the reconnaissance probes to reach the network by placing proper protection on edge nodes. For reconnaissance attacks that originate inside the network, it is needed to consider the use of other mechanisms, such as IDS and firewalls, or rely completely on the authentication process following the techniques suggested in [10].

The work in [13] suggests that is a good idea to have a strong link-layer protection mechanism such as SEcure Neighbor Discovery (SEND) protocol. Works related to WSN sensors proposed different mechanisms for authentication on this layer, e.g. Tesla, TIK and TRANS [10]. For standardization, the use of the RPL protocol is suggested.

If in the previous layer the authentication of the nodes is not handled the authentication must occur in this layer. The key nodes in this layer, such as the border router, must have a better physical security than the other sensors, if they are lost all the nodes will be jeopardized.

4   Upper Layers: Trust and Data Handling

The standardization, format, and integrity of data are aspects that will be defined in the transport, session, presentation and application layers. The transport layer for the Internet is conformed by TCP and UDP. The 6LowPAN protocol supports both of them and adds a third one called 6LoWPAN UDP (6UDP), which is a constrained version of UDP. *As TCP implies a heavy overhead for the sensors, all the communications inside of the 6LoWPAN subnetwork should be using the 6UDP protocol.* Because of the previous restrictions, the protocol HTTP is not a candidate for the standardization of a secure channel between the sensors and the clients; nevertheless, there exist protocols that are friendly with 6UPD, one of them is the Constrained Application Protocol (CoAP) that, roughly speaking, is the equivalent of HTTP for 6UPD. Additionally, the Extensible Markup Language (EXI) protocol has been selected for the Machine to Machine communications (M2M) between sensors. CoAP and EXI are explained in more detail in Sect. 4.1 and are followed by an analysis in Sect. 4.2 of the current state of the art for developing trust mechanisms into constrained networks, finally a review in the handling of the data under the IoT environment is made in Sect. 4.3.

4.1   CoAP and EXI

Protocols based on the paradigm Representational State Transfer (ReST) have been developed in the last years to reach a reliable communication using an intrinsic unreliable protocol, such as UDP. They are, usually, similar to HTTP but are designed for constrained networks requirements, for instance 6LoWPAN [18]. They are ideal for the M2M communication.

The CoAP is a protocol based in ReST and defined by the IETF [19]. CoAP has the same type of messages as HTTP (GET, PUT, POST and DELETE) making them compatibles. It uses a constrained version of TLS called Datagram Transport Layer Security (DTLS) for achieving confidentiality for end-to-end communication over 6UDP. CoAP helps defining both, the session and the way for sending data. A structured way of representing the data helps to standardize a successful M2M communication. The Extensible Markup Language (XML) has been used for that purpose on traditional devices [18] as well as other structured protocols, such as Protobuf developed and used by Google for their own index servers [20]. A weakness of XML is its "verbosity" for defining the data, as it is not ideal for constrained networks. However, the organization W3C released the EXI protocol as a compact representation of XML for constrained environments [21]. ZigBee IP and Contiki have native support for CoAP and DTLS. ZigBee IP has native support for EXI, but Contiki seems not to have it, though the work in [22] has defined an implementation based on the W3 EXI standard [23]. Nevertheless, the work is from 2012 and the definition on [23] has been updated since then.

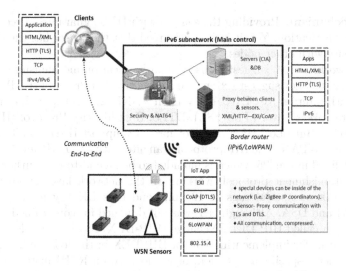

Fig. 5. Representation of one communication ent-to-end

As stated before, the fully IoT environment need to consider issues well known from typical networks, therefore the IPv6 subnetwork needs to have an access control mechanism and advanced security against attacks. The Implementation of IDS as an option, although implementing one IDS in the 6LoWPAN subnetwork could be challenging. Besides of any other devices that by law or administrative criteria are needed to guarantee a secure performance of the network; and a NAT64 gateway for giving support to clients with only IPv4.

4.2   Analysis of the State of the Art on Trustiness for IoT

Many well-known mechanisms exist to reach the trustiness of the applications on development. However, the limited resources on the sensors oblige to consider new mechanisms which bring new challenges for achieving the following goals: (i) A Trust mechanism for all the nodes on the IoT environment. (ii) Privacy of the data being transmitted. (iii) A reliable M2M communication between the sensors and other non-human members.

On the other hand, the implementation of more advanced trust management systems for detecting aberrant nodes (those with malfunctions or compromised) and revoking their trust should be considered [5]. However the limitation of the hardware and the memory in the sensors limits this possibility. But at least, a trust management system with authentication, authorization and accounting (AAA) should be implemented. Additionally to the trustworthy nodes, the way in which the node will treat the data and how it will be transmitted are factors that need to be defined. Yet, for the transmission, are required cryptographic techniques but the sensors only have as a valid option the block or stream ciphers due to their limited resources [6].

Trust Mechanism. Providing the sensors with DTLS guarantee a secure end-to-end communication. Yet, it is no guaranteed that the sensor has the rights to communicate with other nodes.

Other works as [24] suggest to use the authentication mechanisms from real solutions for IP. They suggest Extensible Authentication Protocol (EAP), as well as IPsec with Internet Key Exchange version 2 (IKEv2), Transport Layer Secure with Secure Sokeet Layer (TLS/SSL), DTLS, Host Identity Protocol (HIP) and ID-Moskowitz. But 6LoWPAN does not natively support IPsec and TLS is not optimal in 6LoWPAN. The HIP protocol is an alternative to EAP, an experimental draft defined in the [25] which is intended to be an end-to-end authentication and key establishment protocol, working on the network layer or above. HIP bases its work on special tags of 128 bits and uses DH key management as RSA/SHA1 and DSA. Although HIP was not designed for constrained networks an adaptation called HIP Diet EXchange (HIP-DEX) has been made.

Other works for implementing HIP or HIP-DEX in the IoT are [26–29]. But they are either a specific adaptation, or are focused on RFID instead of WSN, or do not use 6LoWPAN or a mix of those, making them not ideal for standardization. The work in [30] focuses on adapting HIP-DEX to 6LoWPAN, using Contiki as a platform. It operates at the MAC layer, similar to ZigBee IP with PANA, and according to the work, seems to be more efficient than PANA with the use of resources. Yet, they consider that more work is needed to create a more lightweight solution.

HIP and EAP are strong candidates to be used as AAA mechanisms as they are very well known on IP domains. However, an AAA mechanism can be considered as the lowest trust system available. Due to the constraints of the sensors for the IoT environment, many of the best known trust management systems are not available, at least not with the current technology.

Another alternative is the project of Usable Trust in the Internet of Things (uTRUSTit) which has two objectives [31–34]: (i) Create a guideline to identify, produce and manage trustiness on the IoT environments. (ii) Developing the trust feedback toolkit (TFT) which aims to be embedded in smartphones and IoT applications for providing privacy settings and feedbacks to the final user.

In addition to uTRUSTit exists the Social Internet of Things (SIoT) as a change of paradigm to the IoT. With SIoT, the "smart" device "evolves" to "social" device with the objective of fostering resource visibility from the devices [35]. SIoT not only wants the devices to be able to communicate inside of a specific IoT environment, but between multiple environments. Allowing the nodes to interact between themselves, as people do, for delivering data and finding paths [36]. Also, SIoT has developed a trustiness based on social interaction and P2P techniques [37].

The main limitations with SIoT are that all their works are theoretical and only based on simulations. They assume a mix of devices - RFID, mobile devices, sensors, etc. - and the nodes without enough resources can retrieve them from other nodes. Consequently, all the simulations are made without considering the hardware limitations.

In [38] an adaptation to SIoT for adding Quality of Service (QoS) is proposed. Similarly to the original work on SIoT, the testing does not consider the current hardware limitations. Also, 6LoWPAN has removed key elements for QoS, therefore it is needed more work to define how to handle QoS on 6LoW-PAN networks. Similar to SIoT, the work in [39] is able to interconnect devices of different environments, however it takes into consideration the privacy of data as a part of Quality of Context (QoC) for defining the trustiness of the nodes. Yet, again, this work is still on simulation and does not consider the current hardware constraints.

In [38] a key management system similar to PANA is proposed, making it redundant. One approach to a fuzzy trust based access control is defined in [40], however, their trust system is a concept tested with only simulations.

There are other works related to the authentication process, as cited in [41, 42] but their implementations are not standardized and several weaknesses in their works can be found. In [41] is proposed an authentication mechanism aimed for mobile devices on IoT, where a pair of public and private keys are generated based on the nodes and their current network, with a third server used for generating the entropy of the keys. However, we have found their algorithm very susceptible to middleman attacks, as the entropy number does not change, and is sent in an insecure way. The work of [42] is an authorization mechanism based in control lists where each node has a list of the privileges for all the existing nodes on the network. If a node gets a message and the receptor is not authorized in the list, the node will drop the message. However, the IPv6 address is the only way to identify the nodes, and even with the 6LoWPAN short version of 16 bits this will deplete the node memory very quickly as can be thousands of nodes. Also, it is possible to bypass this with only changing the source and destination address.

Data Privacy. CoAP using DTLS guarantee the privacy of the data, due that any pair of nodes is able to configure a unique and temporary symmetric key through the session lifespan. CoAP has four modes for configuring DTLS: NoSec, PreSharedKey, RawPublicKey and Certificate. Each one of them operates in different ways and has different scenarios in mind [43]. NoSec has DTLS disabled. When using PreSharedKey a list of pre-shared keys exists where each key includes a list of nodes. The relation in the list can be used 1:1 to identify each node in the network; the relation can vary for identifying certain nodes as members of specific groups. For this configuration the cipher suite TLS_PSK_WITH_AES_128_CCM_8 is used.

The RawPublicKey mode uses an asymmetric key pairing, without a certificate, that will be validated using the cipher suite TLS_ECDHE_ECDSA_WITH_AES_128_CCM_8. For the mode Certificate, the protocol X.509 will be used for certifying the keys. This mode also uses the cipher suite as RawPublicKey but applying the hash algorithm SHA-256 for the key. Is important to note that previous versions of the SoAP draft stated that the Certificate mode should implement the cipher suite TLS_RSA_PSK_WITH_AES_128_CBC_SHA instead of the current one.

The work in [44] is focused on identifying the cost of many cryptographic suites for 6LoWPAN networks, including SoAP with DTLS, and their own compression technique: Encapsulated Security Payload (ESP) for 6LoWPAN. ESP uses triple Data Encryption Standard (3DES) and AES with keys of 96 bits, a tradeoff between security and performance of the constrained devices. ESP is discarded because its trade-off is too much for the current technology. Yet, the results of its tests with the 3 modes of DTLS are displayed in the Table 1, although the Certificate results are deprecated as they used a previous version of SoAP.

Table 1. Comparative of [44] with a TelosB (48Kb ROM, 10Kb RAM, 16-bit RISC MSP 430).

	PreShared	PreRaw	Certificate[a]
% Memory RAM/ROM	56.2/88.5	88.6/139.2	53.0/78.9[b]
Energy requirement (mJ)	0.0002	10.8900	0.0019
Computational time (mS)	3.6	2019.6	21.9
Max packets/sec	132.1	0.49	38.7

[a]Current CoAP draft uses TLS_ECDHE_ECDSA_WITH_AES_128_CCM_8 for Certificate and RawPublic.
[b]As estimated based on the ROM of the devices used on the testing.

The work in [45] supports the notion of using DTLS, besides they recommend using a Trusted Platform Module (TPM) embedded chip, which performs the RSA algorithm operations in hardware, as is the case for the `Certificate` mode. The chip helps to reduce the times displayed in the Table 1. The TPM also provides hardware protection against tampering attacks, but the price of 20 USD or more per unit and the potential amount of nodes to be used might not be feasible.

Another alternative is suggested in [46] where virtual machines (V.M.) are implemented in the sensors. This is justified as a way to reduce the problem of hardware compatibility, as the application developers will not be concerned anymore about the particulars of the hardware since this is the V.M. duty. However, the use of V.M. comes with the overhead of resources, yet their work suggests that this is a temporary problem, as new and more powerful sensors will become available in the near future. Finally, the DTLS implementation and its performance are not considered in this work.

Data Structure. How the data get stored on the sensors and servers should follow the already defined standards of privacy, and be subject to the regulations and legal framework of the country where it is deployed. Special emphasis must be given to the IoT, as it has received many critiques due to its potential privacy invasion [47–49]. Different works, as [50,51] are useful for handling the selection, storage and manipulation of data.

Another alternative is the EXI structure with the works in [20,22,52] that have validated its use for constrained devices. EXI uses two different schemes for defining the XML structures: schema-less encoding and schema-informed encoding [18]. The first is generated from the XML data allowing other nodes to decode it without prior knowledge about the structure. The second, by contrast, requires that the nodes share the same XML schema to be able to encode and decode the transmitted data.

There exist other works as [53], which propose changes to the EXI protocol; however, this does not seem to be adequate, since it reduces the wished standardization. In [20] an evaluation of EXI and the Protobuf protocols is made and it is concluded that Protobuf is a better candidate for the IoT, due to its better use of energy and bandwidth optimization. Still, more work is needed for justifying a different approach that risks the standardization.

Vulnerability Analysis. A wrong use of ports by the application can entail the loss of communication. As the 6UDP is a compressed version, the port address fields are reduced from 16 bits to 8 bits, and under certain configuration to 4 bits. A wrong formatted EXI on any part of the communication could provide fake information to the receptor, risking an unexpected behavior from the sensors or clients.

Our Threat Analysis. The clients and sensors will be communicating in at least two possible ways: (i) sending compatible messages between CoAP and HTTPS or (ii) in some point of the IPv6 network, a translation occurs from one protocol to the other and vice versa. The clients should be able to use a standardized application for requesting the information from the IoT environment, as a web browser. However, this brings many threats from the client side, for instance: (i) the data can be captured from the client application, (ii) arbitrary orders could be sent from or to the client, (iii) Similar to former case, but in huge quantities for provoking a DoS.

4.3   Discussion

Although IoT implementations have been appearing since 2001, almost all the work has been made on proprietary protocols, which need special devices for translating from the WSN network to the Internet. The protocols listed in this survey are relatively new, 6LoWPAN was first announced in 2009 and products supporting it began to appear since 2012. Something similar occurs with the ReST protocols, such as CoAP that is still a draft. EXI is from 2007, but it was not designed for the IoT. Therefore, *more work for testing the performance of all those protocols combined is needed.*

In the Fig. 5 is shown a generic model for the IoT environment. The clients have IPv6 or IPv4, and they request the data using a typical HTTP/S communication meanwhile the sensors communicate using CoAP, 6LoWPAN and the 802.15.4 standard. As all the communication and operations occur over the Internet, all the inherited security concerns need to be taken into consideration, such as the ones related to HTTP.

5   Conclusions

The objective of the work is to present a review of the state of the art on the secure design for IoT environments. Taking as a starting point the 802.15.4 standard for the WSN platform, and having as primary concerns the security, trust and privacy of each component of the environment. Emphasis is given to those protocols that let the intercommunication between WSNs and the current Internet (e.g. IPv6). The number of works in the surveyed field is still limited, their achievements are modest, and there is plenty of space to investigate further.

References

1. Enterprise, N.D.N., Micro, R.I.G.: Nanosystems, Internet of things in 2020, roadmap for the future, Technical report Version 1.1, May 2008
2. Atzori, L., Iera, A., Morabito, G.: The internet of things: a survey. Comput. Netw. 54(15), 2787–2805 (2010)
3. Haley, K.: 2014 predictions from symantec, November 2013. http://www.symantec.com/connect/blogs/2014-predictions-symantec-0. Accessed 31 March 2014
4. Abreu, F.B., Morais, A., Cavalli, A., Wehbi, B., Montes de Oca, E.: An effective attack detection approach in wireless mesh networks. In: 27th International Conference on Advanced Information Networking and Applications Workshops, pp. 1450–1455. IEEE (2013)

5. Undercoffer, J., Avancha, S., Joshi, A., Pinkston, J.: Security for Sensor Networks, pp. 253–275. Kluwer Academic Publishers, Norwell (2004)
6. Walters, J.P., Liang, Z., Shi, W., Chaudhary, V.: Wireless sensor network security: a survey. In: Security in Distributed, Grid and Pervasive Computing, Chap. 17
7. Wood, A., Stankovic, J.: Denial of service in sensor networks. Computer **35**(10), 54–62 (2002)
8. Vlajic, N., Stevanovic, D.: Performance analysis of Zigbee-based wireless sensor networks with path-constrained mobile sink(s). In: 2009 Third International Conference on Sensor Technologies and Applications, pp. 61–68 (2009)
9. Zen, K., Habibi, D., Member, S., Rassau, A., Ahmad, I.: Performance Evaluation of IEEE 802. 15. 4 for Mobile Sensor Networks, Technical report, School of Engineering, Edith Cowan University, Joondalup, Australia (2008)
10. Chen, X., Makki, K., Yen, K., Pissinou, N.: Sensor network security: a survey. IEEE Commun. Surv. Tutorials **11**(2), 52–73 (2009)
11. Mpitziopoulos, A., Gavalas, D., Konstantopoulos, C., Pantziou, G.: A survey on jamming attacks and countermeasures in WSNs. IEEE Commun. Surv. Tutorials **11**(4), 42–56 (2009)
12. Montenegro, G., Kushalnagar, N., Hui, J., Culler, D.: Rfc 4944: Transmission of ipv6 packets over ieee 802.15, Technical report, IETF, September 2007. Accessed 28 April 2012
13. Shelby, Z., Chakrabarti, S., Nordmark, E., Borman, C.: Rfc 6775: Neighbor discovery optimization for ipv6 over low-power wireless personal area networks (6lowpans), Technical report, IETF, November 2012. Accessed 28 April 2012
14. Hasbollah, A.A., Ariffin, S.H.S., Bahru, J.: Performance analysis For 6loWPAN IEEE 802. 15. 4 with IPv6 network. In: TENCON, pp. 4–8 (2009)
15. Maley, R.: The new zigbee ip specification: Ipv6 control for low-power, low-cost devices, Technical report, 2400 Camino Ramon, San Ramon, CA 94583, April 2013. Accessed 22 April 2013
16. Winter, T., Thubert, P., Brand, A., Hui, J., Kelsey, R., Levis, P., Pister, K., Struik, R., Vasseur, J., Alexander, R.: Rfc 6550: Rpl: Ipv6 routing protocol for low-power and lossy networks, Technical report, IETF, April 2008. Accessed 23 May 2012
17. Gomez, C., Paradells, J.: Wireless home automation networks : a survey of architectures and technologies. IEEE Commun. Mag. **48**, 92–101 (2010)
18. Zanella, A., Bui, N., Castellani, A., Vangelista, L., Zorzi, M.: Internet of things for smart cities. IEEE Internet Things **1**(1), 22–32 (2014)
19. Skarmeta, A.F., Hernandez-Ramos, J.L., Moreno, M.V.: A decentralized approach for security and privacy challenges in the internet of things. In: 2014 IEEE World Forum on Internet of Things (WF-IoT), pp. 67–72 (2014)
20. Gligori, N., Dejanovi, I., Krco, S.: Performance evaluation of compact binary XML representation for constrained devices. In: 2011 International Conference on Distributed Computing in Sensor Systems and Workshops (DCOSS), pp. 1–5. IEEE, Baercelona (2011)
21. Efficient xml interchange (exi) format 1.0 (second edition), Technical report, W3C, February 2014. http://www.w3.org/TR/exi/. Accessed 10 May 2012
22. Caputo, D., Mainetti, L., Patrono, L., Vilei, A.: Implementation of the EXI schema on wireless sensor nodes using contiki. In: 2012 Sixth International Conference on Innovative Mobile and Internet Services in Ubiquitous Computing, pp. 770–774 (2012)
23. Embeddable exi processor in c, Technical report, Embedded Internet Systems Laboratory (EISLAB), October 2013. http://www.w3.org/TR/exi/. Accessed 10 May 2012

24. Garcia Morchon, O., Kumar, S., Hummen, R., Struik, R.: Security Considerations in the IP-based Internet of Things draft-garcia-core-security-06, Technical report, IETF (2014)
25. Moskowitz, R., Nikander, P., Jokela, P., Hederson, T.: Rfc 5201: Host identity protocol, Technical report, IETF, April 2008. Accessed 23 May 2012
26. Urien, P., Elrharbi, S., Nyamy, D., Chabanne, H., Icart, T., Lecocq, F., Pepin, C., Toumi, K., Bouet, M., Pujolle, G., Krzanik, P., Susini, J.-F.: Hip-tags architecture implementation for the internet of things. In: First Asian Himalayas International Conference on Internet. AH-ICI 2009, pp. 1–5 (2009)
27. Urien, P., Nyami, D., Elrharbi, S., Chabanne, H., Icart, T., Pepin, C., Bouet, M., Cunha, D., Guyot, V., Pujolle, G., Gressier-Soudan, E., Susini, J. F.: Hip tags privacy architecture. In: 3rd International Conference on Systems and Networks Communications. ICSNC 2008, pp. 179–184 (2008)
28. Hummen, R., Hiller, J., Henze, M., Wehrle, K.: A hip dex compression layer for the ip-based internet of things. In: 2013 IEEE 9th International Conference on Wireless and Mobile Computing, Networking and Communications (WiMob), pp. 259–266 (2013)
29. Nyamy, D., Urien, P.: Hip-tag, a new paradigm for the internet of things. In: 2011 IEEE Consumer Communications and Networking Conference (CCNC), pp. 49–54 (2011)
30. Meca, F.V., Ziegeldorf, J.H., Sanchez, P.M., Morchon, O.G., Kumar, S.S., Keoh, S.L.: HIP security architecture for the ip basedinternet of things. In: 2013 27th International Conference on Advanced Information Networking and Applications Workshops, pp. 1331–1336 (2013)
31. Hochleitner, C., Graf, C., Unger, D., Tscheligi, M.: Making devices trustworthy: security and trust feedback in the internet of things. In: Pervasive 2012 Fourth International Workshop on Security and Privacy in Spontaneous Interaction and Mobile Phone Use, Newcastle, UK (2012)
32. Leister, W., Schulz, T.: Ideas for a trust indicator in the internet of things. In: SMART, no. c, IARIA, pp. 31–34 (2012)
33. Pietro, D.: Security and trust challenges in the area of IoT. In: INNOSUMMIT (2012)
34. Dunkels, A.: Utrustit website (2013). www.utrustit.eu. Accessed 11 May 2014
35. Atzori, L., Iera, A., Morabito, G.: From smart objects to social objects: the next evolutionary step of the internet of things. Commun. Mag. **52**, 97–105 (2014)
36. Nitti, M., Atzori, L., Cvijikj, I.P.: Network navigability in the social internet of things. In: 2014 IEEE World Forum on Internet of Things (WF-IoT), pp. 405–410. IEEE, Seoul (2014)
37. Nitti, M., Girau, R., Atzori, L., Member, S.: Trustworthiness management in the social internet of things. IEEE Trans. Knowl. Data Eng. **26**(5), 1253–1266 (2014)
38. Nasiraee, H., Mohasefi, J.B.: A novel three party key establishment scheme in the context of internet-of-things. In: Information Security and Cryptology (ISCISC), pp. 1–5. IEEE, Yazd (2013)
39. Machara, S., Chabridon, S., Taconet, C.: Trust-based context contract models for the internet of things. In: 2013 IEEE 10th International Conference on Ubiquitous Intelligence and Computing and 2013 IEEE 10th International Conference on Autonomic and Trusted Computing, pp. 557–562 (2013)
40. Mahalle, P.N., Thakre, P.A., Prasad, N.R., Prasad, R.: A fuzzy approach to trust based access control in internet of things. In: Communications, Wireless, Technology, Vehicular (eds.) Information Theory and Aerospace and Electronic Systems (VITAE), pp. 2–6. Atlantic city, IEEE (2013)

41. Khan, S.U., Pastrone, C., Lavagno, L., Spirito, M.A.: An authentication and key establishment scheme for the ip-based wireless sensor networks. Procedia Comput. Sci. **10**, 1039–1045 (2012)
42. Oliveira, L.M., Rodrigues, J.J., Neto, C., de Sousa, A.F.: Network admission control solution for 6LoWPAN networks. In: 2013 Seventh International Conference on Innovative Mobile and Internet Services in Ubiquitous Computing, pp. 472–477 (2013)
43. Shelby, Z., Hartke, K., Bormann, C.: Constrained application protocol (coap) draft-ietf-core-coap-18, Technical report, IETF, June 2013. Accessed 23 May 2012
44. Granjal, J., Monteiro, E., Silva, J.S.: On the effectiveness of end-to-end security for internet-integrated sensing applications. In: 2012 IEEE International Conference on Green Computing and Communications, pp. 87–93 (2012)
45. Kothmayr, T., Schmitt, C., Hu, W., Br, M.: A DTLS based end-to-end security architecture for the internet of things with two-way authentication. In: Local Computer Networks Workshops (LCN Workshops), pp. 956–963. IEEE, Clearwater (2012)
46. Azzara, A., Alessandrelli, D., Bocchino, S., Pagano, P., Petracca, M.: Architecture, functional requirements, and early implementation of an instrumentation grid for the IoT. In: 2012 IEEE 14th International Conference on High Performance Computing and Communication and 2012 IEEE 9th International Conference on Embedded Software and Systems, pp. 320–327 (2012)
47. Lohr, S.: The age of big data, New York Times the opinion pages: Sunday Review, February 2012. Accessed 27 May 2014
48. Fried, L.: Minimizing risk is easy: Adopt a bill of rights, New York Times the opinion pages: Room for debate, May 2014. Accessed 27 May 2014
49. Bennett, M.: The internet of things will kill privacy, Website TheInquirerDebate.net, March 2014. Accessed 27 May 2014
50. Sanchez Alcon, J., Lopez, L., Martinez, J.-F., Castillejo, P.: Automated determination of security services to ensure personal data protection in the internet of things applications. In: 2013 Third International Conference on Innovative Computing Technology (INTECH), pp. 71–76 (2013)
51. Vermesan, O., Friess, P.: Internet of things - Converging technologies for smart environments and integrated ecosystems, River Publishers' Series in Information Science and Technology, River Publishers, PO box 1657 Algade 43, 9000 Aalborg, Denmark (2013). Accesed by the EU IoT research website
52. Castellani, A., Gheda, M., Bui, N., Rossi, M., Zorzi, M.: Web services for the internet of things through coap and exi. In: 2011 IEEE International Conference on Communications Workshops (ICC), pp. 1–6 (2011)
53. Doi, Y., Sato, Y., Ishiyama, M., Ohba, Y., Teramoto, K.: XML-less EXI with code generation for integration of embedded devices in web based systems. In: 2012 3rd IEEE International Conference on the Internet of Things, pp. 76–83 (2012)

A GPSR Enhancement Mechanism for Routing in VANETs

C. Bouras[1,2(✉)], V. Kapoulas[1,2], and E. Tsanai[2]

[1] Computer Technology Institute and Press "Diophantus", Patras, Greece
{bouras,kapoulas}@cti.gr
[2] Computer Engineering and Informatics Department,
University of Patras, Patras, Greece
{bouras,kapoulas,tsanai}@ceid.upatras.gr

Abstract. Vehicular Ad Hoc Networks (VANETs) are considered as a special case of mobile Ad Hoc Networks (MANETs) and are recently gaining a great attention from the research community. The need for improved road safety, traffic efficiency and direct communication along with the great complexity in routing, makes VANETs a highly challenging field. Routing in VANETs has to adapt to special characteristics such as high speed and road pattern movement as well as high linkage break probability. In this paper, we propose an enhancement mechanism for the GPSR routing protocol and present its performance for urban and highway scenarios. Its performance is compared to the performance of the most common MANET routing protocols adopted in VANETs. The proposed enhancement is shown to be beneficial in most occasions as it outperforms the rest of the tested routing protocols.

Keywords: VANETs · MANETs · Routing protocols · Applications

1 Introduction

Vehicular Ad Hoc Networks (VANETs) are a special class of Mobile Ad Hoc Networks (MANETs) with unique characteristics. Similar to MANETs, VANETs are an autonomous and self-configured wireless network that allows communications without any dependency on infrastructures or a central coordinator. Any vehicle can be an active node in a VANET if equipped with wireless transceivers. Most nodes in a VANET are continuously moving with a wide range of speeds and directions in the same way as a vehicle moves in a roadway or an urban area. The moving rates in a VANET are in the general case higher than that in a typical MANET but more predictable for nodes traveling on the same direction. This means that nodes in a VANET, moving towards the same direction in a roadway maintain similar speeds and thus longer radio communication periods of time than those moving in opposite directions. Another unique characteristic of VANETs is their challenging surrounding environment that contains blocks of buildings, roadways that limit the possible node movements and roadside infrastructures that may provide internet access points along with a rich variety of services and applications.

The unique nature of VANETs provides some key advantages over MANETs but also introduces some challenging issues. A main advantage is the unlimited battery

© Springer International Publishing Switzerland 2015
M.C. Aguayo-Torres et al. (Eds.): WWIC 2015, LNCS 9071, pp. 94–107, 2015.
DOI: 10.1007/978-3-319-22572-2_7

power of the vehicle when moving and the high energy levels that allow exceptionally high bandwidth links and integration with new technologies like LTE systems. However, a very important challenge in VANETs is the routing performance [1]. Importing existing MANET routing protocols directly into VANETs could lead to abyssal network performance and unsatisfactory performance. Compared to MANETs, the node movement in VANETs is more predictable allowing more effective position allocation algorithms and routing protocols that benefit from GPS and electronic maps. However, the node density may vary a lot due to traffic conditions. An important issue in the environment of VANETs is the presence of buildings in urban areas, which adds signal weakening and noise. Implementing a routing protocol able to select the best possible path which avoids passing through buildings and other obstacles in the topology is not an easy task.

Routing in VANETs has been an important field for research the last years. A lot of work exists that studies and analyzes routing in VANETs. In [2–4] several routing protocols in MANETs and VANETs are being studied and categorized according to their routing strategy. A comparative performance analysis of AODV (Ad Hoc On-Demand Distance Vector), DSDV (Destination Sequenced Distance Vector) and DSR (Dynamic Source Routing) is conducted in [5] for rural and urban scenarios. In [6], general design ideas and components are being presented for reliable routing design and implementation and in [7], a quantitative model for evaluating routing protocols on highway scenarios is proposed. In [8], 3 realistic radio propagation models are presented that increase the simulation results' accuracy. A novel routing protocol for reliable vehicle to road-side AP connection is proposed in [9] that uses an algorithm for predicting the wireless links' lifetime. In [10], a road based VANET routing protocol is proposed that uses real-time vehicular traffic information to form the paths and is compared with existing well-known routing protocols. In [11], a cross-layer position based routing algorithm for VANETs is presented that performs better than the GPSR (Greedy Perimeter Stateless Routing) routing protocol. The algorithm, named CLWPR (Cross-Layer Weighted Position-based Routing), uses information about link layer quality and positioning from navigation.

The following of this work is organized as follows: Sect. 2 provides an overview of the communication types in VANETs and the most common routing protocols used in MANETs and VANETs that are the subject of study; Sect. 3 describes the proposed enhancement to the GPRS protocol (named GPRS-Modified or GPRS-M for short); Sect. 4 presents the reference scenarios and the simulations settings; Sect. 5 presents and discusses the results of the simulations and finally Sect. 6 gives the conclusions of this work along with ideas and directions for future work.

2 Routing in VANETs

A VANET is composed of static and mobile nodes, thus the common types of communication are:

- Vehicle to Vehicle (V2V)
- Vehicle to Infrastructure (V2I or I2V)
- Infrastructure to Infrastructure (I2I)

V2V is the direct communication between vehicles, which may occur in every topology as long as there is node movement inside the communication range. V2I is the communication between vehicles and infrastructures, which provide services related to safety, convenience, commercial purposes, internet access and others. I2I is the communication between infrastructures, which may be roadside units (RSUs), tool ways and others. Except from these 3 communication types, a mixed communication may occur, especially in cases of large inter-vehicle spacing and low traffic density. In such scenarios, infrastructures such as RSUs may forward the desired messages to the destination. Vehicles and infrastructures may all interact together and form WLAN, Ad Hoc or Hybrid Networks. The routing protocols that are being tested and evaluated in this work are presented below:

AODV. The Ad Hoc On-Demand Distance Vector [12] is intended for use by mobile nodes in an Ad Hoc network. It offers swift adaptation to dynamic link conditions, low processing and memory overhead, low network utilization, and determines unicast routes to destinations within the Ad Hoc network. It uses destination sequence numbers to ensure loop freedom at all times avoiding common problems associated with classical distance from vector protocols.

DSDV. Destination Sequenced Distance Vector routing [13] is adapted from the conventional Routing Information Protocol (RIP) to an Ad Hoc network routing. It adds a new attribute and sequence number to each route table entry of the conventional RIP. Using the newly added sequence number, the mobile nodes can distinguish stale route information from the new one, thus preventing the formation of routing loops.

DSR. Dynamic Source Routing [14] uses source routing, that is, the source indicates in a data packet's sequence of intermediate nodes the routing path. In DSR, the query packet copies in its header the IDs of the intermediate nodes that it has traversed into. The destination then retrieves the entire path from the query packet and uses it to respond to the source. As a result, the source can establish a path to the destination. If the destination is allowed to send multiple route replies, the source node may receive and store multiple routes from the destination. An alternative route can be used when some link in the current route breaks. In a network with low mobility, this is advantageous over AODV since the alternative route can be tried before DSR initiates another flood for route discovery.

OLSR. Optimized Link State Routing [15] operates as a table driven, proactive protocol, i.e., exchanges topology information with other nodes of the network regularly. Each node periodically constructs and maintains the set of neighbors that can be reached in 1-hop and 2-hops. Based on this, the dedicated MPR algorithm minimizes the number of active relays needed to cover all 2-hops neighbors. Such relays are called Multi-Point Relays (MPR). A node forwards a packet if and only if it has been elected as MPR by the sender node. In order to construct and maintain its routing tables, OLSR periodically transmit link state information over the MPR backbone. Upon convergence, an active route is created at each node to reach any destination node in the network. The protocol is particularly suited for large and dense networks, as the optimization done using MPRs works well in this context. The larger and more dense a network is, the more optimization can be achieved.

GPSR. The Greedy Perimeter Stateless Routing [16] is based on positioning of the routers and assumes that every node has access to a location service and knows its position coordinates. GPSR makes greedy forwarding decisions using only information about a router's immediate neighbors in the network topology. The best next hop is considered the neighbor node with the least distance from the destination. When the greedy forwarding is impossible, the algorithm recovers by routing around the perimeter of the region.

3 Proposed GPSR Enhancement

The proposed GPSR enhancement is implemented in the NS-3 simulator and follows the implementation of [17]. Because of the intense and high speed mobility in VA-NETs, the GPSR forwarding process may not be always efficient. Choosing as next hop the neighbor node with the least distance from the destination may easily lead to recovery state as the link may brake due to opposite directions or great speed difference between the next hop and the destination. The proposed mechanism enhancement is applied on the greedy forwarding process during the best next hop calculation. The modified process handles not only the positions of the routers but also the speed, direction and link quality. The speed and direction is send as a velocity vector attached in the hello messages of the modified GPSR. The destination's position and velocity is added in the packet header in order to be available at the intermediate nodes. The position and velocity for every node is obtained from a location service that in the real world could be the GPS. For link quality assignment, every packet is tagged with an SNR value at the physical layer. This SNR packet tag is extracted at the routing layer during the hello messages receipt. The position, velocity and SNR information is stored in the neighbor table of every node and then is included in the next hop weight calculation.

Except from velocity and link quality, the enhancement mechanism also includes a future position prediction process (getFuturePos), a process for determining if nodes are moving in the same road and direction (inSameRD) and a next hop weight calculation process (CalculateW). The future position calculation uses the formula:

$$FutPos.x = Pos.x + Vel.x * dt(speed);$$
$$FutPos.y = Pos.y + Vel.y * dt(speed);$$

where $dt()$ is a mapping function that returns the time from 1.0 up to 4.0 s based on the speed parameter. As the speed increases the returned time period decreases.

To examine if 2 nodes are moving in the same road and direction, the second process calculates the nodes' velocity vector angle, their line distance, and their dot product. If their velocity vectors are parallel and their line distance is less than the road width, the algorithm decides that they are moving in the same road. The overall process is presented in Fig. 1.

When a need for packet transmission occurs, the Forward procedure of GPSR-M is called. At this point, the decision for the best next hop is made through the Best-Neighbor procedure which triggers the CalculateW procedure.

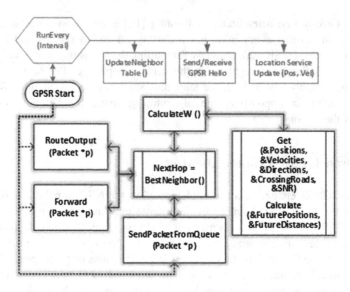

Fig. 1. Mechanism schema

```
1. Procedure Forward(packet)
2.    if neighborTable.isNeighbor(dst) then: nextHop ← dst;
3.    else nextHop ← neighborTable.BestNeighbor(myPos, myVel,
                                                dstPos, dstVel);
4.    if nextHop.addr->isValid() then: route->SetGateway(nextHop);
5.    else RecoveryMode(route);
6.    return;
7. EndProcedure
```

The BestNeighbor procedure iterates through the neighbor table of the index node and triggers the CalculateW for every neighbor in order to return the best next hop.

```
 1. Procedure BestNeighbor(myPos, myVel, dstPos, dstVel)
 2.    initialW ← CalculateW(myPos, myVel,.., dstPos, dstVel, snr);
 3.    W ← CalculateW(myPos, myVel, nTable.Pos, nTable.Vel,
                      dstPos, dstVel, nTable.Snr);
 4.    for i ← nTable.begin() to nTable.end():
 5.       if W > CalculateW(myPos, myVel, i->pos, i->vel, dstPos,
                            dstVel, i->Snr) then:
 6.          W ← CalculateW(myPos, myVel, i->pos, i->vel, dstPos,
                            dstVel, i->Snr);
 7.          nextHop.addr ← i->addr;
 8.    if initialW > W then: return nextHop;
 9.    else return IpV4Address::GetZero();
10. EndProcedure
```

The CalculateW procedure is called for every neighbor node of the index node through the BestNeighbor procedure and returns the calculated weight of the examined node based on the input routing data. The 5 weight factors have been set after extended simulation tests for performance analysis of CalculateW.

```
1. Procedure CalculateW(srcPos,srcVel,indxPos,indxVel,dstPos,
                        dstVel,snr)
2.    W ← +INF, w1 ← 0.25, w2 ← 0.15, w3 ← 0.25, w4 ← 0.15, w5 ← 1;
3.    p1 ← getFuturePos(srcPos, srcVel);    //Source future pos
4.    p2 ← getFuturePos(indxPos, indxVel); //Index future pos
5.    p3 ← getFuturePos(dstPos, dstVel);    //Destination future pos
6.    d1 ← getDistance(p1, p2); //currently not used
7.    d2 ← getDistance(indxPos, dstPos);
8.    d3 ← getDistance(p2, p3);
9.    if inSameRD(indxPos, IndxVel, dstPos, dstVel) then: w2 ← 0;
10.   if inSameRD(indxPos, IndxVel, srcPos, srcVel) then: w4 ← 0;
11.   W ← (w1+w2)*d2 + (w3+w4)*d3 + w5*d3/(snr);
12.   return W;
13. EndProcedure
```

Two basic cases where the GPSR enhancement mechanism significantly improves the network performance are shown in Fig. 2. In the left case, the mechanism forms the green route and avoids the route change that will occur in the red route in a very short amount of time. In the right case, the default GPSR forwarding process chooses the red route and shortly will fall in recovery mode. The proposed mechanism avoids that. The improvement gets more intense as the number of the intermediate nodes rises. The code of the mechanism can be found in the web site: http://ru6.cti.gr/ru6.

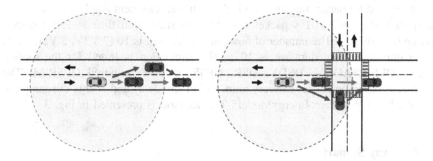

Fig. 2. Routing in a highway (left) and a junction (right). The red arrows represent the GPSR routes and the green the modified GPSR routes (Color figure online)

4   Reference Scenarios

The evaluation of the routing protocols in VANETs is conducted for 2 topology scenarios. The first topology is an Urban Area and the second a highway. For both scenarios, the tools JOSM (https://josm.openstreetmap.de/), SUMO [18] and

BonnMotion [19] were used for the network topology generation. The common network parameters that both scenarios share are shown in Table 1.

Table 1. Network parameters for both scenarios

Node Transmission Range	300 m
Mac Layer	IEEE 802.11p Wave
PhyMode	Ofdm6 mbs10 MHz
Propagation Model	FriisPropagationLossModel
Packet Size	128 Bytes
Packet Interval	0.01 s
Application	Udp Server-Client

4.1   Urban Area Scenario

In this scenario, the road network from the city of Athens is simulated, extending for about 2 × 2 km. The city simulation process includes fetching the city map including all the road elements (traffic lights, junctions, road directions, etc.) with the use of JOSM, preprocessing it with SUMO to generate vehicles and road traffic and then import them to NS-3. The number of nodes is 130 with their movement following random vehicle movements with respect to the imported road network. The nodes are never allowed to move outside the area limits keeping the node density stable. Roads leading outside the selected area are properly edited to lead back any vehicles approaching the limits. The maximum node speed is 85 km/h and the average 60 km/h. All nodes are equipped with Wi-Fi devices and transmission range up to 300 m. The selected Mac layer is the IEEE 802.11p Wave with 6Mbps data rate and 10 MHz channel bandwidth. Except from vehicle nodes, the simulated area contains 2 Base Stations for V2I or I2I communications. During the simulation, all 3 types of VANET communications take place. The application used for packet transmission is the UDP Server-Client Application with 128 bytes packet size and 0.01 s packet interval. The simulation time is 150 s with a warm-up time of 30 s. The number of flows in the network is 10 (7 V2V, 2 V2I, 1 I2I) and the minimum flow duration is 10 s. The simulation is tested for the routing protocols OLSR, AODV, DSDV, DSR, GPSR and the proposed GPSR-M. The evaluation is based on packet delivery ratio, end to end delay and energy consumption (using the NS-3 WifiRadioEnergyModel). The scenario is presented in Fig. 3.

4.2   Highway Scenario

The highway scenario simulates the case of high distance roadways with high vehicle movement speeds and course stability. In this scenario, the node's mobility route is more predictable and tends to keep its current state. Course changes take place mainly when a vehicle moves to another lane. In the tested scenario, 100 nodes are moving with average speeds varying from 20 km/h up to 180 km/h. The communication type is V2V with the source and destination node moving towards the same direction. The distance between them is 1 km and the nodes' transmission range is 300 m.

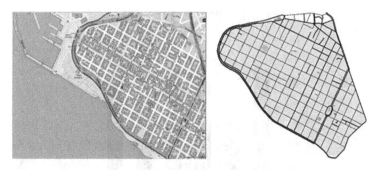

Fig. 3. The simulated Urban area scenario. On the left: The original area from the Open Street Map. On the right: The final road network to be tested.

This scenario type is produced by a custom simple generator which can be found together with the simulation code. Figure 4 depicts the described scenario.

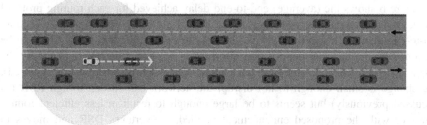

Fig. 4. Highway scenario

5   Simulation Results

5.1   Urban Scenario Results

The results for the simulation of the urban scenario are presented below. Three metrics are presented: packet delivery ratio, end-to-end delay and energy consumption.

Figure 5 shows the packet delivery ratio for each tested routing protocol. The AODV seems to be the worst performer while GPSR seems to be the best choice out of the existing protocols. This is expected as AODV (as a reactive routing protocol) is not very well suited for network with frequent topology changes (such as VANETs). OLSR and DSDV as pro-active routing protocols exhibit better performance in this case. DSR, although a reactive routing protocol, handles topology changes with less messages and adapts better that AODV bringing its performance in par with OLSR. GPSR, taking into account the position of the nodes has a much better performance. Still, the proposed enhancement improves the PDR from approximately 75 % for GPSR up to approximately to 79 %, which is a quite good enhancement. This is due to moving nature of the nodes in a VANET which constantly changes the position of the

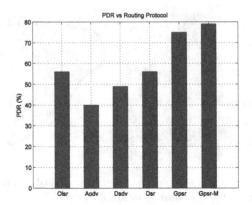

Fig. 5. Packet Delivery ratio VS Routing Protocol

nodes. Thus the information GPRS uses can quickly get a bit outdated. The proposed enhancement anticipates this change and estimates a better position for the nodes at the time they are used to relay a message.

Figure 6 shows the (average) end-to-end delay achieved for each routing protocol tested. AODV is again the worst performer, but OLSR is the best choice for keeping end-to-end delay at a minimum level. GPSR is behind OLSR and DSR. This can be explained by the fact that the position information is getting slightly outdated by the time a node is used (and some time has passed from when its position was acquired). The change is small enough to not disrupt the network and sustain a high PDR (as discussed previously) but seems to be large enough to result in less efficient routes. However with the proposed enhancement applied, it overtakes DSR and moves in second place close to OLSR. The reduction of the end-to-end delay with the application of the proposed enhancement is quite impressive (the end-to-end delay drops to less than half), and is attributed to the better estimation of the then current position of each node.

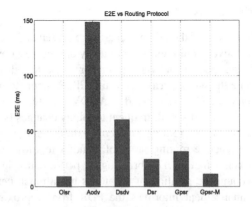

Fig. 6. End to End Delay VS Routing Protocol

Figure 7 shows the total energy consumption for each routing protocol tested. AODV is again the worst performer and must clearly be avoided for VANETs in such urban settings. This is probably due to the frequent topology changes that result in disconnected paths and the need to frequently re-run the route discovery. DSR uses the less energy with all the other protocols following using approximately the same energy. The proactive routing protocols manage to keep the energy consumption at this lower level as they update the routes regularly to avoid disconnections. DSR manages to use slightly less energy as it does not rediscover the route globally but somehow tries to re-route locally, and this proves more than enough. The proposed enhancement shows a very small reduction but no clear improvement. However, its application does not increase the energy consumption footprint of GPSR. This means that the proposed enhancement can be applied without any energy consumption drawbacks.

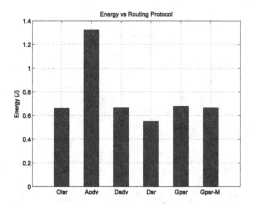

Fig. 7. Total Energy Consumption VS Routing Protocol

Looking at the combined results, GPSR with the proposed enhancement is a quite good choice for VANETs in such urban settings. The small deficits (with respect to DSR) for the end-to-end delay and the energy consumption are a small compromise for the increased packet delivery ratio. In cases where GPSR is used, the proposed enhancement either improves (even slightly) all of these metrics and therefore is a really nice contender to be applied.

5.2 Highway Scenario Results

The results for the simulation of the highway scenario are presented below. The same three metrics (packet delivery ratio, end-to-end delay and energy consumption) are presented. However this time they are shown against the average vehicle speed.

Figure 8 shows the packet delivery ratio for the tested routing protocols against the average vehicle speed. DSDV is the worst performer followed by AODV and OLSR, which seem to drop to very low level of PDR as the average vehicle speed increases. DSR displays an "erratic" behavior with large fluctuation in the PDR for different average vehicle speeds. This is due to the more frequent topology changes that result from the higher speeds. Clearly, these routing protocols are not suitable for such scenarios. GPSR has better PDR but this seems to drop as the average vehicle speed increases. This is explained as the higher speeds result in higher deviation of the actual position of a node from the reported position of that node when it was queried. The higher the speed the higher the variation, the lower the performance as nodes considered neighboring can actually be out of reach. GPSR with the proposed enhancement is clearly the best performer. The enhancement seems to improve GPSR quite a lot for such scenarios and improve the PDR above 90 % in most cases. This is due to fact that this routing protocol takes the speed into account and estimates correctly the actual position of the nodes at each time (as opposed to the reported one). An important consequence of this is that it maintains this high level of PDR for high vehicle speeds, with no indication that higher speeds will present any problem; i.e., it scales very well with the vehicle speeds.

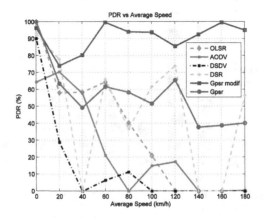

Fig. 8. Packet Delivery ratio VS Average Speed

Figure 9 shows the average end to end delay for the tested routing protocols against the average vehicle speed. The results indicate that OLSR maintains steady levels of delay up to 20 ms for speeds up to 100 km/h. DSDV follows the OLSR and shows lower levels of delay than DSR and AODV for speeds up to 60 km/h. The GPSR shows intense reduction of delay for speeds greater than 60 km/h and performs better than the previously mentioned protocols for high speeds. From this speed onwards, it seems that the error in the node position can be quite high as to result in disconnections (and the lower PDR seen above); however when there is no disconnection the route is good enough to result in low end-to-end delay. The enhanced GPSR mechanism seems to improve significantly the end to end delay of GPSR and performs better for almost all the tested speeds. As explained above this is due to the fact the enhanced protocol does not suffer from a bad knowledge of the actual position of nodes.

Figure 10 shows the energy consumption for the tested routing protocols against the average vehicle speed. AODV seems to be the most energy hungry protocol, while DSR is the best performer. All the other protocols are close together. GPSR with the

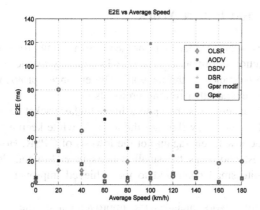

Fig. 9. End to End Delay VS Average Speed

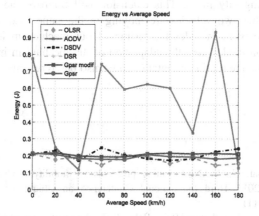

Fig. 10. Total Energy Consumption VS Average Speed

proposed enhancement use slightly more energy than GPSR but the increase is quite low. This is more-or-less the same picture as with the urban scenario.

The combined results demonstrate that GPSR with the proposed enhancement is a quite good choice for VANETs in such highway settings. Again, the small deficits for the end-to-end delay and the energy consumption are a small compromise for the increased packet delivery ratio.

The proposed enhancement improves the PDR of GPSR in all cases and improves the end-to-end delay and energy consumption of GPSR in several cases. In the rest of the cases, the deficit is quite small and tolerable for obtaining the higher PDR.

Therefore, the proposed enhancement is a strong contender to be implemented together with GPSR.

6   Conclusions and Future Work

In this work, we present an enhancement for the GPSR routing protocol that makes use of location and direction information as well as link quality metrics to produce routes that improve the performance of the network. The enhanced protocol is tested (with simulations) against several other routing protocols.

The proposed enhancement is shown to achieve higher packet delivery ratio for the network, a low end-to-end delay (but not the lowest), while keeping the energy consumption at the same low levels (again not the lowest) of GPSR. However, overall is shown to be the best choice as the small deficits in end-to-end delay and energy consumption are quite small compared to the achieved improvement in the packet delivery ratio.

Our plan for future work includes the improvement of the weight calculation algorithm by implementing a more accurate positioning and direction model. This will be achieved by extending the existing location service model and introducing road models from existing city maps. This extension will improve the accuracy of the algorithm for weather two vehicles are moving in the same road and direction. In addition, our future work includes the testing of our mechanism in scenarios with building propagation models and the adaptation of the mechanism in such scenarios. The final goal will be the routing orientation to be also based on environment obstacles and noise.

References

1. Maan, F., Mazhar, N.: MANET routing protocols vs mobility models: A performance evaluation. In: 2011 Third International Conference on Ubiquitous Future Networks, pp. 179–184 (2011)
2. Kakarla, J., Sathya, S.S., Laxmi, B.G., Babu, B.R.: A survey on routing protocols and its issues in VANET. Int. J. Comput. Appl. **28**(4), 38–44 (2011)
3. Kumar, R., Dave, M.: A comparative study of Various Routing Protocols in VANET (2011). arXiv Prepr. arXiv1108.2094
4. Lee, K.C., Lee, U., Gerla, M.: Survey of routing protocols in vehicular ad hoc networks. In: Advances in Vehicular Ad-Hoc Networks: Developments Challenges, pp. 149–170 (2010)
5. Abbas, S.F., Chaudhry, S.R., Yasin, G.: VANET route selection in urban/rural areas using metric base traffic analysis. In: UBICOMM 2013, The Seventh International Conference on Mobile Ubiquitous Computing, Systems, Services and Technologies, pp. 85–91 (2013)
6. Kim, J.-H., Lee, S.: Reliable routing protocol for vehicular ad hoc networks. AEU-Int. J. Electron. Commun. **65**(3), 268–271 (2011)
7. Kaisser, F., Johnen, C., Vèque, V.: Quantitative model for evaluate routing protocols in a vehicular ad hoc networks on highway. In: 2010 IEEE Vehicular Networking Conference (VNC), pp. 330–337 (2010)
8. Martinez, F.J., Toh, C.-K., Cano, J.-C., Calafate, C.T., Manzoni, P.: Realistic radio propagation models (RPMs) for VANET simulations. In: Wireless Communications and Networking Conference, WCNC 2009, pp. 1–6. IEEE (2009)

9. Wan, S., Tang, J., Wolff, R.S.: Reliable routing for roadside to vehicle communications in rural areas. In: IEEE International Conference on Communications, ICC 2008, pp. 3017–3021 (2008)
10. Nzouonta, J., Rajgure, N., Wang, G., Borcea, C.: VANET routing on city roads using real-time vehicular traffic information. Veh. Technol. IEEE Trans. **58**(7), 3609–3626 (2009)
11. Katsaros, K., Dianati, M., Tafazolli, R., Kernchen, R.: CLWPR - A novel cross-layer optimized position based routing protocol for VANETs. In: IEEE Vehicular Networking Conference, VNC, pp. 139–146 (2011)
12. Perkins, C., Belding-Royer, E., Das, S.: Ad hoc On-Demand Distance Vector (AODV) Routing. Internet RFCs **285**, 1–38 (2003)
13. He, G.: Destination-sequenced distance vector (DSDV) protocol. Netw. Lab. Helsinki Univ. Technol. (2002)
14. Johnson, D.B., Maltz, D.A.: Dynamic source routing in ad hoc wireless networks. In: Mobile Computing, vol. 353, pp. 153–181 (1996)
15. Jacquet, P., Mühlethaler, P., Clausen, T.H., Laouiti, A., Qayyum, A., Viennot, L.: Optimized link state routing protocol for ad hoc networks. In: IEEE International Multi Topic Conference, pp. 62–68 (2001)
16. Karp, B., Kung, H.-T.: GPSR: Greedy perimeter stateless routing for wireless networks. In: Proceedings of the 6th Annual International Conference on Mobile Computing and Networking, pp. 243–254 (2000)
17. Fonseca, A., Camões, A., Vazão, T.: Geographical routing implementation in NS3. In: Proceedings of the 5th International ICST Conference on Simulation Tools and Techniques, pp. 353–358 (2012)
18. Krajzewicz, D., Erdmann, J., Behrisch, M., Bieker, L.: Recent development and applications of SUMO - Simulation of Urban MObility. Int. J. Adv. Syst. Meas. **5**(3&4), 128–138 (2012)
19. Aschenbruck, N., Ernst, R., Gerhards-Padilla, E., Schwamborn, M.: BonnMotion: a mobility scenario generation and analysis tool. In: Proceedings of the 3rd International ICST Conference on Simulation Tools and Techniques (2010)

AntWMNet – A Hybrid Routing Algorithm for Wireless Mesh Networks Based on Ant Colony Optimisation

Luis J. Mariscal[1], Alicia Triviño[1], and Fernando Boavida[2(✉)]

[1] Universidad de Málaga, Málaga, Spain
jacob.m.f@gmail.com, atc@uma.es
[2] CISUC, Departamento de Engenharia Informática,
Universidade de Coimbra, Coimbra, Portugal
boavida@uc.pt

Abstract. Routing in wireless mesh networks is of paramount importance to their good performance. As this type of network is becoming key to many application scenarios, it is fundamental to guarantee that routing is as efficient as possible. Despite extensive research work carried out in the past, existing routing algorithms have problems in terms of latency, throughput, network overhead, and/or scalability, depending on their type. In the current paper we propose a hybrid wireless mesh networks routing algorithm that addresses the referred problems, exploring the ant colony optimisation paradigm. The algorithm, named AntWMNet, was extensively studied through simulation using OMNET++, and the results show that it clearly outperforms the reference AODV algorithm.

Keywords: Wireless mesh networks · Routing algorithms · Ant colony optimisation

1 Introduction

As we witness an unprecedented increase in the deployment and use of wireless technologies (mobility management, pervasive sensing, automated object-to-object and object-to-person communications, the Internet of Things, etc.), it is becoming important to revisit wireless mesh networks (WMN) and devise new and more efficient ways for their operation. Despite considerable work done in the past in the area of routing in WMNs [1], the fact is that several challenges persist and there is need to go beyond traditional proactive or reactive routing algorithms and protocols.

Routing is, of course, a key aspect in these self-organized and self-configured networks. Routing protocols used in WMNs can be classified into reactive (also known as on-demand routing protocols) and proactive (also known as table-driven) [2]. The former typically lead to higher throughput and less signaling protocol overhead. The latter lead to lower latency at the cost of higher overhead. Moreover, they have limited scalability. Examples of reactive routing protocols are Ad Hoc on Demand Distance Vector (AODV) [3], Temporarily Ordered Routing Algorithm (TORA) [4], Dynamic Source Routing (DSR) [5], and Link Quality Source Routing Algorithm (LQSR) [6].

© Springer International Publishing Switzerland 2015
M.C. Aguayo-Torres et al. (Eds.): WWIC 2015, LNCS 9071, pp. 108–121, 2015.
DOI: 10.1007/978-3-319-22572-2_8

Examples of proactive routing protocols are Destination-Sequenced Distance Vector Routing (DSDV) [7], and Optimized Link State Routing (OLSR) [8]. Additionally, there are several hybrid WMN routing protocols that use a reactive approach in the general case and a proactive approach in specific network areas, such as the backbone.

In this paper we propose and analyse a hybrid WMN routing protocol – AntWMNet – that uses the ant colony optimisation (ACO) paradigm. The use of ACO for WMN routing is not new, and can be seen in protocols such as AntNet [9], AntHocNet [10], or AntMeshNet [11]. The innovative aspects of AntWMNet are the fact that it uses ACO both in its reactive and proactive operation, and that the proactive component is used for continuously maintaining, updating and optimising selected, promising routes, based on specific routing metrics. Moreover, the algorithm supports local, controlled route fixes when route problems are detected, thus limiting its protocol overhead.

The AntWMNET algorithm is presented in Sect. 2. In Sect. 3 the evaluation set up is detailed, followed by a presentation and discussion of extensive simulation results in Sect. 4. The objective of this discussion is to clearly characterise the benefits of the proposal under study. Section 5 analyses the AntWMNET proposal in light of related work, and Sect. 6 summarises the key findings and identifies guidelines for further work.

2 AntWMNet

AntWMNet is a hybrid ACO-based WMN routing algorithm. Its reactive, on-demand characteristic stems from the fact that it only deals with routing information concerning active destinations. In this respect, it is quite similar to reactive routing algorithms, such as AODV. It is also, nevertheless, a proactive algorithm, as it maintains and tries to improve the active communication routes, anticipating possible route changes and establishing alternative routes, if existing, as a way to prevent route disruption. This is a key factor in such dynamic environments as WMNs and it is, in fact, one of its main innovative aspects. The following subsections provide an overview of key aspects of the algorithm's operation.

2.1 Data Structures

AntWMNet relies on three basic per-node data structures: routing table (or pheromone table), neighbours table, and visits table.

The routing table is a 2-dimensional matrix of $j \times d$. that keeps routing information from the current node i (the node in which the table resides) to destinations d, through neighbouring nodes j. Each matrix value is composed of a pheromone concentration value, F_{ij}^d, a hop count value, H_{ij}^d, and the latest measured delay to the destination, T_{ij}^d. The neighbours table is a vector that keeps information on all the known neighbours of node i. This is used to propagate routing information and to determine possible link failures. The neighbours table is updated periodically, based on beacon packets. The visits table stores the identification of ant packets (either reactive or proactive), in order to discard ants of similar type reaching the same node. In addition, a timestamp is used to discard information of out-dated visits.

2.2 Reactive, On-demand Routing

Whenever there is need to send a packet to a destination for which there is no information on the routing table, a route discovery process is initiated, using an ant colony optimisation approach. For this, special packets called reactive forward ants are sent out to all neighbours of the source node, and subsequently are propagated to the entire network by flooding. Flooding is controlled by the visits table in each network node.

When a reactive forward ant reaches the destination, it carries information on all the nodes visited from source to destination. The reception of the ant by the destination triggers the sending of a reactive backward ant to the source, using the reverse path. The objective of reactive backward ants is to update the pheromone information contained in the routing tables of the nodes along the path from destination to source, according to a cost function, c_i^d. This cost function depends on the used routing metrics and usually takes into account the hop count and the delay, although it may account for other parameters, such as link quality, bandwidth, or even jitter. The value of the cost function will determine the pheromone concentration level that will be stored in each node along the path, which will be given by

$$F_{ij}^d(new) = F_{ij}^d + (1 - \gamma) \cdot \left(c_i^d\right)^{-1}, \gamma \in [0, 1] \tag{1}$$

where γ is a parameter that controls the speed of adaptation to pheromone changes (experimentation led us to use a value of 0.73, although this is obviously configurable).

Once one or more routes to a given destination are known, data packets can be sent. Routes are chosen stochastically, using the respective pheromone concentration values. The probability that node i sends a packet to destination d through node n is given by

$$P_{in}^d = \frac{(F_{in}^d)^\beta}{\sum_{j \in N_i^d} (F_{ij}^d)^\beta}, \beta \geq 1 \tag{2}$$

where β controls the preference for routes with higher pheromone concentration. For instance, low values of this parameter will cause traffic to frequently use multiple routes, leading to better use of network resources, although some routes may have lower quality. Values close to 20 concentrate traffic on better routes, which leads to better flow performance at the cost of uneven route utilisation. In our experiments we used a value of 16 as it turned out to lead to good results both in terms of performance and resource usage.

2.3 Proactive Operation

AntWMNet includes proactive route maintenance mechanisms with the objective of coping with the relatively frequent topology changes and route failures that are typical of wireless environments such as it occurs in WMN. These mechanisms are the following: pheromone diffusion, proactive forward ants, and proactive backward ants.

The objective of pheromone diffusion is to convey pheromone information to new neighbouring nodes, as they become available in the network. New neighbouring nodes are asynchronously discovered by beacon or hello messages. These new nodes may open up new routes to active destinations and, thus, it is important that pheromone information can reach them.

Another important mechanism is that of proactive forward ants. Contrary to reactive forward ants, proactive forward ants use existing pheromone information and are launched periodically or by source or transit nodes affected by topology changes whenever there is some indication of potential improvement (basically, when new nodes are discovered and/or when there is an improvement in terms of hop count or delay in the vicinity of source, destination, or mesh nodes).

Proactive backward ants complete the proactive process by periodically checking and updating the pheromone tables along active routes.

2.4   Link Failures

Link failures are quite frequent in WMNs. Their detection can be done by using MAC layer information or by specific hello packets sent at regular intervals (typically, 1 s) that can additionally be used for maintaining neighbour tables.

Whenever a link failure is detected, the corresponding neighbour is removed from the neighbours table and all the entries in the pheromone table that use that neighbour are set to 0. In case the number of routes to a given destination becomes 0, a local route repair ant is sent out. Local route repair ants are similar to reactive ants, with the exception that flooding is restricted to a limited number of hops (in our experiments, this parameter was set to 3). When they reach the destination or a node that has a route to the destination, a backward ant is sent back that completes the route repairing process.

3   Evaluation Setup

This section details the AntWMNet evaluation setup, namely it describes the scenarios used in the simulations, explains the various studies that were made, and identifies the algorithms against which AntWMNet was compared.

All evaluations were done through simulation, using OMNET++ [12] and the INETMANET package [13] developed by the University of Málaga, Spain.

3.1   Simulation Scenarios

The basic scenario is composed by a wireless mesh network of 9 nodes, of which 7 are hosts and 2 are access points, as depicted in Fig. 1. One of the hosts (hostX) moves along the edge of the network towards the vicinity of hostF at an average speed of 1 meter per second.

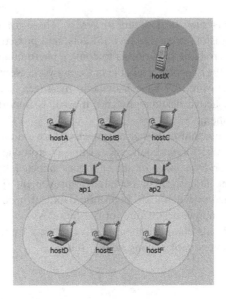

Fig. 1. Basic, 9-node wireless mesh network.

In certain simulations this basic scenario was modified in order to include higher size networks. For this, WMNs of 9 × 10, 14 × 14, 18 × 17, and 20 × 20 nodes were added and connected to the base network through mesh nodes hostA and hostD, thus creating WMNs with 99, 205, 315, and 409 mesh nodes, respectively.

Each experiment was simulated 20 times, with duration of 120 s. Data traffic consisted of 64-byte UDP packets generated at a varying rate (see Sect. 3.2, below). At the physical and data link layers, IEEE 802.11 was used.

3.2   Simulation Studies

Three sets of simulation studies were performed in order to characterise the behaviour of AntWMNet under various situations, as shown in Fig. 2.

In the first set, the objective was to study AntWMNet when subject to an increasing data volume. For this, several simulations were performed in which 2, 4, 6, 8, 10, and 12 data packets per second were generated in each session.

In the second set of simulations, the number of data sessions varied, according to the following cases: (1) a single data session, from hostD to hostX; (2) two data sessions, one from hostD to hostX, and one in the reverse direction that sends a reply to each received packet; (2*) two data sessions, from two distinct source nodes, hostA and HostD; (3) three data sessions, from source nodes hostA, hostD and hostF; (4) four data sessions, one from each hostA and hostD to hostX, and the corresponding replies to each packet; (6) six data sessions, one from each source node hostA, hostD and hostF, and the respective replies.

In the third set of simulations, the number of WMN nodes varied, as mentioned in Sect. 3.1, i.e., with networks of 9, 99, 205, 315, and 409 mesh nodes. In these cases, data transmission always originates in the farthest node.

Set 1: Evaluation varying the data send rate

Set	Source	Data session packets/second
1	hostD	2, 4, 6, 8, 10, 12

Set 2: Evaluation varying number of data sessions

Type	Source nodes	Data reply packets
1	hostD	No
2	hostD	Yes
2*	hostD, hostA	No
3	hostD, hostA, hostF	No
4	hostD, hostA	Yes
6	hostD, hostA, hostF	Yes

Set 3: Evaluation varying the network size

Set	Source	Number of nodes
3	host[0] (farthest)	2, 9, 99, 205, 315, 409

Fig. 2. The three sets of simulation studies.

For the various simulated scenarios we obtained values for the average packet delivery ratio, average packet end-to-end delay, average data packets hop count, and average control packets hop count. The confidence interval of the obtained values is 95 %.

3.3   Algorithms Comparison

AntWMNet was compared with AODV as this is a reference WMN routing algorithm. In addition to comparing it with the basic AODV algorithm, we also compared it with a modification to AODV that performs local route repairing.

Comparison with AntNet and AntHocNet was discarded due to their known inefficiency in what concerns network overhead, especially in environments with frequent topology changes.

In the case of AntWMNet we distinguished two forms of counting the control packets hop count: the normal way, in which we do not consider the pheromone diffusion control messages, and the strict way, in which we consider them. The latter case appears in the graphs as AntWMNet2.

4   Evaluation Results

The following sub-sections present and discuss the results of each set of simulations, namely in what concerns AntWMNet's response to varying data volume per session, number of data sessions, and network size.

4.1   AntWMNet Evaluation with Respect to Data Volume

Figure 3 presents the packet delivery ratio (PDR) as a function of the number of data packets generated per second in each data session.

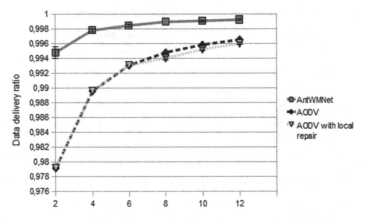

Fig. 3. Average packet delivery ratio as a function of generated packets per second.

We can observe that PDR increases with the data volume, which is normal in uncongested WMNs. With higher data volumes, most routes are already known when there is the need to transmit packets, and are constantly being updated. Naturally, the situation would be different in a congested network.

The important thing to notice is the clear advantage of AntWMNet over the two versions of AODV (with and without local route repairing), which is due to its pro-active route maintenance and repair mechanism.

Figures 4 and 5 present the average packet delay and data packet hop count, respectively.

The figures are quite similar due to the fact that the network is quite homogeneous and most links have similar delay characteristics.

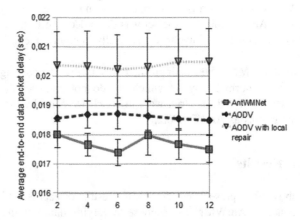

Fig. 4. Average packet delay as a function of generated packets per second.

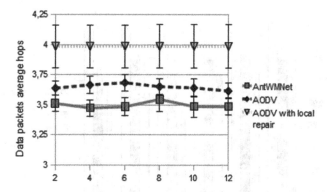

Fig. 5. Average data packets hop count as a function of generated packets per second.

In these figures we can see once more that AntWMNet performs better than any of the AODV versions. This is due to AntWMNet's ability to quickly determine and adapt to new routes, namely the ones that must be determined as destination nodeX moves through the mesh network.

Figure 6 presents the average control packets hop count as a function of data volume. Once again we can see that AntWMNet has lower overhead than AODV, if we do not consider pheromone diffusion control messages. If we consider them (Ant-WMNet2), then the overhead is higher than that of the basic AODV. This is the price to pay for the higher packet delivery ratio and lower packet delay illustrated in the previous figures.

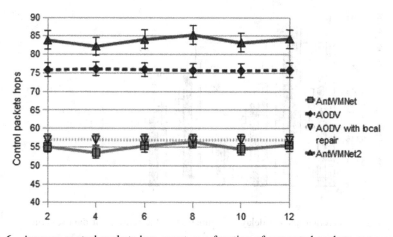

Fig. 6. Average control packets hop count as a function of generated packets per second.

4.2 AntWMNet Evaluation with Respect to the Number of Data Sessions

The second set of simulations had the objective of comparing the algorithms under a varying number of data sessions, as explained in Sect. 3.2.

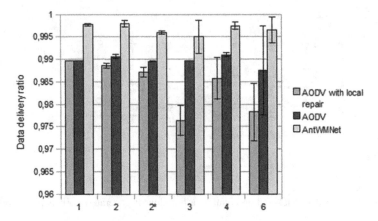

Fig. 7. Average packet delivery ratio as a function of the number of data sessions.

Figure 7 presents the packet delivery ratio (PDR) as a function of the number of data sessions.

AntWMNet elicits a better behavior in all cases and is quite unaffected by the increase in the number of sessions, contrary to what happens with AODV. Moreover, we can see in Fig. 8 that AntWMNet also performs better than AODV in terms of average packet delay. Similar values were also obtained for the average data packets hop count.

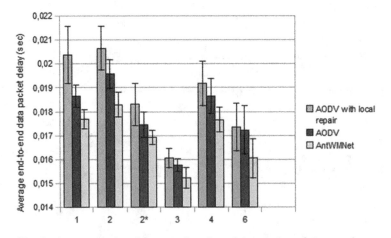

Fig. 8. Average packet delay as a function of the number of data sessions.

Figure 9 presents the average control packets hop count as a function of the number of data sessions. It is interesting to see that AntWMNet performs better than AODV in all cases and that in the cases of higher number of sessions AntWMNet2 also performs better than AODV, which shows the high efficiency and effectiveness of the proactive mechanisms and of pheromone diffusion and localised route repairing that are the distinguishing characteristics of the proposed routing algorithm.

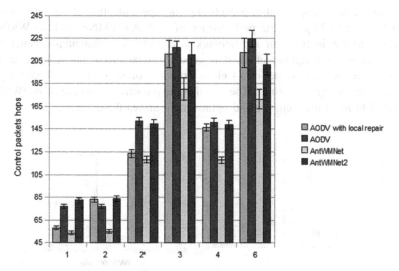

Fig. 9. Average control packets hop count as a function of the number of data sessions.

4.3 AntWMNet Evaluation with Respect to Network Size

The final set of simulations addressed the algorithms' response in WMNs of increasing size.

Figure 10 presents the average packet delivery ratio (PDR) as a function of network size. Here we can see the drastic degradation of the performance of both versions of AODV with the increase of the network size. On the other hand, the performance of AntWMNet is quite stable, thus showing that AntWMNet can adequately cope with

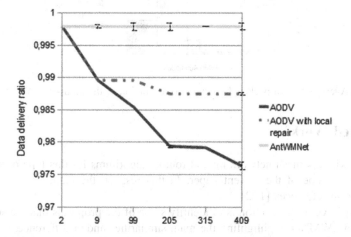

Fig. 10. Average packet delivery ratio as a function of the number of WMN nodes.

WMNs of considerable size. Similar behaviour was also registered for the cases of average packet delay and average data packet hop count.

The excellent performance of AntWMNet in large networks was confirmed when we determined the average control packets hop count as a function of the network size. As can be seen in Fig. 11, the performance of both AntWMNet and AntWMNet2 increases with the increase in the network size and gets substantially better than AODV. This is quite significant, as it is generally recognized that reactive routing algorithms, such as AODV, perform well in large networks, contrary to what happens with proactive routing algorithms. The fact that the proactive operation of AntWMNet is restricted to route maintenance and optimization makes the difference.

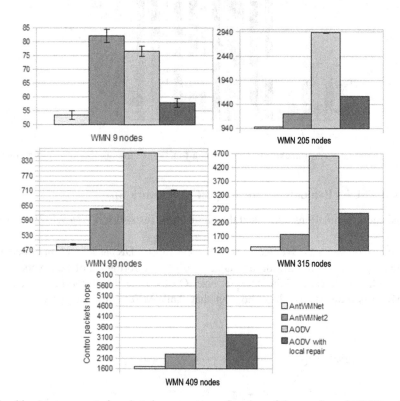

Fig. 11. Average control packets hop count as a function of the number of WMN nodes.

5   Related Work

Surveying wireless mesh networking and routing algorithms for this type of networks is out of the scope of the current paper. In this respect, the reader can find useful information in references [1, 2].

The objective of this section is to identify some of the proposals that are somehow related to AntWMNet, highlighting the main similarities and/or differences.

The use of multiple routes for load sharing and reliability is common to several ACO, such as AntHocNet [10], ARA [14], or Termite [15], or non-ACO algorithms in [16, 17]. In the case of the ACO ones, an important factor is the β parameter, which controls the stochastic dispersion through the various routes, depending on their quality, according to Eq. 2 (see Sect. 2.2). ARA and Termite use a value of 1, which leads to high dispersion, at the cost of higher average delays. AntHocNet uses a value of 20, which concentrates traffic on the best routes only and may lead to quick resource exhaustion or congestion. In AntWMNet we used a value of 16, which we found a very good compromise between load balancing and delay performance.

The algorithms in [16, 17] use the proactive approach for the maintenance of known routes only, as is the case of most ACO-based algorithms, with the exception of Termite and EARA [18] that use blind exploration. AntHocNet is the closest to the AntWMNet algorithm, although less efficient, as AntWMNet takes advantage of backward ants to do route maintenance and these ants update the routing metric values increasing or decreasing them according to the measured values, and not as in traditional ACO-based algorithms that always increase the pheromone level along visited routes. This leads to a better response time to network changes.

To the best of the authors' knowledge, the AntWMNet WMN routing algorithm is the only algorithm that uses all of the following features: reactive and proactive ACO-based routing mechanisms; proactive route maintenance, update, and optimization; proactive exploration of promising routes only, according to the used route metrics; various routing metrics that can take into account and combine hop count, delay, link quality, bandwidth, or jitter; local routes repairing; pheromone diffusion to newly discovered nodes.

6 Conclusion

In the current paper we proposed and evaluated an ACO-based hybrid WMN routing algorithm that combines and explores several basic mechanisms in order to collectively achieve optimal performance in terms of throughput, delay, latency and scalability.

The algorithm, named AntWMNet, was extensively studied through simulation using OMNET++ in a variety of scenarios, in order to compare it with AODV, the reference reactive WMN routing algorithm, and to characterise its behaviour and ability to cope with varying traffic loads per session, increasing number of data sessions, and increasing network sizes.

The results showed that AntWMNet outperforms AODV in all of the studied scenarios. Moreover, the performance differences between AntWMNet and AODV get higher as the network size increases, thus revealing the excellent scalability of the proposed algorithm.

Future work will address the prototyping of the proposed algorithm, in order to confirm its potential in real networks. Additionally, further simulations will target the comparison with other routing algorithms and more dynamic environments involving several mobile devices.

Acknowledgments. The authors would like to thank Marco Dorigo, Frederick Ducatelle, Mudassar Farooq and Alfonso Ariza for their help, influence with their previous work and kindly replied messages.

The work presented in this paper was partially financed by the University of Málaga and by the iCIS project (CENTRO-07-ST24-FEDER-002003, http://icis.uc.pt).

References

1. Akyildiz, I.F., Wang, X., Wang, W.: Wireless mesh networks: a survey. J. Comput. Netw. **47**(4), 445–487 (2005)
2. Siraj, M.: A survey on routing algorithms and routing metrics for wireless mesh networks. World Appl. Sci. J. 30(7), 870–886 (2014). doi:10.5829/idosi.wasj.2014.30.07.1465, ISSN 1818–4952
3. Perkins, C., Belding-Royer, E., Das, S.: Ad hoc On-Demand Distance Vector (AODV) Routing. IETF. RFC 3561, July 2003
4. Park, V., Corson, S.: Temporally-Ordered Routing Algorithm (TORA) Version 1 Functional Specification. Internet Draft draft-ietf-manet-tora-spec-04.txt. IETF, 20 July 2001
5. Johnson, D., Hu, Y., Maltz, D.: The Dynamic Source Routing Protocol (DSR) for Mobile Ad Hoc Networks for IPv4. IETF. RFC 4728, February 2007
6. Corson, M.S., Ephremides, A.: A distributed routing algorithm for mobile wireless networks. ACM/Baltzer Wirel. Netw. **1**(1), 61–81 (1995)
7. Perkins, C., Bhagwat, P.: Highly Dynamic Destination-Sequence Distance Vector, Routing (DSDV) for Mobile Computers. In: Proceedings of the ACM SIGCOMM Computer Communication Review, pp. 234–244 (1994)
8. Clausen, T., Jacquet, P. (eds.): Optimized Link State Routing Protocol (OLSR). IETF. RFC 3626, October 2003
9. Di Caro, G.A., Dorigo, M.: AntNet: distributed stigmergetic control for communications networks. J. Artif. Intell. Res. (JAIR) **9**, 317–365 (1998)
10. Di Caro, G.A., Ducatelle, F., Gambardella, L.M.: AntHocNet: An ant-based hybrid routing algorithm for mobile ad hoc networks. In: Yao, X., et al. (eds.) PPSN 2004. LNCS, vol. 3242, pp. 461–470. Springer, Heidelberg (2004)
11. Sharad, S.P., Kumar, S., Singh, B.: AntMeshNet: An ant colony optimization based routing approach to wireless mesh networks. Int. J. Appl. Metaheuristic Comput. **5**(1), 20–45 (2014)
12. OMNet ++ Discrete Event Simulator. http://www.omnetpp.org. Accessed on 26 February 2015
13. Ariza Quintana, A., Dreibholz, T., Bojthe, Z., Maureira, J.C., Jonsson, K.V., Borbély, T., Mészáros, L., Yousaf, F.Z., Janota, V., Sommer, C.: Inetmanet: An Open Source communication network simulation package for the OMNEST/OMNeT ++ simulation system. Contains models for several Internet protocols: TCP/IP, UDP, Ethernet: PPP, MPLS with LDP and RSVP-TE signalling (2011). https://github.com/aarizaq/inetmanet-2.0 Open Source software
14. Günes, M., Sorges, U., Bouazzi, I.: ARA – The Ant-colony based Routing Algorithm for MANETs. In: Proceedings of the ICPP International Workshop on Ad Hoc Networks (IWAHN) (2002)
15. Martin, R., Stephen, W.: Termite: A swarm intelligence routing algorithm for mobile wireless ad-hoc networks. In: Ajith, A., Crina, G., Vitorino, R. (eds.) Swarm Intelligence and Data Mining. SCI, vol. 31, pp. 155–184. Springer, Heidelberg (2009)

16. Ganesan, D., Govindan, R., Shenker, S., Estrin, D.: Highly-resilient, energy-efficient multipath routing in wireless sensor networks. Mobile Comput. Commun. Rev. **1**(2), 1–13 (2002)
17. Wang, L., Shu, Y.T., Yang, O.W.W., Dong, M., Zhang, L.F.: Adaptive multipath source routing in wireless ad hc networks. In: Proceedings of the IEEE International Conference of Communications (2001)
18. Liu, Z., Kwiatowska, M., Constantinou, C.: A self-organised emergent routing mechanism for mobile ad hoc networks. Europ. Trans. Telecommun. (ETT) **16**(5), 457–470 (2005)

Adaptive Beaconless Opportunistic Routing for Multimedia Distribution

Larissa Pimentel[1], Denis Rosário[1], Marcos Seruffo[1],
Zhongliang Zhao[2], and Torsten Braun[2(✉)]

[1] Federal University of Pará, Belém, Brazil
{larissamp,denis,seruffo}@ufpa.br
[2] University of Bern, Bern, Switzerland
{zhao,braun}@iam.unibe.ch

Abstract. User experience on watching live videos must be satisfactory even under the influence of different network conditions and topology changes, such as happening in Flying Ad-Hoc Networks (FANETs). Routing services for video dissemination over FANETs must be able to adapt routing decisions at runtime to meet Quality of Experience (QoE) requirements. In this paper, we introduce an adaptive beaconless opportunistic routing protocol for video dissemination over FANETs with QoE support, by taking into account multiple types of context information, such as link quality, residual energy, buffer state, as well as geographic information and node mobility in a 3D space. The proposed protocol takes into account Bayesian networks to define weight vectors and Analytic Hierarchy Process (AHP) to adjust the degree of importance for the context information based on instantaneous values. It also includes a position prediction to monitor the distance between two nodes in order to detect possible route failure.

Keywords: AHP · FANETs · Beaconless OR · QoE support

1 Introduction

Collaboration between multiple Unmanned Aerial Vehicles (UAVs) to set up a Flying Ad-Hoc Network (FANET) is a growing trend, since future applications claim for more autonomous and rapid deployable systems. In this context, FANETs have been employed in many kinds of new smart city scenarios, such as disaster recovery, environmental monitoring, and others. For such scenarios, multimedia data plays an important role in helping ground rescue teams to make appropriate decisions based on detailed visual information [1].

Video transmissions require Quality of Experience (QoE) support to deliver the content with a minimal quality level based on the user perspective, which demands low frame loss rate, tolerable end-to-end delay, and low jitter [2]. Many UAVs may also be responsible for transmitting simultaneous videos from monitored areas, resulting in network congestion and buffer overflow. In addition, one of the main challenges to route packets in FANETs is how to mitigate the

© Springer International Publishing Switzerland 2015
M.C. Aguayo-Torres et al. (Eds.): WWIC 2015, LNCS 9071, pp. 122–135, 2015.
DOI: 10.1007/978-3-319-22572-2_9

effects of UAV mobility in a 3D space to avoid communication flaws, delays, and packet loss during video transmissions [3]. This is because UAVs fly in a 3D space, worsening the effects of node mobility, e.g., breaking plenty of communication links. Hence, a routing strategy must consider the nature of network, application, and scenario characteristics to deliver high quality videos [4].

Existing routing protocols for FANETs establish end-to-end routes by taking into account existing information on routing tables. Nevertheless, the dynamic nature of UAVs, e.g., UAV mobility in a 3D space, leads to frequent topology changes, resulting in constant routing table updates, routing inconsistency, or route failures. In this context, beaconless Opportunistic Routing (OR) acts in a completely distributed manner to pick up one of the possible relay nodes to forward packets [5]. Nodes do not need prior establishment of routes for data transmission, avoiding frequent beacon exchange for route maintenance or discovery, and saving scarce network resources, such as bandwidth and energy. Beaconless OR works with the concept of Dynamic Forwarding Delay (DFD), where nodes calculate a short waiting-time (i.e., DFD) before forwarding the received packet [6]. DFD value can be computed as a multi-criteria cost function based on multiple context information, such as energy, distance, etc. By context, we refer to any information that impacts on the routing decision to deliver videos over FANETs with QoE support, e.g., link quality, energy, buffer state, geographic information in a 3D space. However, it is important to first analyse which metric has more impact on the forwarding decision. In addition, the degree of importance for each context metric changes continuously at runtime, and has a great influence on the network performance. In this context, Analytic Hierarchy Process (AHP) provides optimum solutions when multiple contexts are integrated into the routing process, and also supports dynamic weight calculation based on instantaneous network changes [7].

To address the above issues, we introduce an adaptive context-aware beaconless OR protocol (CABR) to deliver simultaneous video flows transmitted over FANETs with QoE support. We take into account multiple types of context information to compute the DFD, which can be acquired locally (node's energy, buffer state, and 3D geographical location) or derived from received packets (link quality and UAV neighbours mobility information). We also include position prediction to monitor the distance between a given node and its forwarding node to detect route failures. We consider a Bayesian Network (BN) to analyse which CABR metrics have more impact on the final video quality level, resulting in a weight vector. We take into account AHP to adjust the degree of importance of each context metric based on the instantaneous network or node conditions. We performed simulations to evaluate CABR performance. In contrast to well known beaconless OR protocols, CABR provides multimedia transmission with QoE support in case of simultaneous video dissemination and mobile nodes.

The remainder of the paper is structured as follows. Section 2 outlines existing routing protocols or mechanisms, and their main drawbacks. Section 3 describes CABR, which was evaluated by means of simulation experiments as shown in Sect. 4. Section 5 presents the main contributions and results of this paper.

2   Related Work

Li et al. [8] introduced mobility prediction to monitor the distance between a given node and its next hop to avoid route failures, and considers only distance for the routing decision. Costa et al. [9] proposed ECORA, a mechanism that combines multiple 3D geographic criteria to select forwarding nodes with short-term speed and direction variations, and low possibility of route failures, i.e., it considers link validation time (LIVE), direction and distance of interception.

However, these protocols [8,9] consider only geographical information for routing decisions, increasing the packet loss ratio and reducing the video quality level, since the most distant node might suffer from poor link quality connectivity [10]. In addition, such protocols assume end-to-end routes to forward packets or rely on beacon-based approaches to acquire information from neighbour nodes, but beacon-based schemes consume scarce network resources and end-to-end route may be subject to frequent interruptions or do not exist at any time, due to the dynamic characteristic of FANETs. Our proposal considers a position prediction mechanism and combines multiple 3D geographic criteria, but we also add other context information for routing decisions.

Heissenbüttel et al. [6] introduced the idea of DFD for forwarding decisions in Beaconless Routing Protocol (BLR), where source nodes broadcast a data packet. Before possible relay nodes forward the received packet, they compute the DFD value based only on location information. The node that computes the shortest DFD forwards the packet first and becomes the forwarding node. As soon as the neighbour nodes recognize the occurrence of relaying, they cancel the scheduled transmission for the same packet. Rosário et al. [11] proposed a Link Quality and Geographic-aware beaconless OR protocol (XLinGO), which combines different context information to compute the DFD, namely link quality, queue length, location, and residual energy. It considers a mechanism to detect and quickly react to route failures. Zhao et al. [12] introduced a context-aware adaptive beaconless OR protocol (CAOR), which also exploits multiple context information to compute the DFD, i.e., link quality, 2D node movement, and residual energy. CAOR considers an AHP method to adjust the degree of importance for each type of context metric according to their runtime values in order to adapt the protocol behaviour.

However, CAOR does not consider 3D location information to compute the LIVE metric and XLinGO only computes distance from a given node to the destination node, and thus CAOR and XLinGO do not mitigate the influence of UAV mobility to avoid communication flaws, delays and packet loss during multimedia transmission. XLinGO gives the same degree of importance to each type of context information, and both CAOR and XLinGO do not analyse which context metrics have more impact on the final video quality level. Finally, both do not consider a prediction mechanism to monitor the distance between a given node and its next hop in the following n seconds, which do not allow both protocols to detect route failures. Our proposal follows the beaconless OR approach with multiple context information to compute the DFD, considering BN to analyse the degree of importance for each context metric and AHP method to adapt the protocol behaviour. In addition, we integrate a position prediction mechanism and combine multiple 3D geographic criteria to select forwarding nodes with short variations in speeds/directions and low possibility of route failures.

Based on the analysis of our related work, we conclude that it is essential to consider multiple types of context information to compute the DFD to provide video dissemination with QoE support, and also it must consider the degree of importance of each metric on the final video quality level. In addition, the protocol must adapt its forwarding decision at runtime, since network or node conditions can be subject to continuous changes, and it must detect possible route failures to avoid communication flaws and packet loss. However, so far not all of these key features have been provided in a unified beaconless OR protocol.

3 Adaptive Context-Aware Beaconless or (CABR)

In this section we describe CABR that relies on multiple context-information to compute the DFD. CABR also includes a position prediction to detect possible route failure. We consider BN to analyse which CABR metrics have more impact on the final video quality, resulting in a weight vector. CABR adapts the protocol behaviour by considering AHP to change the context priority at runtime, allowing more realistic decision-making.

3.1 Network and System Model

CABR delivers high quality video transmitted over FANETs, as soon as the standard fixed network infrastructure becomes unavailable as the result of a natural disaster, such as an earthquake or hurricane. Hence, multimedia content plays an important role in enabling humans in the control center to take action to explore a hazardous area based on rich video information. Figure 1 shows an overview of the main CABR components. We first transmitted videos with different characteristics in an experimental setup in order to collect information about video quality, link quality, buffer state, energy, and connectivity. We take into account such experiment results to define the weight vector, i.e., the degree of importance for each metric, which serves as input to apply in an AHP method to adjust the weights at runtime based on network or node conditions.

We consider a FANET composed of n mobile nodes, i.e., UAVs, deployed in the monitored area. Each UAV has an individual identity denoted as $i \in [1, n]$. These nodes are represented in a dynamic graph $G(V, E)$, where the vertices $V = \{v_1, \cdots, v_n\}$ represent a finite set of nodes, and edges $E = \{e_1, \cdots, e_n\}$ build a finite set of wireless links between neighbour UAVs (v_i). We denote $N(v_i) \subset V$ as a subset of UAV neighbours within the radio range of a given node v_i. Each UAV v_i is equipped with a camera, an image encoder, a radio transceiver, and a limited energy supply. We assume a network scenario with one static Destination Node (DN) $\subset V$ equipped with a radio transceiver, an image decoder, unlimited energy, and also one-to-multiple Source Nodes (SN) $\subset V$ that can be any UAV v_i capturing video flows.

Link quality estimator (LQE) is measured at the physical layer, e.g. Received Signal Strength Indicator (RSSI) or Signal to Noise Ratio (SNR), which has a maximum LQE value (LQE_{max}). LQE can be used to analyse the characteristics of each link e_i, as soon as a given node v_i receives a packet. In addition, each node v_i has a queue (Q) with a maximum queue capacity (Q_{max}) and current queue length (Q_{length}). The queue policy schedules the packet transmission by using the First In First Out (FIFO) algorithm. Each node v_i can estimate its Remaining Energy (RE) and it is aware of its own location (x_i, y_i, z_i) in a 3D space ($\mathbb{R}^3$) by means of GPS, or any other positioning services. The DN location is known a priori by each node v_i, since we assume one static DN.

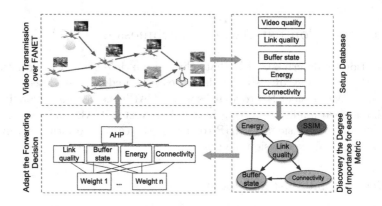

Fig. 1. CABR network scenario and forwarding decision

3.2   Contention-Based Forwarding Mode

In a similar way as existing beaconless OR protocols, where whenever a given Source node (SN) wants to send a video flow, it broadcasts the video packet to its neighbours $N(SN)$. Before the SN transmits a video packet, it must determine its own location (x_{SN}, y_{SN}, z_{SN}), speed (s_{SN}), and direction ($\overrightarrow{dir_{SN}}$) to include them in the packet header. Afterwards, SN neighbours $N(SN)$ compete to forward the received packets in a completely distributed manner, and CABR ensures that only one node forwards the received packet, where $N(SN)$ closer to DN than to SN compute the DFD, i.e., a short time interval for possible relay nodes to wait before forwarding the received packet.

Instead of immediately forwarding the received packet, each possible relay must compute the DFD to start a timer, and wait for the time-out to forward the received packet. The relay node that generates the smallest DFD value forwards the packet first, and becomes the forwarding node. Another possible relay node that overhears the packet transmission must cancel the scheduled transmission, and delete the buffered packet. At the same time, CABR uses the transmitted packet as passive acknowledgement, and thus the SN knows which node has the best conditions to unicast subsequent packets, and it must change to the persistent route mode. The algorithm continues until the packet reaches DN, which sends an explicit acknowledgement. In the persistent route mode nodes transmit packets in unicast, and without any additional delay.

The DFD can be computed as a multi-criteria cost function based on context information acquired locally (node energy, buffer state, and geographical location) or derived from the received broadcast packets (link quality and UAV mobility neighbour information), where there are no additional communication costs involved when collecting this context information. The utility cost function method is used for multi-criteria selection. We suggest to use the following utility function to quantify the DFD for a given node v_i.

$$DFD(v_i) = min(DFD(v_i)) = DFD_{max} \times \left(\sum_{i=1}^{n} c_i \times metric_i \right) \qquad (1)$$

$metric_i$ is the value for a given type of context information i, i.e. link quality, energy, buffer state, and UAV mobility in a 3D space. We consider $f(metric_i)$ $\in [0, 1]$ as a normalized function for each type of context information i, which expresses different unit characteristics in a numerical representation. There are different normalized functions introduced in the literature to solve several problems in communication networks, e.g., linear piecewise, logarithmic, exponential, and sigmoid functions. We consider the sigmoid function to normalize each metric $f(metric_i)$, since sigmoid is well known function often used in communication networks to represent the values for a given metric i [13]. We represent c_i as the weight for each metric i, where $\sum_{i=1}^{n} c_i = 1$. We consider a BN to define the weight vector, by analysing empirically which CABR metric have more impact on the final video quality. Afterwards, CABR considers AHP to adjust the degree of importance for the context information based on instantaneous network or node conditions. Finally, DFD_{Max} means the predefined maximum delay value allowed for each node to wait before forwarding the received packet.

(1) Context Metrics: CABR considers link quality as context information to ensure that the selected forwarding node provides multimedia transmission with packet delivery guarantees. In case of simultaneous video flow transmissions, considering buffer state avoids the selection of a forwarding node with heavy traffic, ensuring video dissemination with a QoE guarantee, since video streaming generates a larger amount of packets, which might cause buffer overflows and interference along the route [14]. Energy is another important type of context information to prevent the selection of a forwarding node with low energy, since UAVs are battery-powered and have limited energy resources. It is not desirable to choose a forwarding node that suffers from energy failures, which might cause packet losses. CABR considers the link quality, buffer state, energy, and progress definitions proposed by XLinGO [11], as shown in Eqs. 2, 3, and 4.

$$f(linkQuality) = \frac{1}{1 + e^{-c(LQE - LQE_{Max}/2)}} \qquad (2)$$

$$f(bufferState) = \frac{1}{1 + e^{-c(Q_{length} - Q_{max}/2)}} \qquad (3)$$

$$f(energy) = \frac{1}{1 + e^{-c(RE - RE_{max}/2)}} \qquad (4)$$

UAV mobility in a 3D space appears as another important type of context information in FANETs, since it worsens the effects of node mobility by breaking plenty of communication links. CABR considers connectivity of given pairs of neighbour nodes computed based on $LIVE$ [9], Direction of Interception ($DirI$) [9], and progress [11], as shown in Eq. 5. Hence, CABR mitigates the influence of UAV mobility effects to avoid communication flaws, delays and packet loss during multimedia transmission. We consider weights (α, β, γ) for each criteria, and the sum of them is equal to 1.

$$f(connectivity) = \alpha \times LIVE_{i,j} + \beta \times DirI_{i,DN} + \gamma \times progress_{v_i,DN} \qquad (5)$$

We compute distances and directions between a given pair of nodes v_i and v_j based on Eq. 6, where $LIVE_{i,j}$ estimates the link duration in the Radio Range (RR) of each other based on speed and direction variations, and θ_i, ϕ_i, θ_j, ϕ_j means mobility directions. High $LIVE_{i,j}$ values indicate that the nodes are moving into opposite directions or with different moving speeds, and this link is more susceptible to communication flaws caused by UAV mobility.

$$dist\,(x, y, z) = (x_i - x_j, y_i - y_j, z_i - z_j)$$
$$dir\,(x, y, z) = ((s_i \sin\theta_i \cos\phi_i - s_j \sin\theta_j \cos\phi_j),$$
$$(s_i \sin\theta_i \sin\phi_i - s_j \sin\theta_j \sin\phi_j),\,(s_i \cos\phi_i - s_j \cos\phi_j))$$

$$\qquad (6)$$

$$a = dir_x^2 + dir_y^2 + dir_z^2$$
$$b = 2dis_x dir_x + 2dis_y dir_y + 2dis_z dir_z$$
$$c = dist_x^2 + dist_y^2 + dist_z^2 - RR^2$$
$$LIVE_{i,j} = \frac{-b \pm \sqrt{b^2 - 4ac}}{2a}$$

$DirI_{i,DN}$ computed based on Eq. 7 indicates whether a given node v_i is moving towards the DN. This is because the selection of the forwarding node moving into opposite direction away from the DN increases the number of hops, reduces robustness, and increases the packet loss ratio. We denote θ_1 as the angle between the positive x-axis and the speed components of a given node v_i. On the other hand, θ_2 means the angle between the positive x-axis of a given node v_i and the imaginary line that connects v_i to DN. Finally, $angleTh$ represents the threshold used for the choice of a node within a predefined area, allowing the selection of forwarding node with better direction towards the DN.

$$\theta_1 = \arctan(s_{iy} s_{ix}) \frac{180}{\pi}$$
$$\theta_2 = \arctan(x_{DN} - x_i, y_{DN} - y_i) \frac{180}{\pi} \qquad (7)$$
$$DirI_{i,DN} = |\frac{\theta_1 - \theta_2}{angleTh}|$$

We attempt to reduce the number of hops by considering the progress from a given node v_i towards the DN ($progress_{v_i,DN}$), since longer routes reduce the packet delivery ratio. For this reason, we prefer to select nodes closer to the DN. Hence, we compute $progress_{v_i,DN}$ according to Eq. 8.

$$progress_{v_i,DN} = \frac{1}{1 + e^{(-c(P(v_i,DN)-RR))}}. \tag{8}$$

(2) Degree of Importance for Each Context Information: We estimate the individual importance of each type of context information to find an appropriate global solution for routing decisions. In this way, we consider BN and K2 Algorithms as data correlation models to find how a given CABR context metrics influence the others to increase or decrease the video quality level. We perform data correlation based on a database with information about the context metrics and the video quality level.

In this way, we performed a set of simulations, where two source nodes transmitted video sequences with different motion and complexity levels via multiple forwarding nodes. We collected information about link quality, buffer state, energy, and connectivity at each possible relay node, as well as the quality level of videos received at the DN. Based on inferences by different context information (i.e., link quality, buffer, energy, and connectivity) on the video quality, we found the weight vector that indicates the degree of importance of each context metric. According to our database, we obtained the following weight vector: $[0.399, 0.269, 0.204, 0.128]$, which means that link quality, buffer, energy, and connectivity have 39.9 %, 26.9 %, 20.4 %, and 12.8 % degree of importance, respectively, in order to provide video dissemination with acceptable quality.

(3) Runtime Context Weight Adaptation Scheme: The degree of importance for each type of context information might change at runtime, since considering fixed weight assignments for each metric is unrealistic and makes it difficult to cope with frequent context switching during the multimedia transmission. In this way, the AHP method provides a structured technique for decision-making problems with multiple parameters, which makes pairwise comparison between numerical values of a given metric and their relative importance to adjust weights at runtime. High weight means more importance should be attached to this particular metric, and we define five importance levels, as shown in Table 1.

Table 1. Pairwise context importance

$c_{i,j}$	Importance degree
3	i is much more important than j
2	i is more important than j
1	i is as important as j
1/2	i is less important than j
1/3	i is much less important than j

Hence, every node v_i constructs its own matrix to compare all context-pairs according to their instantaneous values. We denote $c_{i,j}$ as the comparison matrix, as shown in Eq. 9, where $c_{i,j}$ value means how important the $i - th$ element is compared with the $j - th$ element.

$$C_{i,j} = \begin{array}{c} \\ c_1 \\ c_2 \\ c_3 \\ c_4 \end{array} \begin{array}{cccc} c_1 & c_2 & c_3 & c_4 \\ \left(\begin{array}{cccc} c_{1,1} & c_{1,2} & c_{1,3} & c_{1,4} \\ c_{2,1} & c_{2,2} & c_{2,3} & c_{2,4} \\ c_{3,1} & c_{3,2} & c_{3,3} & c_{3,4} \\ c_{4,1} & c_{4,2} & c_{4,3} & c_{4,4} \end{array} \right) \end{array} \tag{9}$$

Based on previous simulations and existing studies, we defined thresholds for each type of context by mapping its value into three categories: poor, intermediate, and good, as shown in Table 2. We consider real-time context values as input to compare them with the defined thresholds, and then apply AHP to estimate their importance based on pairwise context comparison. For instance, metric i is more important than metric j, as soon as metric i value is in a more critical range (i.e., poor range) than metric j (i.e., good range), and thus metric i has $c_{i,j}$ equals to 3.

Table 2. Threshold definition of the Context Information

Context	Ranges
$f(linkQuality)$ - LQE	$(0, LQE_{bad}), (LQE_{bad}, LQE_{good}), (LQE_{good}, LQE_{max})$
$f(connectivity)$ - C	$(\infty, C_{bad}), (C_{bad}, C_{good}), (C_{good}, C \approx 0)$
$f(energy)$ - E	$(E \approx 0, E_{min}), (E_{min}, E_{good}), (E_{good}, E_{max})$
$f(bufferState)$ - BS	$(BS \approx_{full}, BS_{min}), (BS_{min}, BS_{good}), (BS_{good}, BS \approx_{empty})$

To illustrate the method described above, let us assume a given node v_i with context values in the following ranges: $LQE \in (LQE_{good}, LQE_{max})$, $C \in (\infty, C_{bad})$, $E \in (E_{good}, E_{max})$, and $BS \in (BS_{min}, BS_{good})$. Based on the pairwise context information, the comparison matrix can be represented as:

$$C_{4,4} = \begin{array}{c} \\ M \\ LQ \\ BS \\ E \end{array} \begin{array}{cccc} M & LQ & BS & E \\ \left(\begin{array}{cccc} 1 & 3 & 2 & 3 \\ 1/3 & 1 & 1/2 & 1 \\ 1/2 & 2 & 1 & 2 \\ 1/3 & 1 & 1/2 & 1 \end{array} \right) \end{array} \tag{10}$$

CABR obtains the relative weights vector c_i by normalizing them by dividing each context value by the total sum of each column. The contribution of each criterion in the overall target is obtained by calculating the matrix eigenvector. Based on the comparison matrix of Eq. 10, the new weight vector can be derived as $w = [0.453, 0.142, 0.262, 0.142]$.

3.3   Persistent-Route Mode

CABR avoids the drawbacks of broadcasting transmissions by introducing a persistent route mode, where nodes transmit subsequent packets in a unicast fashion. Video flows must be delivered even in presence of continuous topology changes. CABR relies on a mechanism to detect and respond to route failures, but CABR includes a position prediction mechanism to monitor the distance between a given node and its next hop to detect possible route failures.

CABR considers that every node that composes the route should assess whether the route is still a reliable or valid route to transmit subsequent packets. This is achieved by a given forwarding node n_j sending a reply message to its last hop n_i, and piggyback the exponential average for the link quality and Packet Received Ratio (PRR) perceived in the last k received packets, and also x'_j, y'_j, z'_j, v_j, θ_i, and ϕ_i. In this way, n_i must return to the contention-based forwarding mode, as soon as it detects lower link quality or PRR for the packets received by its forwarding node n_j.

Position prediction enables a given node n_i to estimate the location of its forwarding node n_j ($x_{pred}, y_{pred}, z_{pred}$) based on Eq. 11, which considers coordinates information in the 3D space (x'_j, y'_j, z'_j), speed (v_j), and timestamp (t) from n_j. We denote Δt as the difference between the current timestamp t_c and the timestamp t_l of the last reply message for a given node n_j, i.e., $\Delta t = t_c - t_l$. In addition, θ_i and ϕ_i mean the moving directions of n_j. A given forwarding node n_j might move out of RR of node n_i, and thus the estimated position enables CABR to monitor the distance between a node n_i and n_j to detect possible route failures, i.e. as soon as the distance between both nodes is higher than RR.

$$x_{pred} = x'_j + \Delta t(v_j sin\theta_j \times cos\phi_j)$$
$$y_{pred} = y'_j + \Delta t(v_j sin\theta_j \times sin\phi_j) \qquad (11)$$
$$z_{pred} = z'_j + \Delta t(v_j cos\theta_j).$$

4   Evaluation

This section describes the methodology and metrics used to evaluate the quality level of transmitted videos via CABR compared with the existing beaconless OR protocols. We evaluated the impact of node mobility at different moving speeds and number of multimedia flows on the video quality level.

4.1   Simulation Description and Evaluation Metrics

We used an OMNeT++ framework [15] running on Microsoft Azure. The results are averaged over 33 simulation runs with different randomly generated seeds to provide a confidence interval of 95 %. The simulations run for 200 seconds with the lognormal shadowing path loss model. We set the simulation parameters to allow wireless channel temporal variations, link asymmetry, and irregular radio ranges, as expected in a real FANET scenario.

We deployed 30 and 40 nodes with one destination located at $(75, 0, 0)$, and some source nodes are moving and transmitting simultaneous video flows. Possible relay nodes are moving following the Gauss-Markov mobility model generated by means of the BonnMotion mobility trace generator tool, because it provides a mobility behaviour closest to a FANET [1]. We defined the minimum speed limit equal to 1 and the maximum ranging from 5 to 20 m/s. Nodes are equipped with IEEE 802.11 radio and transmission power of 12 dBm, resulting in a nominal transmission range of 15 m. They rely on CSMA/CA MAC protocol without RTS/CTS messages and retransmissions, on a drop tail mechanism to drop packets in case of buffer overflow, and on a QoE-aware redundancy mechanism [11] to add redundant packets only to priority frames at the application layer.

We conducted simulations with five different beaconless OR protocols to analyse their impact to deliver videos with good quality level. First we consider **BLR** [6] as routing protocol. Afterwards, we consider connectivity to compute the DFD under BLR (**BLR-E**), which is computed based on the combination of geographic information and node mobility in a 3D space, such as introduced in Sect. 3.2. In this way, we can analyse the ability of connectivity to improve the routing decisions. Third, we consider **XLinGO** [11] as routing protocol, where XLinGO takes into account progress, buffer state, and link quality to compute the DFD with fixed degree of importance for each type of context information. Then, we included connectivity to compute the DFD under XLinGO (**XLinGO-E**). Finally, we use **CABR** as routing protocol, which considers multiple type of context information to compute the DFD and also adapts its forwarding decision based on context information at runtime, such as introduced in Sect. 3.

Source nodes transmitted the Hall, Container, UAV_1, or UAV_2 video sequences, which have different video features. These videos are downloaded from the YUV video trace library and YouTube [16]. We encoded those videos with a H.264 codec at 300 kbps, 30 frames per second, GoP size of 18 frames, and common intermediate format (352×288). The decoder uses a Frame-Copy method for error concealment to replace each lost frame with the last received one to reduce frame loss and maintain the video quality.

In terms of video quality evaluation, Quality of Service (QoS) schemes alone are not enough to assess the quality level of multimedia applications, because they fail in capturing subjective aspects of video content related to human experience. In this context, QoE metrics overcome those limitations, and thus we rely on a well-known objective QoE metric, namely Structural Similarity (SSIM). SSIM $\in [0,1]$ is based on a frame-by-frame assessment of three video components, i.e., luminance, contrast, and structural similarity. Higher SSIM value means better video quality. We used the MSU Video Quality Measurement Tool (VQMT) to measure the SSIM value for each transmitted video.

4.2 Simulation Results

In this section, we evaluate the reliability of CABR compared to XLinGO, XLinGO-E, BLR, and BLR-E, in a scenario composed of 30 and 40 mobile nodes moving at different speed limits, i.e. 5, 10, 15, and 20 m/s. In addition, we considered scenarios with 1, 2, and 3 source nodes transmitting simultaneous video flows. Figure 2 shows the quality level of videos transmitted via CABR, XLinGO, XLinGO-E, BLR, and BLR-E. In this way, we can analyse the impact of the moving speed and number of source nodes on the final video quality level.

By analysing results from Fig. 2, we conclude that CABR delivered videos with a high quality level compared to XLinGO, XLinGO-E, BLR, and BLR-E regardless of the moving speed and number of simultaneous video transmissions. For instance, videos transmitted via BLR have poor quality level, since it only considers geographical information to compute the DFD. Due to the unreliability of wireless channels, the most distant node might suffer from a bad connection [10], increasing the packet loss ratio for BLR. BLR-E improves the BLR performance, because BLR-E considers connectivity computed based on 3D geographical information as the metric to compute the DFD, and thus it provides the selection of forwarding nodes with short-term variation in speeds and directions. However, videos transmitted via BLR-E have lower quality than videos transmitted via XLinGO and XLinGO-E, since BLR-E still selects forwarding nodes based on geographical information only, and XLinGO or XLinGO-E compute the DFD based on multiple types of context information. On the other hand, XLinGO-E provides video dissemination with better quality than XLinGO. This is because XLinGO-E includes connectivity to compute the DFD, which also highlight the importance of computing connectivity based on 3D information in order to select forwarding nodes with short variation in speeds and directions.

Quality level of videos transmitted via CABR are around 15 % higher than transmissions via XLinGO and XLinGO-E, in case of different numbers of simultaneous video transmissions and moving speeds. This is because CABR includes position prediction to monitor the distance between a given node and its forwarding node to detect route failures, considers BN to find the degree of importance for each CABR metric and AHP to adjust them based on network or node conditions at runtime. In this way, CABR transmits video packets with a reduced frame loss rate, protecting priority frames in congestion and link error periods. For instance, it reduces the frame loss rate by 20 % compared to XLinGO and XLinGO-E in case of two source nodes transmitting simultaneous videos and nodes moving at 5m/s. It reduces also in 10 % the packet failed below sensitivity than XLinGO and XLinGO-E, which means that CABR reduced route failures.

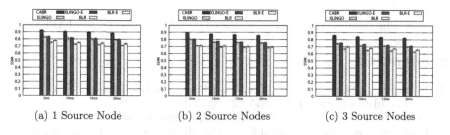

(a) 1 Source Node   (b) 2 Source Nodes   (c) 3 Source Nodes

Fig. 2. Video quality level for a scenario composed of 40 mobile nodes

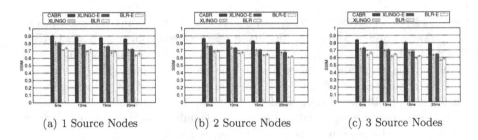

(a) 1 Source Nodes   (b) 2 Source Nodes   (c) 3 Source Nodes

Fig. 3. Video quality level for a scenario composed of 30 mobile nodes

The video quality level reduces when the node density decreases, regardless the routing protocols, by comparing results from Figs. 2 to 3. This is because the number of neighbors decreases, minimizing the likelihood to establish/reestablish a reliable persistent route between SN and DN. It is important to highlight that CABR delivers videos with SSIM higher than 0.8 independent of nodes speed, density, and number of simultaneous video transmission, which is not achieved by existing beaconless OR protocols.

5 Conclusions

This paper introduced CABR, a beaconless OR protocol that supports simultaneous video dissemination with QoE assurance over multimedia FANET scenarios. These videos can be delivered to multimedia platforms for further processing and analysis, in order to guide rescue operations, and allow appropriate action to be taken based on visual information. More specifically, CABR takes into account multiple type of context information to compute the DFD value, namely energy, buffer state, 3D geographical location, link quality, and UAV mobility information. It considers the degree of importance of each metric obtained empirically, and adapts its forwarding decision according to runtime context information. Simulation results highlighted CABR's reliability, robustness, and QoE support in the presence of node mobility and simultaneous video transmissions compared to XLinGO, XLinGO-E, BLR, and BLR-E. This is achieved in scenarios composed of mobile nodes with different moving speeds, number of source nodes, and videos with different motion and complexity levels.

Acknowledgements. This work is supported by CAPES, CNPQ, and FAPESPA.

References

1. Bekmezci, I., Sahingoz, O.K., Temel, Ş.: Flying Ad-Hoc networks (FANETs): a survey. Ad Hoc Netw. **11**(3), 1254–1270 (2013)
2. Dobrijevic, O., Kassler, A.J., Skorin-Kapov, L., Matijasevic, M.: Q-POINT: QoE-Driven path optimization model for multimedia services. In: Mellouk, A., Fowler, S., Hoceini, S., Daachi, B. (eds.) WWIC 2014. LNCS, vol. 8458, pp. 134–147. Springer, Heidelberg (2014)

3. Sahingoz, O.K.L.: Mobile networking with UAVs: opportunities and challenges. In: Proceedings of the International Conference on Unmanned Aircraft Systems (ICUAS 2013), pp. 933–941 (2013)
4. Ehsan, S., Hamdaoui, B.: A survey on energy-efficient routing techniques with QoS assurances for wireless multimedia sensor networks. IEEE Commun. Surv. Tutorials **14**(2), 265–278 (2012)
5. Hsu, C.-J., Liu, H.-I., Seah, W.: Survey paper: opportunistic routing - a review and the challenges ahead. Comput. Netw. **55**(15), 3592–3603 (2011)
6. Heissenbüttel, M., Braun, T., Bernoulli, T., WäLchli, M.: BLR: beacon-less routing algorithm for mobile ad hoc networks. Comput. Commun. **27**(11), 1076–1086 (2004)
7. Saaty, T.: Fundamentals of Decision Making and Priority Theory with the Analytic Hierarchy Process. AHP Series. RWS Publications, Pittsburgh (2000)
8. Li, Y., St-Hilaire, M., Kunz, T.: Improving routing in networks of UAVs via scoped flooding and mobility prediction. In: Proceedings of the IFIP Wireless Days (WD 2012), pp. 1–6. IEEE (2012)
9. Costa, R., Rosário, D., Cerqueira, E., Santos, A.: Enhanced connectivity for robust multimedia transmission in UAV networks. In: Proceedings of the IFIP Wireless Days Conference (WD 2014), Rio de Janeiro, Brazil, November 2014. IEEE (2014)
10. Baccour, N., Koubâ, A., Youssef, H., Alves, M.: Reliable link quality estimation in low-power wireless networks and its impact on tree-routing. Ad Hoc Netw. **27**, 1–25 (2014)
11. Rosário, D., Zhao, Z., Santos, A., Braun, T., Cerqueira, E.: A beaconless opportunistic routing based on a cross-layer approach for efficient video dissemination in mobile multimedia IoT applications. Comput. Commun. **45**(1), 21–31 (2014)
12. Zhao, Z., Braun, T., Rosário, D., Cerqueira, E.: CAOR: context-aware adaptive opportunistic routing in mobile ad-hoc networks. In: Proceedings of the 7th IFIP Wireless and Mobile Networking Conference (WMNC 2014), pp. 1–8. IEEE (2014)
13. Lohier, S., Rachedi, A., Ghamri-Doudane, Y.: A cost function for QoS-Aware routing in multi-tier wireless multimedia sensor networks. In: Pfeifer, T., Bellavista, P. (eds.) MMNS 2009. LNCS, vol. 5842, pp. 81–93. Springer, Heidelberg (2009)
14. Hanini, M., Haqiq, A., Berqia, A.: Multicriteria queuing model to improve intra-user multi-flow QoS in wireless cellular networks. In: Wireless Systems, and Mobile Computing, Multidisciplinary Perspectives on Telecommunications (2014)
15. Rosário, D., Zhao, Z., Silva, C., Cerqueira, E., Braun, T.: An OMNeT++ framework to evaluate video transmission in mobile wireless multimedia sensor networks. In: International Workshop on OMNeT++, ICST, March 2013, pp. 277–284 (2013)
16. Videos used for simulations (2015). http://plus.google.com/117765468529449487 870/videos

Network Architecture and Applications

Invariant Preserving Middlebox Traversal

Ahmed Abujoda[✉] and Panagiotis Papadimitriou

Institute of Communications Technology, Leibniz Universität Hannover,
Hannover, Germany
{ahmed.abujoda,panagiotis.papadimitriou}@ikt.uni-hannover.de

Abstract. Middleboxes, such as firewalls, NATs, proxies, and application accelerators are known for their undesirable implications on traffic
(mainly due to packet headers or payload modifications) and for hindering connection establishment when certain protocols are in use (e.g.,
UDP, SCTP).

Since many of these implications occur in middleboxes within ISPs or
cellular networks, we present a software-defined network (SDN) architecture that can foster the collaboration between end-hosts and ISPs.
In particular, an end-host can express a desirable behavior from the
network, specified as an invariant (*e.g.*, no IP header or payload modification), and the ISP, in turn, can establish a connection through middleboxes that preserve this invariant. We discuss the proposed architecture
and the requirements for invariant preserving middlebox traversal. We
further propose an algorithm for the selection of the best path through
a sequence of invariant-preserving middleboxes. We use simulations to
assess the efficiency of our approach.

1 Introduction

The increasing demand for security and access control along with the need for
better application support has led to the deployment of network appliances,
known as middleboxes, by enterprises, Internet Service Providers (ISP), and
cellular network operators. The proliferation of middleboxes, such as firewalls,
proxies, network address translators (NAT), intrusion detection systems (IDS),
and redundancy elimination boxes, has been reported in recent studies [9,11].

Unfortunately, the additional functionality that middleboxes embed comes
at a cost: middleboxes introduce various undesirable implications on traffic. For
example, NATs rewrite IP addresses and ports, proxies break end-to-end semantics, firewalls may block UDP traffic or cache out-of-order-packets introducing varying delays, while application optimizers can modify the packet payload
[9,10]. Furthermore, the deployment of firewalls and NATs along most Internet
paths may hinder connection establishment with protocols such as Stream Control Transmission Protocol (SCTP) or Multi-Path TCP [8]. To mitigate these
problems, most applications resort to tunneling, *e.g.*, non-HTTP traffic may be
tunnelled over HTTP to traverse firewalls, SCTP usually has to be tunnelled
over TCP (or over UDP in case it is not blocked). Furthermore, traffic may be

© Springer International Publishing Switzerland 2015
M.C. Aguayo-Torres et al. (Eds.): WWIC 2015, LNCS 9071, pp. 139–150, 2015.
DOI: 10.1007/978-3-319-22572-2_10

encrypted at the client device (*e.g.,* using HTTPS) to inhibit payload modifications by application optimizers [10]. However, this increases power consumption in mobile devices.

Most of these implications stem from the middleboxes deployed by access ISPs and cellular networks. To obviate the need for tunneling or traffic encryption for middlebox traversal, we consider fostering the collaboration between end-hosts and ISPs. More precisely, an end-host can express requirements for the establishment of a certain type of connection, *e.g.,* do not modify packet fields or payload, permit UDP traffic or access to public DNS servers. Such requirements can be specified in the form of invariants (*e.g.,* using the API in [10]). Upon the submission of such a request, the ISP may be willing to redirect the traffic through a set of middleboxes (*e.g.,* NAT and firewall) that comply with his security policy and, at the same time, preserve the invariant expressed by the end-host. This can be offered to ISP clients as a value-added service, which may be appealing to a wide range of users (*e.g.,* home network users, mobile users, enterprises) that currently experience limitations in the applications or services they can run.

Establishing connections through a sequence of invariant-preserving middleboxes raises several requirements: (i) the collection of middlebox configurations, (ii) parsing and checking middlebox configurations against requested invariants, (iii) the selection of invariant-preserving middleboxes and shortest paths, and (iv) the insertion of forwarding entries in the ISP's routers to route the traffic through the assigned path. To this end, we present a software-defined network (SDN) architecture for invariant preserving middlebox traversal. Following the trend for (logically) centralized control, we rely on a centralized controller deployed by the ISP, which retrieves middlebox configurations, selects middleboxes and paths that preserve the specified invariant, and configures packet forwarding along the selected path. Middlebox checking against invariants can be performed using recent advances on static analysis, such as Header Space Analysis (HSA) [6] or SymNet [7]. For the installation of flow entries to routers, we employ OpenFlow [5]. Our work is mainly focused on middlebox and path selection. To this end, we present and evaluate an algorithm for the selection of a path through a set of invariant-preserving middleboxes. Our simulation results show that our approach increases substantially the number of established connections, especially under low and moderate levels of network utilization.

The remainder of the paper is organized as follows. In Sect. 2, we review and discuss the different implications of middleboxes on traffic and connection establishment. Section 3 provides an overview of our SDN architecture. In Sect. 4 we discuss our algorithm for invariant preserving path selection. In Sect. 5, we present our simulation environment and results. Finally, in Sect. 6, we highlight our conclusions.

2   Middleboxes Implications

In this section, we discuss the implications of widely used middleboxes on traffic and connection establishment:

- **NATs:** Due to the limited size of IPv4 address space, NATs have become one of most popular middleboxes on ISP networks, especially on cellular networks [9]. They enable the sharing of a public IP address among multiple hosts with private IP addresses by mapping the private IP address and the source port number of a host connection (TCP or UDP) to the public IP address and a selected port number. As a result, hosts sitting behind NATs are not visible to the outside world, *i.e.*, establishing connections with NATed hosts (*e.g.*, a VoIP, P2P applications) requires complicated NAT traversal techniques [14–16] and might need the participation of a third party (*e.g.* a relay [17]). However, even with NAT traversal techniques, connection establishment could fail due to the ISPs policies and configurations. As shown in [9], to perform load balancing cellular network operators may assign multiple NATs to a single device. Subsequently, this hinders NAT traversal techniques that depend on learning the NAT's public IP address by establishing multiple connections with the NAT (since different connections are handled by different NATs). Furthermore, operators might configure NATs to assign random port numbers to the mapped connections which hampers applications (*e.g.*, P2P) performing NAT traversal by trying to infer the mapped NAT port number [9].

- **Firewalls:** They are essential to today's network functionality by providing protection against malicious traffic as well as untrusted and policy-violating accesses. However, despite their importance, firewalls have become an obstacle hindering not only the deployment of new protocols and extensions (SCTP, ECN), but also restricting the connectivity of the traditional protocols. More particular, recent studies have shown that applications and protocols are being forced to tunnel over HTTP/HTTPs to bypass firewalls [9,10]. Even when connections are successfully established, firewalls introduce further implications such as buffering out-of-order packets which impairs the functionality and performance of TCP connections, and terminating long-lived flows due to short timeouts on firewalls, leading to increased power consumption and service disruption [9].

- **Proxies:** They perform several functions to optimize the performance of particular applications or protocols such as caching contents, data compression and TCP connections splitting. Proxies are usually implemented with a specific application in mind which impairs the functionality of new applications passing through them. For example, mobile devices have to tunnel over HTTPS to avoid HTTP optimizers breaking their protocol semantics by modifying their packets payload or by sending a cached reply instead of forwarding the packet to the end server [10].

3   Architecture Overview

In this section, we discuss the requirements of invariant preserving middlebox traversal and present the components of our SDN architecture.

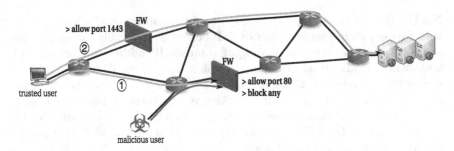

Fig. 1. Example of invariant preserving middleboxes traversal.

Consider the example in Fig. 1, where a trusted user (*e.g.*, an enterprise with well-established relation/contract with the ISP) is trying to access a server through port 1443. Since the firewall on its default path (path 1) blocks any traffic on ports other than port 80, the user fails to establish a connection with the server. A straightforward solution is to request the ISP to reconfigure the firewall on the default path. However this will allow the malicious user's traffic to traverse the network. An alternative solution, which we consider in this paper, is to allow the user to express her requirement as an invariant to the ISP (in this case allow port 1443), and in turn the ISP identifies a path which preserve the invariant and does not violate the the ISP policy (path 2).

To this end, we envision an SDN architecture where a centralized control plane provides invariant preserving routing and redirection through the ISP network. Accordingly, we assume the deployment of OpenFlow switches which serve as the data plane of the network. Furthermore, as in today's ISP network, a set of middleboxes are deployed in the network at different locations to provide services such as protection against malicious traffic (e.g. firewalls), enable the sharing of IPv4 addresses (NAT) and caching of frequently used content (proxies). To provide invariant preserving connection establishment, our SDN architecture needs to fulfil a set of requirements:

- **Efficient Resource Management:** We consider two objectives for resource management in ISP networks: (i) delay minimization, where an ISP aims at routing traffic through the path with the shortest delay and (ii) load balancing, where an ISP aims at balancing the traffic load across the network.

- **Correctness:** Traffic should traverse paths that preserve the invariant while not violating the ISP policy, *e.g.*, a video flow with a particular port number might be redirected through a firewall which grants access to it but still needs to keep an upper bound on the BW consumed by this flow. This requires correct and efficient parsing and checking of the state and configuration of the middleboxes deployed in the network.

- **Traffic Redirection:** The controller should be able to install forwarding entries in the ISP's switches to reroute traffic through the selected path. This should also take into account middleboxes which modify the packets routing header fields such as the IPs addresses (*e.g.,* NATs, load balancer).

To fulfil these requirements, we design a control plane which consists of four components (Fig. 2):

- **MBs Configuration and State Collection:** This component collects and stores the state and configurations (*e.g.,* firewall rules) of each middlebox deployed in the network. It accesses middleboxes through interfaces exposed to the controllers by the vendors. These interfaces could be vendor-specific (*e.g.,* CISCO CLI) or standard interface such as netconf [3] or SIMCO [4].

- **Static Checking:** This component implements tools such as SymNet [7] or HSA [6] to parse and analyse the state and configurations of middleboxes against the requested invariants. It basically identifies the implications the middleboxes have on the flow and hence, specifies the middleboxes which do not violate the flow invariant.

- **Network Monitoring:** This component keeps track of the network topology as well as the network links and middleboxes utilization. It reads the counters of the network switches deployed on the network using OpenFlow [5]. For monitoring middleboxes utilization, it uses again the interface exposed by the vendors.

- **Path Selection:** Based on the output provided by the static checking and the network monitoring component, this component selects a path which fulfils the invariant of the connection while considering the utilization of the network and the middleboxes. It implements our path selection algorithm presented in Sect. 4.

- **Switch Configuration:** It installs the required flow entries in OpenFlow switches to redirect the flow through the path selected by path selection component. For middleboxes (e.g. NAT) which modify some of the flow's 5 tuples (source and destination IP addresses, source and destination port numbers, protocol), the flow can be identified by adding tags to each packet such as in [12,13].

4   Path Selection

We develop an algorithm which selects a network path traversing middleboxes that preserve a connection invariant. In addition to the configuration and the state of each middlebox, our algorithm takes into account the available bandwidth on each network link as well as the available processing capacity of each

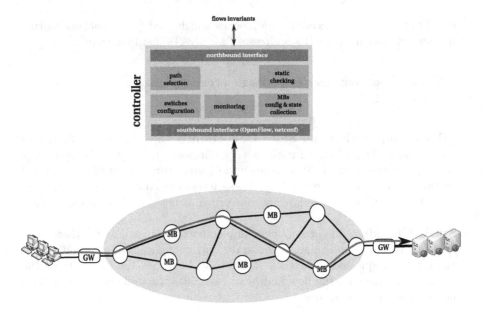

Fig. 2. Architecture components.

middlebox. The algorithm is executed by an SDN controller which has the knowledge of the network topology and utilization, the middleboxes utilization and state, and the connection invariant. We present two variants of our algorithm: the first aims at minimizing end-to-end delay, whereas the second strives to achieve load balancing across the network.

We represent the ISP network as a weighted undirected graph $G = (N, L)$, where N is the set of nodes and L is the set of links between nodes of the set N. Nodes are classified into set of routers R and a set of middleboxes M such that $N = R \cup M$. Each m_i has a processing capacity which is denoted by $CP(m_i)$ and a state $S(m_i)$. Each link $l_{ij} \in L$ between two nodes n_i and n_j is associated with the available bandwidth $C(l_{ij})$. Let P_{ij} represents the set of paths in the network G, between the pair of nodes n_i and n_j. The available bandwidth $C(p)$ of a path $p \in P_{ij}$ is given by the minimum residual bandwidth of the links along the path:

$$C(p) = \min_{l_{ij} \in p} C(l_{ij}) \qquad (1)$$

We further represent a connection demand with a vector $d = \{n_{src}, n_{dst}, r, cmp, v\}$, where $n_{src}, n_{dst} \in N$ denote the connection source and destination nodes, r represents the traffic rate, cmp is the required computing capacity to process the traffic, and v is the connection invariant.

The algorithm selects a path between the source and destination of a connection. It starts by removing all the links with insufficient available bandwidth to fulfil the rate of the connection. This step reduces the size of the graph that

---

Algorithm 1. Path selection

Inputs: $G = (N, L), d$

for each $l \in L$ do
    if $C(l) < r$ then
        delete l from G
    end if
end for

$P_{ij} \leftarrow$ FIND_ALL_PATHS(n_{src}, n_{dst}) // all paths between source and destination
SORT(Pi, j) // sort paths based on their length or available BW

for each $p \in P_{i,j}$ do
    found $\leftarrow$ *true*
    for each $m \in P$
        if $cmp > CP(m)$ or $v \cap S(m) = \emptyset$ then
            Found $\leftarrow$ *false*
            break
        end if
    end for
    if *found* then
        return p
    end if
end for
return $\emptyset$ // no path was found

FIND_ALL_PATHS function has to process to calculate all paths between the source and the destination. This function implements the algorithm in [2] which has a complexity of $O(N + L)$. Reducing the size of N and L results in lower runtime. After identifying all the paths, we sort them in increasing order based on the number of hops or on a decreasing order based on the available bandwidth $C(p)$. Sorting based on number of hops results in delay minimization, whereas sorting based on the available bandwidth achieves load balancing. We term the two algorithm variants as *invariant preserving SP algorithm* and *invariant preserving LB algorithm*, respectively. Finally, the algorithm goes through the sorted paths to find the first one which fulfils the invariant as well as the connection processing demand.

5 Evaluation

In this section, we evaluate the efficiency of our path selection algorithms for invariant preserving middlebox traversal. In particular, we use simulation to measure the connection acceptance rate and the network and middleboxes utilization. Furthermore, we compare our algorithms in terms of load balancing level and path hops counts per connection.

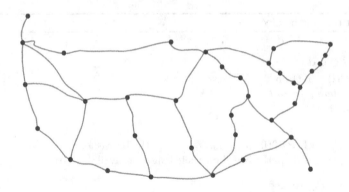

Fig. 3. Simulation OpenFlow switches topology.

5.1 Evaluation Environment

We have developed a Python flow-level simulator to establish invariant preserving connections through a ISP network. To model ISP network, we use internet2 topology [1] which consists of 34 nodes (Fig. 3). Each node in this figure represents an OpenFlow switch, whereas each edge is a network link with 1 Gbit/second bandwidth. At different locations of the topology, we deploy 12 Middleboxes. Each middlebox has 10 GHz CPU capacity and performs access control using a randomly generated list of destination port numbers (each Middlebox works as a stateless firewall). We generate non-expiring connections with destination port numbers, rates, and processing demands sampled out of a uniform distribution. For each generated connection, we randomly select a source and a destination switch. Using the algorithm in Sect. 4, a connection is established if a network path which preserve its invariant, and fulfils its rate and processing demand is found, otherwise it is rejected. For each successfully established connection, the bandwidth of the links and the processing capacity of middleboxes on the path are updated accordingly.

We compare the efficiency of our approach against the traditional shortest path selection. In particular, for each new connection we calculate the shortest path between the connection source and destination, if the shortest path fulfils the connection demand and invariant, the connection is established, otherwise it is rejected.

We conducted our simulation on a machine with Intel Core i5 quad-core CPU at 3.20 GHz and 16 GB of RAM. We repeat each experiment 100 times and report the average.

5.2 Evaluation Results

We start by measuring the *connection acceptance rate*. This represents the percentage of connections' sizes for which invariant-preserving paths were selected. As Fig. 4 shows, our algorithms (invariant-preserving SP and invariant-preserving LB) establish almost 40 % more connections than the traditional shortest path

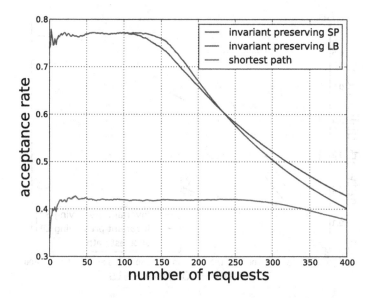

Fig. 4. Connection establishment rate vs. number of arriving requests.

selection. This is because our algorithms select alternative paths when either the invariant or the connection demand are not fulfilled, whereas the traditional shortest path rejects the connection when the shortest path does not meet the connection requirements. This can be also seen through the evolution of network and

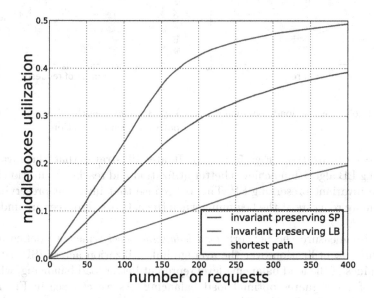

Fig. 5. Total utilization of middleboxes deployed on the network.

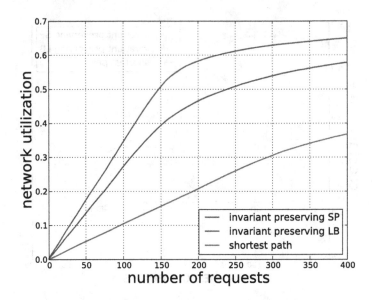

Fig. 6. Total utilization of all network links.

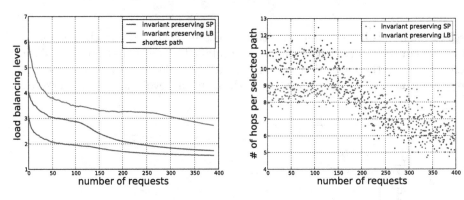

Fig. 7. The network load balancing level.

Fig. 8. The length of each selected path for each connection.

middleboxes utilization (Figs. 5 and 6). It also illustrates that the invariant-preserving LB algorithm achieves better utilization and reaches saturation faster than the invariant-preserving SP. This is because that invariant-preserving LB accepts more requests at the beginning when the network resources are underutilized.

We also measure the network *load balancing level* which we define as the maximum link utilization over the average link utilization across ISP network. Lower values of the load balancing level represent better load balancing, whereas a value of 1 designates optimal load balancing. As we can see in Fig. 7, the invariant-preserving LB algorithm outperforms both our invariant-preserving SP algorithm and the traditional shortest path.

We further look at the path length per selected path in terms of the number of hops. As we expect, the invariant-preserving SP outperforms the invariant-preserving LB algorithm (Fig. 8), however, as the network resources become more utilized the difference between both algorithms diminishes. This is because the number of alternative paths with sufficient capacity decreases which limits the solution search space for both algorithms.

6 Conclusions

In this paper, we presented a SDN architecture for establishing invariant preserving connections traversing middleboxes and fostering the collaboration between end-hosts and ISPs. In particular, an end-host can express a desirable behavior from the network, specified as an invariant (*e.g.,* no IP header or payload modification), and the ISP, in turn, can establish a connection through middleboxes that preserve this invariant. To this end, we developed an algorithm to select redirection paths through a sequence of invariant-preserving middleboxes while considering network and middlebox utilization. Our algorithm can be adapted to fulfil different objectives: load balancing or delay minimization. Using simulations, we showed that our algorithm increases substantially the number (more than 40 %) of established connections with invariant preservation and achieves a network-wide load balance as well as higher network and middleboxes utilization.

We believe that our work indicates the feasibility of invariant preserving middleboxes traversal and takes a step towards providing more flexibility at the core of the network for new service and protocol deployment. As part of future work, we plan to implement and experimentally evaluate the efficiency of our SDN architecture using our Emulab-based network testbed.

Acknowledgments. This work was partially supported by the EU FP7 T-NOVA Project (619520).

References

1. Internet2. http://www.internet2.edu/
2. Sedgewick, R.: Algorithms in C, Part 5: Graph Algorithms, 3rd edn. Addison Wesley Professional, Upper Saddle River (2001)
3. Enns, R.: NETCONF Configuration Protocol, RFC 4741, IETF, December 2006
4. Stiemerling, M., Quittek, J., Cadar, C.: NEC's Simple Middlebox Configuration (SIMCO), RFC 4540. http://tools.ietf.org/html/rfc4540
5. McKeown, N., et al.: OpenFlow: enabling innovation in campus networks. ACM SIGCOMM CCR **38**(2), 69–74 (2008)
6. Kazemian, P., Varghese, G., McKeown, N.: Header space analysis: static checking for networks. In: USENIX NSDI, San Jose, CA, April 2012 (2012)
7. Stoenescu, R., Popovici, M., Negreanu, L., Raiciu, C.: Symnet: static checking for stateful networks. In: ACM HotMiddlebox (2013)
8. Wischik, D., Raiciu, C., Greenhalgh, A., Handley, M.: Design, implementation and evaluation of congestion control for multipath tcp. In: USENIX NSDI (2011)

9. Wang, Z., Qian, Z., Xu, Q., Mao, Z., Zhang, M.: An untold story of middleboxes in cellular networks. In: ACM SIGCOMM, Toronto, Canada, August 2011 (2011)
10. Raiciu, C., Olteanu, V., Stoenescu, R.: Good cop, bad cop: forcing middleboxes to cooperate. In: IAB (2015)
11. Sherry, J., et al.: Making middleboxes someone elses problem: network processing as a cloud service. In: ACM SIGCOMM, Helsinki, Finland, August 2012 (2012)
12. Fayazbakhsh, S., Sekar, V., Yu, M., Mogul, J.: FlowTags: enforcing network-wide policies in the presence of dynamic middlebox actions. In: ACM SIGCOMM HotSDN, Hong Kong, China, August 2013 (2013)
13. Gember, A., et al.: Stratos: Virtual Middleboxes as First-Class Entities
14. Guha, S., Takeda, Y., Francis, P.: NUTSS: a SIP-based approach to UDP and TCP network connectivity. In: ACM SIGCOMM FDNA (2004)
15. Eppinger, J.L.: TCP Connections for P2P Apps: A Software Approach to Solving the NAT Problem. http://reports-archive.adm.cs.cmu.edu/anon/isri2005/CMU-ISRI-05-104.pdf
16. Biggadike, A., Ferullo, D., Wilson, G., Perrig, A.: NATBLASTER: establishing TCP connections between hosts behind NATs. In: ACM SIGCOMM ASIA (2005)
17. Kho, W., Baset, S.A., Schulzrinne, H.: Skype relay calls: measurements and experiments. In: IEEE Global Internet Symposium (2008)

BitWorker, a Decentralized Distributed Computing System Based on BitTorrent

Arnaud Durand[1], Mikael Gasparian[1], Thomas Rouvinez[1], Imad Aad[2],
Torsten Braun[2(✉)], and Tuan Anh Trinh[3]

[1] University of Fribourg, Fribourg, Switzerland
{arnaud.durand,mikael.gasparian,thomas.rouvinez}@unifr.ch
[2] University of Bern, Bern, Switzerland
{aad,braun}@iam.unibe.ch
[3] Budapest University of Technology and Economics, Budapest, Hungary
trinh@tmit.bme.hu

Abstract. In this paper we present BitWorker, a platform for community distributed computing based on BitTorrent. Any splittable task can be easily specified by a user in a meta-information task file, such that it can be downloaded and performed by other volunteers. Peers find each other using Distributed Hash Tables, download existing results, and compute missing ones. Unlike existing distributed computing schemes relying on centralized coordination point(s), our scheme is totally distributed, therefore, highly robust. We evaluate the performance of BitWorker using mathematical models and real tests, showing processing and robustness gains. BitWorker is available for download [1] and use by the community.

Keywords: Distributed computing · BitTorrent · Peer-to-Peer networks

1 Introduction

The processing power requirements in almost every field of study have increased. Due to the ever increasing complexity of problems to solve, single processing units are often no longer able to yield results within an acceptable time. Despite the advances and progress achieved in the fields of photolithography and processor architecture, the processing power is often not enough. Many research works benefit from the ability to test and iterate on the results, which requires computations to be done multiple times. Breaking out of a single processing unit became essential. Distributed computing is characterized by multiple processing units connected together in a network and sharing computation. The goal of distributed computing is to allow multiple processing units (distinct machines) collaborating on the same task. This results in a computational speedup dependent on the number of collaborating machines.

Distributed computing faces challenges and limitations. The first issue is the speedup factor not being linear to the number of machines in the network. On a

© Springer International Publishing Switzerland 2015
M.C. Aguayo-Torres et al. (Eds.): WWIC 2015, LNCS 9071, pp. 151–164, 2015.
DOI: 10.1007/978-3-319-22572-2_11

single machine operations are read and executed locally, in a procedural/multi-threaded fashion. The obvious advantage is the ease of distributed computing as well as synchronization. Moreover, all the results are held in a single location, making data retrieval and exchange very easy. With multiple machines, operations are first distributed among all the machines in the network. Note that all the dependencies for the computation have to be shared, which adds to the computational overhead. Upon reception of a new task, a machine in a distributed computing network will have to process its share of computation and return the result. This involves a complex communication scheme that also adds computational overhead. Furthermore, reliability becomes a prerequisite. All the mechanisms required to guarantee data integrity between the machines in the distributed network, in turn, add to the overhead. All these reasons may affect the speedup.

Beyond the overhead issues, an organizational issue arises with distributed computing. The needs in terms of infrastructure regroup the machines, the complete setup of these machines, and a fully working network. The costs of such infrastructures do not follow a linear curve as more machines in the network increase the complexity of the requirements in terms of power, networking, and administration. Distributed computing allows faster computations but at greater financial cost. With this financial aspect in mind, new developments of distributed computing got oriented toward outsourcing computations to willing volunteers rather than in-house farming. Installation costs are moved to the volunteers but at the expense of security and data privacy. With potentially malicious machines in the network, further data verification is required. Nevertheless, the concept of tapping into the processing power of machines all around the world is attractive.

In this paper, we propose an implementation of a distributed computing system called BitWorker. BitWorker is based on a modification of BitTorrent and performs computations in a fully distributed way. In Sect. 2, known distributed computing solutions are presented. Section 3 presents the fundamentals of our approach to distributed computing based on BitTorrent. In Sect. 4 the general architecture of BitWorker with its workflow is explained. Section 5 shows analytical and experimental performance evaluations. We discuss future work in Sect. 6 and conclude in Sect. 7.

2   Related Work

2.1   Distributed Computing

Distributed Computing is an environment in which a group of independent and geographically dispersed computer systems solve a complex problem, each by solving a part of the solution and then combining the result from all computers [2]. Compared to centralized computing, distributed computing offers more flexibility, fault resilience, and scalability. Furthermore, it can be used to reduce the costs of problem solving in areas of public interest using computing resources of volunteers. The computing power could come from CPUs, GPUs, game consoles, or specialized hardware.

The idea of using computing resources of volunteers is a known concept. A wide variety of distributed computing projects are available, most of which focus on scientific research. Folding@home [3] predicts protein structures ($\approx$40 PetaFlops in September 2014), SETI@home analyzes radio frequencies in search for extraterrestrial life and Milkyway@home [4] models our galaxy from available data. Some of these projects are based on the Berkeley Open Infrastructure for Network Computing (BOINC) [5], an open platform for distributed computing.

A recent approach [6] proposes novel techniques for management of large-scale distributed storage systems. However, there are two key areas which differentiate our approach from this approach. First, the proposed approach [6] focuses on the IP level of the network, whereas BitWorker focuses on the overlay networks. Second, the proposed approach focuses on storage systems, whereas BitWorker can be applied in different computing environments as well.

2.2   BitTorrent and Distributed Hash Tables

BitTorrent is a peer-to-peer file sharing protocol. Using BitTorrent, users can exchange large amounts of data without any data hosting servers. Instead of downloading a file from a server, users request small pieces of the data from other users and start exchanging these as they become available. The file transfer process is thus completely offloaded to peers in the network. The tracker is a dedicated server enabling peers' exchanges by providing a list of connected peers of its registered shared files. The tracker is regularly queried for new peers to connect to, thus enabling disconnected peers to be replaced by newer ones. In this regard the BitTorrent protocol fully handles node discovery and sharing of pieces in a centralized fashion. BitTorrent has been later on extended with PEX (Peer exchange) [7,8]. PEX allows peers to retrieve addresses from other peers rather than from the tracker. This is a semi-decentralized solution, as at least one connection to the tracker is required for bootstrapping. Distributed Hash Tables (DHTs) [9] extend BitTorrent file exchange, enabling BitTorrent to work in a totally decentralized fashion. It only requires an initial bootstrap to start exchanging files from any public torrent.

2.3   Distributed Computing and Peer-to-Peer

Available distributed computing projects such as BOINC use a centralized or semi-centralized approach where a main entity is responsible for coordinating work load distribution among the available resources. The result of the computational task is shared either using (1) a client-server architecture (Folding@home [3], BOINC-based projects, etc.) or (2) a P2P exchange system (BOINC with BitTorrent [10], CompTorrent [11]).

In the client-server case, the processing result of a volunteer is transmitted directly to a server. The clients are not informed about the state of the global computation or the available resources (other clients).

In the second case, task distribution is still coordinated by a centralized entity but the computation results are shared using P2P mechanisms. While having an entity coordinating the resources ensures efficient distribution of the tasks, this approach requires a permanently available infrastructure. Moreover, it presents a single point of failure. Fully decentralized infrastructures involve a P2P data-distribution model: a decentralized mechanism to find and connect to other volunteers. Therefore, it replaces the centralized coordination system with peer signaling. Cryptocoins (Bitcoin [12] and derivative crypto currencies) mining is a good example of decentralized distributed computing systems.

SETI@home [13] is a distributed computing project allowing public clients to contribute. This project aims at searching for extraterrestrial intelligence in the universe through an analysis of radio signals. Based on a classic client/server architecture, packets of data and computation instructions are sent to each client and the computation results are gathered back to the unique server. Since then, new ways to perform distributed computations have appeared, involving different communication schemes and security improvements. A considerable improvement was made when the BitTorrent protocol first helped with data distribution. Efficient and fast data exchange was solved. BitTorrent has been known to work well for data management in distributed computing. BitTorrent can also offer node (peer) discovery, task splitting and distribution. There are implementations of distributed computing using a modified version of BitTorrent, e.g. CompTorrent. However, we did not find any implementation that fully harnesses the capabilities of BitTorrent or fully decentralizes the work distribution process.

2.4   BOINC

Berkeley Open Infrastructure for Network Computing (BOINC) is a project originating from the Space Sciences Laboratory at the University of California. The principle is to harness the processing power left on the host machine (full load - current CPU/GPU load) and to use it for research projects. Upon launching the BOINC client, a registration is performed and a list of available projects is proposed to the user. When a project is selected the client fetches instructions from the project's server. These instructions take into account the capabilities of the client and the project server returns a set of applications and input files for the task to be performed by the client. Upon completion, the client uploads the output files back to the server. Then, according to user preferences, the client restarts this process and asks for a new task. BOINC is, therefore, a centralized distributed computation system based on the classic client-server architecture.

BOINC was originally created for the SETI@home project. After opening BOINC to support other projects, optimizations such as multi-threaded CPU applications and the use of OpenCL appeared. Extensions have been developed to enhance BOINC functionalities and performance. Among these extensions a BitTorrent wrapper has been created to help any BOINC client to fetch large datasets required to make computations. A BOINC client can open a BitTorrent wrapper, which will contact a tracker, get a list of peers, who possess the required input datasets, and perform requests on these peers to obtain the data required.

Therefore, the required data acquisition is performed via P2P networks rather than overloading one or multiple servers with direct downloads. Compared to BitWorker, BOINC does not rely on BitTorrent to distribute the workload on the network. BOINC only uses BitTorrent as a data exchange/retrieval convenience mechanism.

2.5 Gnutella Processing Unit

Gnutella Processing Unit (GPU) [14] organizes clients in a Gnutella network. Each client allows the other users to request CPU resources. The concept of GPU involves trading network resources in exchange of CPU resources. A GPU network usually organises itself in a cluster of 5 to 15 peers. A GPU first determines a list of all the peers connected to the network and establishes a predefined number of connections to each peer. This list of IP addresses is stored in a Web cache and mimics the functionality of a tracker (without performance evaluations). Upon detection of a request, a GPU client will create a set of threads to handle the new task at hand. Each task is then processed thanks to the use of plugins. A GPU client can host multiple plugins that hold the algorithmic logic to handle a given request. For example, such plugins could contain the algorithms required to solve a brute force attack to the discrete logarithm [15], computation of a partial differential equation using the random walkers approach and the Feynman-Kac formula [16], or even computer rendering of images generated with Terragen [17]. Once a task has been processed, the GPU client transmits the result back to the peer that requested it. GPU also uses frontends, which are a complement to plugins as well as serve easing work distribution and result visualization.

GPU uses Gnutella as an underlying protocol and hence it sends requests by flooding the whole network. Since flooding is not an optimal solution to efficiently transmit messages between peers within the same network, Gnutella makes use of "Ultrapeers". An Ultrapeer is a specific node in the network whose role consists of maintaining connections between normal nodes while these simply keep one connection to the Ultrapeer. The result is the formation of a tree-shaped network. Though the concept is close to what we achieve with BitWorker, we do not use Gnutella to manage the network structure as it is inefficient and prone to both failures and flooding attacks. Moreover, no resource trading is done with BitWorker as contributing peers are also interested in the result of the computation. This results in a collaborative work rather than in requests for resources.

2.6 CompTorrent

CompTorrent's [11] approach to distributed computing makes use of BitTorrent. CompTorrent aims at providing an easy to use distributed computing environment by creating a CompTorrent file that holds the description of both an algorithm and a dataset. The CompTorrent file should then be made available for download. Potential peers have to download the CompTorrent file and run it.

Each peer then connects to the "seed". The seed is a super node that handles workload distribution over the network. When a peer connects to the seed, it receives its tasks and starts to process them. When a task has been completed, the seed is informed and the results are transferred to it. The seed also acts as a quality control agent by making sure that each sub-dataset is computed multiple times, hence allowing comparison of the results. When the seed determines that all computations have been carried out and that the data has been verified, it will simply let the other peers share the results among them. Data is verified by seeds that may ask two clients to compute the same work and compare results afterwards. Compared to BOINC with BitTorrent, CompTorrent is more decentralized as it lets BitTorrent distribute the workload by using super nodes. Unlike CompTorrent, BitWorker is completely decentralized and takes advantage of DHT instead of only relying on trackers. Furthermore, it can be downloaded and used by the community.

3   BitWorker Fundamentals

Throughout this paper, we focus on enabling distributed computations by modifying the BitTorrent protocol. BitTorrent has been previously used in distributed computing, but only for data management purposes such as data retrieval from all the machines taking part in the computation process. Our approach aims at fully transforming peers to become both server and client for distributed computations. To solve the issues above, the BitTorrent specification had to be modified to allow the specification of a distributed task in the metadata files. BitWorker supports any parallel computation achievable by using the UNIX shell environment. Distributed computations carried out by BitWorker are enabled thanks to three functionalities originally provided by the BitTorrent protocol, which we modified to fit new purposes:

1. File splitting into pieces.
2. Piece sharing.
3. Node discovery.

File splitting reduces the size of files transmitted between peers. This is achieved by splitting the original file into multiple pieces of predefined equal sizes.

The reasonfor file splitting is explained by the second functionality: piece sharing. The BitTorrent protocol allows a peer to download a file by requesting and offering missing, respectively available, pieces of the torrent to other peers. Upon connecting to another peer, a "bitfield" message is exchanged directly after the handshake. The message payload represents pieces that have been successfully downloaded. When a piece (selected at random) is not available among all the peers, BitWorker will compute it and make it available.

"Have" messages play a major role in piece exchanges and, for BitWorker, in computation distribution. The exchange of bitfields is enabled by the third functionality of BitTorrent: node discovery. Unlike centralized distributed computing, BitWorker relies on a network of directly connected end users (peers).

To start participating in a BitTorrent network, a peer must establish an initial connection to a tracker or use the DHT. In terms of distributed computing, Bit-Worker takes care of distributing computations, respectively storing/retrieving the results. Participating in a task in BitWorker then fully harnesses the Bit-Worker protocol as it takes care of the following essential operations:

- Node discovery using DHT.
- Task splitting.
- Workload distribution.
- Piece sharing.

Therefore, the complete process of distributed computing with BitWorker is managed by the protocol itself. In the following section we present the modifications to the BitTorrent protocol to support distributed computations.

4 Architecture

4.1 Implementation Overview

Upon starting the client, the first process reads the content of the torrent file. The currently owned data is evaluated and a list of peers is retrieved from the announcement provided by the trackers specified within the torrent file. Performing these first tasks allows the client to create the list of pieces it possesses and the list of pieces already available in the network. Once the client knows which pieces are missing, it can request them from any peer it is connected to. With BitWorker, if a piece is present in the list of available pieces, it means that it has already been computed. Therefore, it is only downloaded to speed up sharing among peers and return the results. When a piece is not present in the list of available pieces, it means it is unavailable because no connected peer possesses it. Therefore, the client can choose to start computing the piece and upon completion send a BitTorrent "have" message. When all the pieces have been computed, the torrent enters into seed mode where it only uploads the data to peers requesting it. As explained previously, BitWorker is based on the BitTorrent protocol. We modified three parts of it:

1. Meta-information task file.
2. Missing piece management.
3. Support for variable piece sizes.
4. Peer list acquirement process.

4.2 Meta-Information Task File

A distributed task is described in a bencoded [18] file. A bencoded file is a dictionary (key and value pairs) namely used by BitTorrent to provide meta data of shared files. The task and its parameters are specified in this file. The task file is very similar to torrent files; it contains metadata about the generated files and an announcement (list) (optional with DHT). Unlike a torrent file, it does not contain any hash list as the content is non-deterministic. In other words, we cannot create hashes for the content we do not have yet. Ideally, piece sizes range from 256 kB to 4 MB, according to the recommendations for the BitTorrent network. The piece sizes are specified inside the task file and should be greater or equal to the biggest generated file. The communication protocol is able to deal with varying pieces size by exchanging piece size information among the peers.

4.3   Task Interpretation

Tasks should be described generic enough to fit most of the use-cases. We take advantage of the UNIX architecture and represent a distributed task as a unique shell command. A task is split into work items, the atomic subtasks of the distributed work. A work item is specified using the same command with different environment variables. Environment variables are defined according to piece index, file index, and part index. The pieces are then filled with the standard output of work item executed commands.

4.4   DHT Functionality

Using legacy BitTorrent, the tracker is periodically queried by the clients to obtain an updated list of peers. A peer connects to the tracker, receives a list of peers, and then communicate with these peers to obtain the locally missing pieces. The tracker is the only way to start downloading pieces from peers while using the original BitTorrent protocol. Although being convenient and beneficial in terms of performance, it is also the unique point of centralization, thus, the only critical point of BitTorrent. To solve this issue, we created a new independent DHT service to complement peer discovery. Therefore, we have the ability to run in a completely decentralized fashion.

4.5   Applications and Examples

The content of the pieces is evaluated using the standard output of bash shell commands. Any task that can be divided into a set of bash shell commands can be computed in a distributed fashion using BitWorker. BitWorker uses the results returned in the standard output of the bash shell. An example of such a task could be the computation of squares for integers. The following paragraphs presents two examples and how to process these in a distributed and decentralized fashion with BitWorker.

The first example is a video transcoding task that allows to encode a given video using FFmpeg [19]. FFmpeg is a library for video encoding. With BitWorker each client will encode a part of the video. The parts (pieces) are generated and shared with the peers. The generated piece sizes are non-deterministic. When a peer possesses all the pieces it will merge them to create the complete encoded video and continue to share the parts with connected peers.

The second example uses RainbowCrack [20] to generate rainbow tables in a distributed and decentralized fashion. Rainbow tables are precomputed tables using time-memory tradeoff [21]. The tables allow to reverse cryptographic hash functions. As in the first example, a rainbow table is divided into multiple parts. The parts are generated and shared among the peers.

BitWorker allows to generate tasks both featuring deterministic or nondeterministic piece sizes. The client reads the task run-time command from the bencoded task file to run a task.

4.6 Workload Distribution

In approaches like BOINC or CompTorrent, work distribution is unified and centralized. BOINC uses the client-server architecture, which allows the server to fully control what each client has to compute. GPU is doing the same but the server is a peer that requests help on a specific computation. In CompTorrent special peers called "seeds" act as centralization points that distribute the workload. All these distributed computation systems feature a point of centralization that can optimally handle with minimum costs both the computation distribution and the verification of the work done. However, having a single point of centralization also means having a single point of failure. CompTorrent reduces the risk of the entire network going down by increasing the number of seed instances for redundancy. Considering the case of an attack, all instances of seeds could be targeted and the whole network would collapse. In GPU, since flooding is the only way to transmit computation requests, Ultrapeers are used to reduce the message overhead. Ultrapeers become hubs, which makes them interesting targets, since they are critical to make the network run efficiently. Finally, in BOINC if the main server fails, no more work requests can be issued.

BitWorker focuses on eliminating all critical single points of failure. Indeed there is no distinction between a regular BitTorrent peer and a CompTorrent seed. Therefore, in BitWorker, every peer is both a client and a server. Unlike all the discussed approaches, BitWorker has no point of centralization, which makes it naturally resilient to attacks: with every peer being able to work as a server, there is no need for a centralised entity anymore; the use of DHT removes all centralization during the establishment of the network.

5   Performance Evaluation

In this section we evaluate the performance of BitWorker in terms of processing speedup for a varying number of volunteer nodes. We first start evaluating the completion time of a specific task theoretically, without considering communication overhead. Evaluation is done analytically and using real testbeds. Additional experiments are also performed to evaluate the impact of the number of pieces on the overall performance of the system.

5.1 Expected Completion Time

We want to evaluate the completion time of a task. Assume that we do not have any communication overhead and that peers are perfectly synchronized for task completion, then the average completion time is $E_{n,m} \times t$ where:

$$E_{n,m} = \left(\sum_{j=1}^{n-1} \left| \sum_{k=1}^{j} (-1)^{k+1} \binom{j}{k} k^m \right| \binom{n}{j} \frac{E_{n-j,m}}{n^m} \right) + 1$$

$$= \left(\sum_{j=1}^{n-1} \left\{ mj \right\} \frac{n!}{(n-j)!} \frac{E_{n-j,m}}{n^m} \right) + 1, E_{1,m} = 1$$

with $\left\{ \begin{matrix} n \\ m \end{matrix} \right\}$ being stirling numbers of the second kind using Knuth's [22] notation. n is the number of pieces, m is the number of connected peers and t is the average time to generate a piece.

This model assumes that the churn rate is 0. The churn rate measures the number of nodes moving out of the network over a given time period. We evaluate the average number of computing iterations (rounds) according to the expected number of collisions per iteration. We can assess this by evaluating the completion time of the scenarios and then compute the arithmetic mean. To do so, we start by evaluating $S(m,j)$, the number of possibilities to partition a set of m connected peers into j subsets. Here, j represents the number of remaining pieces. For each scenario, we have $(n-j)!$ possible outcomes for the current round. We should also evaluate the outcomes for the next rounds using the recursive function. We should also add 1 to the summation as there is always at least one round for any $n \geq 1$ and $m \geq 1$, so we only require to compute j from 1 to $n-1$. We always need exactly one round to complete one piece for any $m \geq 1$ so we know $E_{1,m} = 1$. Because of communication overhead, churn rate and task synchronization are not taken into account. This model is optimistic and serves as a reference to experimental results.

5.2   Hypotheses

We expect that the time to complete the task will decrease when increasing the number of peers. A speedup significantly superior to 1 proves that the sharing mechanism is beneficial. The first hypothesis is that the task completion time will closely follow the expected completion time model previously described, with slightly lower performance due to communication overhead. The second hypothesis is that the speedup is higher with more pieces (the same task is split into more pieces).

5.3   Setup of Test Environment

The aim of the experiments is to calculate the completion time of a task given different numbers of volunteers and pieces. We have tested with Amazon small EC2 instances. To make sure that the machine performance variation does not have high impact on the results, we created a task with a deterministic completion time of exactly 64 min when computed locally. The global output size is 64 MB, which is split into pieces. For an experiment with 64 pieces, this simulates a computation that takes 1 min per piece and each piece has a size of

1MB. This allows to minimize machine performance variation and to consider essentially the time it takes to finish the computation in terms of piece selection and sharing among peers. The computation is finished when at least one peer possesses all the pieces.

5.4   Computation Speedup

The test is performed using 4, 8, 12 and 16 peers and for each number of peers we test it with 3 different number of pieces: 64, 128, 192. All tests were executed 5 times. The average computation times for the three different numbers of pieces are shown in the Fig. 1.

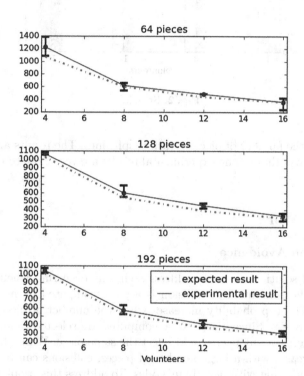

Fig. 1. Completion time (in seconds) using BitWorker, with 4, 8, 12 and 16 peers, computing 64, 128 and 192 pieces.

Figure 1 shows the expected and experienced computation time in seconds. The computation time is always slightly higher than the expected time due to the communication delays neglected in the model. Due to the random nature of piece selection, the completion time can vary using the same setup. This is highlighted with the variance metric.

The speedup chart in Fig. 2 illustrates the relative computing speed improvement, which increases with the number of peers. It further shows the speedup

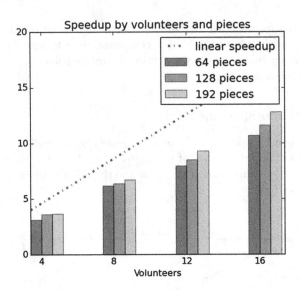

Fig. 2. Speedup

increase with the number of pieces a task is split into. The results are exactly in line with our hypothesis. The experimental results are very close to the expected results.

6   Future Work

6.1   Collision Avoidance

The proposed solution does not address collisions occurring when selecting a new piece to be computed. A collision is a piece computed by more than one peer. This collision probability increases when the number of pieces still to be computed decreases. Since pieces to be computed are selected randomly among the missing pieces, many peers could select the same piece. While the number of collisions decreases with a large number of pieces, collisions can be avoided, at least by collaborating with neighbour nodes. To address this problem, signaling mechanisms can be implemented: when a peer receives a "generating piece N" message, it could give a lower priority to this piece and prefer to generate pieces for which there are no hints whether other peers are working on them. The proposed solution would be, however, only optimal for a small number of peers - in a fully connected swarm - as a torrent peer only communicates with its direct neighbours. In the case of a large number of peers, the connections of each peer are limited to a user-defined threshold value to avoid network and CPU congestion. This results in disjoint networks or low connectivity in extreme cases. In such situations, signaling to every other peer requires flooding, which results in high communication overhead.

6.2   Computation Verification

The peers do not verify downloaded pieces. The system does not provide any protection against data corruption or malicious peers sharing garbage data - the poisoning attacks. This can be avoided using extra security mechanisms such as a peer reputation system and piece verification. There have been some works [23,24] on reputation systems but the proposed solutions are not applicable if the verification is computationally too expensive. Thus, piece recomputation or verification mechanisms can be implemented at the cost of increasing the time to complete a task. Some specific problems can be verified much faster than solved but this is not always the case as most problems require full recomputation. Using recomputation or verification would not only protect against poisoning but also against data corruption.

7   Conclusions

In this paper we presented BitWorker, a fully distributed computing system. Our approach is fully based on BitTorrent and supports new functionalities through an extension of the BitTorrent protocol. Compared to other solutions such as GPU or CompTorrent, BitWorker is fully decentralized. In our experiments, we measured the speedup with varying numbers of volunteers and piece size. In these experiments, we demonstrated that the system works as expected, with a less than linear speedup due to collisions.

From our experiments, BitWorker proved to be scalable and to work autonomously. Compared to the other distributed systems, the only configuration required by BitWorker is the creation of the meta-info file and the installation of our client. Volunteers willing to contribute to a specific computation only have to launch the task using BitWorker. BitWorker then handles data management as well as work distribution. Furthermore, our prototype allows to perform any kind of computation that is splittable into pieces and can run in the shell command. We propose a fully working prototype available to the community [1]. DHT contributes heavily to enhance the robustness of the system by making it fully decentralized.

Acknowledgements. We would like to thank Maxime Petazzoni (Software Engineer at SignalFuse, Inc), original author, main developer and maintainer of the Ttorrent library, a Java implementation of the BitTorrent protocol. The library was used as a basis for our implementation.

References

1. BitWorker. https://github.com/DurandA/bitworker
2. http://www.jatit.org/distributed-computing/grid-vs-distributed.htm
3. http://folding.stanford.edu/
4. http://milkyway.cs.rpi.edu/milkyway/

5. http://boinc.berkeley.edu/
6. Hartman, D., Glass, T., Sinha, S., Bernhard, B., Kiselev, O., Mattly, J.: Decentralized distributed computing system. US Patent Applications 14/535,850, 12 March 2015. http://www.google.com/patents/US20150074168
7. http://www.rasterbar.com/products/libtorrent/extension_protocol.html
8. http://wiki.vuze.com/w/Azureus_messaging_protocol
9. Loewenster, A.: BitTorrent DHT protocol. BitTorrent BEP 5 (2008)
10. Costa, F.e.a.: Optimizing the data distribution layer of boinc with bittorrent. In: IEEE International Symposium on Parallel and Distributed Processing (IPDPS) (2008)
11. Goldsmith, B.: Enabling grassroots distributed computing with comptorrent. In: Joseph, S.R.H., Despotovic, Z., Moro, G., Bergamaschi, S. (eds.) AP2PC 2007. LNCS, vol. 5319, pp. 85–96. Springer, Heidelberg (2010)
12. Nakamoto, S.: Bitcoin: a peer-to-peer electronic cash system. Consulted, vol. 1, 2012, p. 28 (2008)
13. http://setiathome.ssl.berkeley.edu/
14. http://gpu.sourceforge.net/docs/gpu_p2p.pdf
15. Mengotti, T., Petersen, W.P., Arbenz, P.: Distributed computing over internet using a peer to peer network, September 2002
16. Petersen, W.P., Arbenz, P.: Introduction to Parallel Computing. Oxford University, Oxford (2003)
17. http://planetside.co.uk/
18. https://wiki.theory.org/BitTorrentSpecificationd#Bencoding
19. http://www.ffmpeg.org/
20. http://project-rainbowcrack.com/
21. Oechslin, P.: Making a faster cryptanalytic time-memory trade-off. In: Boneh, D. (ed.) CRYPTO 2003. LNCS, vol. 2729, pp. 617–630. Springer, Heidelberg (2003)
22. Graham et al. (1994); Knuth (1997), p. 65
23. Aberer, K., Despotovic, Z.: Managing trust in a peer-2-peer information system. In: ACM Proceedings of the Tenth International Conference on Information and Knowledge Management (2001)
24. Kamvar, S.D., Schlosser, M.T., Garcia-Molina, H.: The eigentrust algorithm for reputation management in P2P networks. In: ACM Proceedings of the 12th International Conference on World Wide Web (2003)

Virtual Network Flavors: Differentiated Traffic Forwarding for Cloud Tenants

Aryan TaheriMonfared[(✉)] and Chunming Rong

IDE Department, University of Stavanger, Stavanger, Norway
{aryan.taherimonfared,chunming.rong}@uis.no

Abstract. Today, a cloud system user can select a specific type of virtual machine for deployment based on needs, for instance memory or storage size. In terms of networking, however, no similar mechanism exists which allows users to select a virtual network based on characteristics such as link speed and QoS. The lack of such a mechanism makes it difficult for users to manage VM instances along their associated networks. This limits the efficacy and scalability of cloud computing suppliers.

This paper presents a novel approach for defining *virtual network flavors* and differentiated forwarding of traffic across the underlay networks. The flavors enable tenants to select network properties including maximum rate, maximum number of hops between two VMs, and priority. Measures such as metering, prioritizing, and shaping facilitate steering traffic through a set of paths to satisfy tenants' requirements. These measures are designed such that the legacy parts of the underlay network can also benefit from them. Software Defined Networking (SDN) mechanisms are an essential part of the solution, where the underlay and overlay networks are managed by a network operating system. The implementation and evaluation data are available for further development [2].

Keywords: Software defined networking · QoS · Virtual network

1 Introduction

Today's cloud infrastructure as a service provider supports a variety of virtual machine types. These types are frequently referred to as *flavors*, which defines a virtual machine's specifications, such as the number of vCPU, memory, and storage size. Flavors aid users by simplifying the selection and specification of VMs. However, there exists no similar mechanism for the virtual networks connecting these VMs. Virtual networks are mostly created with similar specifications, which are also limited. They lack quality of service (QoS) support, path calculation options, etc. Per-tenant virtual network building blocks, as presented in [13], propose an extreme approach where the new architecture delegates all network functions to tenants. While this solution can be beneficial for an enterprise customer, it is a burden for the average customer. Moreover, a tenant is not in control of the underlay network and cannot influence the forwarding decisions. Thus, a provider should deliver more functionality for virtual networks.

© Springer International Publishing Switzerland 2015
M.C. Aguayo-Torres et al. (Eds.): WWIC 2015, LNCS 9071, pp. 165–179, 2015.
DOI: 10.1007/978-3-319-22572-2_12

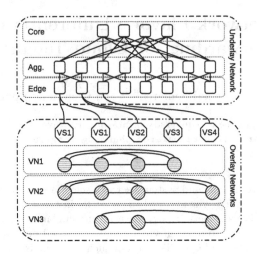

Fig. 1. High level overlay and underlay architecture

Tunnelling is a common technique for creating virtual networks and isolating tenants' traffic in the underlay. However, this technique gives rise to several issues in adapting legacy network functions to handle tenants' traffic. In particular, identifying, classifying, and engineering tenants' traffic in the core network, without decapsulating, are challenging tasks.

Moreover, typical data center network topologies consist of a multi-rooted tree [4]. Therefore, there are multiple paths between any two nodes. Virtual network traffic between two endpoints of a tenant should be forwarded through the path which fulfils the tenant's QoS requirements. A central controller with a unified view of the network can perform significantly better than hash-based Equal-Cost Multi-Path (ECMP) load-balancing [4].

This paper proposes an approach for differentiated forwarding of overlay traffic across the underlay network (Fig. 1), such that it satisfies the virtual network flavor constraints. Initially, the virtual network flavor should be defined as a structure that presents a tenant traffic class, maximum rate, priority, etc. (Sect. 3). Then, the following steps are necessary to enforce the flavor requirements. The first step is to discover the underlay network topology. The underlay topology is later used to find a set of flavor-compliant paths between VMs which are connected to the same virtual network (Sect. 4). Therefore, the tenant's points of presence in the data center should be identified and the topology of its virtual network should be discovered (Sect. 5). Then, tenants' traffic are classified according to their network flavors (Sect. 6). The classification is performed only once, at the endpoint virtual switch (Sect. 7). The overlay traffic is marked such that a legacy network node can also benefit from the classification. Finally, the aforementioned end-to-end paths, for each class, are programmed in the overlay and underlay networks (Sect. 8). In addition, an extensive evaluation framework is developed to study the effectiveness and accuracy of the flavor implementation (Sect. 9).

2   Related Work

Plug-n-Serve [6] is a load-balancing system for web services. It uses the network state and servers load to customise flow routing and update service capacity (e.g. number of hosts).

Wang et al. [14] proposes a proactive load-balancing approach for online services using OpenFlow. It creates a minimal set of wildcard rules to aggregate clients' requests and update the set to reflect the system dynamics.

Hedera [4] focuses on scheduling large flows in a data center with a topology inspired by the fat tree topology. It shows that dynamic flow scheduling can substantially improve network bandwidth in multi-rooted trees, while the deployment cost is moderated. Simulated Annealing and Global First Fit algorithms are compared to ECMP, and the results show that the former outperforms the rest in most cases.

Khan et al. [7] introduces a mechanism for virtual network QoS support in the Multi-Protocol Label Switching (MPLS) transport domain. OpenFlow domains are the ingress and admission points to the MPLS transport network, and have their own disjoint controllers. However, the transport network is configured by legacy means. Each virtual network session admission, at an OpenFlow domain, requires communication with the domain's controller. This requirement imposes an overhead on the session establishment process, which is caused by the communication round-trip time and the decision-making logic in the controller.

3   Virtual Network Flavors

Customers' traffic in a cloud infrastructure can be isolated using different techniques, such as IP block splitting, VLAN tagging, and tunnelling. Maintaining IP blocks is a tedious task – the VLAN field has a limited size (up to 4094 under IEEE 802.1Q), and tunnels introduce additional overheads, in terms of forwarding capacity and traffic volume. However, tunnelling is the most flexible approach and can be widely used if the overheads are reduced by employing hardware acceleration (e.g. Virtual eXtensible Local Area Network (VXLAN) [8]) or hardware-friendly protocols (e.g. Stateless Transport Tunnelling (STT) [5]).

This paper focuses on virtual networks which use tunnelling techniques for traffic isolation and end-to-end forwarding. However, these mechanisms can be expanded, with minor extensions, to cover other virtualization techniques.

Virtual network flavor specifies the quality of end-to-end paths between any two VMs which are connected to a virtual network. Although our proposed mechanisms support varying flavors for the paths in a virtual network (i.e. virtual network path flavor), for the sake of simplicity the case is presented where paths in a virtual network use the same flavor (i.e. virtual network flavor). Path flavor plays an essential role in providing fine-grained QoS for provisioned resources by a tenant. For instance, resources involved in latency-sensitive tasks utilize the shortest path, while high traffic volume operations are forwarded through the least utilized path.

Each flavor has a class that is used for coarse-grained traffic classification and facilitates the legacy network support. Since legacy networks have a limited capacity for traffic classes (e.g. 6-bit Differentiated Services Code Point (DSCP)), multiple flavors may have the same class. In addition to the class, a flavor determines the end-to-end priority and maximum rate of virtual network traffic in the underlay network. In the following text, the underlay refers to the infrastructure's network that is controlled by the infrastructure provider; while overlay refers to the tenant's virtual network that is established on top of the infrastructure network, Fig. 1.

As the virtual switch inside a compute node has high throughput, the inter-VM communication inside a single hypervisor is not shaped. Therefore, traffic engineering takes place for the inter-hypervisor VM's communication.

4   Underlay Topology Discovery and Path Calculation

The data center network has a tree-like topology with redundant paths between any two nodes. Therefore, it can be represented as a weighted directed sparse graph, where an edge has a REFERENCE_SPEED/LINK_SPEED weight. The underlay topology is constructed by processing node and link updates, which are sent from the controller platform.

For a different set of tenants with varying network demands, shortest path routing is not flexible enough [3]. The aim is to calculate the first k-shortest loopless paths (KSP) between any given node pair, where k is a positive integer. A modified version of Yen's algorithm [15] is implemented for path calculation. Moreover, a set of constraints can be used to further limit the result. For instance, the constraints can ensure that packets visit a set of nodes before reaching the destination to apply middle-box functions, or avoid another set to bypass congestion. Modularity of the approach makes it flexible to update the algorithm with another group of policies.

5   Overlay Topology Discovery

Tunnels are established on demand between interested endpoints. Tunnel endpoints are responsible for marking tenants' traffic with their tunnel keys, prior to encapsulation. Two types of tunnel discovery are performed – proactive and reactive. The proactive approach is suitable for OpenFlow 1.0 and 1.3 protocols. It listens to the management plane events which are dispatched from the OVSDB southbound plug-in. When a new tunnel interface is identified, the key, IP address, interface ID, and the corresponding tenant ID are added to a data store. The data store is further processed to build a matrix of tunnel endpoints for each tenant, that represent the tenant's virtual network. The data store reflects the current status of tenants' overlays, and is updated by relevant events (e.g. add, remove, modify). This approach is applicable where tunnels are "port-based" and created with explicit flow keys. In the port-based model each tenant has a separate tunnel and the port fully specifies the tunnel headers [11].

The reactive approach takes advantage of the cloud platform APIs for retrieving the tenant network properties (e.g. tunnel key, provisioning hosts, virtual ports, etc.). By correlating the properties with the information from the SDN controller, tunnel endpoints, which are involved in the tenant overlay, are discovered. This approach is necessary for "flow-based" tunnels, introduced in OpenFlow 1.3. Flow-based tunnels do not strictly specify the flow key in the tunnel interface and one OpenFlow port can represent multiple tunnels. Therefore, the matching flow rule should set the key and other required fields, such as source/destination IP addresses.

6   Tenant Traffic Classification in Underlay Network

Topology discovery for the overlay and underlay networks was explained in the previous sections, as well as path calculation between two endpoints. However, this is not enough for classifying tenants' traffic in the underlay, when it is encapsulated. Classes are essential for differentiated forwarding of overlay traffic.

Irrespective of the isolation technique chosen for the network virtualization, classifying tenant traffic in the underlay network is a challenging task. If IP block splitting or VLAN tagging are used for isolation, source/destination IP addresses or VLAN IDs suffice for tenant traffic identification, respectively. However, distinguishing tunnelled traffic is not trivial. The tenant IP packet is encapsulated in the tunnel packet, and the tunnel ID (64 bits) is inside the tunnel header. OpenFlow 1.3 [9] proposes 40 match fields, and can not match on the tunnel ID in a transit node.

Therefore, either the first packet of a flow should be sent to the controller, for decapsulation, or another field should be used for the classification. The former approach is not practical, since the overhead is significant. For the latter approach, the IPv6 header has a "flow label" field (20 bits), which can be used for this purpose. However, there is no equivalent field in the IPv4 header. In IPv4, the DSCP field is used. This approach has two major benefits: proactive flow programming (i.e. efficient forwarding) and seamless integration with the legacy network DiffServ domains.

A third approach is to use an IP addressing scheme in the underlay which reflects the virtual network tenant and forwarding classes in addition to the location. Further implementation and evaluation are parts of the future work.

7   Endpoint Virtual Switch Architecture

Tenants' tunnelled traffic should be marked, according to its class, before leaving a host. However, when a packet is sent to a tunnel interface, the Linux routing table determines the egress interface. This decision cannot be overridden by the virtual switch. Therefore, the OpenFlow LOCAL port on the switch is configured such that the routing table will choose it as the egress for all tunnelled traffic (Fig. 2). The configuration consists of assigning an IP address from the provider underlay subnet to the LOCAL port.

Since, the LOCAL port is chosen as the egress interface, external interfaces should be added to the virtual switch. The external interfaces connect the host to the underlay network. In addition, the virtual switch is supplied with a set of rules to forward the traffic between LOCAL and external interfaces, and avoid loops in case of persistent broadcast packets.

Moreover, tunnels are created such that they copy the inner IP header ToS to the outer one. This provides visibility to the DSCP value of a packet in transit.

8 Differentiated Forwarding

This section explains the end-to-end network programming steps for implementing the overlay QoS. It consists of controlling endpoint switches of a traffic exchange and underlay transit nodes along the path.

8.1 Programming Endpoints

The tenant's egress IP traffic from VMs is marked with the DSCP value derived from the endpoint pair's flavor (Sect. 6). The encapsulated packets are further processed in the switch and an external interface is chosen according to the provided policy for the tenant and the tunnel destination. The detailed steps are as follows (Fig. 2): (1) Marking the tenant's traffic with the chosen DSCP value. (2) Sending the marked traffic to the tunnel. (3) Resolving the egress port using the Linux routing table. (4) Capturing the tunnelled traffic on the switch LOCAL port. (5) Checking the tunnel packets and marking those without DSCP by the biggest value for the given endpoint pair. (6) Forwarding the traffic through an external interface.

The encapsulated traffic destined for a tenant VM(s) is forwarded through the underlay and received on an external interface of the destination host. It is decapsulated in the tunnel interface and forwarded to the VM(s) or another switch: (7) Receiving traffic on the external interface. (8) Forwarding ingress

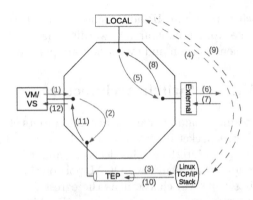

Fig. 2. Virtual switch configuration

traffic from an external interface to the LOCAL port. (9) Resolving the tunnel port. (10) Capturing the traffic on the tunnel port. (11) Decapsulating the packet. (12) Forwarding the packet to the destination.

8.2 Programming Underlay

Underlay (aka transit) nodes are networking devices in the edge, aggregation, and core networks, that are responsible for forwarding tenants' traffic between compute nodes. Tenant traffic identification is explained in Sects. 6 and 8.1 has discussed overlay traffic marking in each endpoint. Transit datapaths should be programmed such that they honour the classification made at the endpoints. The *(in_port, ip_src, ip_dst, mark)* tuple determines the class of a tenant flow in transit. However, efficiently programming the tuple across the network is a challenging task. This section proposes a few approaches for the differentiated forwarding of tenants' traffic in transit nodes.

Programming Transit Nodes on a Given Path Between Two Endpoints. Endpoints are compute nodes which are hosting resources provisioned by a tenant. This approach finds a path between two given endpoints for a tenant, such that it complies with the tenant's virtual network flavor. Then, it programs intermediate nodes to forward the overlay traffic.

It is proactive and utilizes the forwarding table space efficiently. The proactive mechanism reduces the runtime overhead, and responds well to small flows by avoiding further communication with the controller (i.e. slow path).

Programming Complete Reachability Matrix Between All Endpoints for All Classes. This approach calculates routes for all network classes between all endpoints. If provisioned resources by all tenants are uniformly distributed over endpoints, it has less computational cost compared to the previous one, while the storage cost is of the same order. Like the previous one, this is proactive and has a minimal impact on the forwarding speed.

However, if the tenants distribution is not uniform, the forwarding table space is not used efficiently and may cause a state explosion.

Programming on PacketIn Messages. A third approach is to wait for PacketIn messages from intermediate nodes, when they do not have a matching flow rule for a packet. The switch sends a PacketIn message to the controller, which contains the packet and its arrival port. Then, the controller finds the corresponding tenant for the flow and calculates the path for it, according to the network flavor. Finally, it programs all the nodes on the path for that flow. Therefore, other packets will have a matching flow entry, and would be forwarded in the datapath. This is a reactive mechanism for programming the network. Although it uses the table space efficiently, the overhead is significant, specifically for short-lived flows.

The evaluation (Sect. 9) focuses on the first approach, which provides a balance between the number of installed flow entries and the runtime computational complexity. In addition, the path between two endpoints can be updated dynamically, with least disruption. The new path flow entries have lower priorities compared to the old ones. Therefore, the target traffic uses the old path, while the new path is programmed in the underlay. When all flow tables are updated, the old path is removed and the traffic will match the new one. This approach ensures that packets are not forwarded to switches without matching flow entries.

8.3 Traffic Engineering Methods

Implementing traffic engineering using SDN mechanisms can be more flexible and effective compared to IP and MPLS based TEs [3]. Unified views of the networking substrates and applications, through southbound and northbound APIs, provide visibility into the network status and the applications' requirements. The SDN specification abstraction [12] makes the proactive programming and dynamic reprogramming of the network efficient, as devices are not handled individually. Therefore, the controller can efficiently react to the network status and application demand.

In addition to the chosen path between two endpoints, meters and queues of the OpenFlow switches are exploited for traffic engineering and QoS differentiation in the underlay.

Meter. A meter is a part of a flow entry instruction set. It measures the rate of all the packets which are matched to the flows to which it is attached. The meter counters are updated when packets are processed. Each meter has a set of bands which specify the minimum rate at which their action can be applied. A band can support "drop" or "dscp remark" operations [9]. Meter creation, configuration, and flow assignment are performed by the OpenFlow wire protocol version 1.3.0.

In our design, each traffic class has a set of meters, which are attached to the flows mapped to it. The minimum rate of a meter band is specified in the network flavor, otherwise it is REFERENCE_BW/CLASS_NUM, where the REFERENCE_BW represents the physical port speed (i.e. 1 Gbps for our test-bed) and CLASS_NUM is the traffic class specified in the flavor. When the packet rate is over the band rate, the band applies and packets are dropped.

Queue. A port in an OpenFlow switch can have one or more queues, where flow entries are mapped to them. A queue determines how flows are treated, using a set of properties: a minimum rate, a maximum rate, and an experimenter property [9]. The maximum rate of a queue is set to REFERENCE_BW/(MQ-QP), where MQ and QP are the maximum number of queues and the queue priority, respectively. In contrast to the meter, queue configuration is handled by the OVSDB protocol, while flow mapping is done by the OpenFlow wire protocol.

Flows of a tenant are forwarded to a queue according to the virtual network flavor priority. The queue priority determines which one is served first. Therefore, in addition to the rate limiting function, overlay traffic with a higher priority class is forwarded before lower priority ones.

Meters are more useful for fine-grained rate limiting, since a switch can support more meters than queues, and meters are per-flow while queues are per-port.

Therefore, a meters' configuration can be more granular. Although the number of queues in hardware is limited, they provide better guarantees for traffic prioritization and are more effective for coarse-grained policies. A combination of meters and queues can deliver complex QoS frameworks [9].

For the evaluation, minimum rates of meter bands and maximum rates of queues are chosen with significant differences for each flavor to clearly visualize the impact on the network QoS (Table 1).

9 Evaluation

Flavors should create a clear distinction between virtual networks' QoS. An extensive evaluation framework is developed to measure a variety of QoS parameters and study the system behaviour under different scenarios.

9.1 Evaluation Framework

The framework has a modular architecture and allows new experiments to be added as plug-ins. The experiment covers all scenarios that should be assessed. It requires a set of parameters, which are used to create a group of sub-experiments. A sub-experiment is executed according to the specified execution type and the results are comparable. Some of the parameters used for the virtual network throughput analysis are as follows:

- *Instances range*: The minimum and maximum number of virtual machine instances which are involved in the measurements.

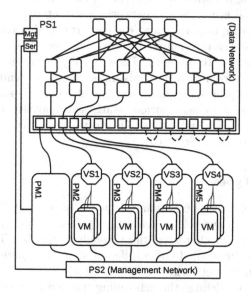

Fig. 3. Evaluation test-bed

- *Networks range*: The minimum and maximum number of virtual networks, created in this experiment.
- *Classes*: The traffic classes (specified in the flavors), assigned to virtual networks, where lower class numbers have higher priorities and better QoS.
- *Instance distribution*: The distribution of instances over networks.
- *Network distribution*: The distribution of networks over classes.
- *Path length*: The maximum number of hops between two instances of a class.
- *Instances execution type*: Determines whether instances should perform the task simultaneously or sequentially (i.e. `i:{true,false}`).
- *Classes execution type*: Determines whether networks of a class should execute the task in parallel or in series (i.e. `c:{true,false}`).
- *TE strategy*: Specifies the traffic engineering method(s) in the underlay network (i.e. `none, meter, queue, meter_queue`).
- *Failure threshold*: The upper threshold for the permitted number of failures before a sub-experiment is terminated.

Before executing a sub-experiment, all the configurations are set to their default values and the cloud platform is reinitialized. This will avoid propagation of side-effects from previous sub-experiments and increase precision. After the reinitialization, virtual networks and instances are created according to the aforementioned parameters. Then, the SDN controller programs the network and the framework waits for the instances to become reachable. Once enough instances are reachable, the framework instructs instances to perform the measurement and report back. If the number of reachable instances is less than the failure threshold, the process is terminated with an error report and the next sub-experiment is started.

When all reachable instances finish their tasks, the reports are stored and processed. Finally, all instances and networks are deleted.

In addition to the input parameters, each report contains a set of task-specific results. For instance, the throughput measurement reports on TCP/UDP rate, Rx/Tx CPU utilization, Round Trip Time (RTT), retransmission occurrence, number of report errors, number of missing values, start/end time and hosting hypervisors. The processing phase consists of report classification based on common parameters, data aggregation, statistical analysis and plotting. The outcomes are presented in two forms, TE strategy comparison (Sect. 9.4) and execution type comparison (Sect. 9.5).

9.2   Execution Types

Evaluating virtual network performance is not a trivial task [13]. Tenants of a cloud service provision and release resources dynamically; they also have workloads with varying traffic characteristics throughout the day. Therefore, virtual network QoS should be studied under different scenarios where a realistic workload is simulated in the network.

An execution type defines the scheduling method of a sub-experiment. It determines how competing networks with different classes and their instances

should perform the measurement. To limit the scope of the evaluation, two parameters are considered: network classes and instances execution types. The network class execution type specifies whether throughput of competing networks
should be measured concurrently. Whereas, the instance execution type controls
the parallel or series measurement between two instances in a network.

The number of concurrent individual measurements (CIM) depends on the
execution type, and estimated values are presented in Table 2. However, it might
not be the exact number in an arbitrary given point of time, because a strict
mechanism is not used for the experiment scheduling. As an example, some
instances of a network class may become reachable sooner than others, when all
networks and their instances have been requested simultaneously. Therefore, it
may show some stochastic behaviours and noises in the results.

Although concurrent execution of the measurements decreases each class
throughput, higher priority classes perform better than lower priority ones.

Table 1. TE method properties

	Meter	Queue	
Class	Min rate	Priority	Max rate
1	1 Gbps	6	1 Gbps
2	500 Mbps	5	500 Mbps
3	333 Mbps	4	333 Mbps
4	250 Mbps	3	250 Mbps

Table 2. Scheduling method properties

Type	# CIM
c:false,i:false	1
c:false,i:true	(#instances choose 2)
c:true,i:false	#classes
c:true,i:true	#classes × (#instances choose 2)

9.3 Evaluation Setup

The platform is deployed on 5 Intel NUCs, with Core i5 processors, 16 GByte
memory, 140 GByte SSD storage, and two Gigabit Ethernets. Each node is connected to the management and data networks. The management network uses an
8-port Gigabit switch, and the data network uses an OpenFlow capable Pica-8
P-3290 switch. The whitebox switch has 8 physical queues (0–7), and the highest
priority queue is dedicated to the switch-controller communication.

As shown in Fig. 3, the SDN (PM1) and cloud (PM2) controllers have dedicated nodes and the rest are compute nodes (PM3,4,5). A Fat-Tree topology
with K-port commodity switch is emulated in the whitebox switch (PS1), where
K is 4. As the switch does not support Open vSwitch patch-port, the remaining
physical ports are connected in pairs to patch the emulated switches.

The SDN controller modules are developed as part of the OpenDaylight
project, and the cloud platform is OpenStack. The implementation has 10,613
lines of code and is available for the community, along with the raw evaluation
data and additional analysis [2]. The virtual machine image is built using Buildroot [1] and the VM flavor is m1.nano with one vCPU and 256 MB memory.

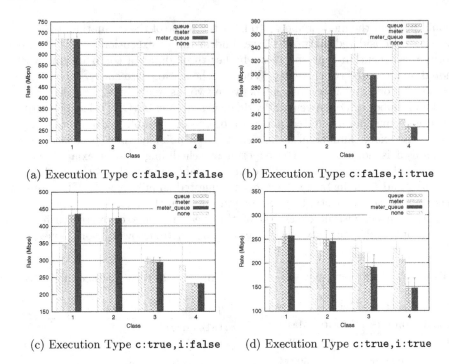

(a) Execution Type `c:false,i:false`   (b) Execution Type `c:false,i:true`

(c) Execution Type `c:true,i:false`   (d) Execution Type `c:true,i:true`

Fig. 4. Comparing the impact of QoS strategies on TCP throughput for different execution types

9.4 Traffic Engineering Strategy Analysis

Figure 4 represents the mean TCP throughput between any two instances on a network, with a distinct class, that are hosted on different hypervisors. Each sub-figure depicts a specific execution type, and data series are different strategies.

Figure 4a plots the TCP throughput when at any point of time measurement is performed between two instances of a single class. As explained in Sect. 9.2, since this scheduling method offers the least concurrency, each class achieves the maximum throughput under different TE strategies. When the only class enforcement method is the chosen path (i.e. strategy is **none**), the differences between classes' throughput are not significant. However, other strategies make considerable differences between classes.

As shown in Figs. 4b, c and d, when instances or networks execute the measurements concurrently, the TCP throughput is decreased.

9.5 Execution Type Analysis

Figure 5 also represents the mean TCP throughput between any two instances, where each sub-figure depicts a specific strategy, and data series represent execution types. It can be observed that the throughput is mandated by the class priority, and it is independent of the scheduling method.

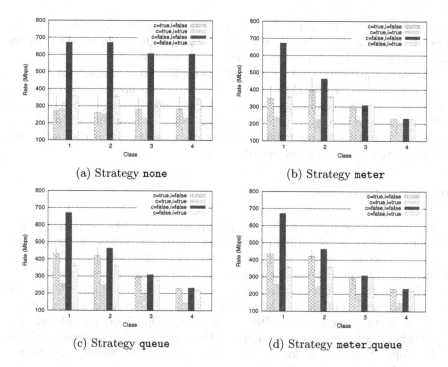

Fig. 5. Comparing the impact of execution types on TCP throughput for different QoS strategies

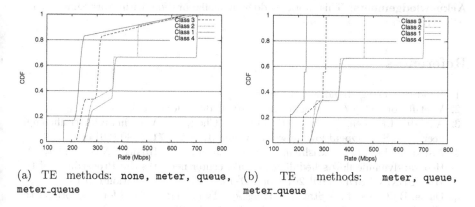

(a) TE methods: none, meter, queue, meter_queue

(b) TE methods: meter, queue, meter_queue

Fig. 6. CDF of the 90th percentile TCP throughput for each class independent of the experiment scheduling approach.

In Fig. 5c, each queue has a maximum rate of REFERENCE_BW/CLASS_NUM; the TCP throughputs of all classes are limited by this constraint. However, if the maximum rate is set to REFERENCE_BW, when classes are not executed concurrently (i.e. c:false,i:*), lower priority classes will perform as good as the strategy **none** case in Fig. 5a; whereas the throughputs in other execution types remain the same. It is due to the queue scheduling mechanisms of the switch, where the higher priority queues are served first.

Figure 6 depicts the CDF of the 90th percentile TCP throughput for each class, independent of the scheduling method. Figure 6a presents the CDF with and without traffic engineering mechanisms explained in Sect. 8.3, while Fig. 6b only includes the 90th percentile throughput when at least one TE method is employed. It can be deduced that higher priority classes (lower class numbers) perform better than the lower priority ones.

10   Conclusion

Virtual network flavor is a crucial feature, but missing in cloud platforms design. The proposed approach utilizes SDN mechanisms for delivering flavors, and providing QoS for overlay virtual networks. SDN abstractions make overlay traffic classification and underlay traffic engineering much more efficient. The logically centralized SDN controller not only provides a unified view of the network through southbound APIs, but also has visibility into applications' demands through northbound APIs. Standard (i.e. OpenFlow 1.3 [9]) and open (i.e. OVSDB [10]) protocols are used for the control and management planes, and all operations are performed using them. Therefore, there is no manual configuration involved for network management and programming.

Acknowledgements. This work is done in collaboration with Norwegian NREN (UNINETT).

References

1. Buildroot. http://buildroot.uclibc.org/
2. Vnet-flavors. http://www.ux.uis.no/~aryan/docs/dc/vnet-flavor/
3. Akyildiz, I.F., Lee, A., Wang, P., Luo, M., Chou, W.: A roadmap for traffic engineering in SDN-OpenFlow networks. Comput. Netw. **71**, 1–30 (2014)
4. Al-Fares, M., Radhakrishnan, S., Raghavan, B., Huang, N., Vahdat, A.: Hedera: dynamic flow scheduling for data center networks. In: Proceedings of the 7th USENIX NSDI, NSDI 2010, pp. 19–19. USENIX Association (2010)
5. Davie, B., Gross, J.: A Stateless Transport Tunneling Protocol for Network Virtualization. Internet Draft (Informational), October 2014
6. Handigol, N., Seetharaman, S., Flajslik, M., McKeown, N., Johari, R.: Plug-n-serve: Load-balancing web traffic using OpenFlow. ACM SIGCOMM Demo **4**(5), 6 (2009)
7. Khan, A., Kiess, W., Perez-Caparros, D., Triay, J.: Quality-of-service (QoS) for virtual networks in OpenFlow MPLS transport networks. IEEE, November 2013
8. Mahalingam, M., Dutt, D., Duda, K., Agarwal, P., Kreeger, L., Sridhar, T., Bursell, M., Wright, C.: Virtual eXtensible Local Area Network (VXLAN): A Framework for Overlaying Virtualized Layer 2 Networks over Layer 3 Networks. RFC 7348
9. Open Networking Foundation: OpenFlow switch specification version 1.3.0

10. Pfaff, B., Davie, B.: The Open vSwitch Database Management Protocol. No. 7047 in Request for Comments, IETF, published: RFC 7047 (Informational), December 2013
11. Pfaff, B.: Open vSwitch manual. http://benpfaff.org/~blp/ovs-fields.pdf
12. Shenker, S., Casado, M., Koponen, T., McKeown, N.: The future of networking, and the past of protocols. Open Networking Summit (2011). http://opennetsummit. org/archives/oct11/shenker-tue.pdf
13. TaheriMonfared, A., Rong, C.: Flexible building blocks for software defined network function virtualization. In: 10th International Conference on QShine (2014)
14. Wang, R., Butnariu, D., Rexford, J.: OpenFlow-based server load balancing gone wild. In: Proceedings of the 11th USENIX Hot-ICE. USENIX Association (2011)
15. Yen, J.Y.: Finding the k shortest loopless paths in a network. Manage. Sci. **17**(11), 712–716 (1971)

Exploiting Communication Opportunities in Disrupted Network Environments

Lefteris Mamatas[1]([✉]), Alexandra Papadopoulou[2], and Vassilis Tsaoussidis[3]

[1] Department of Applied Informatics, University of Macedonia, 156 Egnatia Str., 54636 Thessaloniki, Greece
emamatas@uom.gr
[2] Department of Mathematics, Aristotle University of Thessaloniki, 54124 Thessaloniki, Greece
apapado@math.auth.gr
[3] Department of Electrical and Computer Engineering, Democritus University of Thrace, 12 Vas. Sofias Str., 67100 Xanthi, Greece
vtsaousi@ee.duth.gr

Abstract. The capability of a mobility model to detect certain patterns of user behavior (e.g., favorite walks or walking habits) enables solutions for a number of challenging networking problems, including efficient opportunistic communications and handoff/cellular planning. We argue that the limited viewpoint of a single mobile node and its scarce resources (e.g., energy, memory or processing) are major obstacles for accurate estimations. Targeting at hybrid network environments, we offload prediction capabilities to the fixed nodes that may be available in the area, offering a global view and the capability of resource-demanding calculations.

Here, we introduce a solution running on top of the infrastructure nodes that: (i) implements a mobility model which provides a number of mobility forecasts to the mobile users in the area, (ii) supports proactively the routing decisions of opportunistic mobile devices being taken at times there is not connectivity. We introduce the corresponding semi-Markov model and demonstrate its efficiency using scenarios deployed in a pre-selected city center, where a number of mobile nodes seek for Internet access.

Keywords: Delay-Tolerant Networks · Opportunistic networks · Infrastructure-supported mobile communication · Mobility prediction

1 Introduction

Internet is entering a new era, in which sophisticated devices can be deployed anywhere, run demanding applications and require connectivity occasionally or permanently. Various challenging networks have been introduced, initially as

---

L. Mamatas carried out his main contribution in this paper during his employment at the Democritus University of Thrace, Greece.

© Springer International Publishing Switzerland 2015
M.C. Aguayo-Torres et al. (Eds.): WWIC 2015, LNCS 9071, pp. 180–193, 2015.
DOI: 10.1007/978-3-319-22572-2_13

stand-alone homogeneous networks that were gradually attached to the Internet. Space Networks [22] are the most recent example; other examples include the Mobile ad-hoc networks (MANETs), Delay - and disruption - tolerant networks (DTNs) [11], and Vehicular ad-hoc networks (VANETS) [13]. This inherent heterogeneity is dominant in today's Internet; however, the properties of such internetworks are typically studied in the context of the extended network module alone (e.g., MANETs, DTNs, VANETs) and not in the appropriate context of their influence to the global internetwork.

This hybrid setting requires supportive strategies to exploit even the slightest communication opportunity; let alone the technology to allow for dynamic updates and the capability to continuously seek an optimal solution. In this context, what appears theoretically possible becomes conditionally feasible, only when system granularity and routing accuracy can adequately match user-behavioral and -mobility patterns. Beyond that, the complexity of the task increases if we also consider device constraints, energy aspects and application diversity.

Here, we claim that infrastructure nodes around areas with poor or intermittent connectivity could collectively build and, based on historical data, train a stochastic model capable of predicting future contacts. Actually, each fixed node can trace the coordinates of mobile devices passing by along with their corresponding connectivity times. Such data can be communicated within the infrastructure and constitute valuable input for the mobility model, which, in turn, can produce node-level (i.e., detect mobility patterns of certain nodes), or system-level estimations (e.g., number of nodes at a certain area after some time). This allows each mobile node to query the system for information regarding its future contact opportunities and expect by the neighboring fixed node to reply with a potential suggestion. Such response information could become, for example, a probability value or the coefficients of a known distribution. The latter can represent the inter-contact time PDF between a mobile/class of mobiles and other mobiles or Internet hotspots.

So, the moving device can calculate the cost functions associated with potential tactics - from holding data further, to forwarding to another node and also to which particular direction - and make a decision with respect the delivery time of the data or, perhaps, the certainty to reach the destination within some required timeframe. It is obvious that storing the data in the source mobile until a new hotspot appears is a conservative strategy that misses communication opportunities. Furthermore, 3G networks are often expensive and unavailable. In experiments documented in [3], in places 3G is not available there is WiFi availability roughly half of the time. In our experience, forwarding decisions can be taken with a level of accuracy that can be occasionally high (when the scenario allows) although communication and processing overhead could be low. Other approaches to location-prediction using historical information are based on the limited contact history of a single node (e.g., [12]), group contact-time information of a certain number of users (e.g., based on their social ties [10]) or use offline network traces to evaluate the accuracy of Markov or semi-Markov based approaches (e.g., [9,19]).

In this paper, we employ a semi-Markov model for the prediction of contact opportunities. Semi-Markov models [15] were introduced as stochastic tools with capacity to accommodate a variety of applied probability models: they may provide more generality to describe the semantics of complex models - which, in turn, increases the complexity of analysis. However, the extra-added variables improve the modeling expressiveness of real-life problems. We also note that the increased complexity is assigned to the resource-capable fixed nodes, improving prediction accuracy without damaging the sensitive performance of mobile, battery-powered devices. It is documented (e.g., in [9,25]) that Markov-based location predictors perform very well in practice, but require more complex and expensive mobility data for sophisticated forecasts such as the time and location of the next user movement or duration of stay in an area.

Our approach is characterized by two main advantages: (i) the fixed infrastructure allows for a global view of the system and improved predictions of connectivity opportunities, (ii) the mobile devices delegate resource-expensive operations to the infrastructure nodes in order to exploit their capabilities in terms of energy availability, processing power and memory allocation. Therefore, the performance of mobile devices is preserved without trading prediction accuracy and hence communication efficiency. Decoupling (but also improving) the forecasting capability from the routing strategy enables a number of new efficient protocols to be introduced. Furthermore, the forecasting connectivity opportunities can be a basis for an efficient energy-saving strategy also; the mobiles could be switching off their communication subsystems at times the probability to meet other nodes is low.

To demonstrate the potential of our solution, we consider an urban scenario where mobile users are interested into getting Internet access. Different hotspots are scattered in a city center (i.e., around $60\,km^2$ in Thessaloniki, Greece), covering with Internet connectivity some percentage of that area (i.e., less than 40 %). The hotspots are deployed in real points of interest (central squares, museums and other places attracting people) and are collectively building a communication model. The mobile nodes can request information on neighboring nodes: how often or with what probability they do contact the available hotspots. Such information is passed from the closest hotspot to the mobile contacts. So, a moving user can easily make decisions on whether a neighboring node is more suitable to forward its own data towards the Internet. Indeed, as we show in our experimental results, we were able to identify useful mobility patterns for future efficient network protocol designs.

The paper is structured as follows. In Sect. 2 we review the state of the art that is relevant to the present work. In Sect. 3 we describe a particular scenario, along with the proposed semi-Markov stochastic model. In Sect. 4 we evaluate the above model in three experimental scenarios. Finally, in Sect. 5 we conclude the paper.

2   Related Work

Internet complexity has been increased rapidly since new communication paradigms, other than Infrastructure - based networking, have been incorporated into the internetworking model (e.g., ad-hoc, mesh or space networking). In this context, the network becomes also a storage device - not just a communication vehicle. This new property of the Internet alone challenges all known models and evaluation standards for internetworked systems. Furthermore, approaches such as Delay - and Disruption - Tolerant Networks (DTNs) [11] undergo major standardization efforts that target a unification perspective for the various pieces of the global network jigsaw puzzle. We note that protocols originally designed for a homogeneous network environment are not expected to work optimally in such a hybrid setting. An example work that brings closer different types of networks (i.e., wireless and mobile) is [8], attempting to define a continuum between the different networks.

A number of approaches support mobile communication using the surrounding infrastructure. In the area of VANETs, proposals either exploit infrastructure to support car-to-car communication (e.g., through roadside access points) or the opposite (e.g., [23]). Recent papers consider clouds as a dynamic infrastructure that improves mobile communication through offloading resources from the mobile users (e.g., [18]). The DTN throwboxes have been introduced as stationary, battery-powered nodes, embedded with storage and processing capabilities that are able to enhance the capacity of DTNs [4]. Mobile infostation networks use the infostation nodes to support mobile communications for this specific context (e.g., to keep information close to the mobile users [17]). Other proposals move a portion of the mobile data traffic to WiFi networks, exploiting the significantly lower cost of WiFi technology and existing backhaul infrastructure [24].

In the literature, approaches to mobile connectivity forecasting have been proposed in different contexts, such as resource reservation in cellular networks or handoff planning (e.g., [5,28]). For example, BreadCrumbs [20] maintains a personalized mobility model on the user's device that tracks APs (i.e., using RF fingerprinting) and combines the predictions with an AP quality database to produce connectivity forecasts.

Compared to the related works, our solution decouples the mobility model from the routing protocol and offloads prediction operations to the surrounding infrastructure. This allows a larger number of samples to be considered (i.e., due to the more complete view) and more complicated calculations to be performed, improving the forecasting accuracy in a resource friendly way for the mobile devices. In our proposal, we model user mobility with a semi-Markov process with heterogeneous properties, allowing for flexible definition of different distributions for inter-contact times, under different conditions. Such conditions and other relevant patterns are being explored and associated with practical constraints (e.g., resource availability). Other relevant approaches using semi-Markov processes are [6,29]. Both of them model routing behavior rather than mobility patterns.

3   Case Study and Modeling Considerations

3.1   Studied Environment

In this paper, we consider a heterogeneous network scenario consisting of both mobile and infrastructure nodes. In this context, we assume a communication system that integrates deployed infrastructure (e.g., a network of hotspots) with opportunistic networks, therefore allowing for additional communication opportunities even for uncovered city areas. The infrastructure nodes have been delegated the responsibility of tracking the position of mobile nodes as well as the potential estimation of their future positions.

At this stage, we study an urban scenario where mobiles require Internet connectivity at times they are not covered from deployed hotspots. For methodological reasons, we start from the particular environment and the study of next-place or WiFi connectivity forecasts in order to devise strategies for extended and efficient Internet access. As a next step, we plan to move on to more complicated scenarios, predicting device-to-device connectivity opportunities in heterogeneous deployments (i.e., mixing networked vehicles with pocket switched networks).

Our scenario includes a number of hotspots covering only a percentage of the area with connectivity (e.g., 30–40 %). There is a wide-range of mobile device types moving around the hotspots. Each mobile node may need to access the Internet or to interact with any other node. To address this demand, a dynamic path should be established between the communicating nodes, carrying the data to be transmitted. This is not trivial, since all nodes may be constantly moving and all participating node positions are not known in advance. The communication between the user and the closer hotspot can be handled from variations of well-known opportunistic network protocols, such as the Spray 'n Focus [26], the MaxProp [7] or any other similar.

In our case, the hotspots collectively train a model which is able to estimate the evolution of node topology structure, elaborated in the following subsection. In a more general setting, the source mobile node can query any hotspot for the destination node position or any other relevant information. If the latter node is directly connected to an infrastructure node, data will be carried through the infrastructure to the destination, straightaway. In case the destination mobile user is located in an uncovered area, data will be forwarded through the infrastructure to the hotspot that has the higher probability to be near the user. This hotspot is selected from the source mobile node using forecast information produced by the proposed semi-Markov model and the most recent location information of the destination mobile.

Since the source node may not be always connected to a hotspot, the infrastructure responses regarding the potential destination node positions will be more general, enhancing mobiles with limited but resource - efficient and accurate estimation capabilities. For example, the responses can be coefficients of known distributions, which are functions of time.

3.2   Semi-Markov Model and Basic Equations

In this subsection, we detail the proposed stochastic model and its basic equations reflecting different aspects of users' mobility behavior. The stationary nodes implement collectively the model and communicate the output of the equations to the interested mobile nodes. An efficient routing decision may require one or more calculations, based on its own criteria. We present usage examples along with the model description (denoted in italics), in the context of our proposed infrastructure. We note that all equations can be used as contact predictors for communication between the mobiles as well.

We model the users' mobility behavior using a Discrete - Time Semi - Markov System (DTSMS). A semi-Markov chain is a generalized Markov model and can be considered as a process whose successive state occupancies are governed by a Markov chain (i.e., embedded Markov chain), although state duration is described by a random double variable which associates with the present but also with the next transition state. A relevant model discussion focused on theoretical aspects can be found in [21].

At the beginning of our analysis, we assume a population of users moving around a city center (i.e., in this paper we considered the city of Thessaloniki) and pass through a number of scattered hotspots in real points of interest in the area (e.g., central squares, museums etc.). The users can be stratified into a set of areas $S = 1, 2, ..., N$. We assume that a number of areas have network coverage (e.g., 1 to K) while other areas do not (e.g., K to N). These areas are assumed to be exclusive and exhaustive, so that each user is located at exactly one area at any time. The system state at any given time is described by the vector $N(n) = [N_1(n), N_2(n), ..., N_N(n)]$, where $N_i(n)$ is the expected number of users located at an area i, after n time slots. We consider a closed system with constant total population of users denoted with T. Also, we assume that the individual transitions between states occur according to a homogeneous semi-Markov chain (i.e., embedded semi-Markov chain). In this respect, let us denote by P the stochastic matrix whose $(i,j)th$ element equals to the probability of a user in the system which entered an area i to make its next transition to area j. Thus, whenever a user enters area i selects area j for its next transition, according to the probabilities $p_{i,j}$.

A mobile node may request a specific probability value in the form of $p_{i,j}$ from the infrastructure system. This expresses the probability of a node to reach an area j after being at an area i, in the next transition. This value could be used from a mobile node in order to check if there is a chance for a user to pass by area i and reach area j straightaway. For example, the mobile could perform a quick check if two areas are adjacent.

In our model, the mobile user remains for sometime within area i, prior to entering area j. Holding times are described by the holding time mass function $h_{i,j}(n)$, which equals to the probability that a user entered area i at its last transition holds for n time slots in i before its next transition, given that node moves to area j.

The holding time mass function $h_{i,j}(n)$ could be used by a mobile in order to check the possibility of a direct transition from area i to area j at a given time. Occasionally, the destination area may not matter, but instead, the transition is important: for example, a transition from a non-covered to a network-covered area. *A node, therefore, at an isolated area may evaluate the cumulative probability to move to any area with connectivity, independently of which area it is.*

By the same token, we discuss the following variation of the holding time mass function:

$$h_i(n) = \sum_{j=1,2,\dots N(j \neq i)} p_{i,j} h_{i,j}(n) \tag{1}$$

The $h_i(n)$ function captures the probability of a mobile at state i to make a transition at time n (the particular destination area is irrelevant). Along the same lines, we introduce the probabilities:

$$h_i^{con}(n) = \sum_{j=1,2,\dots K} p_{i,j} h_{i,j}(n) \tag{2}$$

$$h_i^{disc}(n) = \sum_{j=K,K+1,\dots N} p_{i,j} h_{i,j}(n) \tag{3}$$

The functions $h_i^{con}(n)$ and $h_i^{disc}(n)$ capture the probabilities of a mobile to move from area i to any area with connectivity or not at time n, respectively. For example, a forwarding decision could be made based on the possibility of the forwarding node to carry data to an Internet access network.

We also detail equation $^{>}w_i(n)$ which expresses the probability of a user who made a transition to area i to reach the next area in longer than n time slots:

$$^{>}w_i(n) = \sum_{m=n+1}^{\infty} \sum_{k=1}^{N} p_{i,k} h_{i,k}(m) \tag{4}$$

The initial condition is $^{>}w_i(0) = 1$.

Similarly, variations like $^{>}w_i^{con}(n)$ and $^{>}w_i^{disc}(n)$ could be introduced.

The $^{>}w_i$ equations can support the forwarding decisions of the opportunistic routing protocol inline with data transmission deadlines, e.g., delay constraints for real-time or other time-critical applications.

A main aspect of the proposed model is related to the interval transition probabilities which correspond to the multistep transition probabilities of a Markov process. So, let us define as $q_{i,j}(n)$ the probability of a user from area i to be at an area j after n time slots, independently of the required intermediate state changes. *This metric allows multi-path contact predictions, i.e., captures the probability of a node to be at an area after some time (or two mobiles to contact each other, in a general setting), independently of the required steps.*

The basic recursive equation for calculating the interval transition probabilities is the following [14,27]:

$$q_{i,j}(n) = \delta_{i,j} {}^{>}w_i(n) + \sum_{k=1}^{N} \sum_{m=0}^{n} p_{i,k} h_{i,k}(m) q_{k,j}(n-m) \tag{5}$$

The initial condition is $q_{i,j}(0) = \delta_{i,j}$, where $\delta_{i,j}$ is defined:

$$\delta_{i,j} = \begin{cases} 1 \text{ if } i{=}j \\ 0 \text{ elsewhere.} \end{cases} \tag{6}$$

4 Evaluation

4.1 Evaluation Methodology

Here, we detail our evaluation methodology and the experimental scenarios we studied. We extracted a large area of the city center of Thessaloniki, Greece from the OpenStreetMap website [2]. The area's dimensions are 6.2 km × 10.1 km, including 397 streets and 1884 landmarks. We selected twelve representative points of interest, assuming they offer Internet connectivity as well. For simplicity, we consider as area 13 any other area without connectivity. Their locations were extracted from the same information source and selected based on their popularity (e.g., the Aristotles Square, the railway station, the St. Sophia Church, well-known museums etc.). We use theone [16] simulations augmented with real parameters. A map screenshot that includes some of the selected points of interest is shown in Fig. 1. The mobile users walk around the city, following one of the identified streets each time and directing towards an area based on a mobility pattern detailed in the corresponding scenario. The users stay in each area from few minutes to hours and their walking speed ranges between 0.5 and 1.5 m/sec. Our next step is to use alternative mobility traces from the CRAW-DAD database [1] in order to validate the general applicability of our proposal. A real deployment is in our plans as well.

We grouped our experiments into three distinct scenarios, demonstrating the efficiency of the proposed semi-Markov model, assuming corresponding user mobility behavior in the city center:

- A "Home-to-work" scenario, where a mobile node walks occasionally between home, work and the main city square. There is a 33 % probability of the user to be in one of these three areas.
- A "Walking around the city" scenario, where the mobile node occasionally selects one of twelve different areas in the city center as the next visiting area, with equal probability.
- A "Going out" scenario, where the mobile node has a high probability (33 %) to be in the main square (assuming it as a meeting point) and an equal probability for each of the other eleven areas.

For the above scenarios, we show how the proposed equations can be used as prediction mechanisms for a number of different mobility aspects and how different mobility patterns can be detected and exploited by a communication protocol.

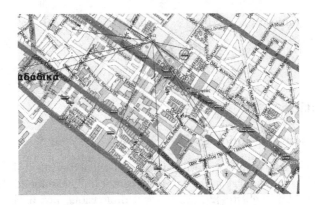

Fig. 1. The experimental scenario

4.2   Evaluation Results

Scenario 1: "Home-to-Work". In Fig. 2(a), (b) we show the equations h_i and $h_{i,j}$, respectively. Both metrics reflect the probabilities of a mobile to move to the next area, at given time slots. In the case of Fig. 2(b), the destination area does not matter, as long as we have a state change. It takes some time (i.e., more than 50 s) for the mobile to change state, a value that is a factor of the movement speed and the distance between the three areas. In Fig. 2(a), we show the probability of a mobile to move to one of the three areas (i.e., home, work or main square), when it is located at an area without connectivity (i.e., area 13). The three h probabilities (i.e., $h_{13,1}$, $h_{13,3}$ and $h_{13,9}$) have often similar values, something not surprising given the experimental setup parameters. This behavior leads to reduced communication overhead of the forecasting request interactions between mobiles and infrastructure: an average value suffices.

The w metric (Fig. 2(c)) reflects the probability of a user who made a transition to an area, to reach to the next area after at least n time slots. In this case, there is a very low probability for a state change, if the mobile stays at a particular area for more than 600 s. The $w_{13}(n)$ value is indeed interesting, since it represents the probability of a mobile node being at an area without connectivity, to move to an area with connectivity in less than n min. In this example, there is an insignificant chance of a connectivity time that exceeds 200 s. Of course, this result is guided by the experimental setup parameters.

Equation q, shown in Fig. 2(d), reflects the probability of a node being at an area without connectivity to move to an area with connectivity at some given time, but without considering the number of areas crossed. We see that after some time, i.e., 200–300 s, the probabilities to move to one of the three areas with connectivity, tend to converge to fixed values. Curve $q_{13,13}(n)$ shows the probability of a mobile being at an area without Internet connectivity to visit an area covered by a hotspot, stay for a while and then leave the hotspot again.

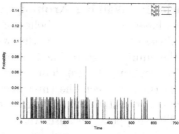

(a) Probability of a user to remain for time n within area i, prior to entering area j - $h_{i,j}(n)$

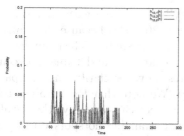

(b) Probability of a user to remain for time n within area i, prior to entering any other area - $h_i(n)$

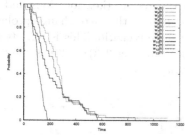

(c) Probability of a user who made a transition to area i to reach the next area in longer than n time slots - $w_i(n)$

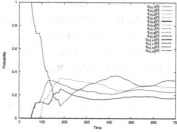

(d) Probability of a user to leave area i and reach area j with multiple steps, after n time slots - $q_{i,j}(n)$

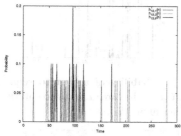

(e) Probability of a user to remain for time n within area i, prior to entering area j - $h_{i,j}(n)$

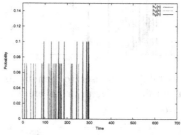

(f) Probability of a user to remain for time n within area i, prior to entering any other area - $h_i(n)$

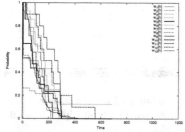

(g) Probability of a user who made a transition to area i to reach the next area in longer than n time slots - $w_i(n)$

(h) Probability of a user to leave area i and reach area j with multiple steps, after n time slots - $q_{i,j}(n)$

Fig. 2. "Home-to-work" and "Walking around the city" scenarios results

Scenario 2: "Walking Around the City". Compared with scenario 1, the h values have an equivalent behavior (see Fig. 2(e), (f)) because the transition probabilities of state changes in the two scenarios are similar. The main difference lies in the number of states (i.e., 12 areas for scenario two and 3 areas for scenario one). In Fig. 2(e), (f), we depict three states only, for clarity and comparison purposes (i.e., between the three scenarios). We note that the h values reflect changes between state 13 (i.e., area without connectivity) and any other available state. This happens because we assume that available hotspots do not have overlaps and have uncovered areas between them. State changes are associated with the parameters of our system, i.e., waiting time at each state. In our case, it is a random value picked from a uniform distribution in the range of $[0, 120]$ s.

Of course, the topological properties of the system (i.e., locations and distances between the hotspots) do matter and impact the state change probabilities between the different areas within the same scenario. This is reflected on the w values (i.e., Fig. 2(g)) and the q values (i.e., Fig. 2(h)). After some time, the different q values converge to fixed values.

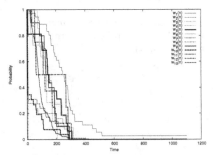

(a) Probability of a user to remain for time n within area i, prior to entering area j - $h_{i,j}(n)$

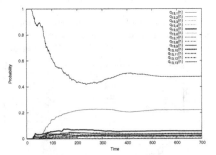

(b) Probability of a user to remain for time n within area i, prior to entering any other area - $h_i(n)$

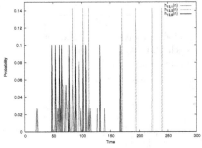

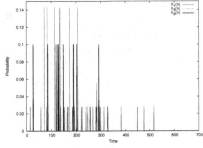

(c) Probability of a user who made a transition to area i to reach the next area in longer than n time slots - $w_i(n)$

(d) Probability of a user to leave area i and reach area j with multiple steps, after n time slots - $q_{i,j}(n)$

Fig. 3. "Going out" scenario results

Scenario 3: "Going Out". Through the h metrics (i.e., Fig. 3(a), (b)), we see a notable difference compared with the previous two scenarios. The h values for area 1 (the main square of the city, the Aristotle Square) are significantly lower. In this scenario, state 1 has been chosen with a probability 0.33. So, there is a high probability for a node to remain at the main square (i.e., same destination state to the source state). This is a pattern that could potentially be detected (i.e., hotspots that have a high probability to host mobile users). The same is reflected in a number of other metrics. For example, the $w_1(n)$, $q_{13,1}(n)$ values are significantly higher than other q, w values, respectively (see Fig. 3(c), (d)).

To summarize, the proposed model allows detection of certain patterns regarding the spatial behavior of the users. Some examples are:

- How probable is a state change between two particular states in a single step (i.e., $h_{i,k}$ values) or in many steps (i.e., $q_{i,k}$ values).
- What is the probability of a state transition from some given state to any other target state (i.e., h_i and w_i values).
- Whether some states have a significantly higher probability to be reached (i.e., $q_{i,k}$, or w_i or h values).

5 Conclusions

In this paper, we detailed a communication paradigm where infrastructure and opportunistic networks can efficiently inter-operate. We argue that:

- Opportunistic networks can bridge distant infrastructure networks (i.e., in areas without connectivity) using sophisticated routing protocols capable of detecting and exploiting user mobility patterns.
- Infrastructure nodes can support opportunistic communication with mechanisms that: (i) detect system - wide mobility patterns, and (ii) perform resource - expensive forecasting calculations for the benefit of the mobile devices.

We introduced a semi-Markov model and detailed a number of equations able to predict different aspects of user mobility behavior. This work focuses on the infrastructure being able to support a variety of network protocols exploiting communication opportunities using a number of accurate user- and system-level forecasts. Our approach allows for more complete and complex mobility models that would be difficult to integrate in a homogeneous network setting. A sophisticated protocol design exploiting the potential of the proposed infrastructure is in our short-term plans.

Acknowledgements. ▓ The research leading to these results has received funding from the European Unions (EU) Horizon 2020 research and innovation programme under grant agreement No 645124 (Action full title: Universal, mobile-centric and opportunistic communications architecture, Action Acronym: UMOBILE). This paper reflects only the authors views and the Community is not liable for any use that may be made of the information contained therein.

References

1. CRAWDAD, a community resource for archiving wireless data at Dartmouth. http://crawdad.cs.dartmouth.edu
2. OpenStreetMap - the free wiki world map. http://www.openstreetmap.org
3. Balasubramanian, A., Mahajan, R., Venkataramani, A.: Augmenting mobile 3G using WiFi. In: Proceedings of the 8th International Conference on Mobile Systems, Applications, and Services, MobiSys 2010, New York, NY, USA, pp. 209–222 (2010)
4. Banerjee, N., Corner, M., Levine, B.: An energy-efficient architecture for DTN throwboxes. In: 26th IEEE International Conference on Computer Communications (INFOCOM 2007), pp. 776–784. IEEE (2007)
5. Bhattacharya, A., Das, S.K.: Lezi-update: an information-theoretic approach to track mobile users in PCS networks. In: Proceedings of the 5th Annual ACM/IEEE International Conference on Mobile Computing and Networking, MobiCom 1999, pp. 1–12. ACM, New York (1999)
6. Boldrini, C., Conti, M., Passarella, A.: Modelling social-aware forwarding in opportunistic networks. In: Hummel, K.A., Hlavacs, H., Gansterer, W. (eds.) Performance Evaluation of Computer and Communication Systems. LNCS, vol. 6821, pp. 141–152. Springer, Heidelberg (2011)
7. Burgess, J., Gallagher, B., Jensen, D., Levine, B.: Maxprop: routing for vehicle-based disruption-tolerant networks. In: IEEE INFOCOM, Barcelona, Spain, vol. 6, pp. 1–11 (2006)
8. Chen, Y., Borrel, V., Ammar, M., Zegura, E.: A framework for characterizing the wireless and mobile network continuum. ACM SIGCOMM Comput. Commun. Rev. 41(1), 5–13 (2011)
9. Chon, Y., Shin, H., Talipov, E., Cha, H.: Evaluating mobility models for temporal prediction with high-granularity mobility data. In: International Conference on Pervasive Computing and Communications (PerCom 2012), pp. 206–212. IEEE (2012)
10. De Domenico, M., Lima, A., Musolesi, M.: Interdependence and predictability of human mobility and social interactions. In: Proceedings of the Pervasive 2012, Newcastle, UK (2012)
11. Fall, K.: A delay-tolerant network architecture for challenged internets. In: Proceedings of the 2003 Conference on Applications, Technologies, Architectures, and Protocols for Computer Communications, pp. 27–34. ACM (2003)
12. Gambs, S., Killijian, M., del Prado Cortez, M.: Next place prediction using mobility markov chains. In: Proceedings of the First Workshop on Measurement, Privacy, and Mobility, p. 3. ACM (2012)
13. Hartenstein, H., Laberteaux, K.: A tutorial survey on vehicular ad hoc networks. IEEE Commun. Mag. 46(6), 164–171 (2008)
14. Howard, R.: Dynamic Probabilistic Systems: Vol.: 2.: Semi-Markov and Decision Processes. Wiley, New York (1971)
15. Iosifescu Manu, A.: Non homogeneous semi-markov processes. Studii si Cercetuari Matematice 24, 529–533 (1972)
16. Keränen, A., Ott, J., Kärkkäinen, T.: The ONE simulator for DTN protocol evaluation. In: SIMUTools 2009: Proceedings of the 2nd International Conference on Simulation Tools and Techniques, ICST, New York, NY, USA (2009)
17. Kubach, U., Rothermel, K.: Exploiting location information for infostation-based hoarding. In: Proceedings of the 7th Annual International Conference on Mobile Computing and Networking, MobiCom 2001, pp. 15–27. ACM, New York (2001)

18. Kumar, K., Lu, Y.: Cloud computing for mobile users: can offloading computation save energy? Computer **43**(4), 51–56 (2010)

19. Lee, J.K., Hou, J.: Modeling steady-state and transient behaviors of user mobility: formulation, analysis, and application. In: Proceedings of the 7th ACM International Symposium on Mobile Ad Hoc Networking and Computing (MobiHoc), pp. 85–96. ACM (2006)

20. Nicholson, A.J., Noble, B.D.: Breadcrumbs: forecasting mobile connectivity. In: Proceedings of the 14th ACM International Conference on Mobile Computing and Networking, MobiCom 2008, pp. 46–57. ACM, New York (2008)

21. Papadopoulou, A., Mamatas, L., Tsaoussidis, V.: Semi markov modeling for user mobility in urban areas. In: Proceedings of the 2nd Stochastic Modeling Techniques and Data Analysis International Conference (SMTDA 2012), 5–8 June 2012

22. Papastergiou, G., Psaras, I., Tsaoussidis, V.: Deep-space transport protocol: a novel transport scheme for space DTNs. Comput. Commun. **32**(16), 1757–1767 (2009)

23. Petit, B., Ammar, M., Fujimoto, R.: Protocols for roadside-to-roadside data relaying over vehicular networks. In: Wireless Communications and Networking Conference (WCNC 2006), vol. 1, pp. 294–299. IEEE (2006)

24. Siris, V.A., Kalyvas, D.: Enhancing mobile data offloading with mobility prediction and prefetching. In: Proceedings of the Seventh ACM International Workshop on Mobility in the Evolving Internet Architecture, MobiArch 2012, pp. 17–22. ACM, New York (2012)

25. Song, L., Deshpande, U., Kozat, U.C., Kotz, D., Jain, R.: Predictability of WLAN mobility and its effects on bandwidth provisioning. In: Proceedings of the 25th IEEE International Conference on Computer Communications (INFOCOM), pp. 1–13. IEEE (2006)

26. Spyropoulos, T., Psounis, K., Raghavendra, C.: Efficient routing in intermittently connected mobile networks: the multiple-copy case. IEEE/ACM Trans. Netw. **16**(1), 77–90 (2008)

27. Vassiliou, P., Papadopoulou, A.: Non homogeneous semi markov systems and maintainability of the state sizes. J. Appl. Probab. **29**, 519–534 (1992)

28. Yu, F., Leung, V.: Mobility-based predictive call admission control and bandwidth reservation in wireless cellular networks. Comput. Netw. **38**(5), 577–589 (2002)

29. Yuan, Q., Cardei, I., Wu, J.: Predict and relay: an efficient routing in disruption-tolerant networks. In: Proceedings of the Tenth ACM International Symposium on Mobile Ad Hoc Networking and Computing, pp. 95–104. ACM (2009)

Next Generation Services

Tiny Network Caches with Large Performance Gains for Popular Downloads

Piotr Srebrny[1]([✉]), Dag Henning Liodden Sørbø[2], and Thomas Plagemann[3]

[1] Nevion, Oslo, Norway
piotrs@ifi.uio.no
[2] Bekk Consulting AS, Oslo, Norway
daghso@student.matnat.uio.no
[3] University of Oslo, Oslo, Norway
plageman@ifi.uio.no

Abstract. File transfers are and will in the future be responsible for a substantial part of the Internet traffic. However, with present solutions transfers of popular files lead to a lot of redundant data transfers in the network. In this paper, we investigate how a link level caching scheme can reduce the number of redundant data transfers. We serve requests from clients that download a file concurrently, but arrived at different times in such a way that they get at a given point in time the same data chunk of the file. This enables link caches to efficiently remove the redundancy. The data chunks are rearranged at the client to compose the original file. Through implementation and experimental studies we show that this approach clearly outperforms traditional file servers in terms of file server capacity and bandwidth consumption; especially when encoding the original file with fountain codes.

Keywords: Link level caching · File server · Fountain codes

1 Introduction

File transfer via protocols like FTP and HTTP is besides streaming of entertainment content one of the applications that dominate the Internet and causes a substantial part of the overall traffic. Increasing popularity of files leads to increasing file server load and increasing redundancy of data transfers from the file server to the clients. In order to distribute popular files and especially to handle flash crowds, P2P solutions have proven to be very useful. The core mechanism in these P2P solutions is to leverage networking and computing resources from the origin server, e.g., a torrent, and from the peers. Thus, the more concurrent downloads of a file, the more peer resources are available. This self-scaling property enables to handle flash crowds, but it leads to increasing overall resource consumption and increasing redundancy of data transfers.

In order to reduce the overall resource consumption and increase the file server performance, we investigate in this paper the feasibility of eliminating

© Springer International Publishing Switzerland 2015
M.C. Aguayo-Torres et al. (Eds.): WWIC 2015, LNCS 9071, pp. 197–210, 2015.
DOI: 10.1007/978-3-319-22572-2_14

respectively reducing the number of redundant data transfers through tiny caches at the link layer. This link level caching approach, called CacheCast, has been originally designed for single-source multiple-destination applications like live streaming [8]. Due to the missing support of Internet-wide IP-multicast, many streaming servers use unicast connections to the clients. If n clients receive a live stream, the file server sends n packets which all have the same payload. This redundancy is eliminated in CacheCast through link level caching. The streaming server sends a data element of the stream to n clients in form of a so-called packet train, which consists of one link level packet containing link, network, and transport layer headers and the data element as payload; and $n-1$ packets without the redundant payload. Furthermore, all packets are marked as CacheCast packets and contain some meta-data for cache management. At the link exit, the payload of the first packet is stored and can be used to reconstruct all following packets from the packet train. This procedure is performed individually at each link (see Sect. 2). The streaming server support simplifies the cache management and allows the use of very small caches that can operate at link speed. This enables a performance that is very close to IP multicast.

Creating a packet train in a streaming server is relatively easy; because the nature of single-source multiple-destination applications imposes that the same data needs to be send to all clients at "the same time". In other words, the transmission of data chunks is timely synchronized. This is different in file servers, because clients might request the same data, but not at the same time. Many clients might download at the same time a popular file, but all of those that arrived at different times at the server will receive different data chunks from the file at a given point in time. One approach to cope with the larger distance in time between redundant transfers is to increase the cache size. However, this comes at the cost of more expensive caches in monetary terms and implementation complexity, which makes it hard or impossible to operate the caches at link speed.

Therefore, we examine the use of the original CacheCast implementation to improve the performance of popular downloads. The key idea to solve this problem is based on the insight that there is no need to sequentially send data chunks of a file to clients. In contrast to streaming applications, clients downloading files consume the data only after the entire file has been received. Out of order packets can be re-ordered at the client before the file is provided to the application. This property can be used at the server to send at a given point in time the same data chunk to clients that arrived at different times. Thus, a packet train can be send over the link and very small caches are sufficient. We show in this paper that fountain codes can be used to alleviate the CacheCast file server implementation. A file is a priori encoded and chunks of the encoded file are sent to the clients. Clients just need to receive data chunks until they have sufficient information to decode the file. With an implementation in ns-3 and extensive simulation studies we show that this solution clearly outperforms traditional file servers, both in terms of file server capacity and of bandwidth consumption. The more concurrent downloads, the more redundancy we can remove. As such this solution is self-scaling like P2P, but not at the cost of peer resources.

The remaining of the paper is structured as follow: the idea and basic functionality of CacheCast is presented in Sects. 2 and 3. The results of our extensive evaluation are presented in Sects. 4 and 5 concludes this work.

2   CacheCast Basics

The server architecture relies on the CacheCast mechanism to deliver the same data chunk to multiple destinations. Therefore, it is essential to understand how applications benefit from CacheCast, and how CacheCast transports data.

CacheCast is a system of packet caches operating on network links. A single cache consists of two processing elements that are installed at the link end-points. The element installed at the link entry is called Cache Management Unit (CMU) and the element installed at the link exit is called Cache Store Unit (CSU). The CMU keeps a short record of payloads that have been recently transmitted over the link. Similarly, the CSU keeps a record of recently received payloads and maintains the consistency of these records[1]. The CMU inspects packet payloads immediately before transmission. If the CMU finds the packet payload in the record of the recently transmitted packets, it substitutes the payload with a short unique identifier. Thus, only the packet header with the identifier is transmitted over the link. Upon receiving the packet on the link exit, the CSU uses the identifier to find the payload in the local record and to reconstruct the packet. The reconstructed packet is processed further in the standard way on the router.

The operation of link caches is transparent to the traffic above the link layer, i.e., the standard IP network and an IP network with link caches provide the same functionality. The IP network with link caches can transport much more efficiently the same data from a single source to multiple destinations. This is achieved by suppressing redundant payload transmissions over the network links. Since the link caches are transparent to the IP layer and above, network hosts can communicate using the standard IP based transport protocols such as UDP, TCP, or DCCP.

Link caches are designed to operate in the Internet infrastructure which is based on fast links transporting large amounts of data. To achieve high efficiency at low implementation costs, the link caches process only packets that are part of single source multiple destination data transfers. This type of transfer creates at the link layer a burst of IP packets that have different headers, but carry the same payload which can be processed very efficiently by link caches. When traversing a link with a link cache the burst of packets resembles a packet train where the first packet in the train carries payload while the remaining packets are truncated by the CMU to the header size. In order to guarantee the minimum time span of the packet burst and consequently to minimise link cache resource requirements, CacheCast introduces a new system call *msend* to the OS. The application uses the system call to send data to multiple destinations. The *msend* API resembles the standard POSIX *send* system call with the difference that

---

[1] The records can be temporally inconsistent due to link transmission errors. For further information please refer to [9].

msend takes a set of file descriptors as the input instead of only one file descriptor taken by the *send* system call. The *msend* system call operates only on the file descriptors, which are referring to network connections.

The choice of transport protocol invoked by *msend* is important, because for CacheCast we require that message boundaries are preserved when passing messages through the protocol layers. Furthermore, one of the approaches we investigate is based on the idea to not send blocks from a file in their given order, but instead adjust this order to the needs of clients. As such TCP cannot be used and we prefer DCCP over UDP since DCCP includes rate control.

3   CacheCast Server Architecture

A file server has to perform two basic tasks: *File Selection* and *File Transmission*. The file selection is initiated by a client, which selects one file from the server repository using a command set provided by the file transport protocol (FTP). The *File Transmission* is the underlying functionality which transfers the file from the server to the client. We assume that the CacheCast file server implements the *File Selection* functionality of the standard FTP server. Thus, the FTP server and the CacheCast file server differ only in how the *File Transmission* is handled. In the standard FTP, the client selects the file to download and tells the server to initiate the file transmission. The server starts forwarding the contents of the file to the client over a TCP connection. The default transfer mode in FTP is Stream mode [7]. When it is enabled FTP sends the data as a sequential stream. TCP ensures that the file is transferred correctly by dividing the data into segments, assigning sequence numbers to these segments, and issuing retransmissions when segments are lost in the network. By using the sequence numbers, TCP assures that all received segments are correctly ordered. TCP also adjusts the transmission rate to the client's available bandwidth.

The CacheCast server is designed to distribute efficiently popular files. Therefore, before we discuss how it solves the problem of reliable file transfer and transmission rate control, first we present how it achieves high efficiency when delivering the same file to multiple clients.

3.1   Synchronous Transmission

An FTP server is a multi user system, i.e. it has support for multiple clients downloading files concurrently. A client can connect to the server at any time and request any file. FTP is designed for single source, single destination transfer. Thus, for each client connected to the server there is one TCP connection. Each client is served separately on each unicast connection. When multiple clients are downloading the same file at approximately the same time, there are overlapping time periods between the download procedures. During these periods the same file is transferred to multiple clients at the same time. When the request rate to a file server is high as in the event of a flash crowd many clients connect to the server within a small time interval, creating multiple overlapping download time periods as shown in Fig. 1. Within these time periods clients are downloading the same file concurrently; however, they are receiving different parts of the file, since TCP transmits data sequentially.

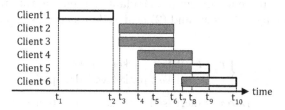

Fig. 1. Multiple clients with different arrival times downloading the same file

In order to optimize the file transmission within the overlapping time periods using CacheCast, it is necessary that individual file blocks are transmitted synchronously to all clients. However, synchronous transmission of blocks to many clients is difficult to achieve due to different arrival times of clients and even if sufficiently enough clients arrive close enough to each other in time they typically will drift apart from each other. The reason is that the available bandwidth on the paths to the clients can differ substantially.

The core idea of our approach is based on the insight that clients use the content first after it has been entirely received. The order in which the blocks of the file are sent and whether the blocks are encoded before transmission or not, is not of relevance for the client. The only important aspect for the client is that the entire file is recreated before it is passed to the client. Therefore, the server can send those blocks that are needed by several concurrent clients to achieve synchronous transmission. In particular, we have investigated two block selection schemes to achieve synchronous transmission, namely, block-by-block transmission and fountain code transmission. In addition to the block selection, rate control and end-to-end reliability has to be supported.

3.2   Rate Control

The rate control works identically for both block selection approaches. For a group of clients downloading the same file, the rate control aligns the transmission rate to the fastest client in the group. Hence, this client can take full advantage of its downlink speed which is not limited by slower clients. Since slower clients are not able to receive all blocks at the selected rate, the congestion control algorithm in DCCP will drop some packets to these clients at the sender side (i.e., it will not be passed to the network layer). With this approach all clients download the file with their individual maximum available speed.

In order to determine the fastest client in the group, the rate control uses status information returned by DCCP after block transmission attempt. The status tells whether the packet has been dropped or sent. By keeping a record of the last N transmission attempts for each client it is easy to identify the fastest client, which is the client with most packets sent. The parameter N can be used to control how fast rate control should adapt to changes. For the results presented in this paper we use $N = 100$. We use the Additive Increase Multiplicative Decrease algorithm to (1) adapt the sending rate to the available bandwidth to the fastest client, and (2) achieve fair share for multiple flows over contented links.

$$r = \begin{cases} r + I & \text{if last packet was set} \\ r/D & \text{if last packet was dropped} \end{cases} \tag{1}$$

The transmission rate r is increased with factor $I > 0$ or decreased by factor D ($0 < D < 1$). We start with an initial transmission rate of $r = 64$ kb/s. The transmission of subsequent blocks is scheduled to match the current rate r.

3.3   Block Selection and Reliability

The block-by-block transmission approach requires from the server to keep track of the blocks each client is missing at any point in time. Thus, the initial state for all blocks for a newly arrived client is MISSING. This information is used to decide to which clients each block should be sent. There are several policies to determine which block should be sent, including most wanted block and round robin. Due to its simplicity we have chosen to implement round robin in our current prototype. With this policy the block selection algorithm selects the blocks from a file in sequential order from the beginning to the end of the file and starts again at the beginning as long as there are clients downloading the file. The selected block is only sent to those clients that are missing it, i.e., the blocks state is MISSING. To achieve reliability retransmission is used. When sending a packet to a group of clients, the server starts a transmission timer for this packet and sets for each client the status of the bock to SENT. The client sends for each received packet an acknowledgement including the sequence number of the packet. If the server receives the acknowledgement before the timer expires it sets the status of the block to RECEIVED and otherwise to MISSING. Retransmission of missing blocks will then naturally happen in the next round when the block is selected again. Negative acknowledgments cannot be used, because the client cannot know which packets have been lost in the network and which ones are dropped by DCCP. One artifact of all block-by-block transmissions is that the last remaining clients can miss disjoint sets of blocks. Thus, it is no longer possible to achieve synchronous transmission.

Block selection and reliability is substantially simpler with the fountain codes [5]. With fountain codes files are encoded in such a way that any block can be used to reconstruct the original file. As such, this scheme provides Forward Error Correction. Thus, adding reliability to DCCP comes for free and all blocks are useful for all clients. No book keeping of packet states, timers, and acknowledgements are needed, a client just receives encoded packets until it is able to reconstruct the entire file. The overall architecture of our prototype with the

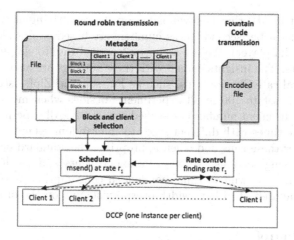

Fig. 2. Architecture of prototype implementation

two approaches is illustrated in Fig. 2. The feedback from each DCCP instance is used to determine the sending rate and to call at the proper point in time the *msend()* system call with a pointer to the selected block and the file descriptors for those clients that should receive the block.

4 Evaluation

We have implemented the above described architecture of the CacheCast file server in ns-3 and performed extensive simulation studies to evaluate it. Since this work aims at the scalability of file servers we focus our study on the outgoing link from the file server, later on called server uplink. The performance advantages of batching several client requests and sending them from a server in form of a packet train are documented in our earlier work through simulation and real world implementation. Furthermore, we have shown in [9] that CacheCast can achieve network-wide close to IP multicast performance and that it can be with great benefits incrementally deployed in the Internet.

Considering the fact that in modern networks congestion occurs at the network edges, i.e., on links attached to the server and the clients, we model those links and ignore the intermediate links. This leads us to a simple topology in which a file server is connected to a router, which in turn has n links to n clients. The bandwidth between the router and the clients is based on measurement results from [4] and ranges between 64 kb/s and 5000 kb/s. It is distributed in this range in six groups as described in Table 1.

To study the scalability of the CacheCast file server, we set the bandwidth of the link between file server and the router to 10 Mb/s such that congestion occurs. The end-to-end propagation delay between the file server and the clients is uniformly distributed between 30 ms and 50 ms, which correspond to a medium sized ISP network. The workload in the experiments consists of a file with the size of 18 MB that is downloaded by clients arriving at the server at a rate of eight clients per second (these numbers are based on download statistics of the VLC media player). We use a constant arrival rate to simplify the analysis of the results. The insights gained with these settings are also valid for more advanced arrival rate distributions, such as Poisson and Zipf distribution. The client number is set to 100 in all experiments besides when measuring system fairness where the client number is specified separately. All experiments are performed multiple times with different seeds to the random generator. We present the average over these runs and when appropriate the standard deviation.

In the following sections, we describe experiments and results of the rate control mechanism, download time, bandwidth consumption, fairness, effect of small file size, and effect of bandwidth overprovisioning on the first link.

4.1   Rate Control

The goal of the CacheCast server is to provide to all clients the shortest possible download time. Therefore, we evaluate how well the rate controller is able to adapt the transmission rate to the available bandwidth to the fastest client.

Figure 3 relates the transmission rate determined by the rate controller with the actual download speed of the fastest client over time, i.e., the ground truth. The transmission rate is, as expected, reduced over time since the fastest clients finish first and the slowest last. Furthermore, the transmission rate aligns very well with the currently fastest client. This is further supported through the data in Table 1 in the row labelled "Last client finish time" which presents the time at which the last client in each downlink speed group finishes.

Looking at the length of the time interval for the different transmission speeds we can distinguish three phases. The first one is defined by the time it takes until

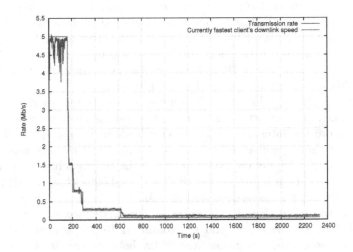

Fig. 3. Transmission rate and currently fastest client

Table 1. Client downlink speed distribution and download performances

Downlink speed [kb/s]	64	256	768	1500	3000	5000
Client share		2.8 %	4.3 %	14.3 %	23.3 %	18 %	37.5 %
Last client finish time [s]		2339.4	622.7	269.3	198.6	161.9	157.8
Single TCP download time [s]	2491	623.5	208.7	106.7	53.7	32.6

the last client with 5 Mb/s downlink speed finishes. In the second phase, the client groups with 3 Mb/s and 1.5 Mb/s downlink speed finish very briefly after the 5 Mb/s group. This can be attributed to the fact that those clients could substantially benefit from the data send during the first phase. In the third phase, the slower clients require more and more time to download the entire file and as such the transmission rate is reduced in increasing larger steps.

4.2 Download Time

We use the same settings as in the previous experiment and compare the distribution of download time for all clients served with (1) a traditional FTP server, (2) CacheCast server with original block transmission, and (3) CacheCast server with a fountain encoded file. To achieve comparability, we related the measured download times to the time it would take a single client to download the file with a TCP connection when accessing all server resources exclusively, i.e., no other clients are present. The download times for this exclusive download (called "single TCP connection") are given in Table 1 in the row labelled "Single TCP download time".

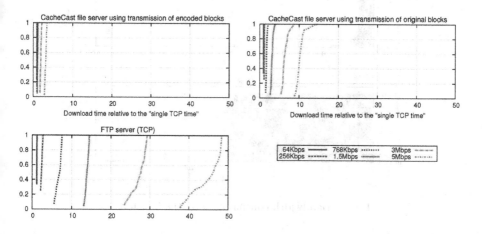

Fig. 4. Download times for FTP server and CacheCast file servers

Figure 4 shows the CDF of the download times for clients grouped by downlink speed. The relative download time increases for all servers with the downlink speed, because fast clients are more affected by congestion than slow clients. Both CacheCast implementations clearly outperform the FTP server due to the reduction of redundant transfers over the first link. There is also a clear difference in performance for the faster clients in the two CacheCast implementations, i.e., transmitting encoded blocks leads to much shorter download times.

In the following studies, we focus only on the comparison of the fountain code based CacheCast server and FTP server.

4.3   Bandwidth Consumption

One important metric for the content provider is the bandwidth consumption, especially for the server uplink. The less bandwidth is consumed per client, the more scalable the server is and less costs incur. Figure 5 illustrates the bandwidth consumption on the server uplink over time for the CacheCast and FTP servers. Both consume in the beginning of the experiment the entire bandwidth.

This seems to be contradicting to the results of the rate adaptation evaluation in Sect. 4.1, which show that the maximum transmission rate in the beginning is very close to 5 Mb/s. However, the transmission rate shows only application layer throughput to a single client while the uplink bandwidth consumption shows the resulting network traffic that carries also packet headers to all receivers. The period in which the bandwidth of the link is fully consumed is substantially shorter for the CacheCast server, since the total amount of data sent over the link is much smaller due to the redundancy reduction.

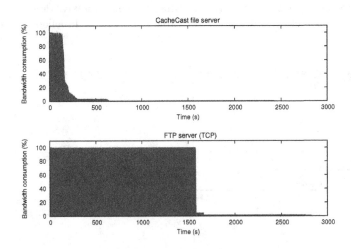

Fig. 5. Bandwidth consumption on the first link

4.4   Fairness

The previous experiments focused on transmission of a single file to multiple clients. In this experiment, we analyse how the CacheCast server distributes the uplink bandwidth capacity between two groups of clients that download different files. The CacheCast server uses DCCP, which ensures fair bandwidth sharing among concurrent data streams in the network. Since the rate controller is build on the feedback from DCCP, the core issue investigated in this experiment is the question whether it preserves the fairness achieved by DCCP.

To simplify the presentation and analysis of results, we study in this section two groups of clients that download each one file. We study how the number of clients impact fairness in experiments with 10 and 200 clients, and with different group sizes. For the 10 clients the two groups comprise of 5/5, 6/4, 7/3, 8/2, and 9/1 members; and for 200 clients the groups comprise of 100/100, 80/120, 60/140, 40/160, and 20/180 members. The download speed of all clients is set to 10 Mb/s to (1) enable each individual group to consume the entire bandwidth on the first link, and (2) to easily compare the bandwidth share. We measure the end-to-end throughput for each client of the groups and show the aggregated throughput per group. The measurements are performed when no clients are arriving or leaving the CacheCast server.

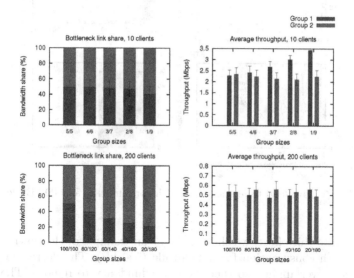

Fig. 6. Bandwidth share on first link and end-to-end throughput

The average bandwidth share on the server uplink and the average client throughput group is shown for the two client populations in Fig. 6. A small client population leads to increasing unfairness in the uplink utilization and end-to-end throughput as the group sizes differ more. However, the results from the experiment with 200 clients show that with larger groups the system achieves more even resource utilization per client. The nature of CacheCast that the ratio between the number of packets sent and the number of bytes sent is unequal leads to the small diversion from the perfect fair share.

4.5   Effect of Small Files

The performance gains with CacheCast are achieved by removing redundant pay-load in packets that are sent during a short time window. Either block reordering or fountain codes is used to send to all concurrent clients the same data block. The more clients concurrently download the same file the higher the perfor-mance gains through redundancy removal. This number of clients depends on the arrival rate and the time they spend to download the file. Given an arbi-trary arrival distribution, the less time the clients need for the download the less clients download the file at the same time. The download time is determined by the file size and the available bandwidth between client and server.

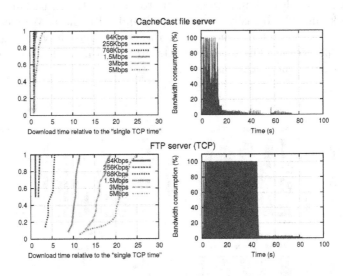

Fig. 7. Download time and bandwidth consumption for 500 kB file

To illustrate this effect, we show in Fig. 7 an example of the download time and bandwidth consumption for a small file (500 kB). The decreased file size results in less overlapping, so there is less redundancy to remove. The perfor-mance gain of the CacheCast file server has decreased compared to the 18 MB file. The average packet train length has decreased from 14 to 6.6, thus the CacheCast file server is not able to benefit as much from CacheCast as in the original experiment.

4.6   Effects of Bandwidth Overprovisioning

So far all experiments have studied cases in which congestion occurs on the first link. To study also the effects of overprovisioning of bandwidth on the first link we set the bandwidth of this link to 300 Mb/s. The results presented in Fig. 8 show that the clients of the FTP and CacheCast file server experience similar

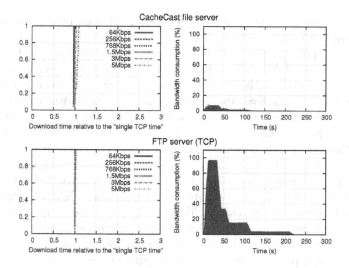

Fig. 8. Download time and bandwidth consumption for 300 Mb/s first link

download times. This is obvious, since there is no need to remove redundant network traffic if the network is overprovisioned. However, it shows also that CacheCast leads to a much lower bandwidth consumption on the first link.

5 Conclusions

This paper presents an approach to increase the scalability of file servers through link level caching with CacheCast. The main difference between the original application domain of CacheCast and file servers is that clients do not all arrive at the same time. This means that they will in a traditional file server be served with different data blocks at any given point in time, which in turn does not allow to create packet trains with the *msend()* system call. The core idea of our solution to this is to re-arrange the data blocks such that the individual data blocks are send with *msend()* to several clients. We implemented and evaluated one version based on round-robin distribution and one on fountain encoded files. The main conclusions from the evaluation are: (1) both approaches can substantially reduce the download time for clients and the bandwidth consumption of the first link, (2) the version with fountain encoded files clearly outperforms the round-robin version, mainly due to problems related to rate control, and it simplifies management tasks of the server; (3) clients of a CacheCast server get a fair bandwidth share; and (4) small files and bandwidth overprovisioning reduces the performance gain of CacheCast over FTP, but still provides benefits in terms of shorter download times (for small files) and lower bandwidth consumption. Thus, if there is more than one client downloading the same file, CacheCast increases the scalability of file servers, both on the server itself through the *msend()* call and the first link; and it reduces traffic related costs. The more concurrent clients the higher the gain without relying on other resources than the host and CacheCast enabled routers.

This paper presents the first study to use CacheCast for asynchronous file transfers. The use of fountain codes has been inspired by previous work combining fountain codes with IP multicast [6]. Many early works in this area assume that all clients have the same amount of bandwidth available. Byers et al. address this unrealistic assumption through layered multicast with several multicast groups [2]. The clients are responsible to subscribe to an appropriate subset of these layers. However, the leave latency of the Internet group management protocol makes it very hard to efficiently adapt to changing bandwidth. The strategy of dynamic layering is introduced in [1] to avoid this bottleneck. However, this results in unfair bandwidth sharing with TCP, especially when the drop tail queue size increases. Gill et al. [3] introduce a client work ahead policy to determine how reception bandwidth is allocated among the layers to protect again short-term bandwidth fluctuations. The major difference between our approach and previous works is the strength of CacheCast to achieve near IP multicast performance and maintain at the same time the end-to-end relation between client and server. In this way DCCP can adjust quickly transmission rate for each individual client to achieve full TCP friendliness.

References

1. Byers, J., Horn, G., Luby, M., Mitzenmacher, M., Shaver, W.: Flid-dl: congestion control for layered multicast. IEEE J. Sel. Areas Commun. **20**(8), 1558–1570 (2002)
2. Byers, J., Luby, M., Mitzenmacher, M.: A digital fountain approach to asynchronous reliable multicast. IEEE J. Sel. Areas Commun. **20**(8), 1528–1540 (2002)
3. Gill, P., Shi, L., Mahanti, A., Li, Z., Eager, D.L.: Scalable on-demand media streaming for heterogeneous clients. ACM Trans. Multimedia Comput. Commun. Appl. 5(1), 8:1–8:24 (2008). http://doi.acm.org/10.1145/1404880.1404888
4. Huang, C., Li, J., Ross, K.W.: Can internet video-on-demand be profitable? SIG-COMM Comput. Commun. Rev. **37**(4), 133–144 (2007)
5. MacKay, D.: Fountain codes. IEE Proc. Commun. **152**(6), 1062–1068 (2005)
6. Mitzenmacher, M.: Digital fountains: a survey and look forward. In: Information Theory Workshop, 2004, pp. 271–276. IEEE, October 2004
7. Postel, J., Reynolds, J.: File Transfer Protocol. RFC 959 (Standard), October 1985. http://www.ietf.org/rfc/rfc959.txt, updated by RFCs 2228, 2640, 2773, 3659, 5797
8. Srebrny, P., Plagemann, T., Goebel, V., Mauthe, A.: CacheCast: eliminating redundant link traffic for single source multiple destination transfer. In: Proceedings of the 2010 30th IEEE International Conference on Distributed Computing Systems (ICDCS). IEEE Computer Society, June 2010
9. Srebrny, P., Plagemann, T., Goebel, V., Mauthe, A.: No more déjà vu - eliminating redundancy with cachecast: feasibility and performance gains. IEEE/ACM Trans. Networking **21**(6), 1736–1749 (2013)

An Openflow-Based Approach
to Failure Detection and Protection
for a Multicasting Tree

Vignesh Renganathan Raja, Abhishek Pandey,
and Chung-Horng Lung[(⊠)]

Department of Systems and Computer Engineering, Carleton University,
Ottawa, ON, Canada
{vigneshrenganathanra, abhishekpandey}@cmail.carleton.ca,
chlung@sce.carleton.ca

Abstract. Software Defined Networking (SDN) has received considerable
attention for both experimental and real networks. The programmability of the
centralized control plane utilizes the global view of the network to provide better
solutions for complex problems in SDN. This results in an increase in robustness
and reliability of network functions running in SDN. This paper is motivated by
recent advancement in SDN and increasing popularity of multicasting applications by proposing a technique to increase the resiliency of multicasting in SDN.
Multicasting is a group communication technology, which uses the network
infrastructure efficiently by sending the data only once from one or multiple
sources to a group of receivers. Multicasting applications, e.g., live video
streaming and video conferencing, are popular and delay sensitive applications
in the Internet. Failures in the ongoing multicast session can cause packet losses
and delay and hence affect quality of service (QoS). In this paper, we present a
technique to protect a multicasting tree constructed by Openflow switches in
SDN. The proposed algorithm can detect link or node failures from the multicasting tree and then determines which part of the multicasting tree requires
changes in the flow table to recover from the failure. We also implement a
prototype of the algorithm in the POX controller and measure its performance
by emulating failures in different tree topologies in Mininet.

Keywords: Software defined networks · Openflow · Multicasting tree protection · POX controller · Mininet

1 Introduction

Multicasting is a group communication technology, which uses the network infrastructure efficiently by transferring the same data only once from a sender to a group of
receivers [5]. The routers involved in the multicasting session are capable of forming
multicasting trees dynamically according to the members joining and leaving the
multicasting group [11]. In the most common multicasting tree, the sender or source is
always connected to the root of the tree and the receivers are connected to the leaf
nodes of the tree. The structure of the tree may change dynamically when receivers join

© Springer International Publishing Switzerland 2015
M.C. Aguayo-Torres et al. (Eds.): WWIC 2015, LNCS 9071, pp. 211–224, 2015.
DOI: 10.1007/978-3-319-22572-2_15

or leave the multicasting session [11]. Multicasting applications like real time video conferencing and live video streaming are getting more popular and the performance of such applications relies critically on the resiliency of the multicasting tree architecture [13]. One key concern of real time multicast traffic is the delay and packet losses due to failures. To decrease the delay due to failures, it is central to protect the traffic involved from the link and node failures. There are various mechanisms proposed to protect multicasting sessions from link failures in the traditional networks [1–5]. In those methods, the failure notifications are sent via other nodes involved in the session to initiate the protection process. In practice, routing protocols and message flooding mechanism are used for topology synchronization. During the convergence period, packet losses and higher delay are inevitable and can be significant.

SDN separates the forwarding plane and the control plane from the physical networking element and runs the control plane in a logically centralized location [12]. This separation and centralization of control plane gives SDN controller the global view of the network, which can be efficiently utilized to monitor and control the network due to dynamic changes in the network. The introduction of the Openflow protocol enables the interaction between the controller and the forwarding elements or switches [10]. Using Openflow, the controller can install the flow entries to the switches according to the control applications running in the controller. Upon a failure, notifications can be sent by a switch that detects the failure directly to the SDN controller instead of flooding in the network to notify each node or as many nodes as possible. This means that the network can be automatically configured according to the way the control plane has been programmed, which reduces tremendous network complexity used in the traditional networks. Specifically, in a multicasting scenario, when a failure happens, the failure notification message can be sent to the controller rapidly and the multicast recovery process can be started immediately.

Further, in traditional networks, it is difficult for a network element to efficiently distinguish between a link and a node failure using the routing protocols [15]. To find out a node failure, routers have to identify if all links of a particular node are down, in which case the node is considered failed, which will result in high delay and packet losses and low QoS. With the combination of programmable control plane and the global view of the network topology in SDN, we can detect, protect, and restore *either link or node failures* in the network efficiently.

This paper is motivated to analyze how fast the control plane can react to protect a multicasting tree from either link or node failures in SDN. Analyzing and understanding failure restoration for real time multicasting is crucial, as multicasting becomes popular in practice. Hence, the main objective of this paper is to design the control plane architecture which responds by installing updated flow tables to the corresponding switches for link or node failures in a multicasting tree. The main contribution of this paper is to present a multicast failure protection and restoration scheme which distinguishes a *link and a node failure* in the multicasting session tree constructed by Openflow switches. The proposed scheme also responds to the failure by installing or modifying flow entries to the Openflow switches for fast recovery. To demonstrate the proposed scheme, we design a prototype in a POX controller and we measure failure detection and controller response time by emulating SDN using Mininet [9].

The rest of this paper is organized as follows. Section 2 describes the related works. Section 3 describes the controller design and the proposed algorithm for multicasting tree protection and restoration. Section 4 demonstrates the evaluation results for the failure localization and protection algorithm proposed in this paper. Finally, Sect. 5 presents the conclusions and future work.

2   Related Work

In the literature, multicasting tree protection and restoration schemes have been advocated for the optical layer or the network layer. This paper focuses on the network layer. This section describes the key component used in the current POX controller, which plays a significant role in failure detection. Following that, an existing approach for multicast protection using fast tree switching in SDN is briefly described.

In IP networks, multicast protection can be supported by proactive and reactive methods [2]. In general, the reactive methods are considered to be inefficient due to the increase in recovery time. The reason is that the backup paths or trees will be cal-culated only after the event of failure. In the proactive method, the backup paths or trees are preconfigured before the failure happens. A few approaches of proactive tree protection for multicasting sessions are discussed in [1–3]. In Dual tree algorithm [1], the protection is performed by switching over the entire primary tree to a preconfigured backup tree whenever a link failure happens. This limits the protection algorithm for a single link failure in the multicasting tree. To accommodate protection for a link or a node failure, a dual forest algorithm is proposed in [3]. The node protection scheme is performed by pre-configuring backup paths covering each link involved in the primary tree. This approach is efficient only when the network topology is capable of providing alternate paths from each node to the leaf of the multicasting tree.

To tackle the problem of switching the whole multicast tree in case of multiple link failures and to make the protection scheme proactive, a subtree based protection scheme for multicast session using MPLS was presented in [5]. According to this approach, when a multicasting tree is built from the source to destinations, it has been divided into several subtrees. A subtree is a subset of the tree that represents a complete tree by itself [5]. There are advantages using the subtree based approach:

- It minimizes the failure detection time by avoiding the notification to be sent all the way to the root of the tree.
- It makes the protection scheme efficient by providing backup paths from root of each subtree to its leaf nodes.
- When a failure happens, the changes are made only to the corresponding subtree instead of the entire tree.

In summary, the failure detection and restoration time are critical, and the pro-tection scheme must support protection for both the link and node failure for a single multicast session tree. However, the algorithm proposed in [5] does not address pro-tection of multicasting session from a node failure.

2.1   SDN Topology Discovery

A topology discovery mechanism is used in the Openflow controller to make switches aware of their neighboring nodes. It is mainly used to detect link or node failures in our approach. The *Topology Discovery* module included in the POX controller [6] is used for the discovery of any network topologies under its control. The *Topology Discovery* module uses the Link Layer Discovery Protocol (LLDP) [7] to detect the connections between the Openflow switches. The controller which executes the discovery module triggers the Openflow switches to send LLDP packets between each other. When a switch receives the LLDP packet from its neighbor, it sends an LLDP packet encapsulated in a Packet-In message to the controller. The Packet-In message has both the datapath id (DPID) and the port number of the sending and receiving switches. The controller then stores this information in the form of links. This stored information will act as a link between two Openflow switches. In this way, the controller learns the topology of the entire network under its domain. In the current POX design, the LLDP sending operation is triggered at a particular interval of time which is known as the *send cycle time* and is defined as follows:

$$\text{send cycle time} = \text{link timeout}/2 \tag{1}$$

By default the *link timeout* is set to 10. Based on the current POX controller design, when a failure happens, the *Topology Discovery* module in the controller will not be triggered until the *send cycle time* interval expires. In other words, failure detection by the controller may be delayed by an entire *send cycle time* in the worst case scenario.

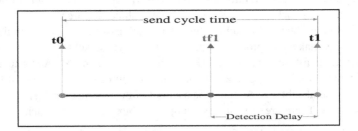

Fig. 1. Detection delay in existing Topology Discovery

As shown in Fig. 1, assume the *send cycle time* is the difference between t1 and t0. If the failure happens at time tf1, then the switches that detect the failure have to wait until t1 to send the notification to the controller. This may affect the failure detection time by several seconds, which will have a significant negative impact on packet losses, delay, and QoS. The exact value of the delay varies as the tf1 can be anywhere between the *send cycle time*. As a result, the failure detection can be much slower than the requirement, e.g., 50 ms, used for the existing carrier grade networks.

2.2 Existing Failure Protection Mechanisms in SDN

In [4], multicast protection is performed by fast tree switching. The redundant tree is calculated as soon as the primary tree is calculated and flows for both primary and redundant tree are installed in the switches. To avoid duplication of the flow tables for the same destination, they are differentiated by using unique ids. If a failure happens in a link in the primary tree, the whole tree will be switched to the pre- calculated redundant tree. This limits the approach from supporting more than one link failure. In addition, a complete diverse redundant tree may not available for some topologies.

3 Multicasting Tree Protection and Restoration for Software Defined Networks

This section discusses the proposed multicasting tree protection and restoration scheme. Figure 2 shows the high level view of SDN with Openflow POX controller for multicasting tree protection and restoration and the POX *Topology Discovery* modules. The existing *Topology Discovery* module in POX detects the failure and sends the information to the proposed *Failure Localization and Protection* module, and the *Failure Localization and Protection* module sends the flow tables to the Openflow switches according to the scheme.

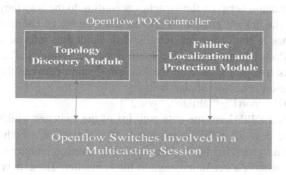

Fig. 2. Proposed Openflow Controller architecture for failure detection and protection

3.1 Assumptions

A few assumptions have been made for our proposed scheme:

- The network has a single Openflow controller. The reason is to validate the behavior and the performance of the protection and restoration algorithm. A single SDN controller is also common to many approaches in the literature.
- The failure detection time is from the time that the *Topology Discovery* module receives the notification. This is due to the limitations existing in the current POX *Topology Discovery* module as explained in Sect. 2.
- A backup path is available in a subtree from the root to the leaf nodes.

- The nodes of all the tree diagrams shown in this paper are Openflow switches and they are all directly connected to the controller. On this understanding we have avoided representing the connection between the switches and the controller in the figures.

3.2 Multicasting Tree Protection and Restoration Method for Openflow Controller

This section describes the four major operations of the multicasting tree protection and restoration algorithm for the Openflow controller. They are listed below:

- Subtree division
- Failure detection
- Failure localization
- Controller response.

Subtree Division. This is the initial stage of the whole algorithm where the unstructured tree information from the emulated topology is sorted and stored in a structured and organized manner. The need for tree sorting in this operation is due to the structure and the order of information the controller receives from the POX *Topology Discovery* module. This is performed by using hash tables, where keys and values are used to identify parents and children nodes of the tree.

When the switches are added to the network, the *Topology Discovery* module creates link information between the switches according to the way they are connected with each other. The link information is created based on the LLDP packets sent by the Openflow switches to the controller. Each switch sends this information to the controller using the Packet-In messages. The controller on receiving the Packet-In message from the switches creates a table with the link information between the two switches. The link information sent is as shown below:

Link ["DPID1", "port1", "DPID2", "port2"].

The DPID1 and DPID2 are the data path ids of the switches which share the link and port 1 is the port for DPID1 and port 2 is the port for switch DPID 2. This information is again generated by the controller in a reversed manner when the switch with DPID 2 sends the Packet-In message to the controller. These data are stored in a two dimensional hash table with switch DPIDs as its keys and the links as its values. So the first step of the tree sorting process is to delete the duplicated link information for a single link between two switches [8]. As a result of this step, we form a two dimensional hash table which has single link information for each pair of switches.

The next step is to reform the sorted link information to parent and children relationship. This step begins with the isolation of the sorted tree from the *Topology Discovery* module. The isolation is necessary to sustain the tree information for later stages when the link failure happens. After the tree is isolated, iteration through the tree is initiated. By iterating through the tree, the parents and children nodes are separated. The parent nodes are saved in a list and the children nodes are saved in a hash table with its parent DPID as its key. The parent and children information is then passed to the subtree division module.

Pseudo Code: Subtree Division

Objective: To divide the existing multicasting tree into subtrees

Components:

Parent_nodes: A list of DPIDs of all the parent nodes in the tree. The first element in this list is the root of the whole multicasting tree.

Chlid_nodes: A hash table which has parent DPID as the key and Children DPID as its value.

Subtree: A hash table which has the subtree root DPID as the key and DPID of members of the subtree as its value.

Subtree_key: A list of root nodes of divided subtrees.

Subtree_search(): A recursive function which starts searching from the root of the tree and divides into subtrees. Firstly it is invoked with the root node and later it is recursively invoked with the current node and the root of the current subtree.

Root_node: Root node of the whole tree. The first element of the *Parent_nodes* list.

Cur_node: Current node being iterated.

Input: *Parent_nodes, Children_nodes.*

Output: *Subtree, Subtree_key*

Algorithm:

```
Root_node = Parent_nodes[0]
Subtree_search (Root_node, Root_node)
Subtree_search(Cur_node,root):
   While (Child of Cur_node is not None)
   If (Child_nodes of Cur_node is > 1)
       Subtree [Cur_node].add(Child_nodes of Cur_node)
       Subtree_search(Child_nodes of Cur_node, Cur_node)
   Else
       Subtree [root].add (Child of Cur_node)
       Subtree_search (Child of Cur_node, root)
```

The subtree algorithm starts searching the tree from its root. It stores the divided subtree in a hash table where the root of the subtree as the key and its members are the values. The root of a subtree is defined when a node has more than one children. The members of a subtree are added to the subtree until the search algorithm reaches a node which has more than one child. It then saves all the roots of the subtree in a list. This is to make the search process efficient when the link failure happens. The operation of the subtree algorithm is described in the pseudo code mentioned earlier.

Failure Detection. The dynamic changes in SDN are monitored by the control applications running in the controller. Link and node failures are among the most important changes in the network that have to be dealt with efficiently. The global view of the controller makes the failure detection more efficient, as switches do not have to flood the network with messages for topology synchronization. The convergence period could be long using the flooding mechanism, which results in packet losses and long delay. Our approach is for concept demonstration and we make use of existing functionalities in POX. Failure detection is conducted using the POX *Topology Discovery* module [7].

The *Topology Discovery* module raises a *LinkEvent* whenever there is a change in the status of the links associated with the Openflow switches. The links here are Layer 2 Ethernet ports of the Openflow switches. Whenever the switch does not send the LLDP packet associated with the port connected to its neighbor, the controller will consider that the link is timed out and will fire the *LinkEvent* for link removal.

Failure Localization. The failure localization begins after the failure is detected. It is the process of identifying where exactly the failure happened and what kind of protection should be provided for the failure. Our proposed tree localization and protection module listens to the *Topology Discovery* module by registering itself to the core of the POX controller. The localization module handles the *LinkEvent* by capturing the events from the *Topology Discovery* module. The link failure is captured by using the *event. removed* part of the *LinkEvent*. This is triggered when the link is timed out. By capturing the *event.removed*, the controller gets the link information of the switches which share the link. The link information contains the DPID and the port number of the two switches which share the link. Using the DPIDs from the link information received, the algorithm searches the failed switches in the divided subtree to find which subtree the failure belongs to. The reason to do this is to identify the subtree for the changes. This search process avoids unnecessary changes to be made to the whole tree upon a failure.

The subtree search algorithm considers three scenarios to exactly find the location of the failure in a subtree. The three scenarios are explained below.

1. When either one of the DPIDs is the root of a subtree.
2. When both of the DPIDs are a root of a subtree.
3. When both of the DPIDs are the children of a subtree.

These three scenarios are important to decide where and what kind of protection to be given for a failure event.

Scenario 1: Either One of the DPIDs is the Root of a Subtree. Consider the tree shown in Fig. 3. It has 3 subtrees as shown. If a failure happens between S3 and S5, the controller receives the link failure between them and will extract the DPIDs of the two switches. With the extracted DPIDs, the localization module searches if either one of the DPDIs is in the root list of the subtree. In this case S3 is the root and S5 is not. Then it checks if the node which is not the root of a subtree is a member of the other node, which is the root of a subtree. So it checks if S5 belongs to S3. If it is, the localization

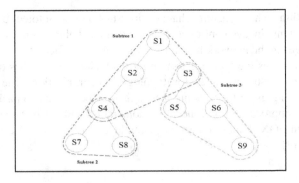

Fig. 3 A sub-divided tree of Openflow switches

module forwards the information to the protection module with root node S3 as its starting point. If the failure is between S2 and S4, the localization module checks if S2 belongs to subtree S4. But it does not, so the localization module sends the root of the subtree where S2 belongs (in this case it is S1) to the protection module.

Scenario 2: Both of the Nodes are a Root of a Subtree. In Fig. 3, if the failure happens between S1 and S3. When the localization module is satisfied that both of them are a root of a subtree, the localization module searches which node belongs to whose subtree. Thus, it searches whether S1 belongs to S3 subtree or S3 belongs to S1 subtree. Here, S3 belongs to S1 and hence the localization module initiates the protection module with S1 as the starting point.

Scenario 3: Both of the Nodes are a Child of the Same Subtree. If the localization module is not satisfied with the above two scenarios, it considers that the DPIDs of the switches are just members of a subtree. The localization module just checks what subtree does one of the nodes belong to and initiates the protection module with the root of the subtree where the failure happened as the starting point for the protection module. In Fig. 3, if the failure happens between S6 and S9, the search process will result in sending S3, the root of the subtree, as the starting point for the protection module.

Pseudo-Code: Failure Localization

Objective: To identify at which part of the subtree the failure has happened and to initialize the protection process according to the switches involved in the failure.

Components:

Failed_switches: A list of DPIDs of the switches involved in a failure event.

Failed_links: A list of the links involved in the failure. A link has DPID and port number of two switches involved in the failure.

Subtree_root: A set of root nodes of the divided subtrees.

S1 and S2: Switches are directly connected to the failed link.

Input: *Failed_link(s)*

Output: Invoking Protection function with the exact switch where the flow table has to be installed.

Algorithm:

```
For all switches in Failed_switches
    If (S1 or S2 is in Subtree_root)
        If (S1 is in Subtree_root but not S2)
            Execute Failure_protection (S1, S1, S2)
        Else if (S2 is in Subtree_root but not S1)
            Execute Failure_protection(S2, S1, S2)
        Else
            If (S1 is the Subtree root of S2)
                Execute the Failure_protection (S1, S1, S2)
            Else if (S2 is the Subtree root of S1)
                Execute the Failure_protection (S2. S1, S2)
    Else
        Find the Subtree_root of S1 and S2 and execute Failure_protection
        (Subtree_root, S1, S2).
```

All the steps to localize the failure explained earlier require tree isolation. The reason is that when a failure happens, the link information gets deleted from the *Topology Discovery* module and hence will change all the information to hash tables associated with it. Without isolation, the entry in the hash tables will also be removed and the search process cannot identify the location of the failure in the subtree.

Failure Protection. Failure Protection is initiated after the failure is localized. This module performs two major functions. One is to determine whether the failure is a link or a node failure and the other one is to send flow table modifications to the switches responsible for protecting the switches from failure. For the traditional networks, network nodes cannot efficiently distinguish link or node (neighbor) failures with the routing protocols. However, with SDN, the controller can distinguish them as switches can send notification directly connected to the controller. The difference is described below:

Determination of Link and Node Failure. Whenever the failure is detected by the *LinkEvent* handler, the ports associated with each switches involved in the failure is added to a *failed_ports*. The *failed_ports* is later used to count whether the number of ports belongs to the switches involved in the failure is equal to the total number of ports in that switch, i.e., all ports of a switch have failed. When the result is true, we initiate the node failure function, if it is not we consider it as a general link failure.

Node Failure. This function performs two quick searches. One is to identify if the node which undergone failure is a root node. If the node is a root, then the controller initiates the flow installation function with the root of the higher level subtree where the failed node belongs to. If the node is not a root, the controller initiates the flow installation function with the root of its own subtree. For example in Fig. 3 if the node S4 has a node failure, then the controller will respond to S1. But if S6 failed, the controller will still respond to node S3.

Link Failure. Link failure is initiated if the condition for the node failure is false. For link failure, the controller just initiates the flow installation function with respect to the node DPID it gets from the flow localization module. For example, in Fig. 3, when a link failure happens between S3 and S5, then the Link Failure function will make changes to S3, as it is the root node of the subtree where the failure happened.

Flow Modification. The flow modification function installs new flows to switches based on the DPIDs it receives. Since we are emulating only the tree topology in Mininet we install flow tables to the responsible switch to show that the controller notifies it successfully.

When the flow modification function receives the DPID of the switch where the new flow has to be installed, the Controller creates the Openflow flow modification message with a unique cookie id. According to Openflow, cookie is an identifier for a flow table installed in an Openflow switch. Each flow table installed in an Openflow switch will have a unique cookie id and the protection module sets the DPID of the switch involved in the failure as the cookie id of the flow table installed to recover the failure. This is done to remove the flows when the primary link is up again. Then the Openflow flow modification messages with the cookie id and action messages are sent to the corresponding Openflow switches.

Pseudo Code: Failure Protection

Assumption: Backup paths are available from the root of each subtree to its leaf nodes

Objective: To determine if it is a link or node failure and to modify or install flow tables to the corresponding switches.

Components:

- *Node_failure()*: A method which determines the switch where the flow table should be modified in case of node failure. Triggers flow installation.
- *Link_failure()*: A method which determines the switch to which the flow table should be modified in case of link failure. Triggers flow installation.
- *Failure_protection()*: A method which determines if it is a link or node failure and triggers the corresponding action for the failure.
- *Flow_installation()*: A method which installs or modifies the flow tables. It takes *root* node as an argument to install flows to recover from the failure.
- *failed_ports*: Tracks the number of ports failed in each switch.
- *fs1, fs2*: DPIDs of the Switches involved in the failure. This argument is passed by the *Failure_Localization* module.
- *failed_root*: Root node identified by the *Failure_localization* module to which flows are to be installed.
- *max*: Maximum number of ports in a switch

Algorithm:

```
Failure_protection (failed_root, fs1, fs2):
    If (failed_ports of fs1 or fs2 == max)
        If (failed_ports of fs1 == max)
            Node_failure (failed_root, fs1)
        Else
            Node_failure (failed_root, fs2)
    Else
        Link_failure(failed_root)


Node_failure (failed_root, fs):
    If (fs not in Subtree [root])
        Flow_installation (failed_root)
    Else
        For (all root in Subtree)
            If (failed_root in Subtree [root])
                Flow_installation (root)


Link_failure (failed_root):
    Flow_installation (failed_root)


Flow_installation (root):
    target = root
    message = Openflow_mod()
    message.command = Add flow table
    connection = Openflow.getconnection(target)
    connection.send(message)
```

4 Experimental Results

This section presents the experimental results and analysis of the proposed multicasting failure localization and protection algorithm with respect to the failure localization time and the failure recovery time using the Mininet environment.

4.1 Experiment Setup

The focus of the experiments is failure localization and protection algorithms which are implemented in the Openflow POX controller. Failure detection is realized using the *Topology Discovery* module in POX which can be replaced with other standards. The real instances of Openflow switches representing a multicasting tree session and the POX controller are emulated in Mininet [9]. Mininet is a network emulation framework, which emulates real instances of OpenVSwitches and an Openflow controller. We run Mininet on a virtual machine (VirtualBox 4.2.16) which is running on top of the Windows 7 64-bit operating system and Intel i7-3770 CPU with 3.40 GHz processing power and has 16 GB of RAM installed.

Figure 3 shows the network topology, which has 9 OpenflowVSwitches connected to the POX controller. Both switches and the controller are running in the same virtual machine. The controller is running the *Topology Discovery* module, the multicasting failure localization module and protection module. The performance of the controller is evaluated by observing the failure localization time and the failure recovery time after the failure has been detected. We create failures by randomly making the link between two switches down by using Mininet s Command Line Interface. We failed each link between each pair of switches and repeated the experiment 10 times per pair. We calculated the average failure localization time and failure recovery time. The results of the experiments are discussed in detail in the following section.

4.2 Experimental Results

Failure Localization Time. Failure Localization time is the time interval from which the multicast localization and protection module gets the link failure information from the *Topology Discovery* module to the time it finds the exact failure location. This shows the time taken by the controller to search through the hash-tables where the subtrees are stored.

Table 1 shows the average failure localization time for failure between different pairs of switches. As depicted in Table 1, the average failure localization time is small, mostly less than 40 μs. The results for the failure between nodes S3-S5 and S2-S4 is higher than others because of the Scenario 1 discussed earlier. The reason is that the search process is performed on both the subtree root list and the hash-table to make sure which node is the root and which is a member of the root. The failure between the non-root nodes takes more time when compared with others due to the increase in the number of searches to find the location of the failure in a subtree.

Table 1. Average Failure Localization Time

Failure between nodes	Average Failure Localization Time (μs)	Standard Deviation
S1-S3	33.6	0.051
S1-S2	40.5	0.042
S3-S6	15.9	0.004
S3-S5	44.2	0.013
S2-S4	65.1	0.048
S6-S9	18.5	0.042
S4-S7	23.8	0.022
S4-S8	26.6	0.024

Failure Recovery Time. Failure Recovery time is the total time taken from which the controller receives the failure notification from the *Topology Discovery* module to the time at which the new flow tables are installed in the Openflow switches. This also includes the failure localization time. Let T_L be the Failure Localization time (as discussed in the previous subsection) and T_C be the time taken by the controller to respond to the failure after the failure localization. Then the Failure Recovery Time T_R is,

$$T_R = T_L + T_C \qquad (2)$$

Table 2 shows the results for the average failure recovery time for the failures between different pairs of switches. As explained earlier, the response time for the failure between S3-S5 and S2-S4 is higher because of the delay in failure localization. But as a whole the total response time falls below 0.5 ms. This indicates that the algorithm is efficient in reacting to failures in a multicasting session in SDN.

Table 2. Average Failure Recovery Time

Failure Between Nodes	Average Failure Recovery Time (ms)	Standard Deviation
S1-S3	0.14	0.057
S1-S2	0.20	0.154
S3-S6	0.14	0.058
S3-S5	0.48	0.254
S2-S4	0.44	0.245
S6-S9	0.31	0.230
S4-S7	0.32	0.222
S4-S8	0.15	0.037

5 Conclusions and Future Work

Multicasting becomes more important in practical applications. This paper presented an approach to multicast tree protection and restoration for SDN. The proposed approach was designed based on subtree protection and restoration and mainly focused on protecting and restoring failure at the network level of the ongoing multicasting session. The main benefit of the proposed scheme is that it is more efficient to identify subtrees as opposed to build an entire redundant backup tree as used in other approaches. A number of experiments have been performed using the Mininet. The results showed that the restoration time was short from the point of failure detection.

Some of the key areas in which this work can be extended are described as follows:

The existing standard *Topology Discovery* module [7] in the POX controller has several limitations on detecting the failure quickly. The reason is that the module is not event triggered; instead it checks the connection between the Openflow switches periodically. We are modifying the existing discovery module event so that the event can be triggered in a much shorter time to reduce failure detection time. In traditional networks, Bidirectional Forwarding Detection (BFD) protocol [14] has been used for fast failure detection. One direction is to integrate BFD into POX or SDN Openflow.

The algorithm assumes a central controller. For large networks, multiple distributed controllers can be deployed. One direction is to covert the algorithm into a distributed algorithm for multiple controllers.

References

1. Fei, J.C., Gerla, M., Cavendish, D.: A "Dual-Tree" scheme for fault-tolerant multicast. In: Proceedings of ICC, pp. 690–694, Jun 2001
2. Zhou, Y., Zhang, Y.: An aggregated multicast fault tolerant approach based on sibling node backup in MPLS. In: Proceedings of ICIECS, pp. 1–4, Dec 2009
3. Saidi, M.Y., Cousin, B., Molnar, M.: Improved dual-forest for multicast protection. In: Proceedings of NGI (2006)
4. Kotani, D., Suzuki, K., Shimonishi, H.: A design and implementation of openflow con-troller handling IP muticast with fast tree switching. In: Proceedings of SAINT, pp. 60–67 (2012)
5. Wei, G., Lung, C.-H., Srinivasan, A.: Protecting a MPLS multicast session tree with bounded switchover time. In: Proceedings of SPECTS, pp. 236–243, July 2010
6. Congdon, P.: Link Layer Discovery Protocol, RFC 2922, July 2002
7. POX Topology Discovery. https://github.com/noxrepo/pox/blob/carp/pox/openflow/discovery.py. Accessed in June 2014
8. POX Spanning Tree. https://github.com/noxrepo/pox/blob/carp/pox/openflow/spanning_tree.py. Accessed in June 2014
9. Lantz, B., Heller, B., McKeown, N.: A network in a laptop: rapid prototyping for soft-ware-defined networks. In: Proceedings of Workshop on Hot Topics in Networks, pp. 20–21 (2010)
10. McKewon, N., Anderson, T., Peterson, G., Rexford, J., Shenker, S., Tuner, J.: OpenFlow: enabling innovation in campus networks. SIGCOMM Rev. **38**(2), 69–74 (2008)
11. Cain, B., et al.: Internet Group Management Protocol, Version 3. RFC 3376, Oct 2002
12. Open Networking Foundation, "Software-Defined Networking: The New Norm for Networks", White Paper, 13 April 2012
13. Xu, X.R., Myres, A.C., Zhang, H., Yavatkar, R.: Resilient multicast support for continuous-media applications. In: Proceedings of NOSSDAV, May 1997
14. Katz, D., Ward, D.: Bidirectional Forwarding Detection, IETF RFCs 5880, June 2010
15. Osborne, E., Simha, A.: Traffic Engineering with MPLS. Cisco Press, Indianapolis (2002)

A Hierarchical Classification Model of QoE Influence Factors

Lamine Amour$^{(\boxtimes)}$, Sami Souihi, Said Hoceini, and Abdelhamid Mellouk

Networks and Telecommunications Department and LiSSi Laboratory - IUT C/V,
University of Paris-Est Créteil VdM, Créteil, France
{lamine.amour,sami.souihi,hoceini,mellouk}@u-pec.fr

Abstract. Quality of Service (QoS) optimization are not sufficient to ensure users needs. That's why, operators are investigating a new concept called Quality of Experience (QoE), to evaluate the real quality perceived by users. This concept becomes more and more important, but still hard to estimate. This estimation can be influenced by a lot of factors called: Quality of Experience Influence Factors (QoE IFs). In this work, we survey and review existing approaches to classify QoE IFs. Then, we present a new modular and extensible classification architecture. Finally, regarding the proposed classification, we evaluate some QoE estimation approaches to highlight the fact that categories do not affect in the same the user perception.

Keywords: Quality of Experience (QoE) · Mobile environment · Quality of Experience Influence Factors (QoE IFs) · Quality of Service (QoS)

1 Introduction

Recently, computer networks shift from traditional paradigms to a new one named: Human-centric networks. In this kind of networks, traditional monitoring and management approaches based only on Quality of Service (QoS) optimization are not sufficient to ensure user's needs. That's why, operators are investigating a new concept called Quality of Experience (QoE), to evaluate the real quality perceived by users. The term of the Quality of Experience has been proposed by Dr. D. Norman in 1986, in the context of designing a user-centered services [9]. Several metrics, called Quality of Experience Influence Factors (QoE IFs) [7], can affect the perceived quality by the user. These factors are closely related to human perception and could potentially serve as more valuable quality indicator for all system's actors (user, service and network provider,...). From the users side, it ensures to have the best perceived service regardless their mobility and their context. From the providers side, the QoE helps them to provide, restore and ensure the best service to their users, into decrease the churn rate and increase their benefit.

Although many works addressing QoE concept have been proposed in the literature, this concept is still hard to estimate. For example, in the case of

© Springer International Publishing Switzerland 2015
M.C. Aguayo-Torres et al. (Eds.): WWIC 2015, LNCS 9071, pp. 225–238, 2015.
DOI: 10.1007/978-3-319-22572-2_16

mobile environments, the QoE is used in several contexts (Video on Demand (VoD), Gaming, Voice over IP (VoIP), ...). In each one of these, QoE IFs (network parameters, application parameters, localization, context, ...) impacting it [3, 4, 7]. That's why, to try to deal with the QoE estimation issue, a fundamental methodological reorientation is needed. To address this issue three steps were required. (i) Find all QoE IFs; (ii) propose a modeling architecture to organize them; (iii) propose an adaptive QoE estimation method which ensure the real perception for the user. In this paper we focus on the first two steps. In Sect. 2, we present an overview of a set of modeling QoE IFs. In Sect. 3, we detail our contribution by explaining the proposed modular and hierarchical architecture in order to organize these factors. Then, we compare the discriminant versus the non discriminant aspect in order to evaluate the importance of the impact of each QoE IFs category on the user perception. Finally, we conclude our work by giving some perspectives.

2   Related Work

With a telecommunication's industry progress, a rapid technological development in networks had been made. This development allows user to use a lot of services in different context (VoD, Gaming, VoIP, ...). It's implying also that the user is influenced by a huge number of parameters in addition to their specific factors (level studies, gender, knowledge...). These parameters can be provided by different system entities such as service provider, network operator and/or the user itself.

Ickin et al. [7] call all these parameters: Quality of Experience Influence Factors (QoE IFs), and define them as *"any characteristic of a user, system, service, application, or context whose actual state or setting may have influence on the Quality of Experience for the user"*. To present these factors, many works have been proposed to classify the QoE IFs. In this section, we will present some of them:

- Stankiewicz and Jajszczyk [17] classified the QoE IFs into three groups: QoS factors, Grade of Service (*GoS*) factors, and Quality of Resilience (*QoR*) factors. The authors underline that the implementation of each factor in the appropriate group is crucial for achieving high QoE.
- Matulin and Š. Mrvelj [11] presented an evaluation of the factors affecting QoE in four levels: *Core network* is the first level, which can be measured by the parameters of quality of service. The *access network* is the second one. Authors explain that to obtain an accurate level of user perception desired, a minimum access network performance levels must be ensured. The third level is the *hardware quality*. It presents Quality of design (interfaces), perception, service price, security and reliability. The last level concerns the *user*. It is affected by various psychological measures, as the previous user experience, the expectations, the emotional states (status, feelings) and other parameters that must be scrutinized by subjective tests (usually through surveys).

- Ickin et al. [7] organize the QoE IFs into two parts: *applications* and *contexts*. In the first part, the authors have collected QoE factors in thirteen categories based on mobile applications (e.g.: Android standard, Web or e-mail applications). In addition, they also mention: Application Interface's Design, Application Performance and Battery. In the second part, they describe the user context and the conducted experimentation has been done. The applications were used of 80 % of the time (in home, in the office and in the school).
- Callet et al. [4] organize QoE IFs into three categories, namely *Human IF*, *System IF* and *Context IF*. The authors define *Human IF* as any variant or invariant property or characteristic of a human user. It can indicate the demographic and socio-economic background, the physical and mental constitution, or the user's emotional state. *Human IFs* are complex, since they refer to the inner world of the individual, their ideas, their background, their feeling and sensations. They explain also that *System IFs* refers to properties and characteristics that determine the technically produced quality of an application or service as: coding, transmission, storage, rendering, reproduction/display and ROM (Read Only Memory) content. Moreover, they explain also that *Context IFs* refer to:
  - spatial aspects: such as the location and space characteristics,
  - temporal aspects: such as the time of day,
  - economic aspects: such as the device cost and telephone subscription price,
  - social aspects, such as the presence of other people in the same hall during a video conference.
- Song et al. [16] summarize seven frames by dividing all parameters in three categories, as follows:
  - User: Emotion, Needs, Prior experiences, Perceptions, Expectations Motivation, Profile (age, sex, preference, skill/knowledge), Physical resources.
  - Product/System/Service: Product appearance, Complexity, Functionality, Usability, Aesthetic quality, Interactivity.
  - Context: Context of use, Physical context, Social context, Culture context, Temporal and task.
- Using the same summarization as the last one, Brooks et al. [3] resume seven services (Data conferencing, Real-time text, Multimedia conferencing .. etc) to give off a bucking with six categories:
  - User choice (Reliability, Cost-benefit...).
  - Technical parameters (Delay, Packet loss, Frame-rate).
  - User appearance (Head only or Head-and-torso, Eye contact).
  - Group communication (Multi-point communication, Window configuration).
  - Purpose of communication (Business communication, Decision making).
  - User groups (Using a foreign language, Elderly persons at home).
- Moor et al. [12] propose a modular architecture based on layers using web agents. This architecture consists of four layers: *QoS monitoring entity* (Device, Infrastructure, Network, Application), *contextual monitoring entity* (Location, mobility, sensors, other running applications), *experience monitoring entity* (feedback) and *user module* (rules, experiences). The authors

indicate that the parameters of a third layer are explicitly obtained while the other layers are obtained implicitly. This model has the advantage that it's a robust measurement approach that allows the modeling of QoE IFs for mobile multimedia applications. In addition, it is easy to implement and it combines the objective and subjective experimental components.

According to Balachandran et al. [2], despite this broad consensus, our understanding of Internet video QoE is limited. The author explained that the reason is that Internet video introduces new effects with respect to both quality and experience. In fact, traditional methods of quantifying experience through Mean Opinion Scores (MOS) are now replaced by metrics from the SLA (Service-Level Agreement) such as viewing time and number of visits that more directly impact content provider's business objectives. The study highlights the complex relationship between these parameters and the decision to drop the viewing of the video in *NetFix* provider.

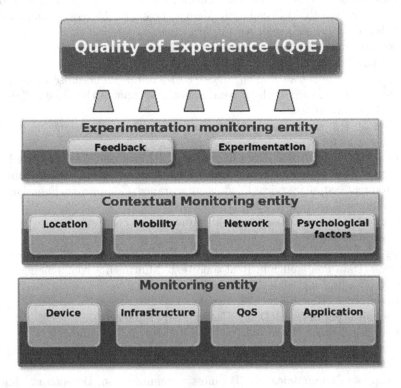

Fig. 1. Hierarchical architecture classifying QoE influence factors (QoE IFs).

3   New Modular Architecture QoE Influence Factors (MaQoEiFs)

There are many publications in the literature that address the problem of modeling parameters affecting user perception (QoE IFs). In the Sect. 2, we have given some of them. Despite of these works, we focus our proposal in this paper to propose a generic model for mobile applications.

Our proposal is based on a new hierarchical and modular architecture to classify QoE IFs. This architecture considers a large number of QoE IFs and it can be extended according to the future expectations of system's actors. In fact, it can model the various service's factors used (real-time services, IPTV, VoD, social networking, gaming, ...), and different communication technologies types (User centric network, Centric network information, Internet of Thing, Spontaneous networks ...). Furthermore, it takes account a new metrics from the SLA engagement measures such as viewing time and number of visits. Our classification is composed of three layers: Monitoring entity, Contextual monitoring entity and Experience monitoring entity. In addition, each layer is composed of modules as shown in Fig. 1. Other way, a key aspect of our work is also the classification method of the QoE IFs into subcategories (QoD, QoS, QoA ... etc.) presented in Sect. 3.2.

3.1   Monitoring Entity

This first layer contains four modules which are described as follows (Fig. 2):

Terminal Parameters: With the rapid advances in technology, there has been a proliferation of new multimedia services. In fact, different terminal types are deployed such as computers, smart phones, tablets, TV and PDA, which also differ from each other by several parameters: screen resolution, processor, SDK version, ...

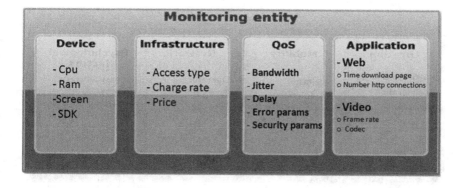

Fig. 2. Monitoring entity.

Infrastructure Parameters: Network providers may evaluate the subscriber QoE using QoS parameters, but also taking into account information related to the used infrastructure such as: *access type*, *cell's loading rate*, *telephone subscription prices*, ...

QoS Parameters: QoS parameters reflect the network state and have direct impact on the QoE. Their degradation necessarily involves a bad user perception.

Applications Parameters: The huge number of services and applications implies different properties and characteristics that have a significant impact on the QoE. As an example, we can note: (i) video streaming affected by *the buffer* and *the codec type*. (ii) web service influenced by *web page downloading time* and *Http sessions number*.

3.2   Contextual Monitoring Entity

This second layer covers all contextual information about the user. It is composed of four parts (Fig. 3):

Location Parameters: User can easily be located through GPS coordinates, cell identifier or the cell location (x, y, z).

Mobility Parameters: In the community of ubiquitous and context management, mobility remains an important research field. The estimation of this parameter can be based on terminal characteristics as sensor acceleration and terminal velocity.

Network Parameters: To evaluate the QoE, various information regarding network can be collected: operator name, network type or network BSSID identifier.

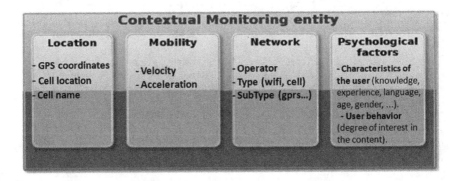

Fig. 3. Contextual monitoring entity.

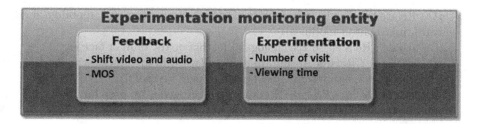

Fig. 4. Experimentation monitoring entity.

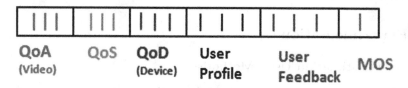

Fig. 5. Sample dataset presentation.

Psychological Factors: The user's perception can be different from one person to another, and it depends on several factors that are related to his experience, his environment and preferences. In this context, we can characterize the parameters that are set as follows:

- User characteristics (knowledge, experience, language, age, gender, ...).
- User behavior (degree of interest for the content).
- Physiognomy characteristic (Galvanic skin response).
- Sensors (temperature places, luminosity ...).

3.3 Experimentation Monitoring Entity

This layer shows the experimental methodology and collecting feedbacks. In the case of subjective measurements. It lets towards gathering explicit feedback in the form of questionnaires and pictograph feedback (e.g. pushing a red button if things go wrong) (Fig. 4).

3.4 Categories

Let's define a set of notations used to present our QoE IFs categories. The developed notation is defined according to the source parameters (System's actors: user, service provider, network operator...) as shown in the following figure (Fig. 5):

  Where:

- QoA : Related to Application parameters.
- QoS : Related to Infrastructure and QoS parameters.

- *QoD* : Related to Device parameters (Device module, location, mobility and network information modules).
- *UserProfile* : Related to Psychological factors or the human factors.
- *UserFeedBack* : Related to information collected from the experimentation entity (the user answers some questions that will be useful).
- *MOS* (*MeanOpinionScore*) : Represents score given by user for the global quality of the service (application).

This notation allows us to obtain as much as possible the influence degree of each category on the MOS.

4   Experimentation

4.1   QoE Estimation Used Methods

To evaluate our proposed approach of QoE IFs classification, we conducted two evaluations using six QoE estimation methods based on [2,8,13], shown in Table 1. The first one is a non discriminant evaluation (considering all QoE IFs) and the second one is a discriminant evaluation to highlight the fact that categories do not affect in the same the user perception.

(a) Naive Bayes (NB). Bayes (NB) classifier is based on Naive Bayes theorem. It simplifies learning assuming that the features are independent for a given class. With Naive Bays, the parameters for each term can be learned separately. Furthermore, it simplifies and speeds up the calculation operations. Note that parameter estimation for naive Bayesian models can be based in some cases on the maximum likelihood [13].

(b) Decision Tree. A decision tree is a decision support tool that is based on the representation of the problem in tree form. The different results are represented by the leaves. This algorithm is characterized by legibility, execution speed and the limited number of needed hypothesis. One of the most used implementation is the "*C*4.5" proposed by John Ross Quinlan in 2003 [15].

Table 1. QoE estimation used methods.

Method
Native Bays (NB) [13]
Decision Trees (DT) [15]
Random Forest (RF) [10]
Support Vector Machine (SVM) [6]
Random Neural Network (RNN) [1]
Adaptive Neuro Fuzzy Inference System (ANFIS) [14]

(c) **Random Forest (RF).** Random Forests (RF) is a classifier that uses multiple decision trees to improve prediction results. It combines the random subspaces concepts and modern statistical inference methods (bagging). In RF classification, the input vector is submitted to each RF tree for a vote (choose his class). The selected class is the one with the highest number of votes [10].

(d) **Support Vector Machines.** Support Vector Machines (SVM) is a classification method, used to solve the two-class-pattern recognition problem. It analyzes the data and tries to identify patterns so that a classification can be done. The main idea is to find the optimal separating hyper-plane between two classes, by maximizing the margin between the closest points of these two classes [6].

(e) **Random Neural Networks.** Random neural networks (RNN) are a variant of neural networks. In RNN, neurons may not function continuously, but exchange signals periodically. These signals can be either excitatory or inhibitory: excitatory, they will increase the potential of the neuron that receives them; inhibitors, they are going to reduce this potential. If this potential is positive, then the neuron may itself transmit signals [1].

(f) **ANFIS (Adaptive Neuro Fuzzy Inference System (ANFIS)).** ANFIS is a Fuzzy Inference System (FIS), which membership function parameters are adjusted using either a back propagation algorithm or a combination of this latter and a least squares method. This method is based on Takagi-Sugeno fuzzy inference system and it integrates both neural networks and fuzzy logic principles proposed by Zadeh in 1965 [14].

Table 2. Overall tested conditions.

Parameter	Description
Video	- **Types:** High motion, average motion and slow motion
	- **Duration:** 10 s
	- **Video resolution:** 500 × 300
	- **Video codec:** 360p (SD)
Device	- **Types:** Smartphone, Laptop and Netbook
Send bit rate (kbps)	600, 800, 1000
Frame rate (frps)	10, 15, 30
Link bandwidth (Mbps)	1, 1.5, 2
Packet loss rate (%)	0, 5, 10
Jitter (ms)	0, 5, 10

4.2 Dataset

For all the experiments shown in this paper, we used a dataset collected in our laboratory. It concerns the video service where the MOS value for each sample was calculated using the ACR (Absolute Category Rating) according to the recommendations of the ITU-T (Telecommunication Standardization Sector: forth in ITU-T recommendation P.910). In this experiment, each user has tested 81 combinations. All members were students or researchers from different disciplines aged 17 to 40 years with few or no experience of this kind of evaluation.

This database contains 243 samples with 9 parameters: device type (QoD), device resolution (QoD), screen (QoD), video content (movement level) (QoA), send bit rate (QoA), video frame rate(QoA), bandwidth (QoS), jitter (QoS) and packet error rate (QoS). Table 2 summarize the tested conditions.

In fact, two studies were performed in this experimentation. In the first one, we evaluate the impact of our classification on the user perception including all parameters (Non discriminant study). In the second one, we evaluate the impact using just one of the QoE IFs categories (Discriminant study).

These evaluations are performed under $Weka$ [18] or R software [5]. These tools have produced many outputs providing information about the estimation and the error rate calculating.

4.3 A Non Discriminant Study

The first evaluation concerns a non discriminant study (considering all QoE IFs parameters). We measure the Mean Absolute Error rate (MAE) (shown in equation 01) for each studied QoE estimation method (shown in Table 1) and compare them.

$$MAE = \frac{1}{n} \sum_{1}^{n} |f_i - y_i| \tag{1}$$

where: f_i is the prediction of MOS, y_i is the true value of the MOS and n is the total number of the considered samples. The results are illustrated in the Table 3.

Table 3. Mean Absolute Error (MAE) -All parameters-.

Method	NB	DT	RF	SVM	RNN	ANFIS	Average
MAE	0.1392	0.1156	0.1170	0.1119	0.1156	0.1143	0.1195

As we see, there are not a huge difference among the error rate of these methods, where the difference between the best estimation method and the less one is: 2 %. The results are illustrated in the Fig. 6. A (All $QoE\ IFs - QoE$).

Despite these estimation methods have acceptable results (approximately), using QoE IFs categories without weighting can produce a worse estimation result then expected. In fact, QoE IFs are inter-dependent. For example, according to [2], streaming video at a higher bitrate would lead to better quality. However, it would take longer for the video player buffer to sufficiently fill up in order to start playback. In order to improve the QoE estimation we need to study the importance of each QoE IFs category on the estimation and their interdependence. That's why, we will address separately the impact of the QoE IFs categories (Discriminant study) in the next section.

4.4 A Discriminant Study

Figure 6 (B, C and D) represents the obtained results by the different studied estimation methods considering one category at a time (summarized in Table 4).

Table 4. Mean Absolute Error (MAE) -QoD/QoS/QoA-.

Method	NB	DT	RF	SVM	RNN	ANFIS	Average
QoD	0.2209	0.2224	0.2232	0.1514	0.2213	0.1917	0.2052
QoS	0.1480	0.1400	0.1288	0.1004	0.1300	0.1227	0.1283
QoA	0.1622	0.1681	0.1601	0.1284	0.1624	0.1295	0.1518

As shown these figures, the SVM estimation gives better results than others studied methods in term of Mean average error independently of the QoE IF category (where the MAE of the SVM presents: 12 % compared to $ANFIS = 14\,\%$,

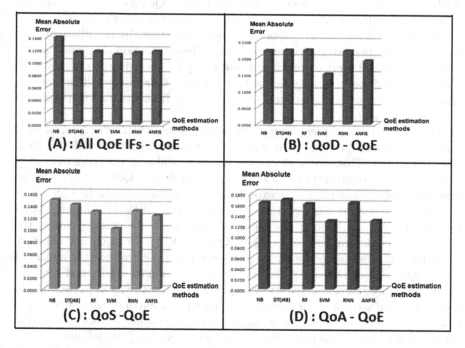

Fig. 6. Mean Absolute Error (MAE) for the parameter chosen using No discriminant and discriminant study.

$RNN = DT = RF = 16\%$ and $NB = 17\%$). In addition, these figures show that we can estimate roughly the user perception using only one category. Another conclusion is in some cases (QoS category), the obtained results using one category is better than the obtained ones using all categories. This fact, confirms the assumption made by [2] about the interaction between metrics: "Naturally, the various quality metrics are interdependent on each other".

4.5   Discussion

Except for the SVM approach, using all QoE IFs categories produces a better user's perception estimation than using each one of them separately (average MAE based on only one QoE IF category: $QoD = 25\%$, $QoS = 13\%$ and $QoA = 15\%$ versus considering all categories 10%). However, the interaction between parameters may lead to worse results than expected (e.g. SVM).

The experiment allowed us to confirm that the user perception estimation accuracy can be improved by considering a large number of QoE IFs. In addition, these QoE IFs should be weighed according to the context. Our hierarchical classification model takes into account this weighting.

5   Conclusion

With the emergence of the human-centric-networks, Quality of service (QoS) is being not enough to evaluate the system's performance. That's why Quality of Experience metrics have being more and more important. In fact, these metrics tends to be widely used as an input to measure the satisfaction of system's actors (user, network and service provider). However, QoE is very hard to estimate. To address the QoE estimation issue, the first step is to determinate all factors that influence the user perception commonly called: QoE Influence Factors (QoE IFs) and organize them.

This paper starts by presenting and reviewing some of QoE IFs classifications. Each one of them has some advantages, but remained however suffering from some drawbacks. That's why we propose a new modular architecture to classify QoE IFs. This architecture considers a large number of QoE IFs and can be extended according to the future expectations of system's actors. In addition, it can be used in several user's contexts (Video on Demand (VoD), Gaming, Voice over IP (VoIP), ...). Another key aspect of our work is the classification of the all QoE IFs on several categories (QoD, QoS, QoA ...). To study and compare the impact of these categories on the user perception, we evaluate the impact of our classification on the user perception (Non Discriminant study) and compare them separately (Discriminant study). QoS category is the most impacting the user perception according our experimentation results. Furthermore, using all the QoE IFs categories with the same importance can produce a worse estimation results then expected. As perspective, we continue working on QoE weights and improve the experimentation in order to build bigger and consistent dataset.

Acknowledgment. This work has been funded by LiSSi laboratory from the UPEC university in the framework of the French cooperative project PoQEMoN, *Pôle de Compétitivité Systematic* (FUI 16).

References

1. Olugbara, O.O., Abe, B.T., Marwala, T.: Hyperspectral image classification using random forests and neural networks. In: Proceedings of the World Congress on Engineering and Computer Science 2012, vol. I, WCECS 2012, San Francisco, USA, 24–26 October 2012
2. Balachandran, A., Sekar, V., Akella, A., Seshan, S., Stoica, I., Zhang, H.: Developing a predictive model of quality of experience for internet video. In: Proceedings of the ACM SIGCOMM 2013 conference on SIGCOMM, pp. 339–350, October 2013
3. Brooks, P., Hestnes, B., Heiestad, S., Aaby, C.: Communicating quality of experience data for the development of multimedia services. In: Proceedings of the 20th International Symposium on Human Factors in Telecommunication, Sophia Antipolis, France, 21–23 March 2006
4. Callet, P.L., Moller, S., Perkis, A. (eds.): Qualinet white paper on definitions of quality of experience (qoe) and related concepts. Lausanne, Switzerland, Output version of the Dagstuhl seminar 12181, European Network on Quality of Experience in Multimedia Systems and Services (COST Action IC 1003), 3 June 2012
5. Institute for Statistics and Mathematics of WU. R software. (Wirtschafts universität Wien). http://www.r-project.org/
6. Hall, M., Frank, E., Holmes, G., Pfahringer, B., Reutemann, P., Witten, I.H.: The weka data mining software: an update. ACM SIGKDD Explor. Newsl. **11**(1), 10–18 (2009)
7. Ickin, S., Wac, K., Fiedler, M., Janowski, L., Hong, J., Dey, A.K.: A factors influencing quality of experience of commonly-used mobile applications. IEEE Commun. Mag. **50**, 48–56 (2012)
8. Khan, A., Sun, L., Ifeachor, E.: Qoe prediction model and its application in video quality adaptation over umts networks. IEEE Trans. Multimedia **14**(2), 431–442 (2012)
9. Harris, R., Nguyen, L.T., Punchihewa, A.: An enhanced analytical framework integrating aspects of network and application performance, psychology, and content in qoe assessment for web browsing. Int. J. Comput. Inf. Technol. **2**(5) (2013) (ISSN: 2279 0764)
10. Malekipirbazari, M., Aksakalli, V.: Risk assessment in social lending via random forests. Expert Syst. Appl. J. **42**, 4621–4631 (2015)
11. Matulin, M., Mrvelj, Š.: State-of-the-practice in evaluation of quality of experience in real-life environments. Inf. Commun. Technol. Preliminary Commun. **25**(3), 255–264 (2013)
12. De Moor, K., Ketyko, I., Joseph, W., Deryckere, T., De Marez, L. (eds.): Evaluating quality of experience of mobile applications and services in a living lab setting, vol. 15(3), pp. 378–391. Mobile Networks and Applications Archive, New York (2010)
13. Mushtaq, M.S., Augustin, B., Mellouk, A.: Empirical study based on machine learning approach to assess the qos/qoe correlation. In: 2012 17th European Conference on Networks and Optical Communications (NOC), pp. 1–7, June 2012
14. Septem Riza, L., Bergmeir, C., Herrera, F., Benitez, J.M.: Learning from data using the r package "frbs". In: 2014 IEEE International Conference on Fuzzy Systems (FUZZ-IEEE), pp. 2149–2155 (2014)

15. Rodriguez-Teja, F., Grampin, E.: Wekatie, a traffic classification plugin integrating tie and weka. In: Proceedings of Wireless Communications and Mobile Computing Conference (IWCMC), pp. 623–628, August 2014
16. Song, W., Tjondronegoro, D.W., Docherty, M.: Understanding user experience of mobile video: framework, measurement, and optimization. In: Tjondronegoro, D. (ed.) Mobile Multimedia: User and Technology Perspectives, pp. 3–30. INTECH Open Access Publisher, Vukovar (2012)
17. Stankiewicz, R., Jajszczyk, A.: A survey of qoe assurance in converged networks. Comput. Netw. **55**(7), 1459–1473 (2011)
18. Weka 3: Data Mining with Open Source Machine Learning Software in Java. http://www.cs.waikato.ac.nz/ml/weka/downloading.html

Network Traffic Analysis and QoE Evaluation for Video Progressive Download Service: Netflix

Francisco Lozano[1](✉), Mari-Carmen Aguayo-Torres[1], Gerardo Gómez[1],
Carlos Cárdenas[2], and Juana Baños[1]

[1] Departamento de Ingeniería de Comunicaciones, Universidad de Málaga,
Campus de Teatinos, 29071 Málaga, Spain
{flg,aguayo}@ic.uma.es
http://www.ic.uma.es
[2] Performance Testing Solutions, AT4 wireless, S.A.U., Severo Ochoa, 2,
29590 Málaga, Spain

Abstract. Over the Top video streaming services has grown very rapidly in recent years, with the emerge of diverse online video stores. One of the popular over the top services is Netflix. The significant increase of user data consumption by this type of services affects the performance of communications networks, and operators need methods to estimate how well the network behaves. In this paper a network traffic analysis of Netflix is presented. The traffic study has been performed with diverse devices and access technologies. A model for quality of experience (QoE) evaluation, based on application performance metrics, has been applied to estimate Mean Opinion Score (MOS) by end users.

Keywords: Traffic pattern · Quality of experience · Mean opinion score · Netflix™

1 Introduction

Mobile video traffic represents today 50 % of all data traffic and, according to forecasts for 2017, video traffic on mobile devices will account for 66 % of the total traffic for these terminals [1]. Netflix is a providing services platform mainly via streaming video on demand. It began in the United States and is slowly expanding its services to other countries in America and Europe. Online distribution began in 1999 and in 2015 has more than 50 million subscribers. This outstanding traffic demand growth represents a serious challenge for network operators, who should engineer their wireless networks architecture to handle the huge volume of traffic in efficient ways while providing the highest Quality of Experience (QoE) to end users. Netflix platform has adapted to computers, TVs and mobile devices, allowing users access to digital content from smartphones and tablets via wireless networks. In terms of communication protocols, Netflix uses Hypertext Transfer Protocol (HTTP) to transfer video instead of Real-time Transport Protocol (RTP) over User Datagram Protocol (UDP), as could be expected for a real time service.

© Springer International Publishing Switzerland 2015
M.C. Aguayo-Torres et al. (Eds.): WWIC 2015, LNCS 9071, pp. 239–246, 2015.
DOI: 10.1007/978-3-319-22572-2_17

Perceived user quality results from a mix of performance indicators that are different from one application to another. In the case of video applications, any stop during the rendering of the image when the user is watching a video is identified as lack of quality.

A traditional way to evaluate the quality perceived by users is by performing a user survey under various network conditions. The ratings are averaged over a large sample of users in order to obtain a single parameter known as "Mean Opinion Score" (MOS) [3]. This approach has several drawbacks such as the difficulty in ensuring repeatability of the network conditions and the cost of the survey itself. Hence, it would be more appropriate to automate the measurement procedure so that it could be performed without human intervention. To this end, MOS models have to be developed in order to substitute direct user opinion on services' performance. Once models that correlate specific measurable parameters to user perceived quality are available, network operators can estimate the perceived user quality from the measurement of those parameters.

The rest of this paper is organized as follows. Section 2 presents an analysis of the network traffic pattern of Netflix. In Sect. 3, a QoE evaluation model for the type of traffic of Netflix is described. Finally, some concluding remarks are given in the last section.

2   Network Traffic Patterns

Netflix is based on adaptive video streaming over HTTP [5]. The main difference between this type of service and real-time video streaming is that the video content has been previously stored in multimedia server. The service provider settles copies of the same movie classified by different qualities. Each movie file is also segmented into fragments.

Basic functionality description of this mechanism is illustrated in Fig. 1. At the beginning the player client requests a manifest, which includes the information of the coding rates available of the movie selected. Then, the client requests an specific fragment of video file from server. The adaptive mechanism is based in changing the quality of the movie fragment as function of bandwidth available or congestion detection.

The adaptive mechanism is based on changing the next movie fragment quality, as function of the bandwidth available or network congestion. For example in Fig. 1 at time t = 2, the client request at best available encoding rate fragment for the already video playing, then a congestion episode occurs so the client requests a fragment with lower encoding rate avoiding stalls during the video playback. When the conditions are acceptable the client will request fragments at higher available quality.

The profile of the traffic generation mechanism in an ideal scenario shows two main phases, Initial data burst and Control algorithm. Figure 2 shows both phases, being blue zone the Initial Burst and the red one the Control Algorithm phase.

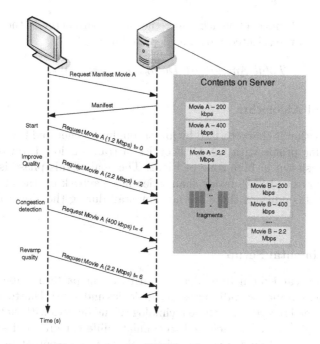

Fig. 1. Adaptive HTTP video streaming

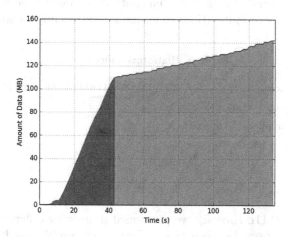

Fig. 2. Phases of video download (Color figure online)

2.1 Initial Data Burst

Corresponds to data transmission before video playback at the client. This state is also known as buffering time, which is the time to download a certain amount of data to play the video with the best quality available, avoiding stalls at the beginning. The amount of data downloaded during the buffering time matches with 300 s of real video playback time, the input parameter is the video rate encoding (V_r) of the selected video, as depicted in Eq. 1.

$$Total\ Amount\ of\ Data_{buffering} = 300V_r. \tag{1}$$

2.2   Control Algorithm

Control Algorithm is characterized by low throughput generated from server and a typical traffic profile with ON-OFF cycles of transmission, throwing a curve with steps as shown in blue zone of Fig. 2. The goal of this phase is to ensure progressive download 25 % faster than video file playback on the client player. Hence, in ideal conditions there are not any stall during the video playback at client viewer.

2.3   Experimental Setup

A test plan was carried out to model the Netflix traffic pattern. Table 1 presents multiple devices to analyze radio access technologies under test. Due to availability, we just performed records over these technologies and devices with Netflix access.

Two type of movies was selected to simulate different group of source. The classification is based on the characteristics of the movie content by the image transitions as presented in Table 2. The capture of video traffic was performed during 200 s with several iterations to ensure a reproducible measurement.

Table 1. Platforms under test

Device	WLAN (802.11n)	Cellular (LTE)
Laptop (Windows)	X	
Smartphone (Android)	X	X
Tablet (Android)	X	

2.4   Comparison

Under WLAN 802.11n coverage we performed records for different devices and establish a comparison between them. First result we obtained is the traffic pattern with two phases, previously described, but with significant differences between client players. Figure 3 displays the amount of data downloaded versus time. The initial data burst corresponds to a lineal function with diverse slope for

Table 2. Video traces

Video trace	Description	Acquisition time
#1	Slower image transitions	200 s
#2	Colorful and faster image transitions	200 s

each device tested. For tests in PC under WLAN connection, the initial data burst downloads more amount of data but over more time, on the opposite side, smartphones running Android OS with native Netflix client, adopts a criteria with less data downloaded during this phase. The Control algorithm also shows a distinctive behavior, while PC and Tablet download more periodically but less amount of data, Smartphones download more data per chunk, but with less periodicity.

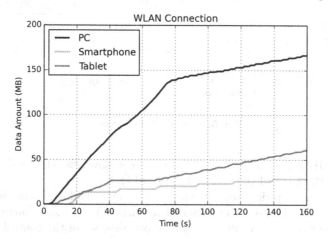

Fig. 3. Comparison between devices

In-depth analyze of the Control algorithm exhibits a different pattern usage in time and data downloaded. The experiments describe a reproducible CDF in both magnitudes. Figure 4 illustrates the out of line operation on Smarthphone devices, in terms of elapsed time between every chunk of data, with a mean value of 24 s. For PC and Tablet the response are quite similar nearby 4 s.

The amount of data received per chunk, under the Control algorithm, also shows diverse operation over the devices tested. Smarthphone presents a mean

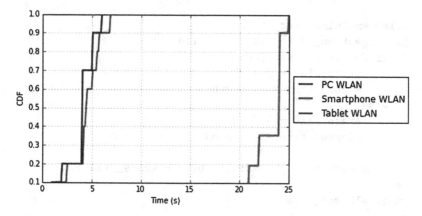

Fig. 4. Time CDF by device

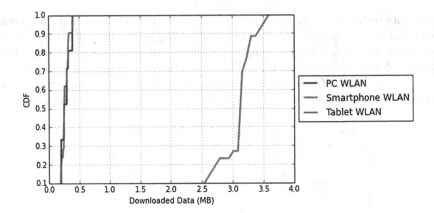

Fig. 5. Data CDF by device

value of 4 MB per chunk while PC and Tablet have less than 0.5 MB, as is depicted by the CDF of the received data in Fig. 5.

Based on our empirical study we propose a Netflix traffic model, classified by two phases, initial data burst and control algorithm. Table 3 summarize the parameters of the model for Netflix. A detailed pseudo-code of the control algorithm is also presented.

Table 3. Proposed Netflix traffic model

Phase	Initial data burst	Control algorithm
Amount of data to send (bits)	$300V_r$	Video length - $300V_r$
TCP packet size	MSS	MSS
Source speed	Full buffer TCP	Client platform function (code below)

```
Function Control Algorithm():
begin
    while(remaining_bits >0)
      if congestion_buffer_full == False
        if device == Smartphone
            trace_size = 3.1 MB
            elapse_time = 24 segundos
        else
            trace_size = 0.3 MB
            elapsed_time = 4 segundos
        end
        remaining_bits = remaining_bits - trace_size
      end
      wait elapsed_time
    end
end
```

3   QoE Evaluation

We have employed the QoE evaluation for multimedia services based on the ITU-T Recommendation P.800 [3]. This opinion scale, the most frequently used for multimedia services, allocates qualitative values from Bad to Excellent by mapping the quantitative MOS as depicted in Table 4. A minimum value of 3 has to be obtained to establish quality as Fair, being 5 the maximum score and 1 the lowest mark.

Table 4. ITU-T Recommendation P.800 MOS scale [3]

Quality	MOS
Excellent	5
Good	4
Fair	3
Poor	2
Bad	1

In adaptive HTTP video streaming service the following APMs are required by the model in [2,4]:

- Initial buffering time (T_{init}): period between the starting time of loading a video and the starting time of playing it.
- Rebuffering frequency (f_{rebuf}): frequency of interruption events during the playback.
- Mean rebuffering time (T_{rebuf}): average duration of a rebuffering event.

Finally, the MOS is computed as a linear model as [2,4]:

$$MOS = 4.23 - 0.0672L_{T_i} - 0.742L_{f_r} - 0.106L_{T_r} \qquad (2)$$

where L_{T_i}, L_{f_r} and L_{T_r} are quantized values of the respective levels T_{init}, f_{rebuf} and T_{rebuf}, following Table 5.

Table 5. APMs quantification levels

	T_{init}	f_{rebuf}	T_{rebuf}	L_x
Low	0–1 s	0–0.02	0–5 s	1
Medium	1–5 s	0.02–0.15	5–10 s	2
High	>5 s	>0.15	>10 s	3

Note that the parameter which affects worst to proposed mean opinion score model, is related to the rebuffering frequency. In terms of the user perception this parameter measure the number of stalls may occur during the video playback.

4   Conclusion

This work has presented main characteristics of traffic generation mechanism of Netflix with two clearly different parts, an Initial data burst and a Control algorithm. Our research conducts to describe the transmission of amount of data which corresponds to 300 s of real video playback, depending of the video encoding employed.

The QoE evaluation has been performed with a proposed model, based on application performance metrics by the client side. The goal of the model is to obtain a mean opinion score with just 3 parameters.

Acknowledgements. This work has been partly supported by the Spanish Government and FEDER under grant TEC2013-44442-P.

The authors would like to thank Noelia Guerra Melgares for her collaboration and technical support during the measurement process.

References

1. Cisco Systems Inc.: Cisco visual networking index: Forecast and methodology, 2013–2018 (2013). http://www.cisco.com
2. Gómez, G., Hortigüela, L., Pérez, Q., Lorca, J., García, R., Aguayo-Torres, M.C.: Youtube QoE evaluation tool for Android wireless terminals. EURASIP J. Wireless Commun. Networking 2014(164) (2014)
3. ITU-T: Recommendation P.800. Methods for subjective determination of transmission quality, August 1996
4. Mok, R., Chan, E., Chang, R.: Measuring the quality of experience of HTTP video streaming. In: 2011 IFIP/IEEE International Symposium on Integrated Network Management (IM), pp. 485–492, May 2011
5. Rao, A., Legout, A., Yeon-sup, L., Towsley, C., Barakat, C., Dabbous, W.: Network characteristics of video streaming traffic. In: Proceedings of the Seventh Conference on Emerging Networking Experiments and Technologies (2011)

A Tool to Estimate Roaming Behavior in Wireless Architectures

Rute Sofia[⊠]

COPELABS, University Lusófona, Lisboa, Portugal
rute.sofia@ulusofona.pt

Abstract. This paper describes a software-based tool that tracks mobile node roaming and infers the time-to-handover as well as the preferential handover target, based on behavior inference solely derived from regular usage data captured in visited wireless networks. The paper presents the tool architecture; computational background for mobility estimation; operational guidelines concerning how the tool is being used to track several aspects of roaming behavior in the context of wireless networks. Target selection accuracy is validated having as baseline traces obtained in realistic scenarios.

Keywords: Mobility tracking · Social mobility behavior · User-centric networks

1 Introduction

The introduction of new, cooperative technologies and in particular of low-cost wireless access, allowed the regular citizen to profit from the Internet as a commodity. Such pervasive Internet access is giving rise to networking architectures that seem to spread in a self-organizing manner, *User-centric Networks (UCNs)* [1,2]. UCNs rely on an Internet end-user that exhibits frequent roaming patterns, and that owns/carries one or more portable devices with a good multimedia support. Hence, the majority of today's mobile devices, which have been considered, up until recently, plain consumer devices, are now also networking nodes. As a consequence, the movement that these devices exhibit impact the underlying Internet connectivity models and the overall network operation. Hence, being able to capture such movement and also to estimate some features is highly relevant to optimize different aspects of network operation e.g. resource management, or routing.

Movement estimation has been a research field for long, with the aim of improving network operation. For instance, in cellular networks, several attempts have been provided to estimate movement as explained in Sect. 2. Fast handing over based on movement anticipation techniques (e.g. tunneling) has been a topic

---

COPELABS, Building U, First Floor, University Lusofona. Campo Grande 388, 1749-024 Lisboa, Portugal.

© Springer International Publishing Switzerland 2015
M.C. Aguayo-Torres et al. (Eds.): WWIC 2015, LNCS 9071, pp. 247–258, 2015.
DOI: 10.1007/978-3-319-22572-2_18

extensively addressed, e.g., within the context of the *Internet Engineering Task Force (IETF)*.

Estimating roaming behavior is therefore becoming more relevant, and today, due to an extensive effort derived from several initiatives as well as from extensive and wide traces collections [3], it is globally accepted that there is a relation between social behavior and the user's roaming behavior [4]. It is the social behavior that assists in defining user movement patterns, both from an individual perspective, and from a group perspective [5]. Being capable of estimating such behavior is therefore relevant to optimize network operation, be it from a mobility management perspective (e.g., handover optimization), from a resource management perspective (e.g. performing a more intelligent load-balancing), or from a routing perspective (e.g. making routing more stable by selecting a priori paths that have a chance to be more stable in the light of node movement).

This paper is dedicated to the topic of mobility prediction in wireless networks. We provide a debate on notions related to social interaction analysis and mobile networks as well as a debate on guidelines to better address mobility prediction. Our work proposes a non-intrusive wireless sensing tool, the MTracker[1], which provides a way to track properties of a user's visit to preferred networks, and to estimate a potential move towards a more preferred network, based on the learnt history of the user's roaming behavior.

The paper is organized as follows. Section 2 is dedicated to related work, while Sect. 3 addresses our proposed mechanism to estimate social mobility, and validate the mechanism against real traces in Sect. 4. The paper concludes in Sect. 5, where guidelines for future work are also provided.

2   Related Work

Within the context of cellular works, there are several studies dedicated to movement prediction. First attempts related with prediction based on *Signal-to-Noise (SNR)* ratio levels [6], being the main purpose to anticipate a potential handover and not to predict such handover in terms, e.g., of preferential target. Improvements to this line of research have been considered, for instance, via probabilistic selection based on user *Global Positioning System (GPS)* coordinates. Such related work fell short in terms of adequately estimating movement, partially due to the fact that at the time there was not a solid understanding on users' roaming behavior.

The current availability of large-scale data sets, such as mobile-phone records and GPS data, allows researchers from multiple scientific fields to gain access to detailed patterns of human roaming behavior, greatly enhancing our understanding of human mobility. The extensive traces that are available today lead to a better understanding of social movement, having given rise to a few mobility models with roots on social network theory [7,8].

---

[1] Software is available as a beta version available directly via Google Apps, https://play.google.com/store/apps/details?id=eu.uloop.mobilitytracker, via http://copelabs.ulusofona.pt/~uloop/ or at http://copelabs.ulusofona.pt/scicommons/index.php/publications/show/489.

In terms of human movement, Barabási et al. have been active in giving insight into human movement patterns [4]. As follow-up of their research, Song et al. research showed that human movement behavior is not compatible with Brownian approaches and showing also some level of predictability in such movement [9]. By measuring the entropy of each individual's trajectory, they have found that there is a 93 % predictable behavior across the studied universe.

Noulas et al. have analyzed roaming behavior features exploiting information on transitions between types of places, mobility flows between venues, and spatio-temporal characteristics of user check-in patterns, showing that supervised models based on the combination of multiple features assist in reaching high prediction accuracy [10]. Their analysis is focused on mobility prediction targetting location-based services. Our work has in common with the latter the intention to consider social behavior aspects that can be extracted from visits to networks, to improve mobility prediction. We do not, however, consider location-based services as the target to address. Instead, our perspective is derived from data captured passively by the user device only, in a non-intrusive way.

3   A Tool to Estimate Movement in Wireless Networks

The MTracker solution is a proof-of-concept software-based mechanism that intends to optimize wireless networking in the following aspects: (i) handover optimization by improving resulting end-to-end delay (and node reachability time), as well as by reducing signaling overhead associated to handovers; (ii) optimize resource management by estimating potential attachment points, and assisting the network in self-organizing, thus providing stations with the optimal wireless base stations.

3.1   Functional Aspects

There are three main tasks that the MTracker performs [11]. The first is **Data Capture**, namely, non-intrusive data capture based on visited and surrounding wireless networks. The second is **Target Handover Selection**, i.e., preferential target selection based on a seamless ranking of all wireless networks on a device's list. The third one, **Time-to-Handover**, concerns estimating the time for the next handover to occur, based on the learnt roaming behavior of the device.

Figure 1 provides a flow-chart for the MTracker operation. Its main three tasks are explained next.

Data Capture. Once the MTracker is activated, it relies on the usual 802.11 MAC Layer scanning mechanism to periodically obtain data concerning the list of networks in range, as illustrated in Fig. 1.

The MTracker list of visited networks is kept locally on the device. The tool devised is capable of periodically provides output to a local system (e.g. local

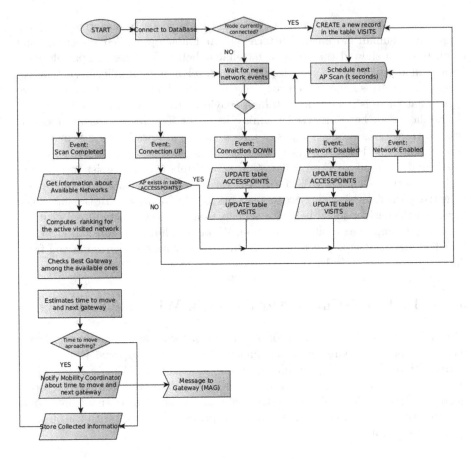

Fig. 1. MTracker Flow-chart.

database); or to external entities that reside on the network, e.g. a mobility management solution that has the responsibility to decide based on other external conditions whether or not a move should be anticipated.

The MTracker captures parameters via the Wi-Fi interface that are either overheard or that can be computed based on overhead data - it does not perform intrusive probing. The initial set of parameters considered in the MTracker are described in Table 1[2].

The mentioned parameters are here provided as a potential example of the type of parameters that can be used to characterize a user's roaming behavior in terms of preferred networks without recurring to probing or to explicit location tracking. These parameters are used to compute the visited networks' rank, as explained next.

---

[2] The MTracker as proof-of-concept has already given rise to the tool WiRank (https://play.google.com/store/apps/details?id=eu.uloop.wirank), intended to improve Android connectivity and to integrate some aspects of prediction with other features, such as context-awareness based on location.

Table 1. Some parameters collected by the MTracker.

Parameter	Name	Definition
$v_{ij} \in [0, \propto]$	Visit	A visit from node i to node j implies that node i is authorized (by j) to use its networking resources
$v = \sum_{j=0}^{n} v_{ij} \; j \in [0, n]$	Total visits	Number of visits that node i does to node j
d_{ij}	Visit duration	Time interval (seconds) since node i is authorized by node j to be attached, until node i deattaches
$d_{avg} = \gamma * d_{avg} + (1 - \gamma) * d_{ij}$	Average duration of a visit	Time interval (seconds) that node i is in average attached to node j, based on nan exponential moving average formula
a_{ij}	Visited network attractiveness	A parameter that a user sets by hand (e.g. gives more preference to using network1 than network2) or it can be passively collected via, e.g., distributed trust schemes that are present in the network (e.g. provided by the operator)
rej_{ij}	Rejected visits	Number of times a node i is not authorized by node j to access its resources
te_{ij}	Visit gap	Time gap (in seconds) since the last visit from node i to a specific visited network j

Target Handover Selection, Ranking Visited Networks. The MTracker tool has been designed to integrate any utility function to rank visited networks. In this paper we consider a potential equation, Eq. 1, where r_{ij} corresponds to the ranking (cost) that node i computes towards the network controlled by node j. The rationale for such equation is that the longer and the more often a node visits a specific network, the higher the preference of that network to the node, provided that such visits are recent. Hence, the function described in Eq. 1 has enough sensitivity to distinguish between targets that seem to be preferential (for instance, high a_{ij} and long d_{avg}) but that have actually been heavily visited a long time ago (long te_{ij}). The function also takes into consideration the number of rejected connections rej_{ij} against the total number of visits v_{ij}.

The rank provided by r_{ij} is computed from the perspective of node i towards a potential visited network identified by node j (e.g. an AP) based on parameters passively collected over time, by relying on the exponential moving average function of Eq. 2, where $r_{ij_{t-1}}$ corresponds to the last computed value for r_{ij} and r'_{ij} stands for the instant computation of r_{ij}. By tuning α one shall be providing more weight to more recent or to older instances of r_{ij}.

$$r_{ij} = a_{ij}^2 * \left(\frac{\sqrt{d_{avg}}}{te_{ij}+1}\right)^{\frac{v}{re_{ij}}} a_{ij} \in [0,1] \tag{1}$$

$$r_{ij} = \alpha * r_{ij_{t-1}} + (1-\alpha) * r'_{ij}, \alpha \in [0,1]. \tag{2}$$

Time-to-Handover Estimate. Estimating a potential move is a task processed by a node in background and has as motivation to provide an estimate of time, as well as a target identifier for the next handover to be performed by the node. We highlight that the MTracker only notifies an entity (a user, some entity on the network, or even some other process in the local device) that a potential move may occur, so that a decision may assist the device in reaching some form of reliability in terms of active communication flow. For instance, it is still up to a mobility management solution to perform such a move, or not, based on the information provided by the MTracker.

To compute the estimate for a potential move, the MTracker periodically checks its list of ranked visited networks. Based on the computed average visit time of the active network as well as on the error time gap derived from prior learning about roaming habits of the node, the MTracker verifies which network(s) attain the best ranking in comparison to the active network.

The time to handover, *TTH*, estimated during an active connection of node i to node j is based on Eq. 3. The equation takes into consideration the average visit duration to the network controlled by node j, d_{avg} as well as the time gap $\triangle t$.

$$TTH_t = d_{avg} \pm \triangle t, \text{ where } \triangle t = d_{t-1} - TTH_{t-1}. \tag{3}$$

3.2 Operational Example

Figure 2 illustrates a wireless scenario where three wireless visited networks are respectively served by AP1, AP2, and AP3. The application MTracker resides on the *Mobile Node (MN)*, which periodically visits the three networks. Moreover, each visited network is served by a specific *Mobility Anchor Point (MAP)* agent which can be co-located to the AP, or placed somewhere else on the network, as occurs today.

MN exhibits a regular trajectory e.g. during a day, where it crosses the three different visited networks. Following the regular IEEE 802.11 operation MN is set to perform *passive scan*ning, i.e., while roaming it passively receives *Beacon* frames sent by the surrounding APs. It can therefore get a list not only of APs that it regularly attaches to, but also of neighboring APs that it did not visit. We highlight that there is no relation whatsoever with GPS location or tracking of the nodes; the MTracker simply captures data that is already provided by today's devices, and has the capability to infer roaming behavior in terms of characteristics for the next handover.

In this operational example, intended to illustrate the benefits of prediction in mobility management, MN also integrates a mobility management solution, e.g. *Mobile IPv6* (MIPv6) or *Proxy Mobile IPv6* (PMIPv6). On its list of visited locations, it keeps track of multiple parameters such as the ones described in Table 1.

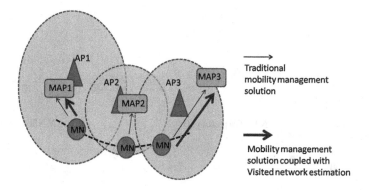

Fig. 2. Example of the potential impact of mobility estimation f.

For instance, MN has recorded an average visit duration (d_{avg}) of 15 min to AP1. On the current visit, 6 min have elapsed. Periodically, MN analysis its list of visited networks and checks whether or not the average duration visit is being reached. From a computational perspective, this means that MN integrates a time-window based mechanism to reach and eventually send a notification to an entity in the current visited network (e.g., AP, MAP, etc.), e.g. every minute.

In our example, after 6 min, MN realizes that there is still a gap of 9 min and therefore does not send any information. When MN1 realizes that the current visit has reached 14 min, it sends a notification about the best possible visited network which, in our example, is the visited network served by AP3. In that notification, it therefore sends information to MAP1 about the best next MAP – MAP3, and also about how much time in average is left for a move. MN does not perform, however, any decision concerning moving (handover).

This outcome can then be fed to a mobility management process, which can then decide whether or not to activate a handover, as we have addressed in prior work [2]. However, this outcome can also be fed into other control-based processes as a way to estimate aspects of roaming behavior.

4   Target Selection Accuracy Validation

In this section we provide input concerning the performance of mobility prediction based on an analysis performed by considering realistic traces. The validation contemplates the **accuracy** of the tool in terms of adequately ranking preferencial networks. The traces selected are from University of South Carolina and available via the CRAWDAD repository [3]. The full set of USC traces[3] comprise 150 nodes which have been tracked over several months across different visited networks. Extracted traces provide information such as identifier of each visited network; duration of each visit; timestamp for the visit start. As there are no traces that consider rejection rates as well as attractiveness level,

---

[3] http://uk.crawdad.org/usc/mobilib/.

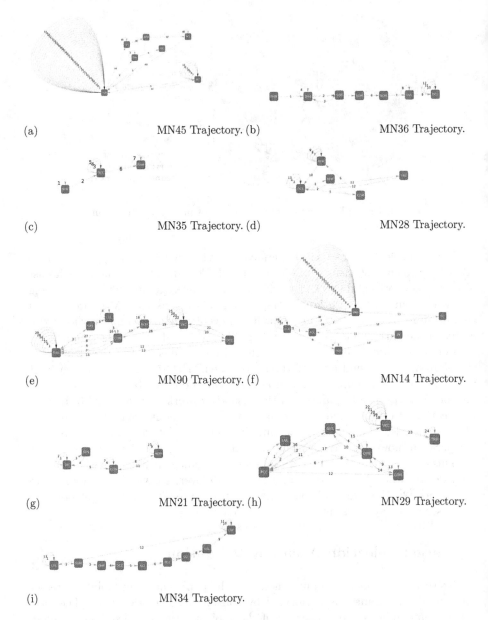

(a)   MN45 Trajectory. (b)   MN36 Trajectory.

(c)   MN35 Trajectory. (d)   MN28 Trajectory.

(e)   MN90 Trajectory. (f)   MN14 Trajectory.

(g)   MN21 Trajectory. (h)   MN29 Trajectory.

(i)   MN34 Trajectory.

Fig. 3. Trajectories of the nine selected nodes, MN45, MN36, MN35, MN28, MN90, MN14, MN21, MN29, MN34. Edges numbering refers to waypoints.

we have considered attractiveness to be similar to the number of visits v and did not assess the impact of rejected visits in our experiments.

Out of the available traces, we have categorized nodes in terms of trajectory, namely: trajectory duration (short; long); number of visited APs (small

Table 2. Results, ranking accuracy based on movement of 9 nodes collected in the USC CRAWDAD trace set.

MN	Number of visited APs	Total waypoints	Roaming path main features	Average visit duration (seconds/minutes)	Total roaming duration (s/days)	Ranking accuracy error margin(%)
MN45	7	55	1 AP heavily visited; remainder APs visited in average 3 times	2793/46	621978/7	20
MN36	6	12	Most APs visited once; 2 visited more than twice	2112/35	1656107/19	25
MN35	3	8	2 APs visited twice; 1 visited 4 times	162757/2712	1303008/15	38
MN28	5	14	3 APs visited once only	8336/139	3334673/38	43
MN90	7	29	All APs visited at least twice; Most APs visited frequently for a specific timeslot, but not revisited	1908/31	1295067/15	54
MN14	6	41	1 AP accounts for circa 50 % of visits; all APs revisited	9250/154	1346709/16	29
MN21	4	12	1 AP visited only once; all APs revisited at least 3 times sequentially	5803/98	366220/4	33
MN29	7	24	Most APs visited twice only; 1 AP visited often	3819/64	1225566/14	28 %
MN34	9	14	7 APs visited only once	1993/33	949480/11	7.14

number, large number); number of waypoints (high or low number of waypoints in the trajectory). Then, for the different categories, we have randomly selected again nine representative node trajectories. These nodes, numbered respectively as MN45, MN36, MN28, MN90, MN14, MN21, MN29, MN34, have their trajectories represented in Fig. 3.

The ranking accuracy has been validated by computing the ranking of each visited AP over time and then selecting the AP with the highest rank, among all possible APs.

Table 2 provides results for the set of selected nodes. The first column represents the selected nodes. The second column contains the total of visited networks for that node during a single trajectory, while the third column provides the total number of visits across different networks. The fourth column provides details concerning the roaming paths extracted of the traces for each node, while the fifth and six columns provide details concerning the average visit

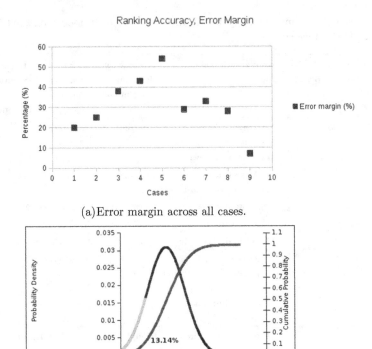

(a) Error margin across all cases.

(b) Probability Density and Cumulative Density.

Fig. 4. Ranking error margin.

duration (seconds and minutes) and total duration of the traces (seconds and days), respectively. The relative error percentage is provided in column seven.

MN45 stands for an example of a node that exhibits a long trajectory with a high number of waypoints, across a small number of visited networks (7). MN45 exhibits frequent visits to two different visited networks, represented as FSA and IRC. These are regular visits over time. In this case, the ranking capability provides an error estimate of around 20%, which is quite relevant given the fact that the other visited networks are in average visited only 3 times, are not necessarily visited sequentially.

MN36 stands for an example of a node that shares a similar trajectory in terms of time and visited networks, with the difference that its trajectory holds less waypoints in comparison to MN45 - 12 instead of 55. For this case, the accuracy is similar, as even though the visited networks have in average been less visited. The reason for this is that visits have been in average longer, which compensates for the lack of visit frequency.

MN28 and MN90 are worst-cases in terms of predicting next handover targets, as the MTracker has reached respectively an error rate of 43% and 54%.

The reason relates to the fact that only two networks are visited more than once, with short visits.

MN34 stands for the best-case in terms of target accuracy (7 % of error margin), being the reason the fact that only the first and the last networks of the trajectory have been frequently and sequentially visited. These networks also exhibit in average longer visits than the others.

The results obtained show that the MTracker can predict with reasonable accuracy future handover targets, as the error margin stands between 20 % and 30 %.

The error margins obtained accross all cases are provided in Fig. 4a and b (Cumulative Density and Probabilistic Density Functions).

5   Summary and Conclusions

This paper contributes to the debate concerning the validity of mobility estimation as an operational improvement to networks, and one that can be easily implemented. It goes over the main concepts concerning movement estimation for portable devices, in particular in UCNs, where the end-user device often assumes the role of a network device.

The work describes the tool MTracker explaining how it can be used to assist in predicting roaming behavior in terms of handover target and time to handover.

We have validated the tool against traces obtained from devices realistic environments, showing that without considering GPS, MTracker is capable of predicting with reasonable accuracy future targets (20–30% error margin for most cases).

As current work, our mobility estimation framework is being validated in the context of IP mobility management solutions. It is also being extended to capture additional parameters that may assist other aspects of the network operation, e.g., routing. Traces are starting to be collected and will be provided to the global community. Last, but not the least, mobility estimation aspects are also being used to feed visualizing tools online, as a way to further analyze mobility behavior of Internet users, in a seamless, anonymous and yet pervasive way.

Acknowledgments. This work has been developed within the EU IST FP7 project *ULOOP - User-centric Wireless Local Loop* (grant number 247158). The author thanks Jonnahtan Saltarin for the implementation of the second version of the proof-of-concept software MTracker.

References

1. Sofia, R., Mendes, P.: User-provided networks: consumer as provider. IEEE Commun. Mag. **46**, 86–91 (2008)
2. Aldini, A., Bogliolo, A.: User-Centric Networking - Future Perspectives. Lecture Notes in Social Networking. Springer (2014). ISBN 978-3-319-05218-2
3. Kotz, D., Henderson, T., Abyzov, I.: Crawdad trace dartmouth. http://crawdad.cs.dartmouth.edu

4. Gonzalez, M.C., Hidalgo, C.A., Barabasi, A.L.: Understanding individual human mobility patterns. Nature **453**, 779–782 (2008)
5. Rhee, I., Shin, M., Hong, S., Lee, K., Kim, S.J., Chong, S.: On the levy-walk nature of human mobility. IEEE/ACM Trans. Networking (TON) **19**, 630–643 (2011)
6. Denko, M.K.: Mobility prediction schemes in wireless ad hoc networks. In: Furht, B., Wysocki, T.A., Dadej, A., Wysocki, B.J. (eds.) Advanced Wired and Wireless Networks. Multimedia Systems and Applications, vol. 26, pp. 171–186. Springer, US (2005)
7. Musolesi, M., Mascolo, C.: Designing mobility models based on social network theory. SIGMOBILE Mob. Comput. Commun. Rev. **11**, 59–70 (2007)
8. Ribeiro, A., Sofia, R.C.: A survey on mobility models for wireless networks. Technical report SITI-TR-11-01, SITI, University Lusófona, February 2011
9. Song, B.C., Qu, N.Z., Barabasi, A.-L.: Limits of predictability in human mobility. Nature **327**, 1018–1021 (2010)
10. Noulas, A., Scellato, S., Lathia, N., Mascolo, C.: Mining user mobility features for next place prediction in location-based services. In: ICDM 2012, pp. 1038–1043 (2012)
11. Sofia, R.: Mobility management method and apparatus. EP 13186562.9, Method and Apparatus for Ranking Visited Networks

Distributed and Efficient One-Class Outliers Detection Classifier in Wireless Sensors Networks

Oussama Ghorbel[1(✉)], Mohamed Wassim Jmal[1], Mohamed Abid[1],
and Hichem Snoussi[2]

[1] National Engineers School of Sfax, CES Research Unit,
Sfax University, Sfax, Tunisia
oussama.ghorbel@ceslab.org, wassim.jmal@gmail.com,
mohamed.abid@enis.rnu.tn
[2] LM2S Research Unit, University of Technology of Troyes, Troyes, France
hichem.snoussi@utt.fr

Abstract. In the data mining literature, many outlier detection models can be found. However, these models are not suitable for the energy constrained WSNs because they assumed the whole data is available in a central location for further analysis. In this paper, we propose Distributed and Efficient One-class Outliers Detection Classifier (DEOODC) based on Mahalanobis Kernel used for outlier detection in wireless sensor networks (WSNs). For this case, the task amounts to create a useful model based on KPCA to recognize data as normal or outliers. Recently, Kernel Principal component analysis (KPCA) has used for nonlinear case which can extract higher order statistics. Kernel PCA (KPCA) mapping the data onto another feature space and using nonlinear function. On account of the attractive capability, KPCA-based methods have been extensively investigated, and have showed excellent performance. Within this setting, we propose Kernel Principal Component Analysis based Mahalanobis kernel as a new outlier detection method using Mahalanobis distance to implicitly calculate the mapping of the data points in the feature space so that we can separate outlier points from normal pattern of data distribution. The use of KPCA based Mahalanobis kernel on real word data obtained from Intel Berkeley are reported showing that the proposed method performs better in finding outliers in wireless sensor networks when compared to the One-Class SVM detection approach. All computation are done in the original space, thus saving computing time using Mahalanobis Kernel.

Keywords: Wireless sensor networks · Outlier detection · Kernel methods · Mahalanobis kernel · Kernel principal component analysis (KPCA)

1 Introduction

With the increasing advances of digital electronics and wireless communications, in the past decade a new breed of tiny embedded systems known as wireless sensor nodes has emerged. These wireless sensor nodes are equipped with sensing, processing, wireless communication, and more recently actuation capability. They usually are densely

© Springer International Publishing Switzerland 2015
M.C. Aguayo-Torres et al. (Eds.): WWIC 2015, LNCS 9071, pp. 259–273, 2015.
DOI: 10.1007/978-3-319-22572-2_19

deployed in a wide geographical area and continuously measure various parameters (e.g. ambient temperature, relative humidity, soil moisture, wind speed) of the physical world. A large collection of these sensor nodes forms a wireless sensor network (WSN) [1]. However, raw sensor observations collected from sensor nodes often have low data quality and reliability due to the limited capability of sensor nodes in terms of energy, memory, computational power, bandwidth, dynamic nature of network, and harshness of the deployment environment. Use of low quality sensor data in any data analysis and decision making process limits the possibilities for reliable real-time situation-awareness. Wireless sensor networks are widely used and have gained attention in various fields including traffic control, health care, precision agriculture, etc. [2, 3]. KPCA has been used in several applications, such as voice recognition, image segmentation, face detection, feature extraction, data denoising and etc. Most WSN's applications require precise and accurate data to provide reliable information to the end user. Although the importance of information quality provided from WSNs, collected sensor data may be of low quality and reliability due to the low cost nature and harsh deployments of WSNs [4]. To ensure the quality of sensor measurements, outlier detection methods allow cleaning and refinement of collected data and let providing the most useful information to end users, while maintaining low energy consumption and preserve high computational efforts due to the limited energy resources of sensor nodes. To detect outliers, a detection model is built upon historical data structure of WSN. This model should be able to detect outliers among new observations with good precision [5].

By means of an alternative way of computing the principal axes through the use of inner product evaluations, Principal Component Analysis has been extended to a kernel-based PCA. The use of non-linear dimensionality reduction to expand in many applications as recent research has shown that kernel principal component analysis (KPCA) can be expected to work well as a pre-processing device for pattern recognition. The use of KPCA is a new field on wireless sensor networks (WSN) which are composed of interconnected micro-sensors that are able to collect, store, process and transmit data over the wireless channel. KPCA has found a new field which is integrated in application of novelty detection.

Our work is a comparative study of One Class outlier detection method in wireless sensor networks. So, the main contribution of this paper is the uses of Mahalanobis kernel based KPCA for outlier detection method in wireless sensor networks. To identify outliers, we use Mahalanobis distance induced feature subspace spanned by principal components as obtained by Kernel PCA. If the distance of a new data point is above a prefixed threshold, the observation is considered as an outlier, which is also established experimentally. It assumes that the principal subspace represents the normal data. The model is tested on real data from Intel Berkeley. The obtained results are competitive and the proposed method can achieve high detection rate with the lowest false alarm rate.

The remainder of this article is organized as follows. Section 2, present the related work for KPCA. Section 3, describes outliers detection and its different category in wireless sensor networks. Section 4, describes adopted method. Section 5, showcases the obtained experimental results, and Sect. 6 concludes and summarizes the main outcomes of the paper.

2 Related Works

Principal component analysis (PCA), first introduced by Hotelling [27], is a well-established dimension-reduction method. It replaces a set of correlated variables by a smaller set of uncorrelated linear combinations of those variables, such that these linear combinations explain most of the total variance. It is also a way of identifying inherent patterns, relations, regularities, or structure in the data. Because such patterns are difficult to detect in high-dimensional data, PCA can be a powerful tool. As a linear statistical technique, PCA cannot accurately describe all types of structures in a given dataset, specially nonlinear structures. Kernel principal component analysis (KPCA) has recently been proposed as a nonlinear extension of PCA (Scholkopf, Smola, and Muller, 1998). See also Scholkopf and Smola (2002).

Kernel based principle components analysis is a non linear PCA created using the kernel trick. KPCA maps the original inputs into a high dimensional feature space using a kernel method [6].

Mathematically, we transform the current features into a high-dimensional space and the calculate eigenvectors in this space. We ignore the vectors with really low eigen-values and then do learning in this transformed space. KPCA is computationally intensive and takes a lot more time compared to PCA. The reason being that the number of training data points in KPCA is much higher than PCA. So number of principle components that need to be estimated is also much larger. The KPCA method has exhibited superior performance compared to linear PC analysis method in processing nonlinear systems [7, 8]. The detail introduction of the basic KPCA can be viewed in [7, 9]. Kernel PCA (KPCA), as presented by Scholkopf et al., is a technique for nonlinear dimension reduction of data with an underlying nonlinear spatial structure. A key insight behind KPCA is to transform the input data into a higher-dimensional feature space. The feature space is constructed such that a nonlinear operation can be applied in the input space by applying a linear operation in the feature space.

Lee et al. [19] and Cho et al. [20] used kernel PCA with Gaussian kernel for fault detection and identification of process monitoring in the field of chemical engineering. Franc and Hlavac [24] used the greedy KPCA which essentially works by *filtering* or *sampling* the original training set for a lesser but representative subset of vectors which span approximately the same subspace as the subspace in the kernel induced feature space spanned by the training set. The training set is then projected onto the span of the lesser subset, where PCA is carried out. Other sampling-based methods exist [22, 25]. Current KPCA reconstruction methods equally weigh all the features; it is impossible to weigh the importance of some features over the others. Some other existing methods also have limitations. Some works only considers robustness of the principal subspace; they do not address robust fitting. Lu et al. present an iterative approach to handle outliers in training data. At each iteration, the KPCA model is built, and the data points that have the highest reconstruction errors are regarded as outliers and discarded from the training set. However, this approach does not handle intra-sample outliers. Several other approaches also considering Berar et al. propose to use KPCA with polynomial kernels to handle missing data. However, it is not clear how to extend this approach to other kernels. Furthermore, with polynomial kernels of high degree, the objective function is hard to optimize. Sanguinetti & Lawrence propose an elegant framework to handle missing data. The framework is based on the probabilistic interpretation inherited from Probabilistic PCA. However, Sanguinetti & Lawrence do not address the problem of outliers.

We present also the OCSVM method used on our work which belongs a family of classifiers based on the SVM of [31] that constructs a hypothesis which estimates the support of the normal distribution, the decision surface constructed separates the normal and anomaly data vectors in the data set and is able to classify unseen data with a decision function. The one-class SVM has two formulations; the hyperplane version of [32] operates by denoting the origin as the only member of the anomalous class, and then separating the majority of the data from the origin with a hyperplane. The alternative formulation is the hypersphere [33] where normal data is enclosed in a hypersphere with those data points outside the hypersphere being considered as anomalies.

This paper presents a novel cost function based on Mahalanobis kernel using Mahalanobis distance that unifies the treatment of outliers in KPCA. Experiments show that our algorithm outperforms existing approaches.

3 Outlier Detection in Wireless Sensor Networks

Sensor data is highly susceptible to various sources of errors such as changing environmental conditions which may produce noise or noise from other sources [10]. These noises can severely affect data transmitted to central base. These abnormal data are called outliers. It is used for finding errors, noise, missing values, inconsistent data, or duplicate data. This abnormal value may affect the quality of data and reduces the system performance. There are three sources of outliers occurred in WSNs: errors, events, and malicious attacks as described above. The use of Outlier detection technique is very important in several real life applications, such as, environmental monitoring, health and medical monitoring, industrial monitoring, surveillance monitors and target tracking [11].

3.1 Errors

An error refers to a noise-related measurement or data coming from a faulty sensor. Outliers caused by errors may occur frequently, while outliers caused by events tend to have extremely smaller probability of occurrence. Erroneous data is normally represented as an arbitrary change and is extremely different from the rest of the data.

3.2 Events

An event is defined as a particular phenomenon that changes the real-world state, e.g., forest fire, chemical spill, air pollution, etc. This sort of outlier normally lasts for a relatively long period of time and changes historical pattern of sensor data. However, faulty sensors may also generate similar long segmental outliers as events and therefore it is hard to distinguish the two different outlier sources only by examining one sensing series of a node itself.

In wireless sensor networks, the sensors have low cost and low energy, so to improve the quality and performance, the better solution is to use outlier detection technique. Evaluation of an outlier detection technique for WSNs depends on whether it can satisfy the mining accuracy requirements while maintaining the resource consumptions of WSNs to a minimum. Outlier detection techniques are required to maintain a high detection rate while keeping the false alarm rate (number of normal data that are incorrectly considered as outliers) low [12, 13]. A receiver operating characteristic (ROC) curves usually is used to represent the trade-off between the detection rate and false alarm rate. For the problem, we can summarize many problems in detection of outliers in WSNs as follows:

- High communication cost
- Modeling normal objects and outliers effectively
- Application specific outlier detection
- Identifying outlier source
- Distributed data
- Communication failures frequently
- Dynamic network topology.

4 Proposed Model

A sensor network consist a collection of sensor that can measure characteristics of their local environment from real world physical phenomenon. It performs certain computation, and transmits the collected data samples to base station. Then it is partitioned onto groups or clusters. Each group consists of a cluster head and a number of members. Nodes which belong to the same cluster are geographically close and monitoring generally similar phenomenon (Fig. 1). In this work, we will not take into consideration clustering details. We assume that the network is pre-partitioned and the clusters are predefined: every cluster is defined by his cluster head and members.

A wireless sensor network consists of several sensors nodes which collect data samples from real world physical phenomenon. Let s consider a set of m sensor nodes measuring each one a multi-real valued attribute at each time instant where $X = (X_1, \ldots, X_m)$ is an m-dimensional random variable [21]. To detect outlier, we present our methodology described in the figure below:

We first propose the Distributed and Efficient One-class Outliers Detection Classifier (DEOODC) based on Mahalanobis Kernel used for outlier detection in wireless sensor networks (WSNs).

Our DEOODC algorithm has some advantages such as lower training time, lower classification time, and lower memory requirements. So, the aims of our algorithm are presented in the following points:

- In DEOODC, the training is conducted using only one class which is the normal class since we do not have labeled training data that contains anomalies as the labeling is difficult and costly.

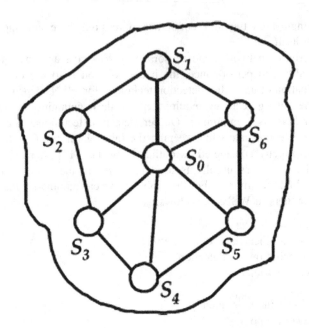

Fig. 1. Example of a closed neighborhood $N(S_i)$ of the distributed sensor node S_i

- The result of applying Automated Cluster Discovery Threshold (ACDT) procedure is only one threshold that separates the normal data from anomalies. This feature is very important for online detection in sensors because in the online testing phase it use only one value.
- In our proposed algorithm, the clustering threshold (Cl_{th}) in the ACDT procedure varies according to the WSN application. Our experimental results reveal that (Cl_{th}) is in the range [1 2] for IBRL dataset.

Our DEOODC model, like other classification models, has two main phases which are training phase and testing phase. We implement the model in each sensor node locally. The following subsections explain each phase in some details.

4.1   Training Phase (Offline)

The normal data measurements in the training phase are collected at each sensor node to build the normal model. This latter will be used in testing phase for real time outlier detection. The procedure used to build the normal model is described after.

In this step, we present the training procedure. First, the collected normal data measurements DM_{tr} are centered and normalized by the mean (ρ) and standard deviation -. Second, PCA is applied on the normalized measurements to obtain the Eigenvector Matrix (EV), and their corresponding eigenvalues (ev_i). Finally, the projection of each data measurement in the training data (PDM_i) on the new PC space is calculated by Eq: (1):

$$PDM_i = DM_{tr}(i) * EV(i) \tag{1}$$

Our proposed training phase of EOODC model (offline) is described as follow:

We start by normalize the normal training data. Then, apply the PCA on the training data and obtain the Eigenvector Matrix (EV), eigenvalues (ev_i) and the training data scores in the PC space (PDM_i). Then, select the number of PCs suitable for the application. After that, calculate the dissimilarity measure $Diss_{tr}$ using the training data measurement scores (PDM_i) and their corresponding eigenvalues (ev_i). Finally, apply the ACTD procedure to find the thresholds vector (TV_i) that separates between the different classes of data and will be used in testing phase.

The dissimilarity measure $Diss_{tr}$ is calculated for each data measurement in the training set using Eq. (2) and the number of PCs suitable for the application is chosen.

$$Diss_{Tr} = \sum \frac{PDM_i^2}{\lambda_i} \tag{2}$$

To find the threshold vector (TV_i), we apply the ACTD procedure [26] which will be used for classifying each real time measurement as normal or outlier. For the proposed EOODC, it is important to know that the vector (TV_i) contains a maximum of 2 values and one threshold value depending on the comparison threshold (Cl_{th}).

4.2 Testing Phase (Online)

For every new data measurement, in online method, collected at each sensor node is tested using the normal model built in the training phase of that particular node. This normal model is composed of the normalization parameters of the training measurements (mean (ρ), standard deviation (Std)), Eigenvector Matrix (EV), eigenvalues (ev_i) and the threshold vector (TV_i). Each measurement is classified as normal or outlier based on the comparison of its projection on the PC space with the threshold computed in the training phase. The procedure used to classify each new measurement in real time is described after.

The new data measurement is first normalized and centered using the same normalization parameters computed from training measurements in the training phase. Then, the projection score of new measurement on the PC space is calculated using the normal model parameters as in Eq. (3):

$$PDM_i = DM_{test} * EV \tag{3}$$

Our proposed testing phase of DEOODC model (online) is described as follow:

We start by normalize the real time data measurement using the same normalization parameters computed from the training data (Mean and Std). Then, calculate the D_{test} measure of the real time threshold in the same way of training phase. So, calculate the dissimilarity measure $Diss_{tr}$ using the training data measurement scores (PDM_i) and their corresponding eigenvalues (ev_i). Finally, compare D_{test} value with each value in the threshold value and assign the class index (i) that satisfies:

$$D_{test} > TH_i \ - \ - \ - > Outlier$$
$$0 \ - \ - > Normal$$

After that, the dissimilarity measure D_{test} for the new measurement is computed using Eq. (4).

$$D_{Test} = \sum \frac{PDM^2}{\lambda} \tag{4}$$

Finally, the D_{test} value is compared with the threshold value stored in the node and assigned the appropriate class (either normal or outlier) to the measurement if its D_{test} is smaller or greater than the threshold respectively.

4.3   Mahalanobis Kernel

In literature, many types of kernels were employed in the nonlinear transformation of data points (polynomial kernel, sigmoid kernel, etc.) but as we know, Mahalanobis kernel was not used yet in the field of wireless sensor networks. The Mahalanobis kernel (MK) is defined as:

$$K(x_i, x_j) = \exp\left(\frac{-1}{2\sigma^2} (x_i - x_j)^T Q^{-1} (x_i - x_j) \right) \tag{5}$$

Transformation results of such a kernel are similar to those of a density estimator as it gives a weighted value w_i for every sample x_i of input space. This weighting is not defined for each variable separately although some variables may be more relevant than others in the practice [14]. Let $\{x_1, \ldots, x_N\}$ be a dataset composed of N data points of dimension m, we define the data center c and the covariance matrix Q:

$$c = \frac{1}{N} \sum_{i=1}^{N} x_i \tag{6}$$

$$Q = \frac{1}{N} \sum_{i=1}^{N} (x_i - c)(x_i - c)^T \tag{7}$$

The Mahalanobis distance between a point and the center is defined as:

$$d(x) = \sqrt{(x - c)^T Q^{-1}(x - c)} \tag{8}$$

We define the Mahalanobis kernel function as follow, where H is a positive semi definite matrix:

$$A(x, x') = \exp(-(x - x')^T H (x - x'))$$ (9)

In this case, the Mahalanobis distance is calculated between every data point pair x and x'. The Mahalanobis kernel is an extension of the RBF kernel when $H = \gamma I$ with $\gamma > 0$ is a parameter that controls the depth of the kernel and I is the identity matrix. In practice, the Mahalanobis kernel (MK) is calculated only for one class:

$$A(x, x') = \exp(-\frac{\delta}{m}(x - x')^T Q^{-1}(x - x'))$$ (10)

Where $\delta > 0$ is a scale factor to control the Mahalanobis distance.

The MK kernel differs from the Gaussian kernel in the fact that for every dimension of the input space data it defines a specific depth value or weight. This makes the calculated decision boundary has a non-spherical shape relative to the center of data points. Using kernel PCA in a learning task has to be well carried out. Choosing the better parameters is important in order to establish the best model with higher accuracy and lower false alarm rate. The outlier detection method of kernel PCA depends generally on kernel type and kernel parameters. In this work, Mahalanobis kernel given by (10) is chosen to resolve the nonlinearity of data distribution. This type of kernel depends on kernel width and number of principal components [23]. We present below the pseudo code algorithm of the training phase and the pseudo code algorithm of the detection phase.

4.4   Outlier Detection Metric

Outlier detection is aim to detect the outlier based on Detection rate and False Alarm Rate described on following equation:

$$Detection\ Rate = \frac{Number\ of\ correctly\ classified\ instances}{total\ number\ of\ instances} * 100\%$$

$$False\ Alarm\ Rate = \frac{Number\ of\ incorrectly\ classified\ instances}{total\ number\ of\ instances} * 100\%$$

Detection Rate: It is defined as the ratio between the numbers of correctly classified instances to the total number of instances.

False Alarm Rate: It is defined as the ratio between the numbers of incorrectly classified instances to the total number of instances.

5   Experimental Results

5.1   Datasets

To validate the proposed models, some data samples were extracted from three WSN deployments which represent static and dynamic environments. The next subsections introduce the datasets and explain the data labeling procedure. The datasets that are used in this paper are extracted from the following WSN deployments:

- *Intel Berkeley Research Lab (IBRL):* IBRL dataset [16] was collected from the WSN deployed at Intel Berkeley Research Laboratory, University of Berkeley. The network consists of 54 Mica2Dot sensor nodes and was deployed in the period of 30 days from 15/04/2004 until 14/05/2004.
- *Grand St. Bernard (GStB):* GStB dataset [17] is one of sensorscope project deployment dataset was gathered using WSN deployment at the Grand St. Bernard pass that is located between Italy and Switzerland. The network is formed of 23 sensors that record metrological environmental data that include temperature and humidity.
- *Sensorscope Lausanne Urban Canopy Experiment (LUCE):* LUCE dataset [18] was collected by a sensorscope project in the École Polytechnique Fédérale de Lausanne (EFPL) campus between July 2006 and May 2007. The measurement system was based on a WSN of 110 sensor nodes deployed on the EPFL campus to measure key environment quantities which include; ambient temperature, surface temperature, and relative humidity.

5.2   DEOODC and OCSVM: Comparative Study

This section specifies the performance evaluation of our technique based DEOODC using Mahalanobis kernel and one class SVM. In our experiments, we have used a real data gathered from a deployment of WSN in the Intel Berkeley Research Laboratory, Grand St. Bernard and Sensorscope Lausanne Urban Canopy Experiment. We simulate our protocol both in Matlab and consider a closed neighborhood as shown in Fig. 2, which is centered at a node with its 6 spatially neighboring nodes. Here, we use Intel CPU (centrino 2) with the MATLAB version R2009a. Mahalanobis kernel is used recently in the field of WSN, specially based outlier detection, was introduced in several works. Kernel PCA performance was showcased in comparison to other established kernel-based methods [17]. To compute the Kernel PCA transform of a set of test patterns, this approach chooses a training set and a suitable projection dimensionality p, and, finally, computes the Mahalanobis distance (MD) for each of these test patterns. Given the projection dimensionality p, outliers are identified as data points, whose MD exceeds an appropriately established threshold value *TH*. Our method has been tested on real data as seen in Table 1.

When comparing the results given on our experimentation by DEOODC and OCSVM, we see that using Mahalanobis distance is more beneficial to detect outliers. The value presented in the in bold represent the best value compared to the other values. For example, in IBRL dataset, the bold value (99.12) represents the percentage of accuracy using in MD which is the best one compared to OCSVM. Then, this comparison reveals that OCSVM may not be an effective measure of deviation from normalcy, when compared to using the DEOODC. Thus, it does not satisfactorily fit the normal data because many potential outliers would not be detected. So, our proposed method has an important advantage compared to OCSVM that detects perfectly the

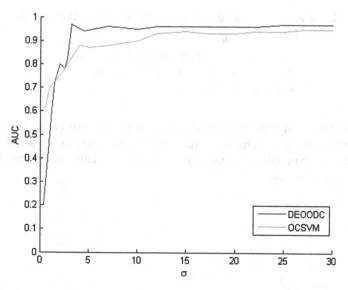

Fig. 2. IBRL dataset: Maximum AUC value versus kernel parameter value.

Table 1. DEOODC and OCSVM on the real world Datasets.

	DEOODC	OCSVM
Intel Berkeley	**0.9912**	0.9783
(IBRL)	0.9635	**0.9743**
	0.9727	0.6152
	0.9551	**0.9642**
	0.9760	0.6396
Grand-St- Bernard (GStB)	**0.9891**	0.7528
	0.9752	0.8457
	0.9675	**0.9732**
	0.9686	0.8593
	0.9841	**0.9876**
Sensorscope (LUCE)	**0.9837**	0.9641
	0.9206	**0.9360**
	0.9172	0.7533
	0.8336	0.7997
	0.9611	**0.9673**

outliers as observed in our experiments and as mentioned by the table. Then, it is clear that DEOODC is more sensitive to the detection of FPR and DR (as shown in Table 2) than OCSVM. However, it seems to capture much better the overall structure of the normal data.

Based on the following figures (Figs. 2, 3 and 4), we presents a comparison between DEOODC and OCSVM. The ROC curve shows that DEOODC based

Table 2. Detection rate and false alarm based DEOODC on IBRL real dataset.

	Nodes					
	N25	N28	N29	N31	N32	Average
DR (%)	100	98	95	97	100	98
FPR (%)	14	0	8	1	0	4.6

Mahalanobis Kernel are much better than that of OCSVM in terms of outliers detection varied by sigma in our experiments. After the following figures we see that Mahalanobis kernel is more efficient either by simulation on Matlab or on real dataset in Wireless Sensors Networks.

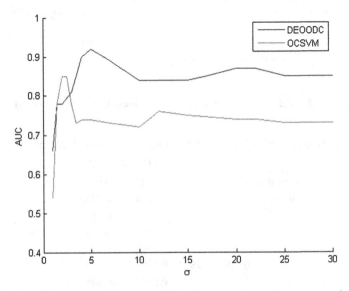

Fig. 3. GStB dataset: Maximum AUC value versus kernel parameter value.

Our methodology can be applied on both small and large datasets. Our Approach is scalable and very efficient in the WSN application because when the dataset used are large, this give a better accuracy, increase the percentage of detection rate and decrease the false alarm rate. So, the use of other datasets doesn t affect the result because our solution is efficient and specially in WSNs domain. Our method is tested on control of fire in a wheat field application, so, it gives us a good detection rate with a minimum false alarm rate compared to Great-Duck-Island: [28], Volcano Monitoring: [29] and Sensorscope [30].

5.3 Computational Complexity

We present the computational complexity of our proposed model on the testing phase in online manner. In this phase, the upper bound computational complexity involved in this process is O (M), where M is the number of observed variables. The training phase

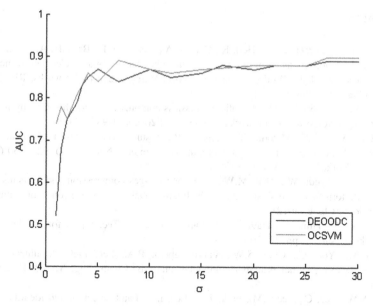

Fig. 4. LUCE dataset: Maximum AUC value versus kernel parameter value

which involves the calculation of the PCs has a time complexity of O (NM^2) where N and M are the size and the dimension of the training set respectively. The complexity of online testing phase in our model structure is O (M) which is O (N^3) for the training phase of the OCSVM. The retraining of the OCSVM will cause a high power consumption which makes it unsuitable for anomaly detection in these types of environments compared to our DEOODC model.

6 Conclusion

In our work, we presents a comparative study between Distributed and Efficient One-class Outliers Detection Classifier (DEOODC) based on mahalanobis Kernel and One Class Support Vector Machine (OCSVM) for outlier detection in wireless sensor networks (WSNs). Our DEOODC demonstrated a higher classification performance on a real database used compared with OCSVM. So, our method demonstrated to be more robust against outlier detection within the training set. In order to showcase the merits of our proposed approach, we performed a number of experiments that compared the capability of detecting outliers in data of the One-Class SVM and DEOODC detection methods. As a future work, we focus on improving the performances of the proposed model and extending it to be able to detect events that may occur instead of only considering outliers in an adaptive method. Also, we intend to utilize this model as a core for a cooperative framework for the whole network to achieve the energy efficiency.

References

1. Naumowicz, T., Freeman, T., Heil, R., Calsyn, A., Hellmich, E., Brandle, A., Guilford, T., Schiller, J.: Autonomous monitoring of vulnerable habitats using a wireless sensor network. In: Proceedings of the Workshop on Real-World Wireless Sensor Networks, REALWSN 2008, Glasgow, Scotland (2008)
2. Marcelloni, F., Vecchio, M.: An efficient lossless compression algorithm for tiny nodes of monitoring wireless sensor networks. Comput. J. **52**(8), 969–987 (2009)
3. Akyildiz, A., Ian, F., Melodia, T., Kaushik, R.: A survey on wireless multimedia sensor networks. J. Comput. Netw.: Int. J. Comput. Telecommun. Netw. **51**(4), 921–960 (2007). Inc. New York, NY, USA, United State
4. Ghorbel, O., Ayedi, W., Jmal, M.W., Abid, M.: Images compression and transmission in WSN: Performances Analysis. In: 14th International Conference on Communication Technology, Chine (2012)
5. Zhang, Y., Meratnia, N., Havinga, P.: Outlier detection Techniques for wireless sensor networks: A survey, pp. 11–20 (2008)
6. Lee, J.-M., Yoo, C., Choi, S.W., Vanrolleghem, P.A., Lee, I.-B.: Nonlinear process monitoring using kernel principal component analysis. Chem. Eng. Sci. **59**(1), 223–234 (2004)
7. Choi, S.W., Lee, C., Lee, J.M., Park, J.H., Lee, I.B.: Fault detection and identification of nonlinear processes based on kernel PCA. Chemometr. Intell. Lab. Syst. **75**(1), 55–67 (2005)
8. Scholkopf, B., Smola, A., Muller, K.-R.: Nonlinear component analysis as a kernel eigenvalue problem. Neural Comput. **10**(5), 1299–1319 (1998)
9. Kapitanova, K., Son, S.H., Kang, K.D.: Event detection in wireless sensor networks. In: Second International Conference, ADHOCNETS 2010, Victoria, BC, Canada, August 2010
10. Zhang, Y., Meratnia, N.P., Havinga, J.M.: Distributed online outlier detection in wireless sensor networks using ellipsoidal support vector machine. Ad Hoc Networks, December 2012
11. Koupaie, H.M., Ibrahim, S., Hosseinkhani, J.: Outlier detection in stream data by machine learning and feature selection methods. Int. J. Adv. Comput. Sci. Inf. Technol. (IJACSIT) **2**, 17–24 (2013)
12. Rajasegarar, S., Leckie, C., Palaniswami, M., Bezdek, J.C.: Quarter sphere based distributed anomaly detection in wireless sensor networks. In: Proceedings of IEEE International Conference on Communications, pp. 3864–3869 (2007)
13. Zhang, Y., Hammb, N.A.S., Meratniaa, N., Steinb, A., Van de Voorta, M., Havingaa, P.J. M.: Statistics-based outlier detection for wireless sensor networks. Int. J. Geogr. Inf. Sci. **26** (8), 1373–1392 (2012)
14. Chakour, C., et al.: Adaptive kernel principal component analysis for nonlinear time-varying processes monitoring. In: ICEECA 2012 (2012)
15. IBRL, Intel Berkely Reseach Lab Dataset (2004). http://db.csail.mit.edu/labdata/1120labdata.html
16. GStB, Grand-St-Bernard dataset (2007). http://lcav.epfl.ch/cms/lang/en/pid/86035
17. LUCE, Lausanne Urban Canopy Experiment (2007). http://lcav.epfl.ch/cms/lang/en/1122pid/86035 ed
18. Werner-Allen, G., Lorin, C.Z.K., Welsh, M., Marcillo, O.: Johnson, J, Ruiz, M., Lees, J.: Deploying a wireless sensors network on an active volcano. IEEE Internet Comput. **10**, 18–25 (2006)

19. Szewezyk, R., Mainwaring, A., Polastre, J., Culler, D.: Analysis of alarge scale habitet monitoring application. In: Proceedings of the second ACM Conference on Embedded Networked Sensors Systems (SenSys), Baltimore (2004)
20. Verma, K., Kumar, V., Samparthi, S.: Outlier detection of data in wireless sensor networks using kernel density estimation. Int. J. Comput. Appl. **5**, 28–32 (2010). Published By Foundation of Computer Science
21. Nguyen, M.H., Torre, F.: Robust Kernel Principal Component Analysis (2008)
22. Ding, M., Tian, Z., Xu, H.: Adaptive kernel principal component analysis. Signal Process. **90**, 1542–1553 (2010)
23. Zheng, W., Zou, C., Zhao, L.: An improved algorithm for kernel principal component analysis. Neural Process. **22**, 49–56 (2005)
24. Franc, Vojtěch, Hlavč, Václav: Greedy Algorithm for a Training Set Reduction in the Kernel Methods. In: Petkov, Nicolai, Westenberg, Michel A. (eds.) CAIP 2003. LNCS, vol. 2756, pp. 426–433. Springer, Heidelberg (2003)
25. Hoffmann, H.: Kernel PCA for novelty detection. Pattern Recogn. **40**, 863–874 (2007)
26. Xie, Z., Quirino, T., Shyu, M.-L., Chen, S.-C., Chang, L.: UNPCC: a novel unsupervised classification scheme for network intrusion detection. Presented at the Proceedings of the 18th IEEE International Conference on Tools with Artificial Intelligence (2006)
27. Hotelling, H.: Analysis of a complex of statistical variables with principal components. J. Educ. Psychol. **24**, 498–520 (1933)
28. Szewezyk, R., Mainwaring, A., Polastre, J., Culler, D.: Analysis of alarge scale habitet monitoring application. In: Proceedings of the Second ACM Conference en Embedded Networked Sensors Systems (SenSys), Baltimore (2004)
29. Werner-Allen, G., Lorin, K.C.Z., Welsh, M., Marcillo, O., Johnson, J., Ruiz, M., Lees, J.: Deploying a wireless sensors network on an active volcano. IEEE Internet Comput. **10**, 18–25 (2006)
30. Barrenetxea, G., Ingelrest, F., Schaefer, G., Vetterli, M., Couach, O., Parlange, M.: SensorScope: out-of-the-box Environmental monitoring. In: Proceeding of the 7th International Conference on Information Processing in Sensor Networks, pp. 332–343, 22–24 April 2008
31. Vapnik, V.: The nature of statistical learning theory (Information Science and Statistics) (1995)
32. Scholkopf, B., Platt, J., Shawe-Taylor, J., Smola, J., Williamson, R.C.: Estimating the support of a high-dimensional distribution. Neural Comput. **13**(7), 1443–1471 (2001)
33. Tax, D.M., Duin, R.P.: Support vector data description. Machine Learn. **27**(4), 45–66 (2004)

Brain-Computer Interface as Networking Entity in Body Area Networks

M.A. Lopez-Gordo[1,2,3(✉)] and F. Pelayo Valle[4]

[1] Department of Engineering in Automatic and Electronics, Electronic,
Architecture of Computers and Networks, University of Cadiz, Cádiz, Spain
malg@nicolo.es
[2] Department of Signal Theory, Communications and Networking,
University of Granada, 18071 Granada, Spain
[3] Nicolo Association, Churriana de la Vega, Granada, Spain
[4] Department of Computer Architecture and Technology, University of Granada,
c/Periodista Daniel Saucedo, 18071 Granada, Spain
fpelayo@ugr.es

Abstract. Modern BCIs are non-invasive, wireless, wearable and EEG-based systems capable to transduce brain signals into cognitive information and stream it out in form of data. BCIs have rarely been considered as part of the network. Thus, data communication approaches have not even tried. The consequence is a suboptimal communication in terms of performance, usability and reliability. In this paper we present BCI as a paradigm in Wireless Body Area Networks (WBANs) that interfaces multisensorial sources with the user brain. The BCI-WBAN concept treats cognitive processes as communication end-points in which sensorial information is consumed by cognitive processes. In the context of WBAN, BCIs implement the functionalities of the lower layers of communication open system: signal transduction into data, access control to the physical and cognitive media and data transmission. The BCI-WBAN paradigm extends the scope of WBAN from mere biosignal sensing by adding interpretation of neural correlates of cognitive information.

Keywords: Telemedicine · EEG · WBAN · Brain-computer interface

1 Introduction

The main purpose of BCI systems is to enable users to communicate with computers without muscles by interpreting and transmitting cognitive information from electrophysiological correlates. Along the last two decades, many definitions have been proposed for Brain-computer interfaces (BCIs), the most popular one, established that a BCI "is a communication system that does not depend on the brain's normal output pathways of peripheral nerves and muscles" [1]. Originally, it was intended for people with severe motor impairment (e.g. locked-in syndrome, Amyotrophic Lateral Sclerosis (ALS), etc.) with no other way of communication but the direct detection of the user volition from neurosignals. Currently, there are BCI works in diverse areas, such as cognitive rehabilitation, entertainment, education, neuromarketing, etc. [2]. The majority

© Springer International Publishing Switzerland 2015
M.C. Aguayo-Torres et al. (Eds.): WWIC 2015, LNCS 9071, pp. 274–285, 2015.
DOI: 10.1007/978-3-319-22572-2_20

of BCIs are based on EEG signals because they can be sensed with non-invasive techniques and their price is relatively low even for small labs.

There are several types of BCI systems. For instance, BCIs based on Event-related potentials (ERPs) are ones of the most popular. ERPs are indicators of brain activities that occur in preparation for or in response to discrete external events [3]. Other BCIs use repetitive stimulus to evoke a permanent response (e.g. visual steady-state responses (SSVEP) [4], auditory steady-state response (ASSR) [5], etc.) whose energy can be modulated by cognitive task such as selective attention [6]. These potentials are narrow-bandwidth responses with high signal-to-noise ratio (SNR) that facilitates their processing and detection. Furthermore, there are BCIs based on the modulation of the amplitude of spectral bands. In this classification, we include those based on the amplitude modulation of sensory-motor rhythm by means of motor imagery [7], alpha band by means of mental switching from relaxation to arousal states, slow cortical potentials by means of own-user strategy, etc.

BCIs have improved usability and user comfort thanks to new advances in wireless technology and the use of new polymers and substrates for dry sensing (see [8] for a complete review). Now, the range of potential users is much larger, with applications in ambulatory EEG sensing for clinic testing, entertainment and other uses [9, 10]. The most advanced BCI are low-cost, wearable and dry EEG headsets devices with wireless transmission that allows mobile EEG services [11, 12]. However, and despite all these new features, both classical and current BCIs suffer from the same inconvenients.

Current and classical EEG-BCIs have some problems in common. First, EEG is a very noisy signal and any feature considered for the interpretation of the corresponding cognitive or mental state gives rise to poor inference. Typically, this problem has been overcome by grand-averaging trials (e.g. approximately one hundred for visual evoked potentials [13]). Assuming EEG to be stationary, the improvement in SNR follows Eq. (1) with N the number of trials

$$\text{SNRnew(dB)} = \text{SNRoriginal(dB)} + 10\log10(N) \qquad (1)$$

SNR improvement is the first step for throughput improvement. Throughput is other problem. Typically, BCI achieve an information transmission rate (ITR) of approximately between 0.3 to 0.6 bits/s [14]. Furthermore and as far as we know, the maximum reported ever, was 1.13 bits/s in 2003 [15]. Since then, and despite technologic advances, performance has not significantly improved. One of the reasons that could justify this disappointment is that other important aspects of BCI have not been changed. In this regards we could point out two aspects: data processing techniques and psycho-physiologic paradigms.

Apart of few exceptions, BCIs has not been treated as a technology suited for data networks. Brain signals are typically processed with intelligent algorithms of extraction, dimension reduction and classification of features that include complex multivariate analysis. In this regards we just cite some BCI studies based on Self-Organizing Map [16], Support Vector Machine theory [17], Artificial Neural Networks (ANNs) such as multilayer perceptron (MLP), etc. However, a simple analysis of the fundaments of BCIs would conclude that they really represent interfaces of a dta network.

Then, typical data transmission issues such as media access and control, signal transduction, throughput improvement or data error correction deserve to be considered and applied to the brain as an entity of the data network. In summary, in BCI-WBANs a biological organ, our brain, is part of the network.

In this paper we present BCIs as a specific link of the data network that interface input sensorial information with cognitive processes in the context of WBAN. Taking this approach, conventional network procedures and assumption can be reused, thus giving rise to a much efficient interface.

The most important contribution in the BCI-WBAN paradigm is the definition of a cyber area network composed by electric and biologic entities in which data and information flows bidirectional and transparently

2   The BCI-WBAN Concept

2.1   Definition and Overall Concept

BCI Definition. In BCI literature there are many definitions of BCI. For instance, the first one was given in 1973 by Vidal who stated "The BCI system is geared to use both the spontaneous EEG and the specific evoked responses triggered by time-dependent stimulation under various conditions for the purpose of controlling such external apparatus as e.g. prosthetic devices" [18]. Another definition giving in 2002 by expert established that a direct brain-computer interface is a device that provides the brain with a new, non-muscular communication and control channel [1]. However, the most popular definition was given in 2000 by a group of prestigious neuroscientifics during the First International Meeting of BCIs [19].

BCI-WBAN Definition. We define BCI-WBAN as the networking area that encompasses from sources of multi-sensorial information to our brain. Multisensorial sources are multimedia devices, speakers, TV, audio-head set, traffic lights, etc. Other devices related to clinic and rehabilitation are also considered (e.g. electric, tactile, haptic, visual, auditory or somatosensory stimulators). There are also biological sources. For instance, voices in multi-taker scenarios (e.g. cocktail party phenomenon [20]), human faces, etc. Conversely, in the brain side we consider cognitive processes that perceive, attend, interpret these sensorial signals and finally take a decision. Decisions can be taken either directly based on these sensorial signals or not.

Then, BCIs constitute the communication interface in the WBAN that, based on brain signals, extract relevant cognitive information generated by brain structures and generates and output stream of data. Typically, this data stream is used to feedback the sensorial source, thus closing the communication loop. Also, it can be used for communication of cognitive states (e.g. level of attention, tiredness, arousal), interest or endogenous context update as response to a novel and relevant sensorial information. Some examples of application of BCI-WBAN [21] could be the online measure of cognitive load in dangerous works, a communication speller for people suffering from locked-in syndrome or ALS [22], or as an attention/interest detector with potential application in neuromarketing or Ambient Assisted Living (AAL).

2.2 Architecture

BCI. BCI architecture was firstly defined by [23]. A typical implementation is the EEG-BCI, which is compounded of the following blocks (see Fig. 1):

- EEG Acquisition System: electrodes, front-end amplifier, A/D converter.
- Signal processing: Signal pre-processing, feature extraction and classification.
- Application Interface: This block provides feedback to the BCI user and also interfaces devices, sensors and actuators.
- User interface: Any communication system needs mechanism to feeback emisor with the state of the communication. In BCIs, a display is typically used to present the BCI user the results. Then BCI users can on-line modify their cognitive actions to obtain the optimal result.

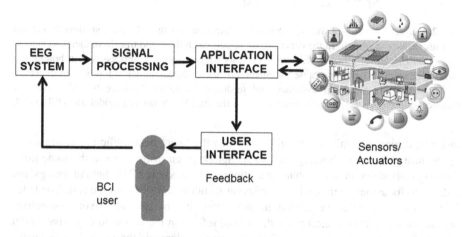

Fig. 1. BCI architecture. Adapted from [23].

BCI-WBAN. BCI-WBAN architecture is compounded of the blocks and elements needed to present multisensorial information to user and transmit out cognitive information. Figure 2 illustrates a layered version of the BCI-WBAN architecture. Firstly, a source transmits sensorial signals to the user. User receives the signals by means of receptors or sense organs. Receptors transduce this sensorial information into electrical currents that reach cortical regions in our brain via afferent pathway.

- If the context of the OSI model these processes occur in the physical layer. In the context of BCI-WBAN,these processes occur in the physiological layer.

These electro-physiological signals reach cognitive structures in the cognitive media and trigger concomitant cognitive processes, such as perception, attention, cognition and volition. Typically, these processes temporally correlate with middle-latency potentials (approx. 100 ms. after stimulus onset). In our daily routine, we are rarely surrounded by just a sensorial source. Conversely, we are always immersed in a mess of multi-sensorial stimuli that fight to grab our attention. For

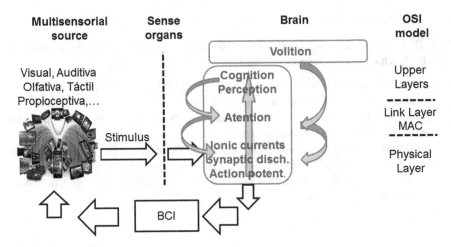

Fig. 2. Layered version of the BCI-WBAN architecture. On the left, external devices present BCI user sensorial stimuli. In the center, sense organs catch them and transform their mechanical energy into electrical currents. Electrical currents trigger cognitive processes in a bottom-top directon. Executive functions cause modulation of the electrical signal in top-bottom direction. BCI measure this top-down influence and feedback the external source (or other network enteities). On the right, the equivalence between the BCI-WAN layered model and OSI model.

instance, during our daily commuting we listen the radio, hear traffic noise, see traffic lights, hear policeman shouting and our navigator given instructions at the same time. Although attention in more than one stimulus is possible [24], human beings are tailored to focus our attention in one relevant stimulus and filter out the rest. The latter is the so-called selective attention. Attention, in its several flavors (selective, pre-attentional, dichotic, etc.) plays the role of referee in the access to cognitive media where cognitive processes occur. Then, attention implements the media-access layer.

- If the context of the OSI model, control to the access media ocurr in the link layer. In the context of BCI-WBAN, the access to the cognitive media is executed by the cognitive task called attention.

  Once user have perceived, recognized and interpreted the external information, then decides and action. A simple action that user could take could be switch attention to another stimulus. When that happens, top-down mechanisms occurs that cause modulation of the energy of signals in physical layer by enhancing of that of the target stimuli and attenuating that of the distracters. In turns, the latter causes and diminishing of the energy in the bottom-up direction toward upper cognitive layers. In turns, that facilitates the attentional effort needed as media-access controller of the incoming stimuli. The latter constitutes a loop (see Fig. 2).

- If the context of the OSI model, execution of actions as a consequence of volition is introduced by users via the application layer. In the context of BCI-WBAN, the access to the cognitive media is executed by executive system of our brain.

2.3   BCI-WBAN in the Network

Figure 3 shows full application model that includes not only the elements of BCI-WBAN described in previous sections, but elements of remote connections in the context of Wide Arena Networks (WANs). This general model would enable tele-services based on on-line cognitive rehabilitation. Currently there studies of telematics services for remote cognitive rehabilitation. However, these proposal lack of interactivity [25]. The BCI-WBAN architecture complements these services by offering the user mobility, usability and on-line feedback during the execution of the program. The components and elements of the BCI-WBAN concept of the proposed tele-service are:

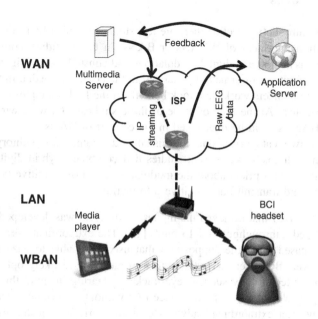

Fig. 3. Application model of BCI-WAN for a remote service.

WAN

- Application server: The main application runs in this server. It is responsible for:
  - User control interface: It offers a GUI to person in charge of the execution of the session (e.g. in the context of application such as remote EEG testing for clinical purposes, rehabilitation programs, etc.)
  - Sensorial stimulation control: It triggers sensorial programs stored in a multi-media server that, in turns, streams down them to the media player.
  - Signal processing: This function inputs EEG signals form EEG headset and process them to obtain an output data stream.
- Multimedia server: It stores a collection of multimedia programs that users could use.

LAN

- Access point: Typically, a wireless router.

WBAN

- Media player: It plays the multimedia stimulus streamed from Multimedia server.
- BCI headset: It acquires EEG signals and transmit them toward the Application server.

3 Related Works

As stated in the introduction section there are few studies in which BCIs are considered as communication interfaces of WBANs or BANs. In these studies, communication techniques such as analog and digital modulations and constellation of signals are used to detect and transmit out information generated in the cognitive media. In this section we mention some pioneers works that took benefits of the BCI principles to achieve an efficient performance. At the time of some of these studies, BCI were wired devices. Then, BCI-WBANs should be interpreted in the context of BANs.

We present two categories, one for visual and another for auditory sensorial information. In both cases, we present studies that combined hybrid digital communication techniques with priors about the modulating effect of cognitive task on brain signals to detect and transmit out cognitive information.

Visual BCIs. The BCI that achieved the highest throughout was developed by Gao in 2003 and achieved a throughput of 1.13 bits/s [15]. The extraordinary performance in this study was based upon the supposition that user were able to gaze at different stimulus. However, BCI users with the ability to gaze would likely opt for a much faster and simpler technology such as eye-trackers. Bearing in mind this limitation, authors in [26] developed a high performance BCI without the need of gazing. At that moment, this was an extraordinary advantage in comparison with the rest of visual BCIs that requested gazing. Despite this handicap, the maximum throughout achieved was 0.64 ± 0.27 bits/s with peaks of 1.16 bits/s and accuracy (or 1-BER) of 90 ± 7 %, which is an excellent performance for a binary BCI. The most important factor that contributed to this excellent performance was the use of customized visual stimulation whose corresponding brain response constituted a constellation of two signals. Then, detection was performed with a coherent on-off keying receiver (OOK) based on a bank of two correlators (see Fig. 4.1).

With the idea use digital receiver to detect symbols in a constellation of brain signals described in the previous paragraph, in [27, 28] the number of symbols in the EEG constellation increased by reusing the same frequency (see Fig. 4.2). This was a novel approach in visual BCIs. Till that moment, phase was not been widely used in on-line detection. Instead, most of the visual BCI just asynchronously measure energy of brain activity. The reason for that is the difficulty to keep accurate synchrony between the stimulation unit and the EEG acquisition system. The advantage introduced in these two studies was the use of a coherent detection, in which information of

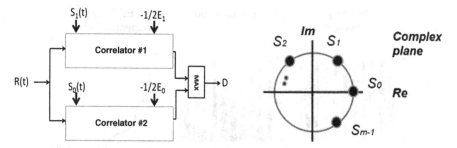

Fig. 4. (1) Bank of correlators that implement a coherent OOK receiver with decisions based on maximum a posteriori criterion. The signal in reception ($R(t)$), passed through two correlators that also input a replica of the signals of the constellation ($S_1(t)$ and $S_2(t)$) and the energy of each one (E_1 and E_2); (2) Constellation of m signals of a PSK modulation. Adapted from [27, 28].

phase is used to detect the correct symbol from the constellation. According to theory, the gain introduced by a coherent OOK receiver is approximately 3dBs in comparison with the non-coherent. Then, this efficient design of BCI attained better performance.

Auditory BCIs. Originally, BCIS were meant for people unable to do muscular movements. However, visual BCIs contradict the original definition of BCIs because they require the subjects to gaze, explore and coordinate the eyes, thus causing muscular movement [29]. One important reason of the existence of auditory BCIs is that they do not require the user to gaze, thus being suitable even for people with visual impairment.

In [30], a tailored auditory stimulation was design to evoke auditory steady-state responses (ASSR). ASSRs are composed of a train of superimposed auditory brainstem responses, that added in phase, conforms an averaged response with most of the energy located around the frequency of repetition [6]. In this case, detection of cognitive information was performed by building a constellation of two signals. The authors of this study took advantage of well-known properties of the physiology of the human auditory system that, when stimulated with an AM modulated signal, can be described as a non-coherent AM demodulator. Figure 5 illustrates the following example: when we present a stimulus consisting of a carrier (e.g. 1 kHz) AM modulated by a sinusoidal wave (e.g. 100 Hz) the transduction from mechanical energy into electrical nerve impulses is performed in such a way that only semi-cycles of the same sign (e.g. positive) of the incoming wave evoke electrical nerve impulses. The overall effect is a rectification of the shape of the sound that, after low-band filtered, works as envelope detector. Then, the modulating signal of 100 Hz, is recovered from EEG as if it were an AM receptor. This principle, which is broadly used in clinical testing for assessment of hearing impairment [31] was first used in this study to detect and transmit out information from the cognitive media.

The most clear example in BCI literature of the use of the BCI as a digital communication system in the context of BANs was developed in [32]. The authors of this study presented a procedure based on the binary phase-shift keying (BPSK) receiver that permitted detection of selective attention to human speeches in real-time. They used barely-audible counter-phased perturbations of the speeches in such a way that the joined EEG response (speeches-perturbations) elicited a robust BPSK constellation (see

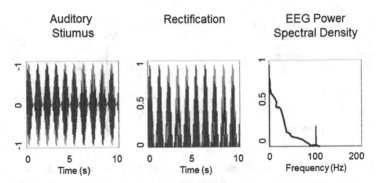

Fig. 5. Rectification of an AM modulated stimulus by human auditory system. The first plot shows one second window of a sinusoidal wave of frequency 1 kHz (carrier) AM modulated by a pure tone of 100 Hz. The plot in de middle shows the rectification process caused by hair cells in the cochlea and other neural structures of the human auditory system. The plot on the right shows the Power Spectral Density of a typical EEG acquisition in which the modulating pure tone of 100 Hz appears with high SNR. In summary, behavior of the human auditory system when stimulated with a AM modulated signal, corresponds to that of a non-coherent AM receiver.

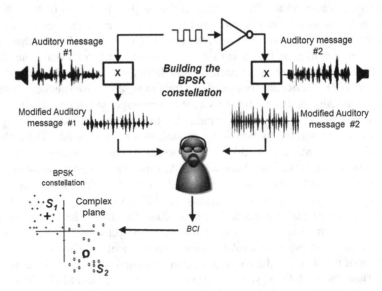

Fig. 6. BPSK system for detection of attention. This schema is part of a dichotic listening task, in which user must pay attention to one stimulus and ignore the other. To facilitate detection of the attended stimulus, both stimulus were perturbed by modulating their envelope by two counter-phases pure tone of the same frequency. The effect of the perturbation was the generation of a BPSK constellation on brain signals. Adapted from [32].

Fig. 6). Then attention was detected and transmitted by mean of BPSK receiver. The results confirmed the expected generation of the BPSK constellation by the human auditory system. Furthermore, evaluation of performance in terms of throughput and

BER was measured under different conditions of SNR and the results fairly matched the theoretical. The latter was an extraordinary advance in the context of BCI as communication system in BANs. Other studies such as [33, 34] tried similar approaches with similar success.

The PLAT-EEG project. The BCI-WBAN is a concept still to develop. Despite some pioneers studies mentioned in previous section, more steps must be takenamong BCI researches. In this section we briefly present a project that, based on the principles of BCI-WBAN, moves forward this direction.

PLAT-EEG aims for the development of a high performance platform for the acquisition, processing of neurosignals, detection and remote transmission of cognitive information (see Fig. 7). The platform will support common services and resources to offer tele-services and BCI applications, for instance, on-line sensing of neurosignals, or cognitive programs for rehabilitation. Among potential users of this platform, we mention people with sever motor and muscular impairment, people suffering from attention disorders, etc.

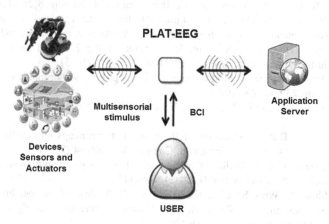

Fig. 7. Basic architecture of PLAT-EEG Adapted from [35].

4 Conclusions

Traditionally, BCIs have not been considered as part of WBANs. The consequence is a suboptimal communication interface in terms of performance. In this paper we have introduced the BCI-BAN concept as a novel paradigm in data communication between biological and electronic entities that encompass the area network between multimedia sources and the user brain. In the context of BCI-WBAN, cognitive processes are communicating entities that inputs sensorial information originated by multimedia devices and output cognitive information by means of a BCI. In the context of WBAN, BCIs implement the functionality of the lower layers of an interconnection open system, namely physical and access control to the cognitive media, thus providing output transmission functionality to cognitive structures. BCIs extends the scope of Personal or Body Area Networks by including the brain in the last mile of the communication network.

Acknowledgement. This study has been co-financed by Nicolo Association for the R + D + i in Neurotechnologies for disability, the regional project P11-TIC-7983, Junta of Andalucia (Spain), the National Grant TIN2012-32030 (Spain), co-financed by the European Regional Development Fund (ERDF) and the CASIP research group TIC-117.

References

1. Wolpaw, J.R., Birbaumer, N., McFarland, D.J., Pfurtscheller, G., Vaughan, T.M.: Brain-computer interfaces for communication and control. Clin. Neurophysiol. **113**, 767–791 (2002)
2. Ohme, R., Reykowska, D., Wiener, D., Choromanska, A.: Application of frontal EEG asymmetry to advertising research. J. Econ. Psychol. **31**(5), 785–793 (2010)
3. Cacioppo, J., Tassinary, L., Berntson, G. (eds.): Handbook or Psychophysiology, 2nd edn. Cambridge University Press, Cambridge (2000)
4. Middendorf, M., McMillan, G., Calhoun, G., Jones, K.S.: Brain-computer interfaces based on the steady-state visual-evoked response. IEEE Trans. Rehabil. Eng. **8**(2), 211–214 (2000)
5. Kim, D.-W., Cho, J.-H., Hwang, H.-J., Lim, J.-H., Im, C.-H.: A vision-free brain-computer interface (BCI) paradigm based on auditory selective attention, pp. 3684–3687 (2011)
6. Hillyard, S.A., Hink, R.F., Schwent, V.L., Picton, T.W.: Electrical signs of selective attention in the human brain. Science **182**(4108), 177–180 (1973)
7. Pfurtscheller, G., Neuper, C.: Motor imagery activates primary sensorimotor area in humans. Neurosci. Lett. **239**, 65–68 (1997)
8. Lopez-Gordo, M., Morillo, D., Pelayo, F.: Dry EEG electrodes. Sensors **14**(7), 12847–12870 (2014)
9. Nijholt, A., Bos, D.P.-O., Reuderink, Y.B.: Turning shortcomings into challenges: Brain-computer interfaces for games. Entertain. Comput. **1**(2), 85–94 (2009)
10. Chang, P., Hashemi, K.S., Walker, Y.M.C.: A novel telemetry system for recording EEG in small animals. J. Neurosci. Methods **201**(1), 106–115 (2011)
11. Lee, S., Shin, Y., Woo, S., Kim, K., Lee, Y.H.-N.: Review of wireless brain-computer interface systems. In: Fazel-Rezai, R. (ed.) Brain-Computer Interface Systems - Recent Progress and Future Prospects. InTech (2013)
12. Dias, N.S., Carmo, J.P., Mendes, P.M., Correia, J.H.: Wireless instrumentation system based on dry electrodes for acquiring EEG signals. Med. Eng. Phys. **34**(7), 972–981 (2012)
13. Odom, J.V., Bach, M., Brigell, M., Holder, G.E., McCulloch, D.L., Tormene, A.P., Vaegan: ISCEV standard for clinical visual evoked potentials (2009 update). Documenta Ophthalmologica, 120(1), 111–119 (2010)
14. Cheng, M., Gao, X., Gao, S., Senior Member, IEEE, Xu, D.: Design and implementation of a brain-computer interface with high transfer rates. IEEE Trans. Biomed. Eng. 49(10), 1181–1186 (2002)
15. Gao, X., Xu, D., Cheng, M., Gao, S.: A BCI-based environmental controller for the motion-disabled. IEEE Trans. Neural Syst. Rehabil. Eng. **11**, 137–140 (2003)
16. Liu, H., Wang, J., Zheng, C.: Using self-organizing map for mental tasks classification in brain-computer interface. In: Wang, J., Liao, X.-F., Yi, Z. (eds.) ISNN 2005. LNCS, vol. 3497, pp. 327–332. Springer, Heidelberg (2005)
17. Liao, X., Yao, D., Li, C.: Transductive SVM for reducing the training effort in BCI. J. Neural Eng. **4**(3), 246–254 (2007)
18. Vidal, J.J.: Toward Direct Brain-Computer communication. Annu. Rev. Biophys. Bioeng. **2**, 157–180 (1973)

19. Wolpaw, J.R., Birbaumer, N., Heetderks, W.J., McFarland, D.J., Peckham, P.H., Schalk, G., Donchin, E., Quatrano, L.A., Robinson, C.J., Vaughan, T.M.: Brain–computer interface technology: a review of the first international meeting. IEEE Trans. Rehabil. Eng. 8(2), 164–173 (2000)
20. Cherry, E.C.: some experiments on the recognition of speech, with one and with two ears. J. Acoust. Soc. Am. 25(5), 975–979 (1953)
21. Blankertz, B., Tangermann, M., Vidaurre, C., Fazli, S., Sannelli, C., Haufe, S., Maeder, C., Ramsey, L., Sturm, I., Curio, G., Müller, K.-R.: The Berlin brain–computer interface: non-medical uses of BCI technology. Front. Neurosci. 4, 1–17 (2010)
22. Birbaumer, N., Ghanayim, N., Hinterberger, T., Iversen, I., Kotchoubey, B., Kübler, A., Perelmouter, J., Taub, E., Flor, H.: A spelling device for the paralysed. Nature 398(6725), 297–298 (1999)
23. Moore, M.: Real-world applications for brain-computer interface technology. IEEE Trans. Neural Syst. Rehabil. Eng. 2(2), 162–165 (2003)
24. Müller, M.M., Malinowski, P., Gruber, T., Hillyard, S.A.: Sustained division of the attentional spotlight. Nature 424(6946), 309–312 (2003)
25. García Vázquez, C., Moreno Martínez, E., Valero Duboy, M.A., Martínez Juez, M.T., Torre Calero, M.S.: Servicio ubicuo de estimulación cognitiva orientado a personas con enfermedad de Parkinson. In: XI Jornadas de Ingeniería Telemática (JITEL 2013), Granada, October 2013
26. Lopez-Gordo, M.A., Pelayo, F., Prieto, A.: A high performance SSVEP-BCI without gazing. In: The 2010 International Joint Conference on Neural Networks (IJCNN), Barcelona, Spain, pp. 193–197 (2010)
27. Lopez-Gordo, M.A., Prieto, A., Pelayo, F., Morillas, C.: Use of phase in brain-computer interfaces based on steady-state visual evoked potentials. Neural Process. Lett. 32(1), 1–9 (2010)
28. Lopez, M.-A., Pomares, H., Prieto, A., Pelayo, F.: Multiple AM modulated visual stimuli in brain-computer interface. In: Cabestany, J., Sandoval, F., Prieto, A., Corchado, J.M. (eds.) IWANN 2009, Part I. LNCS, vol. 5517, pp. 683–689. Springer, Heidelberg (2009)
29. Lopez-Gordo, M.A., Ron-Angevin, R., Pelayo Valle, F.: Auditory brain-computer interfaces for complete locked-in patients. In: Cabestany, J., Rojas, I., Joya, G. (eds.) IWANN 2011, Part I. LNCS, vol. 6691, pp. 378–385. Springer, Heidelberg (2011)
30. Lopez, M.A., Pomares, H., Damas, M., Prieto, A.G., de la Plaza Hernandez, E.M.: Use of kohonen maps as feature selector for selective attention brain-computer interfaces. In: Mira, J., Álvarez, J.R. (eds.) IWINAC 2007. LNCS, vol. 4527, pp. 407–415. Springer, Heidelberg (2007)
31. Moreno-Aguirre, A.J., Santiago-Rodríguez, E., Harmony, T., Fernández-Bouzas, A., Porras-Kattz, E.: Analysis of auditory function using brainstem auditory evoked potentials and auditory steady state responses in infants with perinatal brain injury. International Journal of Audiology 49(2), 110–115 (2010)
32. Lopez-Gordo, M.A., Pelayo, F.: A binary phase-shift keying receiver for the detection of attention to human speech. Int. J. Neural Syst. 23(04), 1350016–12 (2013)
33. Lopez-Gordo, M.A., Pelayo, F., Prieto, A., Fernandez, E.: an auditory brain-computer interface with accuracy prediction. Int. J. Neural Syst. 22(3), 1–14 (2012)
34. Lopez-Gordo, M.A., Fernandez, E., Romero, S., Pelayo, F., Prieto, A.: An auditory brain–computer interface evoked by natural speech. J. Neural Eng. 9(3), 1–9 (2012)
35. Lopez-Gordo, M.A., Ángeles Martín Sánchez, Mª., de la Plaza Hernández, E.M., Pelayo Valle, F.: Plataforma de Altas Prestaciones para la Adquisición, Extracción y Procesamiento Inteligente de Señales EEEG y Telemonitorización (PLAT-EEG). Cognitive Area Networks, vol. 1, nº 1, Junio 2014, Asociación Nicolo, ISSN: 2341-4243 Actas del 6º Simposio CEA Bioingeniería 2014, Interfaces Mente-computador y Neurotecnologías, Granada Junio 2014

Resource Management

A Modification of DYMO Routing Protocol with Knowledge of Nodes' Position: Proposal and Evaluation

Enrica Zola[✉], Francisco Barcelo-Arroyo, and Israel Martin-Escalona

Universitat Politècnica de Catalunya,
C/Jordi Girona 1-3, Mòdul C3, 08034 Barcelona, Spain
{enrica,barcelo,imartin}@entel.upc.edu

Abstract. Knowledge of the physical location of the nodes is known to improve performance in wireless networks. This is especially true in MANETs, where routing protocols face a continuously changing topology. In the past, routing protocols such as Beacon-Less Routing (BLR) used the location information of the nodes to build the forwarding path in a distributed manner. In this work, we borrow the forwarding approach in BLR and apply it in the route discovery process of DYMO. Under the assumption of nodes knowing their own location, the receiving nodes will compute a delay. The node with lower delay will resend the RREQ first. The rest of forwarding nodes will drop the RREQ once they receive this first RREQ. Thus the best forwarding node is selected in a distributed manner. This modification is expected to reduce the amount of RREQs circulating in the network, lessening the routing overhead.

Keywords: MANET · Routing protocol · DYMO · DFD · Localization

1 Introduction

Routing has been one of the hot topics in Mobile Ad-hoc Networks (MANETs) for years. The frequent changes in the network topology became a challenge for researchers, used to deal with networks in which routes were stable. Several solutions to MANET routing have been proposed, but they brought a new issue: protocol scalability. A very well-known solution for MANET routing is the Dynamic MANET On-demand (DYMO) routing protocol [1]. As a reactive protocol, DYMO establishes a route from a source node to a destination node before sending data. What makes DYMO different from classic approaches, such as AODV, is that intermediate nodes are able to learn the route to all the predecessor nodes in the path, thus lessening the number of RREQs generated in the network.

Nowadays, mobile network receivers are commonly integrated with positioning technologies. The nodes' position information can be exploited to improve the efficiency of routing in MANETs. Several proposals use positioning to minimize the search space for route discovery towards the destination node [2] or to

© Springer International Publishing Switzerland 2015
M.C. Aguayo-Torres et al. (Eds.): WWIC 2015, LNCS 9071, pp. 289–298, 2015.
DOI: 10.1007/978-3-319-22572-2_21

apply source routing in order to establish the geographical path that a packet must follow towards its destination [3]. The approach followed by Beacon-Less Routing Algorithm (BLR) [4] is different. In this case, the source node broadcasts data packets without the need to discover the path to the destination beforehand. Knowing the nodes' positions is a requirement in the BLR approach. On the other hand, beacon-based protocols periodically share location information among neighbouring nodes to maintain routing tables up to date. However, the more accurate positioning information the more protocol overhead (i.e. location data is flooded more frequently). Thus, the authors in [5] proposed the Dynamic Route Maintenance algorithm for self-configuring the node's beacon interval according to the mobility pattern of the neighbouring nodes (i.e., shorter intervals for higher mobility nodes).

This paper is focused in assessing the benefits of applying the forwarding strategy of BLR to the route discovery process of DYMO. This approach is named DYMOselfwd (DYMO with selective forwarding) in this paper. It relies on two assumptions: (1) nodes always know their own position (e.g., through GPS) and (2) nodes always know the destination node's position. The specific procedure followed to discover destination node's position is out of the scope of this work. Anyway, the reader can assume that positioning information is provided by an external location management system, as commonly assumed in the literature [4,6]. In next generation wireless networks (i.e., 5G), the ad-hoc network may be used in order to reach a fixed router (i.e., LTE eNodeB or public 802.11 access point in malls, sport centers, libraries, etc.) that provides fixed connection to the Internet; in such scenario, the position of the destination node may be easily assumed to be known. The use of positioning information in DYMOselfwd is expected to reduce the routing overhead, which means (1) fewer nodes contending the access for re-broadcasting the RREQs (i.e. lower probability of collision) and (2) less traffic in the network (i.e. longer network lifetime and less congestion issues). The reduction in collisions is awaited to compensate for the increased delay of DYMOselfwd and therefore the actual delay of the route set-up will be almost the same as provided by DYMO.

There are several works that propose using location information to improve the route-discovery stage in AODV. For instance, authors in [7] propose that only nodes in the *forwarding region* forward RREQs, so that the overhead is reduced. A similar approach is followed in [8], but forwarding nodes are selected according to nodes' mobility information. To the best of our knowledge, the methodology described here, which has been proposed for flooding approaches [4], has never been applied to the route discovery process of AODV or DYMO protocols. The modified version of the DYMO with location information was already proposed in [9], but no evaluation was provided. The simulation results shown in this paper prove the improvement expected by the proposed algorithm.

2   Using Position Information in DYMO

Route discovery and route management can be considered the basic operations of the DYMO protocol [1]. The route discovery starts when a source node (A) has to send data to a target node (O) and there is no established route between nodes A and O yet. In that case, the source node A broadcasts a special message called Route Request (RREQ). Every neighbouring node of A receiving the RREQ (i.e., K_i) will add A as next hop in its own routing table (i.e., direct transmission). At this point, each node K_i will check whether it knows the path to O. If so, K_i will send a Route Reply (RREP) back to A; otherwise, K_i has to broadcast the RREQ again after adding its own address in the path accumulation field. This means that the RREQ size grows with the number of hops required. The benefit of this path accumulation is twofold: any intermediate node is able to learn its next hop (1) towards A and (2) towards all the predecessor nodes in the accumulated path. Once the RREQ has reached (1) a node with established route to O or (2) the destination node O, a RREP is unicasted back to A. This last message is the responsible for setting up the path (i.e., next hop) at all the intermediate nodes.

2.1 Modified Route Discovery

As described before, A will broadcast a RREQ packet if it has not yet a route to reach its destination O. DYMOselfwd will include the transmitter's (TX_pos) and the destination's position (DST_pos) in the RREQ packet. Any intermediate node that will rebroadcasts the RREQ will substitute the TX_pos field with its own position. In the case of no RREP being heard, we propose that only one node broadcasts the RREQ again. The selection of this node is explained in Sect. 2.2. With this approach the amount of RREQ circulating in the network is expected to reduce if compared to DYMO, thus lessening the routing overhead.

DYMO and AODV require the same number of RREQs for a given path. This amount is equal to the number of nodes (N) in the network, since every node receiving a RREQ is expected to rebroadcast it. On the other hand, in DYMOselfwd the number of RREQs linearly depends on the number of hops between source and destination (num_hops). DYMOselfwd is expected to significantly reduce the amount of routing overhead even though RREQ packets are actually larger (due to the embedded positioning data). In the worst-case scenario, three neighbours of the source node will rebroadcast its own RREQ since they do not see each other (i.e., hidden node problem). Accordingly, the amount of required RREQ packets will be, at most, 3 times the num_hops, which is always less than in the figure required by original DYMO algorithm.

2.2 *Best Node* Selection

The procedure followed to select the *best node* (i.e., the intermediate node in charge of rebroadcasting a RREQ first) is inspired in the BLR algorithm [4]. In BLR, data packets are broadcasted through the network until they reach the destination, without the need to set-up or maintain routing tables. The *best node* is selected in a distributed fashion, by applying different delays to each candidate node for broadcasting the packet. BLR will set the shortest delay to the best forwarding node, which is defined as the node with the best position in the *forwarding area*. Accordingly, the *best node* is the first to rebroadcast the data packet. The same idea is applied to broadcast the RREQ in DYMOselfwd. Any node receiving a RREQ regarding an unknown route follows this procedure (see Fig. 1):

1. It computes the distance between the transmitter and the destination nodes ($dist_{tx\_node}$). Remind that *TX_pos* and *DST_pos* data are included in each RREQ packet.
2. It computes its distance to the destination (*own_dist*).
3. If it has an *own_dist* shorter than $dist_{tx\_node}$, it becomes a candidate for rebroadcasting the RREQ. Otherwise, the node discards the RREQ. This prevents nodes in the opposite direction from rebroadcasting the RREQ (i.e., node *E* in Fig. 1).

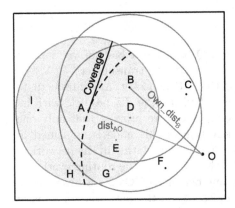

Fig. 1. *Best node* selection for rebroadcast the RREQ sent by *A*. *D* has the shortest *own_dist*.

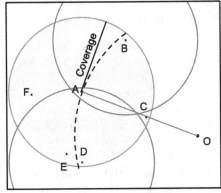

Fig. 2. Up to three nodes may rebroadcast the RREQ due to the hidden node problem (Color figure online).

At this point, the Dynamic Forward Delay (DFD) [4] approach is used to select the *best node* in a distributed way. This approach consists of each candidate node delaying the rebroadcast of the RREQ according to the values previously computed. Hence, the *best node* is the node with the lowest forward delay. A complete discussion on the best DFD function is out of the scope of this paper. However, it is likely to think that the DFD depends on the node's *own_dist*, so that the node with the best position in the *forwarding area* is pushed to be the first rebroadcasting the RREQ.

Candidate nodes hearing a RREQ defer from rebroadcasting any pending RREQ. In case of multiple RREQs reaching the destination node (i.e., because of the hidden node problem), the first RREQ received at destination is selected. The sequence number in the RREQ preserves from looping. In the case that noise or other unexpected events prevent a node from hearing the RREQ sent by the *best node*, more than one node will be rebroadcasting the RREQ, thus ending up with a behaviour similar to the original DYMO protocol.

Figure 1 illustrates the algorithm of the *best node* selection. In this example, source node A is looking for a route towards destination node O. The transmission range (i.e. the maximum distance at which the signal transmitted is heard, under ideal radio conditions) is labeled as *Coverage*. The RREQ sent by A is received by nodes B, D, E, G, H, and I, which are the nodes that lay inside the blue coverage area of A. The dashed line represents the points at $dist_{tx\_node}$ (i.e., $dist_{AO}$ in Fig. 1), highlighting the area in which candidate forwarding nodes can be. Thus, only nodes B, D, E and G are candidates for rebroadcasting the RREQ since their *own_dist* to O is shorter than $dist_{tx\_node}$. Among all of them, D has the shortest *own_dist*. Therefore, it is the first node to rebroadcast the RREQ, i.e., D is the *best node* at this hop. The other candidates inside the coverage range of D (i.e., green circle in Fig. 1) defer from rebroadcasting the pending RREQ once they hear the new RREQ from D (i.e., using a higher sequence number).

According to the geometry depicted in the scenario of Fig. 2, up to three nodes may rebroadcast a RREQ due to the hidden node problem. In this scenario, nodes B, C and D do not hear each other and consequently they all rebroadcast the RREQ. In scenarios like Fig. 2, the RREQ rebroadcasted by C will first reach the destination node O, since C has shorter *own_dist* if compared with B and D.

The advantage expected after applying the DYMOselfwd definition is twofold. First, the routing overhead will decrease if compared with the original DYMO algorithm, even in the worst-case scenario. This aspect has been studied through simulation in Sect. 4. Second, the establishment of a route before sending data packets will guarantee higher throughputs, since DYMOselfwd confines broadcasting to RREQ packets while data packets can be unicasted at higher rates (i.e., IEEE 802.11 nodes must use basic transmission rates for broadcasted frames). This approach can be considered as an improvement over the DFD as used in BLR. This second conjecture has not been tested in this work and requires further research.

3   Simulation Tool and Scenarios

Some tests have been run using simulation. The tool used is Omnet++ 4.3 [10]. The INET framework has been used to build the network models used in this work. INET provides a complete implementation of several network protocols (e.g. IP, UDP, TCP, ARP, etc.), wireless technologies (e.g. IEEE 802.11) and network approaches (e.g. ad hoc). At the same time, this framework provides a complete set of radio models and mobility patterns. The DYMOselfwd was implemented starting from the module described in [11]. After testing other modules it proved to be the most adequate to carry out the modifications successfully. Several upgrades have been implemented to the DYMO module in order to properly work as described in the draft and to allow the achievement of statistics.

All simulations have been run along 1,250 s; the transmitter sends a UDP segment every 250 ms, allowing 5,000 segments. Independent means have been obtained by averaging over five repetitions of each experiment. In all cases, the confidence interval is better than 95 %. Two scenarios have been designed for testing purposes with 9 and 13 nodes respectively. For each scenario, simulations have been run for static and dynamic (i.e. moving) cases. The mobility model assumed for dynamic has been the Random Waypoint without pause times. Different pedestrian speeds have been considered in order to test the ability to recover from changing topologies. The area is 150 × 150 m. The coverage has been set to 71 m so, even in the case of 9 nodes there are always two nodes at sight at least. Other parameters of the configuration are summarized in Table 1 along with other parameters that have been configured as usual in other similar works [11].

Table 1. Configuration parameters used in simulation

Speed	0 | 1 | 2 m/s
Protocol	DYMO | DYMOselfwd
Propagation model	Two Ray Ground Model
Shadowing	0 dB
Frame size	512 Bytes
MAC Protocol	802.11 g
Bit Rate	54 Mbps
Carrier frequency	2.4 GHz

Figure 3 shows the scenarios. These layouts are used for the static cases and as the starting layout for the dynamic cases. The scenario with 9 nodes (3 × 3) represents the case of low density and is considered in order to check this constraint situation. In this scenario, each node has no more than 2 neighbouring nodes in the direction of the sink. The scenario with 13 nodes represents a medium density. In the remaining of the paper we refer to the 9 and 13 scenarios as low and normal density respectively. In all scenarios, there is one node sending UDP segments to a *sink*. They are both represented by black circles in Fig. 3 and labelled as *TX* and *sink* respectively. The coverage range of *TX* is represented by a red circle. The *best node* for retransmitting the RREQ is represented by a grey circle; *own_dist* is also displayed in each layout.

The metrics obtained from the simulations in order to evaluate the performance of DYMOselfwd and compare to the standard protocol are listed below:

- Troute: Time to establish the route (when the source receives the first RREQ from the *sink*).
- ColMAC: number of collisions at MAC level.
- MACPdu: Total number of MAC frames sent by all nodes.
- REQtot: Total number of requests sent by all nodes.

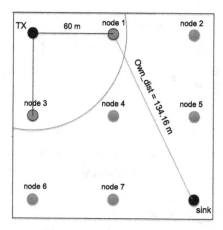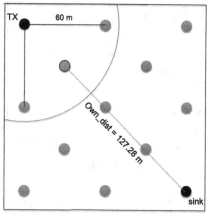

Fig. 3. Nodes' locations in the simulation area for the 9 (low density, on the left) and 13 (normal density, on the right) nodes scenarios. *TX* is the node sending UDP segments to the *sink*. Its coverage area is represented in red (Color figure online).

Table 2. Results with static nodes in the two density scenarios.

	Low density		Normal density	
	DYMO	DYMOselfwd	DYMO	DYMOselfwd
Troute [ms]	5.21	5.72	5.71	5.79
ColMac	15.8	20.2	30.2	0.0
MACPdu	20,253.0	20,262.4	20,351.6	20,176.0
REQtot	180.2	178.4	265.6	84.0

4 Results

4.1 Static Nodes

This scenario suits the case of a sensor network; the results are displayed in Table 2. For low density, DYMO performs better than DYMOselfwd: the three first metrics in the table are better while the last one is slightly worse. This is due to the symmetry: since there are two nodes placed at the same distance from the *sink* (node 1 and node 3 in Fig. 3), they re-send the RREQ from *TX* at the same time and they do not listen to each other. Thus the number of nodes sending the RREQ is the same in both protocols and they achieve similar results. However, due to the modified algorithm, the establishment of the first route takes longer in DYMOselfwd due to the extra delay in the retransmission of the RREQ. Moreover, this extra delay causes a larger number of collisions, mainly occurring in the node located in the middle of the layout, and consequently a higher number of MACPdu sent out in the medium.

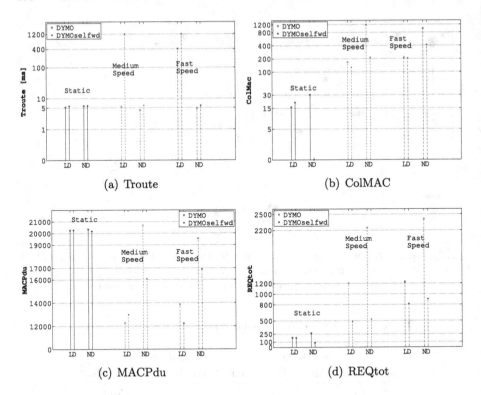

Fig. 4. Results for DYMO (o) and DYMOselfwd (*) for the static (solid black line), medium speed (dashed blue line) and fast speed (dash-dot green line) scenarios. For each, the low density (LD) and the normal density (ND) cases are shown (Color figure online).

In order to confirm that the worst results obtained here are due to the symmetry in the layout, we have slightly changed the location of the nodes in the low density scenario as follows: node 1, node 2, node 5 and *sink* have been moved 5 m left along the horizontal axis, and node 5 and *sink* have been also moved 5 m up along the vertical axis. As expected, after breaking the symmetry the number of collisions decreases for both protocols (i.e., ColMac is 7.0 for both) and the performance still remains similar for both protocols. However, now DYMOselfwd performs slightly better than DYMO (i.e., Troute, MACPdu and REQtot are slightly smaller in DYMOselfwd).

For normal density, the metrics are better for DYMOselfwd with the only exception of the time to establish the first route. The conclusion of this experiment is that DYMOselfwd does not respond so well to the situation of low connectivity but achieves an obvious improvement in other cases. It is important to notice that the number of REQtot is always smaller in DYMOselfwd.

In the next sections results with different mobility settings will be shown. In order to facilitate comparison, results are shown in Fig. 4. Figure 4(a) shows the results for Troute, Fig. 4(b), (c) and (d) those for ColMAC, MACPdu and

REQtot, respectively. Values for the static case are shown with a solid black line, those for the medium speed case with a dashed blue line and those for the fast speed with a dash-dot green line. Results for the DYMO protocol are marked with a circle while those for the DYMOselfwd with an asterisk.

4.2   Medium Speed

This scenario represents the case of MANET with medium pedestrian speed (1 m/s). The results are represented in blue in Fig. 4 and the conclusions are quite similar to those obtained for static nodes: DYMOselfwd improves the performance only after a certain degree of connectivity is present in the network. In this case, the consequence of the low connectivity is worse than in Sect. 4.1 and the longer time to finish the first route must be highlighted. This is because in the static case the node at the upper corner was always at sight of two others, while now because the random movement this amount of two can decrease to one or none. A diffusion-like strategy is more efficient. However, it must be stressed that the number of RREQ sent by all nodes is always smaller for DYMOselfwd.

4.3   Fast Speed

Now all results represented in green in Fig. 4 are worse than for medium speed. This could be expected as connected to the well-known concept of "mobility cost" in mobile networks: movement and speed show always consequences in the performance, network management and signalling needs. This said, the conclusions are not far from the ones drawn in the former cases: DYMOselfwd gets noticeable improvements when a reasonable degree of connectivity is present. Moreover, again the number of RREQ is always smaller in DYMOselfwd. Here it is relevant to stress that the upgrade to DYMOselfwd is more noticeable for fast speed: the collisions are reduced from 14,581 to 1,671 at fast speed while the reduction is from 1,082 to 158 at slow speed (also the total number of MACPdu shows a better improvement).

5   Conclusions

Routing in MANETs is still a challenging topic for researchers, who aim at finding a solution that is scalable but also flexible enough to adapt to the changing mobile scenario. The algorithm proposed in this paper (DYMOselfwd) takes advantage of the location information that many devices have at hand and increases the scalability of the DYMO routing protocol by dramatically reducing the number of route requests (RREQs) sent by the nodes in the network. DYMOselfwd is inspired by the forwarding strategy of BLR [4] for which a node retransmits a frame (i.e., the RREQ here) after delaying its transmission for a given time interval. Since nodes closer to the destination node will apply a smaller delay, the shortest route will be established and less RREQs will circulate in the network. Simulations run in scenarios with different density and speed show that the overall throughput always improve with DYMOselfwd if compared to DYMO. Moreover, the extra delay introduced does not have an impact on the throughput. We can conclude that, in common scenarios in MANETs, the benefits of the DYMOselfwd are evident. In case of more sparse scenarios, the protocol requires larger time to establish the first route and MAC collisions may increase due to the hidden node problem; however, the overall throughput in the network remains high.

The error in the destination node's position may have a negative impact on the performance of DYMOselfw. In the future, we aim at analyzing this impact. Moreover, we aim at extending the present evaluation by comparing our model with another location-based routing protocol and by assessing the tradeoff between the protocol simplicity and its scalability.

Acknowledgment. We would like to express our gratitude to Jordi Ruiz Paños and Raúl Ruiz Díaz who were in charge of implementing the simulations.

This research was partially supported by the Spanish Government and ERDF through CICYT project TEC2013-48099-C2-1-P.

References

1. Perkins, C., Chakeres, I.: Dynamic MANET On-demand (AODVv2) Routing, IETF Internet Draft (Standards Tracks, work in progress) (2012). <http://tools.ietf.org/html/draft-ietf-manet-dymo-22#page-33>
2. Ko, Y., Vaidya, N.H.: Location-Aided Routing (LAR) in mobile ad hoc networks. In: Proceedings of ACM MobiCom, pp. 66–75 (1998)
3. Giruka, V., Singhal, M.: A self-healing on-demand geographic path routing protocol for mobile ad-hoc networks. Elsevier Ad Hoc Netw. 5(7), 1113–1128 (2007)
4. Heissenbüttel, M., Braun, T., Bernoulli, T., Wälchli, M.: BLR: beacon-less routing algorithm for mobile ad-hoc networks. Elsevier Comput. Commun. J. (Spec. Issue) 27, 1076–1086 (2003)
5. Chou, C.H., Ssu, K.F., Jiau, H.C.: Dynamic route maintenance for geographic forwarding in mobile ad hoc networks. Elsevier Comput. Netw. 52(2), 418–431 (2008)
6. Endo, K., Inoue, Y., Takahashi, Y.: Performance modeling of beaconless forwarding strategies in multi-hop wireless networks. Elsevier Comput. Commun. 35(1), 120–128 (2012)
7. Reno, R.: Enhanced AODV for directional flooding using coordinate system. In: Proceedings of International Conference on Networking and Information Technology (ICNIT), pp. 329–332 (2010)
8. Khamayseh, Y., Darwish, O.M., Wedian, S.A.: MA-AODV: mobility aware routing protocols for mobile ad hoc networks. In: Proceedings of Fourth International Conference on Systems and Networks Communications, pp. 25–29 (2009)
9. Zola, E., Barcelo-Arroyo, F.: DYMO routing protocol with knowledge of nodes' position. In: Proceedings of Joint ERCIM eMobility and MobiSense Workshop, pp. 9–14 (2012)
10. Omnet++ release 4.3. <http://www.omnetpp.org/>
11. Sommer, C., Dietrich, I., Dressler, F.: Simulation of ad hoc routing protocols using OMNeT++. Springer Mob. Netw. Appl. 15(6), 786–801 (2010)

DTN Routing Optimised by Human Routines: The HURRy Protocol

Susana Pérez-Sánchez[✉], Jose Maria Cabero, and Iñigo Urteaga

Fundación Tecnalia Research and Innovation,
Parque Tecnológico Bizkaia 700, 48160 Derio, Spain
{susana.perezsanchez,josemari.cabero}@tecnalia.com
http://www.tecnalia.com/

Abstract. This paper proposes the HURRy (HUman Routines used for Routing) protocol, which infers and benefits from the social behaviour of nodes in disruptive networking environments. HURRy incorporates the contact duration to the information retrieved from historical encounters among neighbours, so that smarter routing decisions can be made. The specification of HURRy is based on the outcomes of a thorough experiment, which highlighted the importance of distinguishing between short and long contacts and deriving mathematical relations in order to optimally prioritize the available routes to a destination. HURRy introduces a novel and more meaningful rating system to evaluate the quality of each contact and overcome the limitations of other routing approaches in social environments.

Keywords: Challenged networks · DTN · Probabilistic routing · Social behaviour

1 Introduction

A Disruption-Tolerant Network (DTN) is a network architecture that reduces intermittent communication issues by addressing technical problems in heterogeneous networks that lack continuous connectivity. DTN defines a series of contiguous network data bundles that enable applications. This architecture serves as a network overlay that bases new naming on endpoint identifiers. DTN uses a shared framework algorithm that temporarily connects data communication devices. DTN services are similar to email, but DTN includes enhanced routing, naming and security capabilities. Typically, DTN nodes use network storage to manage, store, and forward operations over multiple paths and longer periods. Exploring self-* properties of nodes belonging to a DTN and learning from neighbour encounters (context awareness), becomes of a great value in order to design an optimized transport strategy to improve service performance in this specific type of networks. Connectivity in DTN scenarios implies that nodes do not have permanent physical paths to certain destinations, but only to some of their closest neighbours instead. This work aims at the development and implementation

© Springer International Publishing Switzerland 2015
M.C. Aguayo-Torres et al. (Eds.): WWIC 2015, LNCS 9071, pp. 299–312, 2015.
DOI: 10.1007/978-3-319-22572-2_22

of a mechanism that helps the node take a decision regarding packet routing and forwarding. There is a wide range of combinations that could be validated for several specific situations where delay tolerant transmissions would be optimized so as to be characterised by a certain expected Quality of Service (QoS). Our aim is to design and implement a prototype that makes use of a valuable subset of these properties and is able to exploit them for a smart management of the connectivity in DTNs formed by human-carried devices. This paper states why the inter-contact time between historical encounters is not sufficient so as to derive probability values in certain scenarios. People usually behave according to routines or patterns that are seamlessly introduced in their daily activity.

The remain of this article is organised as follows: Sect. 2 summarizes the state of the art in related areas of interest and states the motivation for a new routing solution based on human routines, Sect. 3 describes the HURRy protocol we propose including its main component specification and description of components; in Sect. 4 the protocol implementation is outlined, as well as the scenario and configuration simulated as proof of concept, in order to present some results regarding the performance evaluation of HURRy compared to PRoPHET; finally, Sect. 5 presents the most relevant conclusions, while opening some discussion lines and future work.

2   Related Work

Collecting data about people interactions based on wireless technologies is a quite recent activity. Its potential usage did not seem to transcend beyond the biological or sociological fields [1,2], but the irruption of new paradigms in communication networks, which dynamics play a key role for, became a powerful tool in the study of human behaviour. Detecting one or several aspects related to human behaviour like people's social activity [3], the reason why people move to certain places, in which specific moments, or with whom, together with human ability to associate, could be of a great value in order to optimise both network design [4,6], as well as societal structures [5,7]. Thanks to frequent changes in the activity and communication patterns of individuals, the associated social and communication network is subject to constant evolution [11,12]. Barabási studied human dynamics with special focus on the exploration of scaling properties [8] and the limits of predictability in human mobility patterns [9].

Eagle and Pentland [10,11] performed experiments regarding proximity interactions (based on short-ranged Bluetooth technology) using people's mobile phone as a contact sensor; they worked on the identification of communities and patterns of behaviour. In the same line Cabero et al. [12,13] designed Bluetooth medallions specially intended for the monitoring of human Mobile Ad-hoc NETworks (MANETs). They collected a voluminous database with contact traces of people during labour hours in the same office building for several weeks. The outcome of these experiments served as valuable motivation for the work presented in this article [20,21].

Human based networks are complex environments that demand networked applications operating in very challenging conditions. [14] comprises the RFC for PRoPHET, a probabilistic routing protocol based on the history of encounters, which defines a method for deriving a proportional relation between the frequency of past encounters among nodes, and the probability of having a new contact. Lindgren et al. [15] already showed that PRoPHET is able to deliver more messages than epidemic routing approaches [16] with a lower communication overhead. Our protocol continues in the line of PRoPHET, incorporating the concept of human profiling as a key factor for the probability estimation. Our solution incorporates some modifications to PRoPHET, in order to help the routing decision with other parameters that we consider relevant for inferring human profiles from the history of their contacts with neighbours. Some of these enhancements are: a new and refined algorithm for estimation of direct probabilities, a configurable parameter to allow the user or application decide which rating value is prioritized, a new transitivity formula to derive probability values learnt via others, the aging formula and the exchange process of transitivity values have been tuned, among others.

3   The HURRy Protocol

3.1   Motivation

It is assumed that connectivity in disrupted scenarios implies that nodes do not have permanent physical paths to all possible destinations, but only to their closest neighbours instead. When a DTN node receives a packet addressed to a certain destination, a set of steps are triggered in order to find the most suitable way of reaching this destination node. The easiest situation (apart from being the destination node) would be that the destination is one of the node's direct neighbours: in that case, the packet is just at one hop distance from its final destination, and there is a physical connection available. Otherwise, the node will need to analyse its available routing information and take an action according to one or several of the following aspects: accept or discard the packet (buffer constraints), store the packet and wait for a suitable forwarding instant (based on the probability of reaching the destination node within a certain time period), forward the packet immediately to an intermediate node with higher probability of contacting the destination (based on connectivity or mobility pattern estimation, learning process...), etc.

In the HURRy protocol this routing decision is based on probabilistic routing techniques (like PRoPHET), although it incorporates the contact duration of encounters (unlike previous approaches), and it proposes a novel reasoning algorithm for a DTN node to estimate the rating probabilities of all possible paths to a certain destination (i.e. to construct its routing table). HURRy introduces an estimation formula to evaluate the Goodness (G) of a contact, as explained later with Eq. 2.

As per the inherent nature of the connectivity established in a DTN environment, the end-to-end concept is no longer true and/or available. Figure 1 represents a typical scenario, where several nodes are part of a mobile DTN topology and eventually, one user terminal (Node C) might have access to the outside world (i.e. the Internet) through a wireless interface (apart from its available DTN physical interface, which might be based on the same or different wireless technology).

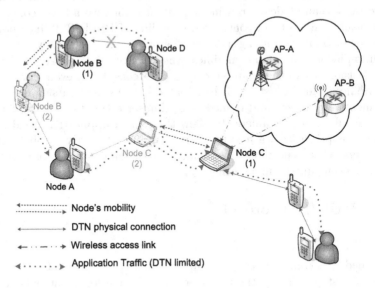

Fig. 1. Dynamic DTN scenario with diverse wireless connectivity

Each DTN node is responsible for interchanging information regarding previous encounters and estimated path-ratings with its neighbouring nodes. A probabilistic algorithm will then come up with quantitative rating values for all possible routes. The best next hop (node with the highest rating value, or probability) to reach a certain destination is decided according to a mathematical equation where the accumulated mean values of inter-contact and contact-duration times in historical encounters are considered (see Eq. 1 below). In Fig. 1 imagine that Node A must find a route towards Node C and gain access to the outside world. If Node A demands a specific content (e.g. a video from Youtube) from the Internet, it will need to decide how to reach Node C (i.e. decide which intermediate neighbour would most probably contact Node C, or in a more reliable way). DTN nodes are mobile, and they register information about who contacts whom, with which frequency and for how long. In Fig. 1 nodes B and C are moving back and forth from position (1) to (2), which induces the establishment of new connections (with nodes A and D), and the intermittent disruption of the link between B and D. Once Node A contacts Node B, they exchange information about the probability with which they expect to reach Node C (this value is merely based on their history of contacts with D and C). The nature of these encounters regarding frequency or duration will vary depending on specific features of the scenario considered. Outdoor and indoor topologies might result in very different contacting routines, for instance. In the same way, people

do not show the same social behaviour with colleagues during labour days, as
with friends during the weekend. Human routines are affected by the surrounding
environment and conditions, but they also affect the resulting connections established in a mobile DTN. Not only is the frequency of contacts used in PRoPHET
[15] insufficient for estimating the probability of a new contact, but it may also
lead to non-optimal routing decisions. Previous works like [7,11] highlight the
necessity of an enhanced characterisation of social patterns in order to design
an optimised probability estimation mechanism. HURRy intends to incorporate
a more elaborated model of human routines to the estimation of contact probabilities by a DTN node.

3.2   Description of Components

In this section we introduce the principles of the HURRy protocol. The operation
of HURRy in a DTN node is represented in Fig. 2.

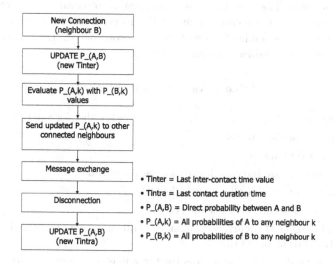

Fig. 2. Sequence of components implemented in a DTN node

Figure 2 shows the flow chart of the whole mechanism from a node's perspective, node A, when it detects a new physical connection to node B. P_(A,B) is
the direct probability of node A contacting its neighbour node B, and calculated
using the inter-contact time since their last encounter (new T_{inter}). After that,
node A would update the rest of its own probabilities, P_(A,k), through the transitivity values learnt from B (node B informs about its probability of reaching
the rest of nodes, P_(B,k)). If node A detects any other simultaneous connection (other direct neighbours), it will exchange its own stored probabilities with
them. If physical connection with node B is lost due to disconnection, the value
of P_(A,B) is calculated again with the last contact duration (new T_{intra}). From

this outline, we can already notice a couple of modifications to PRoPHET, where there is no check for updates in transitivity values while connected to node B, and there is no need for updating P_(A,B) at disconnection, since PRoPHET does not consider contact duration times. The specific components to calculate direct and transitivity probabilities are further described later in Figs. 3 and 4.

Nodes in a challenged network can easily register the inter-contact (T_{inter}) and contact-duration (T_{intra}) time values of their historical contacts with others. But the process of estimating a representative average value, considering the history of values registered, might not be so immediate. HURRy bases this estimation on the statistical features that characterise both mathematical distributions. Assuming these distributions are highly dependant on several factors, such as the minimum time slot detected, or the aggregation of values into certain time intervals, it seems that a good approximation can be achieved deriving a histogram for each magnitude. A node implementing HURRy will have predefined time intervals, both for inter-contact times and for contact durations, which will register an incremental number of repetitions according to the history of encounters. The size of these configurable intervals does not need to follow a linear basis, so we can define smaller interval sizes for the lower range and larger sizes for the higher range of the scale considered. Table 1 summarizes the meaning of the variables used in Eq. 1 below.

Table 1. Variables used in Eq. 1

$\bar{T}_{\mathcal{I}}$	Mean value of T_{inter} or T_{intra}, where $\mathcal{I}$ stands either for *inter* or *intra*
n	Sequence of discrete time
n_{curr}	Current time instant
V	Maximum range interval defined for each magnitude
v_i	Individual values of all intervals defined
e_n^i	Number of occurrences per interval
E_n	Total number of occurrences, number of all encounters registered up to the current time instant
α_n	Weightening factor that awards the three most recent occurrences of v_i in the summation

Equation 1 represents the formula applied by a node to derive a representative mean value of T_{inter} or T_{intra}:

$$\bar{T}_{\mathcal{I}} = \sum_{n=0}^{n_{curr}} \sum_{i=0}^{V} \frac{v_i e_n^i}{E_n} \alpha_n \qquad (1)$$

According to Eq. 1 $\bar{T}_{\mathcal{I}}$ is calculated at a certain instant, using the history of values registered. Introducing α_n factor prioritizes the values registered in most recent encounters in the same proportion as older encounters are penalized. In the case that only three (or less) encounters have occurred, α_n does not modify the average value calculated (i.e. $\alpha_n = 1$).

Each of the HURRy components is implemented by a specific algorithm. Figure 3 shows the detail of the component that estimates a direct probability P_(A,B).

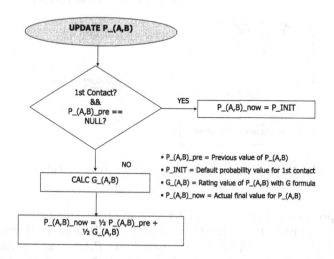

Fig. 3. Detail of the estimation of direct probabilities

In Fig. 3 the functional block $CALC\ G\_(A,B)$ estimates the Goodness (G) of a contact. If node A has its first contact with node B, their direct probability is initialized with a default value P_INIT. Otherwise, this component is in charge of deriving a neighbour's quality by using the G formula:

$$G = \frac{F(T)^{1-\gamma}}{(1 - FT)^{\gamma}}, \gamma \epsilon [0, 1] \qquad (2)$$

Assuming both parameters are normalized to the same period in Eq. 2, F denotes the inverse value of $\bar{T}_{inter}$ and T stands for $\bar{T}_{intra}$. The goodness G of a neighbour is proportional to the frequency of contacts occurred (inversely proportional to the inter-contact time), and to the mean contact duration of past encounters. HURRy introduces a tuning factor γ in order to allow the user or application service to balance the priority among both parameters. It is easy to verify that when $\gamma = 1$ the frequency of contacts is being prioritized, whereas if γ takes values near 0 the goodness is prioritizing the contact duration. This will also influence the transitivity formula described by Eq. 3 below. The last block in Fig. 3 smooths the evolutionary slope of accumulated mean values of the probability under calculation.

Figure 4 shows the detail of the component that updates the values of transitive probabilities in node A. $P\_(A,k)$ represents the transitive probabilities stored by node A to reach any of its historical neighbours in the DTN (denoted by k).

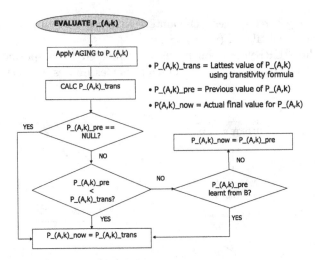

Fig. 4. Detail of the estimation of transitivity probabilities

Unlike previous approaches, HURRy's aging process distinguishes if a third neighbour k is either (i) currently connected or (ii) not. If (i), and because HURRy considers the contact duration, the value of $P_-(A, k)$ will be incremented since last update; if (ii) the $P_-(A, k)$ value will be decremented since last update. This way, the aging may result in a positive factor if node A has been permanently connected to node k since last calculation of $P_-(A, k)$. Furthermore, node A updates its $P_-(A, k)$ values of other currently connected neighbours before sending that information to node B. This enhancement results in a smarter management of the information exchanged within each encounter among nodes in the vicinity. It helps reducing the transitory events of intermittent connections: for instance if a third node is not simultaneously detected by two previously present neighbours due to unstable links, the first node detecting a third entity would immediately inform its connected neighbour through transitivity (e.g. PRoPHET did not exchange new neighbours detected during a previously established connection at once). Equation 3 represents the transitivity formula applied in the module named $CALC\ P_-(A,k)\_trans$ in Fig. 4:

$$\left(\frac{1}{P_-(A, k)}\right)^{\frac{1}{\gamma}} = \left(\frac{1}{P_-(A, B)}\right)^{\frac{1}{\gamma}} + \left(\frac{1}{P_-(B, k)}\right)^{\frac{1}{\gamma}} \qquad (3)$$

If we only considered contact durations (i.e. $\gamma \simeq 0$), transitivity would come from the minimum value of the comparison between $P_-(A, B)$ and $P_-(B, k)$. If we only considered frequency of contacts (i.e. $\gamma = 1$), transitivity would be given by the inverse combination of both probabilities. Since we introduced γ as a tuning factor, it also influences the combination law for transitivity, where Eq. 3 provides a good intermediate approximation function.

4   Validation Results Through Simulation

In order to evaluate the performance of our approach, this section presents the validation of the HURRy protocol in a simulation environment specially designed for opportunistic networks: The ONE simulator [17]. We took the PRoPHET release for The ONE simulator as a starting point, and developed the HURRy modifications of functional blocks in Java code to be integrated and compiled in the simulator environment. Apart from specific functionality tests we executed for the validation of the protocol components, we aimed at the simulation of a significant scenario where the enhancements proposed could be proven and compared with the performance of PRoPHET. We selected the scenario represented in Fig. 1 and we used the simulation results as proof of concept and verification of our solution. We considered Bluetooth interfaces and four nodes in this scenario (A, B, C and D), where node A intends to send information packets to node C, but there is no permanent path established from A to C. Position (1) in the picture represents an initial situation where nodes A and C have no neighbours (they are out of range of any other surrounding node), and nodes B and D are connected through a physical link. When the simulation starts, node C is continuously moving back and forth from position (1) to (2), so the links established by node C with A and D are intermittently active. Moreover, the movement of C is quite fast so the contacts between C and D, and C and A, are very short but with a high frequency. On the contrary, node B has a slower pace: it alternates positions (1) and (2), but once the link with D is broken in (2), node B establish long connections with A before getting back to (1). One of the first results obtained from the comparison between PRoPHET and HURRy in this scenario regards the convergence time needed for all nodes to be aware of the whole topology. If we define the convergence time, *conv_time*, as the time period until all nodes learn about all the rest, and assume generic time units, *t.u*, HURRy outperforms with a gain factor above 2.5, as shown in Table 2.

Table 2. Convergence time in simulated scenario

conv_time(**PRoPHET**)	746.9t.u
conv_time(**HURRy**)	281.8t.u

This is due to the fact that, for instance with HURRy, node B learns about node C during the first contact between C and D (the link B-D is still active), which does not happen with PRoPHET until the second contact. The same happens for the rest of intermittent connections.

The simulation setup includes the following configuration:

- Node A creates 8 information packets headed to node C, and C creates 3 packets headed to node A (11 packets created).
- The packet size is 15 MB.
- The transmission rate of Bluetooth links is 250 kbps.

- The γ parameter has taken three possible values: 0.05 (priority to contact duration); 0.95 (priority to contact frequency); and 0.5 (intermediate balance).
- The intervals predefined for the histogram of contact duration times have been configured with different granularity: (P.G) poor granularity (contact durations below 5t.u are not distinguished); and (H.G) high granularity (v_i of 0.5t.u, 1t.u and 5t.u are distinguished).

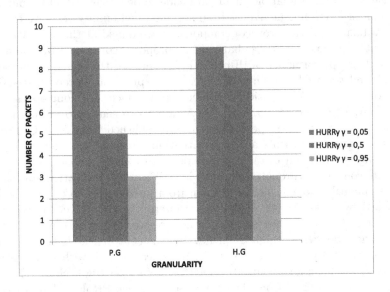

Fig. 5. Results in terms of number of packets delivered

Figure 5 shows the relevance of considering the contact duration in the routing decision. PRoPHET is not represented in the chart, since it delivered zero packets in the simulation. In this scenario, the packet size is considerably large, taking into account the transmission rate, so the frequency of direct contacts between nodes A and C forces PRoPHET to select the direct path as the best route, but in reality those direct contacts between A and C are too short for the messages to be successfully delivered, and that is the reason why a delivery ratio of 0/11 is obtained. HURRy performs differently according to the balance configured for the priority associated to the frequency and the duration of contacts, but at least some of the transmission attempts are successful in all configurations. If $\gamma = 0.05$ HURRy is merely rating available contacts according to their duration, and so, node A is selecting node B as its best next hop to reach C. That is the reason why 9 out of 11 packets are delivered, even with poor granularity in the duration intervals. The opposite configuration with $\gamma = 0.95$ implies that HURRy is prioritizing the frequency of contacts, just like PRoPHET, but the difference in the results obeys to the fact that HURRy selects the upper path in Fig. 1 until a number of encounters between A and C has occurred and then, the direct probability $P_-(A, C)$ increases its value. The intermediate configuration, $\gamma = 0.5$, shows the importance of defining an appropriate precision for the scenario considered. In this case, the number of packets delivered increases considerably if HURRy performs with high granularity in the range of duration intervals.

The comparison of the evolution experimented by $P_-(k, C)$ in the scenario during simulation time is also quite revealing. Figure 6 presents the final status of the key probability values evaluated by node A when selecting a route towards C. All results in Fig. 6 referred to HURRy correspond to the case of high granularity (H.G).

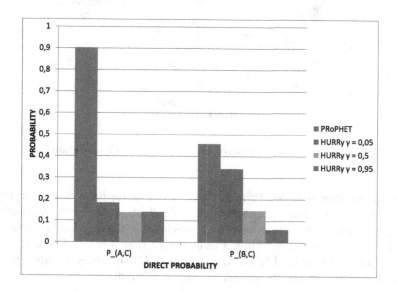

Fig. 6. P_(k,C) values compared by node A

It can be observed that node A will always choose the direct path towards C with PRoPHET, since $P_-(A, C) > P_-(B, C)$, and that is the reason why none of the transmission attempts succeeds, because the packet is too big to be delivered within the short duration of each contact between A and C. The probability values obtained with HURRy depend on γ, of course: the comparison between the two possible paths results in $P_-(A, C) < P_-(B, C)$ when $\gamma = 0.05$ and $\gamma = 0.5$; but if $\gamma = 0.95$ the final status ends with $P_-(A, C) > P_-(B, C)$, like in PRoPHET. The rating difference is much higher for the case $\gamma = 0.05$, which is the most opposed to PRoPHET. On the contrary, when HURRy uses a similar prioritization to PRoPHET, it is only in the beginning of the simulation that certain packets manage to reach node C.

Finally, we would like to highlight some results associated with the precision defined for the intervals of the contact duration. Figure 7 shows the different values obtained for $P_-(k, C)$ for configurations of high and poor granularity.

For $\gamma = 0.05$ the comparison in Fig. 7 results in $P_-(A, C) < P_-(B, C)$ both for poor and high granularity, although the difference is much bigger for the H.G case. When $\gamma = 0.5$, the comparison provides opposed results depending

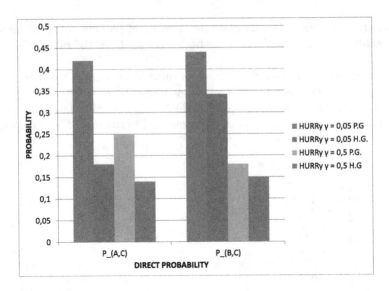

Fig. 7. P_(k,C) values compared by node A with different granularity

on the granularity defined. Provided that the intermediate case is trying to balance the rating parameters considered in Eq. 2, an appropriate granularity to distinguish contact durations with high precision is the key factor influencing the final probability values. Thus, Fig. 5 showed that if $\gamma = 0.5$, the H.G case obtained a delivery ratio of 8/11, whereas the P.G case delivered only 5 packets out of 11. Figure 7 states the reason for such a different performance.

5   Conclusions and Future Work

The work presented in this article summarises the design principles, protocol components and simulation results obtained for the specification of a novel probabilistic routing approach based on human routines: the HURRy protocol. The motivation for this research came from the study of challenged networking in scenarios where the social behaviour of people highlighted some deficiencies in existing approaches. We analysed the statistical distributions followed by the inter-contact and contact duration times in some previous experiments cited as related work, and derived a way of combining these statistical features in order to evaluate the quality of a neighbour. We propose a solution where DTN nodes register the parameters of their contact history to estimate a weighted mean value and calculate the goodness of their contacts accordingly. HURRy incorporates some other enhancements that result in an optimised performance in terms of convergence time and packet delivery ratio for scenarios in which the duration of contacts shows high variability. Some of the most relevant results obtained in simulation have been presented as a proof of concept for the HURRy protocol implementation. There is still much work ahead in order to extend this research line in several directions: we are currently working on the complete specification of the HURRy protocol, and have implemented its functionality into the Byte-walla3 project for Android phones [18]. The resulting Android implementation is called HURRywalla and it is made available through [22]. We would like to incorporate more parameters to the profiling of human routines and we plan to perform a more thorough experimentation plan using real smart phones. Our implementation of HURRy for Android is actually supporting the Bundle Protocol Query (BPQ) [19] extension block for DTN2, and so we can start testing scenarios comprising Content Delivery Networks, content caching and the like.

Acknowledgement. The research leading to these results has received funding from the European Unions (EU) Horizon 2020 research and innovation programme under grant agreement No 645124 (Action full title: Universal, mobile-centric and opportunistic communications architecture, Action Acronym: UMOBILE). This paper reflects only the authors views and the Community is not liable for any use that may be made of the information contained therein.

References

1. Scott, J., Crowcroft, J., Hui, P., Diot, C.: Haggle: a networking architecture designed around mobile users. In: Proceedings of Third Annual Conference on Wireless On-Demand Network Systems and Services (2006)
2. Bagrow, J.P., Wang, D., Barabási, A.-L.: Collective response of human populations to large-scale emergencies. PLoS One **6**(3), 1–8 (2006)
3. Brockmann, D., Hufnagel, L., Geisel, T.: The scaling laws of human travel. Nature **439**, 462–465 (2006)
4. Ebel, H., Davidsen, J., Bornholdt, S.: Dynamics of social networks. Complexity **8**, 24–27 (2002)
5. Palla, G., Barabási, A.-L., Vicsek, T.: Quantifying social group evolution. Nature **446**, 664–667 (2007)
6. Szabó, G., Barabási, A-L.: Network effects in service usage. Physics, subject: Physics and Society (2006)
7. González, M.C., Hidalgo, C.A., Barabási, A.-L.: Understanding individual human mobility patterns. Nature **453**, 779–782 (2008)
8. Song, C., Koren, T., Wang, P., Barabási, A.-L.: Modelling the scaling properties of human mobility. Nat. Phys. (Advanced Online Publications) **7**, 713 (2010)
9. Song, C., Qu, Z., Blumm, N., Barabási, A.-L.: Limits of predictability in human mobility. Science **327**, 1018–1021 (2010)
10. Eagle, N., Pentland, A.: Reality mining: sensing complex social systems. Pers. Ubiquit. Comput. **10**, 255–268 (2006)
11. Eagle, N., Pentland, A.: Eigenbehaviours: identifying structure in routine. Behav. Ecol. Sociobiol. **63**, 1057–1066 (2009)
12. Cabero, J.M., Unibaso, G., Sanchez, A., Arizaga, I.: The Bluetooth Medallion: a wearable device for human MANETs. In: 3rd International Symposium on Wireless Pervasive Computing, pp. 776–780 (2008). ISBN: 9781424416523
13. Cabero, J.M., Molina, V., Urteaga, I., Liberal, F., Martin, J.L.: Acquisition of human traces with Bluetooth technology: Challenges and proposals. Ad Hoc Netw. **12**, 2–16 (2012)

14. Lindgren, A., Doria, A., Davies, E., Grasic, S.: Probabilistic routing protocol for intermittently connected networks. RFC Active Internet-Draft (2012). https://datatracker.ietf.org/doc/draft-irtf-dtnrg-prophet/
15. Lindgren, A., Doria, A., Schelén, O.: Probabilistic routing in intermittently connected networks. ACM SIGMOBILE Mob. Comput. Commun. Rev., 19–20 (2003). ISSN: 1559-1662
16. Vahdat, A., Becker, D.: Epidemic routing for partially connected ad hoc networks. Technical Report CS-200006 (2000)
17. The Opportunistic Network Environment simulator. http://www.netlab.tkk.fi/tutkimus/dtn/theone/
18. Communication System Design (KTH, Stockholm): Android application version 3 of the project Bytewalla (2010). http://sourceforge.net/projects/bytewalla3/
19. Farrell, S., Lynch, A., Kutcher, D., Lindgren, A.: Bundle protocol query extension block. RFC Active Internet-Draft (2012). http://tools.ietf.org/html/draft-irtf-dtnrg-bpq-00
20. Cabero, J.M., Olabarrieta, I., Gil-López, S., Del Ser, J., Martin, J.L.: A novel range-free localization algorithm to turn connectivity traces and motion data into localization information. Ad Hoc Netw. 20, 36–52 (2014)
21. Cabero, J.M., Molina, V., Urteaga, I., Liberal, F., Martin, J.L.: Reliability of Bluetooth-based connectivity traces for the characterization of human interaction. Ad Hoc Netw. 24, 135–1461 (2015). Part A
22. Pérez-Sánchez, S., Errondosoro, N.: HURRywalla project. Implementation of HURRy protocol within the DTN stack of Bytewalla3 project for Android phones (2013). http://sourceforge.net/projects/hurrywalla/

On the Performance of Caching and Forwarding in Information-Centric Networking for the IoT

Mohamed Ahmed M. Hail[1], Marica Amadeo[2]([⊠]), Antonella Molinaro[2], and Stefan Fischer[1]

[1] Telematics Institute University of Lübeck,
Ratzeburger Allee 160, 23562 Lübeck, Germany
{hail,fischer}@itm.uni-luebeck.de
[2] University Mediterranea of Reggio Calabria,
Via Graziella Loc. Feo di Vito, 89100 Reggio Calabria, Italy
{marica.amadeo,antonella.molinaro}@unirc.it

Abstract. *Information-Centric Networking* (ICN) is a communication paradigm for the future Internet that matches the pattern of information-oriented applications and provides in-network caching. Thanks to such properties, ICN has been recently considered as a solution for the IoT. However, IoT shows challenging features: many devices are resource-constrained and applications usually originate transient information. As a consequence, ICN-IoT solutions requires new design choices. Among them, it is crucial understanding if constrained devices can successfully implement ICN caching and forwarding functionalities, and what are the delivery performance.

To provide hints in such a context, in this paper we evaluate the performance of different caching/replacement policies and forwarding strategies in an ICN-IoT wireless network. A novel forwarding scheme is also defined to reduce the load on constrained devices. Simulation results show that the devised caching and forwarding operations are beneficial for delivery performance: they reduce the traffic volume and save the devices' energy resources.

Keywords: Information-Centric Networking · Internet of Things · Caching · Forwarding

1 Introduction

The Internet of Things (IoT) envisions a future in which everyday objects undergo a transformation into smart entities able to interact with each other and/or with humans therefore enabling new classes of applications in different domains, like smart home, smart city and smart transportation [13]. But unlike traditional networks, IoT is a highly heterogeneous and challenging environment, characterized by both resource-constrained and more powerful devices, heterogeneous wireless and wired access technologies and peculiar traffic patterns.

Several research efforts and standardization activities are underway to define proper networking solutions for the IoT. In addition to *evolutionary* IP-based

© Springer International Publishing Switzerland 2015
M.C. Aguayo-Torres et al. (Eds.): WWIC 2015, LNCS 9071, pp. 313–326, 2015.
DOI: 10.1007/978-3-319-22572-2_23

approaches, e.g., 6LoWPAN, the research community is considering a novel communication paradigm called Information Centric Networking (ICN), aka Content Centric Networking (CCN), which has been specifically conceived for data dissemination from information-oriented applications [4] and may also offer several advantages in IoT. In ICN each content is named uniquely and independently from the location of the producer thus facilitating caching at intermediate nodes. A consumer requests a content by sending the so-called *Interest* packet, which carries the content name; the producer or any node that maintains a copy of that content may answer the request. By enabling anycast, connectionless delivery and in-network caching, ICN allows to decouple senders and receivers, speed up data retrieval and limit the massive data access to the same producer [5].

But research on ICN-IoT systems is still at its infancy and there are several open challenges to address. IoT data are usually *transient*: they can be frequently updated by the producer, and also the consumers could be interested in data with a specific *freshness* requirement [15]. This complicates the caching operation. Moreover, the ICN networking functionalities, namely advanced packet processing, caching and forwarding, can be quite expensive for *constrained wireless IoT nodes* like sensors. When a multi-hop scenario is considered, in fact, an ICN node receiving an Interest must decide whether *forwarding* it or not towards the producer. If the Interest is transmitted and a content packet is then received, the node should decide if *caching* the content before *forwarding* it back to the original consumer. When the content is cached, the node can act as a source and answer to future requests. As a result, ICN communication could be highly energy consuming for resource-constrained devices.

The ICN Research Group (ICNRG) of the Internet Research Task Force (IRTF) is currently investigating what could be the role of constrained nodes in ICN-IoT systems. As discussed in [11], a design choice may be to separate IoT functionalities (e.g., sensing and measurement transmission) from ICN functionalities. The constrained node could implement only the IoT functionalities and let ICN tasks to the powerful nodes. However, results in [8] obtained with a preliminary testbed showed that caching is very useful in IoT because it shortens the path length to the content and reduces the network load. In summary, to enable Interest forwarding and consequent data caching in constrained nodes has pros and cons that deserve to be investigated. This is indeed the objective of this paper, which explores the potentials of in-network caching and forwarding in wireless ICN-IoT systems.

In this context, it is the authors' opinion that IoT nodes should perform a *simple distributed caching scheme* and an *adaptive Interest forwarding (AIF) strategy* that considers the status of the node resources (e.g., energy level), which vary over time. Nodes with higher capabilities (e.g., fully charged) have priority in the Interest forwarding and they are candidate to cache the data; constrained nodes, instead, can implement ICN functionalities only if it is strictly necessary, e.g., in a sparse network, where their participation is fundamental to connect different network segments.

After discussing caching and forwarding strategies in ICN-IoT systems by referring related literature, in this paper we present the AIF strategy and deploy an extensive simulation campaign by means of the reference simulation tool of the ICN community, ndnSIM [3]. Obtained results show that a simple probabilistic caching scheme coupled with the Least Recently Used (LRU) policy can be particularly beneficial in ICN-IoT systems, where consumers are usually interested in the freshest copy of the content. But the benefits of caching can be further improved by using proper forwarding schemes like AIF, which is aware of the node's resources.

The rest of the paper is organized as follows. Section 2 describes the ICN paradigm; Sect. 3 discusses ICN caching and its applicability in IoT, while Sect. 4 introduces the forwarding process and presents the AIF strategy. Section 5 discusses the simulation results. Finally, Sect. 6 concludes the paper.

2   Information Centric Networking: General Concepts

ICN replaces the *host-centric conversational model* of the TCP/IP protocol suite with *information-centric communications* where named data are disseminated in the network in a connectionless fashion. Different ICN architectures have been proposed so far [4], which share the same networking principle. Without loss of generality, in the following we refer to the Named Data Networking (NDN) [20] architecture to show the content retrieval procedure by focusing on forwarding and caching operations.

NDN communication is initiated by the consumer which transmits an Interest to request a Data packet by name. Every node maintains three data structures: *(i)* the Content Store (CS) that caches incoming Data; *(ii)* the Pending Interest Table (PIT) that keeps track of the forwarded Interest(s) that are not yet satisfied; *(iii)* the Forwarding Information Base (FIB) that is used as a routing table to relay Interests towards content source(s). When an Interest is received, the node first looks in its CS to find a matching Data packet and send it back. If the Data is not found in the CS, the node looks in the PIT. If a matching PIT entry is found, it means that an equal request has been already forwarded and the node is waiting for the response. Therefore, the entry is updated with the arrival interface and the Interest is *discarded*. Otherwise, a new PIT entry is created and the Interest is forwarded to the interface stored in the FIB.

The Data packet follows the chain of PIT entries back to the consumer(s), and it can be cached in intermediated nodes.

The NDN forwarding fabric together with the caching operation can provide several benefits in IoT scenarios. The PIT look-up is specifically designed to deal with massive data access and reduce the traffic load. In fact, by identifying multiple Interests for the same Data and discarding duplications, intermediate nodes forward only a single request to the producer. Retrieval performance is further improved by in-network caching, which makes data available closer to consumers also under intermittent connectivity, e.g., due to low-power operation.

However, forwarding and caching mechanisms need to be further investigated and properly extended to cope with the challenges of IoT wireless systems, as discussed in the following.

3   In-Network Caching

3.1   Caching Strategies and Replacement Policies

The caching system in a node consists of two main parts: the caching decision strategy and the replacement policy.

The default caching strategy in ICN is the so-called ALWAYS (aka universal) caching, where all incoming packets are cached by all nodes without any actual selection criterion. This simple strategy, however, has been shown inefficient because it generates high redundancy without maximizing the data diversity in the network [9]. Therefore, other solutions are usually used in the literature as benchmark, including PROBABILISTIC caching [17], where the node randomly caches incoming Data with a certain probability p.

Several advanced caching strategies have been proposed so far to minimize redundancy and maximize the cache hit ratio [19]. However, they are not designed for IoT scenarios, they mainly target Internet contents with Zipf distributed request patterns and propose schemes with *implicit* or *explicit* coordination, which leverage information about network topology or content characteristics, e.g., popularity. For instance, in [14], a probabilistic strategy is proposed where the caching probability is inversely proportional to the distance between the requester and the caching node. If this latter is closer to the requester, the content will be copied with higher probability thus quickly pushing it to the network edge and reducing the number of copies. Vice versa, an explicit coordination scheme called Cooperative In-Network Caching is proposed in [10], where nodes in the neighbourhood cooperate to cache the data without duplications. When a Data packet arrives at a caching node, it uses a hash function to determine in which of its neighbours (including itself) to cache the packet. However, in [16], the authors argue that explicit coordination policies would likely violate ICN line of speed constraint, while simple randomized caching policies could perform almost as well as more complex ones.

The most common replacement policies in ICN are LEAST RECENTLY USED (LRU), LEAST FREQUENTLY USED (LFU) and RANDOM. LFU is computationally more expensive than LRU, which is therefore considered for line speed operations. To maintain ICN simple and scalable, the RANDOM replacement, which is agnostic of the frequency and timing of requests, is sometimes preferred [16].

3.2   Caching in ICN-IoT

Caching strategies defined for Internet contents and wired networks are not generally suited to IoT. As a matter of fact, IoT contents are different from Internet contents because they are usually transient and small, and IoT devices are different from Internet hosts because they have usually constrains in terms of energy and storage capabilities, e.g., the CS size is only of a few kbytes [8].

So far, only a very limited number of works have studied in-network caching and related issues in IoT.

The importance of the freshness parameter from the perspectives of both producers and consumers have been recently discussed in [15]. The authors argue that in presence of transient IoT contents both Interest and Data packets should carry a freshness value to perform accurate caching and retrieval operations. On one hand, stale contents are automatically discarded from a CS that honours the freshness declared by the producer; on the other hand, a CS matching can be considered valid if the freshness requested by the consumer is in accordance with the freshness of the cached data.

The work in [18] proposes a distributed probabilistic caching algorithm for IoT contents in the Internet, where routers dynamically update their caching probability by considering information about the network topology, the data freshness, the rate and freshness requirement of incoming requests. However, by taking into consideration those large set of parameters and routers with large storage capacity, the proposed coordination scheme is not well suited for low-power networks and constrained devices. Vice versa, in [8], the focus is on a wireless IoT system where nodes have limited storage. By leveraging a real testbed, the authors compare data retrieval with ALWAYS caching and without caching. They find that, thanks to in-network caching, the number of radio transmissions is reduced by up 50 % thus proving that the caching operation is useful even in presence of nodes with limited capabilities.

In this paper, we extend through simulations the analysis started in [8] with the objective of understanding the performance of the standard caching and replacement policies in wireless ICN-IoT systems.

4   The Forwarding Decision

4.1   Controlled Flooding

IoT systems are often characterized by battery-powered, sometimes mobile, nodes that communicate through the unreliable broadcast shared medium in a multi-hop fashion. In such environments, FIBs are usually not populated in advance by routing information and Interests are broadcasted hop-by-hop with controlled flooding mechanisms, as discussed in [6–8] and reference therein. Flooding is indeed a simple and robust solution in finding a path to the requested content even under intermittent connectivity: the Interest packet is broadcasted over the wireless medium by the consumer and re-broadcasted by intermediate nodes until a producer is located; then, the Data packet is transmitted by the producer and forwarded by intermediate nodes that maintain a PIT entry.

To reduce overhead and redundancy, the forwarding strategy is enhanced with timer-based packet suppression techniques that exploit packet overhearing, i.e., the node defers the packet of a specific delay and drops it if the same packet is overheard over the broadcast medium. The defer (and listening) time can be selected in different ways: it can be randomly computed, or based on some specific information about the network topology, if available. For instance, if nodes are aware of their distance to the producer, the forwarding scheme can prioritize the nodes closer to the producer with shorter defer times [7,12].

Controlled flooding can also be used as the initial discovery phase to set a temporary FIB entry on the reverse path taken by the first Data packet [8]. After the producer is discovered, subsequent Interests can be unicast using the established path, while flooding is used again only if the producer becomes unreachable. Unicast transmissions, however, hinder the possibility of sharing information over the wireless channel.

4.2 Adaptive Interest Forwarding

In this work, we present a simple forwarding strategy that implements controlled flooding but uses a novel technique for the calculation of the defer time. Our focus, in fact, is on constrained IoT devices, which should implement ICN forwarding depending of their capabilities like the energy level, whose value varies over time making the device less (or more) prone to participate in ICN functionalities.

The rationale of the designed defer time calculation is to prioritize forwarding from the nodes with higher capabilities, while the constrained nodes calculate longer defer times and transmit only if they do not overhear the Interest transmission from the neighbours. This should limit the number of packet transmissions, which are indeed the main cause of energy consumption.

The proposed *Adaptive Interest Forwarding* (AIF) strategy extends the so-called Blind Forwarding (BF) presented in [6]. It assumes that Interest and Data rebroadcasting events are deferred by $T_{Interest}$ and T_{Data} time values, respectively, and Data have always higher access priority than Interests. Both defer times are randomly computed by considering a defer window (DW), an integer value that indicates the maximum length of the time intervals, as follows:

$$T_{Data} = rand[0; DW - 1] * DeferSlot \tag{1}$$

$$T_{Interest} = (DW + rand[0; DW]) * DeferSlot \tag{2}$$

where *DeferSlot* is a fixed, short time interval[1].

During $T_{Interest}$, the potential forwarder listens to the channel: if it overhears the requested Data or the same Interest, then it cancels its own transmission and the related PIT entry.

The AIF strategy maintains the logic of the Blind Forwarding but modifies the $T_{Interest}$ calculation in order to set the defer time of a constrained node in a way that is proportional to its available resources, whose values are usually monitored by the node itself. We do not consider additional parameters (e.g., about the network topology or the neighbourhood) because we do not want to introduce additional complexity (e.g., signalling or coordination).

In this paper we focus on a single resource, the energy level of the node, En, but the algorithm can be easily extended to include also other inputs. En is modelled as a normalized parameter with $0 \leq En \leq 1$, where the values 0 and 1

---

[1] Different values for DW and *DeferSlot* parameters are considered in [6]. In this paper, the selected values are reported in Table 1.

mean that the battery is fully discharged or charged, respectively. The Interest defer time is then calculated as:

$$T_{Interest} = (DW + \Gamma_{En} + rand(0; DW)) * DeferSlot \qquad (3)$$

where the term $\Gamma_{En} = (1 - En) * DW$ is the defer time extension related to the energy level of the node.

By following the above computation, the nodes with higher energy level will transmit with higher priority, while the others will not participate in the forwarding and, consequently, they will not be involved in the caching decision of the correspondent Data packet. Such advantages come at the expense of only a little energy consumption due to the overhearing operation.

5 Performance Evaluation

5.1 System Description

To evaluate the impact of caching and forwarding in wireless ICN-IoT systems, we use the ns-3 simulator [1] and the open-source ndnSIM [3] module, specifically designed to support NDN networks.

Our scenario is a *400* m × *400* m area with 36 nodes deployed in a lattice topology, as shown in Fig. 1. Each node uses the IEEE 802.11 g radio interface, where physical and medium access control parameters are set according to [2], a small form factor, low power networking module available on the market. The distance between two adjacent nodes is 80 m and the nominal coverage range of each node is about 120 m. However, the received signal power can vary during the simulation because the Rayleigh fading distribution is selected to reproduce realistic propagation in urban environments.

Four consumers, each one located in a corner of the square, are interested in the retrieval of contents with specific *freshness* values from a set of nodes in the

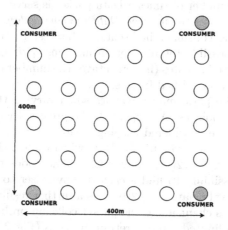

Fig. 1. Simulation scenario: lattice topology with 36 nodes.

topology. Six nodes are randomly selected as producers, which generate *transient* contents, each one composed by N_d Data packets, i.e., the consumer has to transmit N_d different Interests to obtain the overall information. Each consumer periodically sends novel Interests to obtain the fresher (novel) information. We assume the update period is 1 min (e.g., the consumer requests the content at t = 0 s, t = 60 s, t = 120 s, etc., and each time the Interests also carry the freshness requirement).

Performance evaluation is divided into two main parts.

First, we focus on the caching performance in presence of devices with very small CSs. Since our study targets constrained wireless devices, we do not consider burdensome caching schemes based on explicit or implicit cooperation. We instead focus on two simple decision strategies, ALWAYS and PROBABILISTIC with $p = 0.5$, coupled with two replacement policies, LRU and RANDOM. The LFU policy is not included in the analysis since it is computationally more complex than LRU and RANDOM.

Then, we focus on the forwarding schemes (BF and AIF) and their effects on the traffic load and the network energy consumption. To this purpose, the energy model in ns-3 is used to calculate the energy consumption in the simulated scenario. Simulation results are averaged over 10 independent runs.

Table 1 summarizes the main simulation parameters.

5.2 In-Network Caching Analysis

The objective of this first study is to evaluate the impact of small CSs over content retrieval. Therefore, we vary the CS size from 1 to 4 kbytes. Nodes are fully charged and do not run out of energy during the simulation, which lasts 10 min during which the four consumers request contents according to the previously described pattern. Packet forwarding is based on BF, without the AIF extension.

As performance metrics, we consider: *(i)* the *cache hit ratio*, which indicates (in percentage) the number of times a Data packet is served by a CS instead of the original producer; *(ii)* the average *Data retrieval delay*, which is computed as the time since the consumer has sent the Interest to the reception of the Data and includes possible Interest retransmissions; *(iii)* the average *Interest retransmissions*, which indicates (in percentage) the number of times a consumer has to re-transmit an unsatisfied Interest.

Figure 2 shows the performance metrics when varying the CS size and the caching/replacement policies. As expected, the greater the CS size the better the performance of the considered caching strategies, e.g., the cache hit ratio with ALWAYS(LRU) passes from 6 % to 31 %, when the CS size varies from 1 to 4 kbytes, respectively (Fig. 2(a)). Larger CSs allow nodes to cache more data and increase the possibility to find a cached copy closer to the consumer thus shortening the retrieval delays (Fig. 2(b)). As a further result, the transmissions over the lossy wireless channel and the packet collision probability are reduced, which correspond to limited Interest retransmissions (Fig. 2(c)).

Table 1. Simulation parameters

Category	Parameter	Value
Application	Data payload size	256 bytes
	Data freshness	rand (5:20)
	Consumer's freshness	rand (1:10)
	N_d	15
	Update period	1 min
Scenario	Coverage area	400 m × 400 m
	Number of nodes	36
	Distance between nodes	80 m
	Number of consumers	4
	Number of producers	6
NDN	CS size	1–4 kbytes
	Caching strategy	ALWAYS, PROBABILISTIC (with $p = 0.5$)
	Replacement policy	LRU, RANDOM
	Forwarding strategy	Controlled flooding with (or w/o) AIF
		$DW = 255$
		$DeferSlot = 28\,\mu s$ (= IEEE 802.11 g DIFS)
Access	Technology	IEEE 802.11g
	Rx sensivity	$-84\,dBm$
	Propagation model	Rayleigh

When focusing on the replacement policies, an important trend is that LRU performs better then RANDOM when both PROBABILISTIC (shortened as *Prob* in Fig. 2) and ALWAYS strategies are considered. This is due to the fact that IoT consumers are generally interested in fresher data, and the LRU policy naturally favours fresher contents, by discarding the least recently used packets. Therefore, a LRU policy is recommended in IoT systems that honour the freshness requirement.

Under the same replacement policy, it can be observed that PROBABILISTIC caching always performs better then ALWAYS. In particular, PROBABILISTIC caching coupled with LRU gives the highest performance in terms of hit ratio and, consequently, in terms of retrieval delay and Interest retransmissions. This result is due to the fact that the ALWAYS strategy generates high redundancy in the network, a condition already pinpointed in general literature about ICN caching [17]. In presence of small CSs, the negative effects of the ALWAYS strategy are even exacerbated. Vice versa, a PROBABILISTIC scheme improves the data diversity in the network and provides a more efficient utilisation of available cache resources.

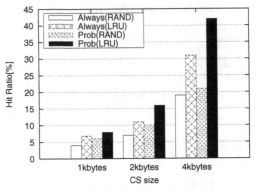

(a) Cache hit ratio.

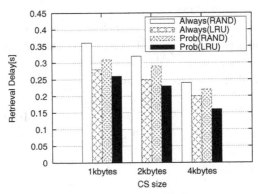

(b) Data retrieval delay.

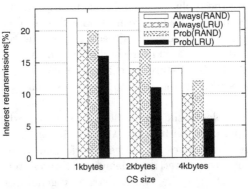

(c) Interest retransmissions.

Fig. 2. Caching analysis: metrics varying the cache size, the caching strategy and the replacement policy.

5.3 Forwarding Analysis

Our second evaluation study compares BF and AIF schemes and it is structured into two parts: *(i)* energy efficiency and *(ii)* delivery performance analysis.

We select as caching strategy the PROBABILISTIC scheme coupled with LRU, which obtained the highest performance in the previous analysis. The CS size is fixed to 2 kbytes.

Our first focus is to estimate the energy efficiency of the forwarding by considering the *network lifetime*, which is defined as the time interval during which the network is connected and there is at least one path between the consumers and the requested contents. When nodes start to run out of energy the communication opportunities reduce as well and, eventually, the data retrieval becomes totally infeasible. The ns-3 energy model allows to specify the initial energy of each device and during the simulation such value decreases on the basis of the activity of the node. In the experiment, the four consumers are fully charged, while the rest of the nodes are provided with low levels of initial energy and they are meant to quickly run out of energy. Simulation ends when such nodes have exhausted their energy and data retrieval becomes infeasible.

Table 2 shows the network lifetime together with the retrieval delay and the percentage of Interest retransmissions for BF and AIF schemes.

Table 2. Comparison of BF and AIF in low-energy conditions

Metric	BF	AIF
Network lifetime [s]	366	425
Retrieval delay [s]	0.23	0.24
Interest retransmissions	12 %	9 %

It can be observed that AIF, by enabling an energy aware forwarding, can improve the network lifetime w.r.t. BF. In fact, nodes with a higher energy level transmit first and let the others to save their resources. AIF can also automatically *balance* the charge in the network because when a node decreases its energy level, due to a high number of transmission operations, its defer time $T_{Interest}$ increases as well. As a result, its transmission opportunities decrease.

This advantage is at the expense of a slightly higher retrieval delay, which is due to generally longer defer times. However, longer delays have a beneficial side effect: they limit the packet collision probability and therefore reduce the number of Interest retransmissions from consumers.

To obtain further insights into the delivery performance of AIF, we consider a different simulation campaign where we vary the number of consumers from 1 to 4. We assume that nodes are provided with different levels of initial energy, which is sufficiently high to guarantee that they do not run out of energy during the simulation, which last 10 min.

Figure 3 shows the number of Interest and Data packets transmitted by all the nodes in the network (i.e., consumers, forwarders, producers) during the simulation. It can be observed that AIF is able to reduce the overall traffic load since

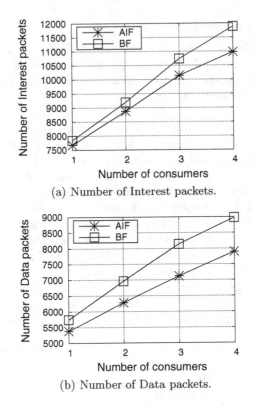

(a) Number of Interest packets.

(b) Number of Data packets.

Fig. 3. Traffic load varying the number of consumers.

it originates a lower number of Interest and Data packets, if compared with BF. This is due to the fact that the $T_{Interest}$ computation includes the additional term Γ_{En}, which increases the listening period and reduces the number of concurrent transmissions. Less transmissions also imply less energy consumption, with consequent advantages in terms of network lifetime.

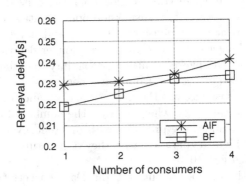

Fig. 4. Data retrieval delay when varying the number of consumers.

The price to pay, as briefly discussed above, is the slightly higher retrieval delay. However, this is not a big matter since, as shown in Fig. 4, the difference in the AIF and BF retrieval delay is less than 10 ms.

6 Conclusion

In this paper, we have studied in-network caching and forwarding in wireless ICN-IoT systems characterized by constrained devices. Simulation results obtained with ndnSIM have shown that ICN caching is very useful in IoT, even if the content store of a constrained device is only of a few kilobytes. In particular, by facilitating the data diversity in the network, PROBABILISTIC caching can improve the cache hit ratio w.r.t. the ALWAYS caching strategy, while the LRU replacement policy results very suited to IoT because it naturally matches the freshness requirements of consumers.

To improve the performance of Interest forwarding in presence of constrained devices, the AIF scheme has been proposed, which considers the node energy level. Such awareness allows AIF to outperform the Blind Forwarding algorithm by guaranteeing longer network lifetime and reducing the traffic load.

As future work, we plan to further extend the simulation campaign by considering mobile scenarios and different content request patterns and node density values.

Acknowledgement. This work was supported by a fellowship within the FITweltweit programme of the German Academic Exchange Service (DAAD) and by the national research project PON03PE_00050 DOMUS "Home automation systems for a cooperative energy brokerage service".

References

1. The network simulator-3 (ns-3). http://www.nsnam.org/
2. RN-171 802.11 b/g Wireless LAN Module, Rowing Networks, Datasheet available on line at: http://www.microchip.com/
3. Afanasyev, A., Moiseenko, I., Zhang, L.: ndnSIM: NDN simulator for NS-3. Technical report NDN-0005, NDN, October 2012
4. Ahlgren, B., Dannewitz, C., Imbrenda, C., Kutscher, D., Ohlman, B.: A survey of information-centric networking. IEEE Commun. Mag. 50(7), 26–36 (2012)
5. Amadeo, M., Campolo, C., Iera, A., Molinaro, A.: Named data networking for IoT: an architectural perspective. In: European Conference on Networks and Communications (EuCNC), Bologna, Italy (2014)
6. Amadeo, M., Campolo, C., Molinaro, A.: Forwarding strategies in named data wireless ad hoc networks: design and evaluation. Elsevier J. Netw. Comput. Appl. 50, 148–158 (2015)
7. Amadeo, M., Campolo, C., Molinaro, A., Ruggeri, G.: Content-centric wireless networking: a survey. Comput. Netw. 72, 1–13 (2014)
8. Baccelli, E., Mehlis, C., Hahm, O., Schmidt, T.C., Wählisch, M.: Information centric networking in the IoT: experiments with NDN in the wild. In: ACM Conference on Information-Centric Networking (ICN-2014) (2014)

9. Chai, W.K., He, D., Psaras, I., Pavlou, G.: Cache "less for more" in information-centric networks (extended version). Elsevier Comput. Commun. **36**(7), 758–770 (2013)
10. Li, Z., Simon, G.: Time-shifted TV in content centric networks: the case for cooperative in-network caching. In: IEEE ICC (2011)
11. Lindgren, A., et al.: Applicability and tradeoffs of information-centric networking for efficient IoT. In: Internet-Draft, January 2015
12. Meisel, M., Pappas, V., Zhang, L.: Ad hoc networking via named data. In: ACM International Workshop on Mobility in the Evolving Internet Architecture, pp. 3–8 (2010)
13. Miorandi, D., Sicari, S., De Pellegrini, F., Chlamtac, I.: Internet of things: vision, applications and research challenges. Elsevier Ad Hoc Netw. **10**(7), 1497–1516 (2012)
14. Psaras, I., Chai, W.K., Pavlou, G.: Probabilistic in-network caching for information-centric networks. In: ICN Workshop on Information-Centric Networking, pp. 55–60 (2012)
15. Quevedo, J., Corujo, D., Aguiar, R.: Consumer driven information freshness approach for content centric networking. In: IEEE Infocom NOM Workshop (2014)
16. Rossi, D., Rossini, G.: Evaluating CCN multi-path Interest forwarding strategies. Comput. Commun. **36**, 771–778 (2013)
17. Tarnoi, S., Suksomboon, K., Kumwilaisak, W., Ji, Y.: Performance of probabilistic caching and cache replacement policies for Content-Centric Networks. In: IEEE 39th Conference on Local Computer Networks (LCN) (2014)
18. Vural, S., Navaratnam, P., Wang, N., Wang, C., Dong, L., Tafazolli, R.: In-network caching of internet-of-things data. In: IEEE International Conference on Communications (ICC), pp. 3185–3190 (2014)
19. Zhang, G., Li, Y., Lin, T.: Caching in information centric networking: a survey. Comput. Netw. **57**(16), 3128–3141 (2013)
20. Zhang, L., et al.: Named Data Networking (NDN) Project. Technical report. NDN-0001, PARC, October 2010

Empirical Analysis of the Minkowski Distance Order in Geographical Routing Protocols for VANETs

Luis Urquiza-Aguiar[1]([⊠]), Carolina Tripp-Barba[2], José Estrada-Jiménez[3], and Mónica Aguilar Igartua[1]

[1] Department of Network Engineering, Universitat Politècnica de Catalunya (UPC), C. Jordi Girona 1-3, 08034 Barcelona, Spain
{luis.urquiza,monica.aguilar}@entel.upc.edu
[2] Faculty of Informatics, Universidad Autonóma de Sinaloa (UAS), De Los Deportes Avenue and Leonismo Internacional, 82107 Mazatlán, Mexico
ctripp@uas.edu.mx
[3] Department of Electronics, Telecommunications and Networks, Escuela Politécnica Nacional (EPN), Ladrón de Guevara E11 253, Quito 170413, Ecuador
jose.estrada@epn.edu

Abstract. This paper offers an empirical study of the impact of the way how the distance between two nodes is measured by a geographical routing protocol for VANETs in order to take its forwarding decision. The distance equations used in this work are obtained by setting the order parameter of the Minkowski distance function. Simulation results from the topology of a real city indicate that the use of dominant distance can improve some classical performance metrics like the packet delivery ratio, average number of hops or end-to-end packet delay.

Keywords: VANET · Geographical routing protocol · Minkowski distance · GPSR

1 Introduction

Vehicular *ad hoc* networks (VANETs) [5] are seen as a special case of mobile *ad hoc* networks (MANETs), where nodes are vehicles. Nevertheless, VANETs face particular challenges compared to MANETs, such as faster topology changes, a lower link lifetime or a potentially greater number of nodes taking part in the network, among others. Particularly, the two formers have encouraged researches to propose new routing protocol for VANETs that do not need to construct end-to-end paths and that make their routing decision based only on local information.

Geographical routing protocols have emerged as an alternative to the classical topological routing approach. This kind of routing protocols considers the geographical (euclidean measured) distance between nodes in their forwarding criteria. On the other hand, the Minkowski distance function [1] provides a general equation to measure the level of dissimilarity between two points. The Euclidean

© Springer International Publishing Switzerland 2015
M.C. Aguayo-Torres et al. (Eds.): WWIC 2015, LNCS 9071, pp. 327–340, 2015.
DOI: 10.1007/978-3-319-22572-2_24

distance is a particular case of the Minkowski distance function. In this work, we analyze the performance impact of a distance-based VANET routing protocol, when it employs distance equations (obtained from the Minkowski distance function) different from the Euclidean one in the computation of its routing metric, when selecting the next hop.

The rest of the paper is organized as follows: Sect. 2 summarizes geographical routing strategy in VANETs and the Minkowski distance family. Then, Sect. 3 describes how using a different distance function changes the forwarding decision made by a distance-based VANET routing protocol. Next, Sect. 4 is devoted to describe the simulation scenario, the evaluation of the different Minkowski distances in the selected protocol and the results obtained from the statistical tests. Finally, conclusions are drawn in Sect. 5.

2   Background

2.1   Geographical Routing Protocols in VANETs

A widely accepted classification of VANET routing protocols is presented in [9] where routing protocols are divided into two big categories: (1) *Topology-based* routing protocols perform packet forwarding by using the information of the existing links in the network, and *Geographic (position-based)*, in which nodes make their forwarding decisions based on the position of a packet destination and the positions of the one-hop neighbors. The latter approach was developed taking into account the inherent fast topology changes in VANETs. Many geographical protocols store packets while they do not have a suitable forwarding node, a process called carry-and-forwarding. This specific type of protocols are appropriate for delay-tolerant networks (DTN) and applications due to the delay introduced by the carrying process.

In the following, we summarize the main features of one of the most extended proposals of geographical routing called Greedy Perimeter Stateless Routing (GPSR) [6]. We also describe our proposal, Greedy Buffer Stateless Routing protocol (GBSR) [14], based on GPSR [6], which improves the performance in terms of packet losses.

Greedy Perimeter Stateless Routing (GPSR) [6] operates in two modes: *greedy forwarding*, which is used by default; and *perimeter forwarding*, which is used in those regions where greedy forwarding cannot be used. With greedy forwarding, the neighbor geographically closest to the packet's destination (greedy choice) is chosen as the packet's next hop, Fig. 1. When there is not a closest neighbor to destination, GPSR uses the right-hand rule to route packets around voids. The sequence of edges traversed by the right-hand rule is called *perimeter*, Fig. 1. GPSR poses two important drawbacks: the first one reported in [10] is the use of outdated information; the second one is the inefficient perimeter forwarding scheme [4]. Greedy Buffer Stateless Routing protocol (GBSR) [14] is an improved version of GPSR since GBSR uses a precise knowledge of the neighbors and destination positions. Furthermore, instead of using the perimeter mode, we propose to use a buffer solution. GBSR includes the location information of the

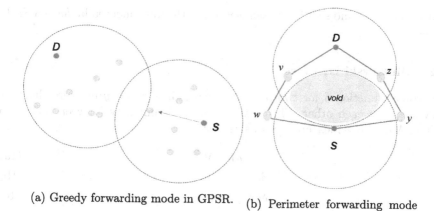

(a) Greedy forwarding mode in GPSR.   (b) Perimeter forwarding mode in GPSR.

Fig. 1. Greedy forwarding mode in GPSR.

neighbors to choose the optimal next forwarding node. The general idea of GBSR is to store packets in a local buffer of the node and try to send them later if the node detects a neighbor as a possible forwarding node. A possible forwarding node is any node that satisfies two conditions:

- It is in the transmission range of the current forwarding node. This estimation based on the position an speed of the neighbors.
- It is the nearest neighbor to destination, deciding among all the neighbor nodes.

GBSR tackles the important issue of which neighbors are actually reachable. This feature is of paramount importance to determinate if a neighbor in the neighbor list could be a good forwarding node. Accurate information about the current position of a neighbor has a strong impact in the performance of GBSR, because knowing this information makes the node aware of which neighbors are reliable to be next forwarding nodes. At the same time, it avoids sending packets to an unreachable node.

In order to take a forwarding decision, GBSR uses the same criterion as the original GPSR. It consists of choosing the nearest neighbor to destination based on the geographical distance. However, GBSR stores the packets in a buffer when there is no neighbor that satisfies all the requirements needed to be a next forwarding node. If at least one of the two conditions (i.e., being actually a neighbor and being closer to destination than the current carrier node) required to be the next hop is not satisfied, then packets are stored in the buffer. If the buffer is full, packets are dropped.

GBSR stores packets in the buffer, while it periodically tries to forward them to a new neighbor that meets the requirements to be a proper forwarding node. This period of time was established in 1 s, because this value was frequently enough to detect a topology change. For each destination the packets are stored in arriving order and sent in the same order, so the implemented buffer is a FIFO queue.

2.2   Minkowski Distance

A distance function δ for two n-dimensional points x and y measures how far they are from each other. This is the level of dissimilarity between these two points. A distance measure $\delta(x, y)$ satisfies:

$$\delta(x, y) = \delta(y, x) \tag{1a}$$

$$\delta(x, y) \geq 0 \tag{1b}$$

$$\delta(x, x) = 0 \tag{1c}$$

The Minkowski distance [1] of order r between the points x and y is defined as:

$$\delta_r(x, y) = \left(\sum_{i=1}^{n} |x_i - y_i|^r \right)^{1/r} \tag{2}$$

If $r < 0$, the Minkowski distance function δ (2) can be seen as a similarity measure instead of quantify how different are two points. Particular cases of the Minkowski distance family are the Manhattan and Euclidean distances. These distances are obtained with the order r equal to 1 and 2, respectively, in the Minkowski distance function δ. When the order $r \to \infty$ the Minkowski distance function is:

$$\delta_r(x, y) = \lim_{p \to +\infty} \left(\sum_{i=1}^{n} |x_i - y_i|^p \right)^{\frac{1}{p}} = \max_{i=1}^{n} |x_i - y_i| \tag{3}$$

This distance is called "dominant" because its value is equal to the maximum of the absolute value of the differences between their components x and y.

Figure 2 shows all the points that are at a distance of 1 from the center, which is the definition of a circle in Euclidean distance ($r = 2$). Notice how that circle grows progressively until reaching the square form in the infinity ($r \to +\infty$). This is because when r increases, the influence of the highest component $|x_i - y_i|^r$ in Eq. 2 increases notably compared to the other components in the distance computation. On the other hand, when $r < 2$, the area defined by the perimeter is smaller than the Euclidean case ($r = 2$).

3   Minkowski Distance in Geographical Distance Routing Metric

As was explained in Sect. 2, geographical routing protocols mostly base their forwarding decision on the geographical distance from their neighbors to destination. On the other hand, the Minkowski distance function provides a whole

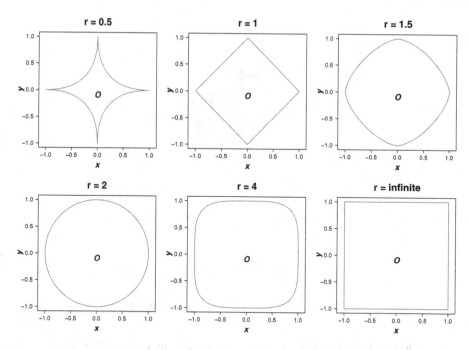

Fig. 2. Points in a 2-dimensional space at a distance of 1 from the center (O) using the Minkowski distance function with different values of the order r. Special cases are: Manhattan distance ($r=1$), Euclidean distance ($r=2$) and Dominant distance ($r \to +\infty$)

family of distances to measure the dissimilarity between two points. This section provides a short explanation of how the forwarding decision is affected by considering alternative ways to measure distance.

The use of order $r \neq 2$ (Euclidean distance) in the Minkowski distance function will affect the operation of a geographical routing protocol in the following parameters:

1. The size and form of the searching area to find a the next forwarding node.
2. The decision of which neighbor is the closest to destination.

To give an example, Figs. 3 and 4 show a comparison among the use of Euclidean distance ($r = 2$), Manhattan ($r = 1$) and dominant distance ($r \to +\infty$), respectively.

As it can be seen in both figures, the Euclidean distance ($r = 2$) between source and destination is the radius of the circle that contains all the nodes closer than the source to the destination, which are called next-hop candidates. For the case of the Manhattan distance ($r = 1$), this area is a diamond. For dominant distance ($r \to +\infty$) the area has a square shape. The selected next forwarding node will be in the intersection area that contains the next hop candidates that are also within the coverage area of the source (pink circle around source node

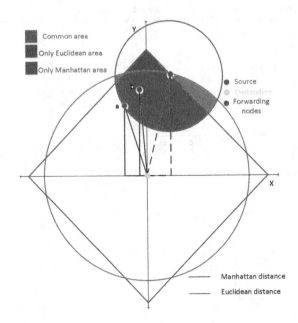

Fig. 3. Euclidean distance ($r = 2$) vs. manhattan distance ($r = 1$).

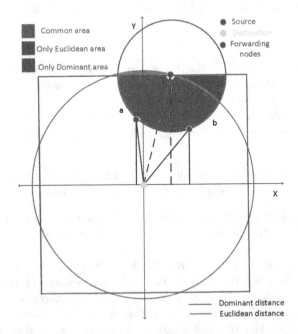

Fig. 4. Euclidean distance ($r = 2$) vs. dominant distance ($r \to +\infty$).

in Figs. 3 and 4). Notice that this area changes depending on the Minkowski order r. For instance, in the aforementioned figures, red areas mean searching zones only valid if we consider Manhattan distance (Fig. 3) or dominant distance (Fig. 4), but not for Euclidean distance. Conversely, the blue areas, are searching regions only valid for the Euclidean distance.

In both figures, Figs. 3 and 4, node a is closer than node b to destination, according to the Euclidean distance. But it is just the opposite if the routing protocol employs the other Minkowski distance orders to make the routing decision. Summarizing, the previous two examples show how the use of other Minkowski distance order values r, will affect the influence area where the next hop is selected. Moreover, the selected next forwarding node will not be the same as the chosen one with the Euclidean distance in most of the cases.

4 Empirical Analysis

4.1 Simulation Settings

The simulation scenario consists of a multi-hop VANET, where we analyzed the impact of the order parameter r of Minkowski distance function in the routing operation of our distance-based proposal GBSR [14]. To do this, we carried out several simulations using the Estinet Network Simulator and Emulator [2]. Estinet is a simulator that includes the standard IEEE 802.11p and a simple and accurate way to design VANET realistic scenarios.

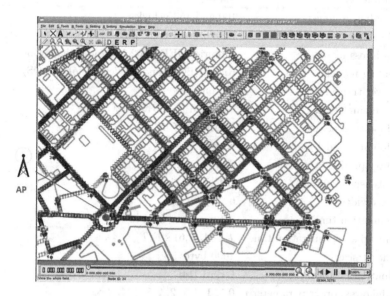

Fig. 5. Simulation scenario. Eixample district of Barcelona, Spain, with an access point (AP). buildings (*orange lines*) from OpenStreetMap are included (Color figure online).

We used a real scenario of $1.5 \,\mathrm{km}^2$ taken from the Eixample district of Barcelona (see Fig. 5) to model an urban Manhattan-style scenario, which consists of streets and crossroads. In our realistic scenario, the mobility model was obtained with CityMob for Roadmaps (C4R) [3], a mobility generator that uses the SUMO engine [7]. C4R is able to import maps directly from the Open-StreetMap [11] and to generate NS-2 compatible traces. Furthermore, the scenarios have building information (orange lines in Fig. 5) extracted from the Open-StreetMap using the SUMO tools. We exported the NS-2 traces to be compatible with Estinet and the buildings information using our own translating software, available at www.lfurquiza.com/research/estinet [15].

We considered two amounts of vehicles: 100 and 150 vehicles, which correspond to densities of 67 and 100 vehicles per km^2, respectively. There was one fixed destination, the access point (henceforth called AP) in Fig. 5, that receives vehicles' traffic information.

We used a single AP in the scenario because in this way we obtained a long range of route lengths, which depends on the position of the source vehicles in the scenario. All nodes sent 1000-byte packets every T seconds to the unique destination during 300 s. T follows a uniform distribution from 2 to 6 s. Simulations were carried out using the IEEE 802.11p standard on physical and MAC layers.

Table 1. Simulation settings.

Parameter	Value
Number of nodes	100 and 150 vehicles
Map zone & area	Eixample district of Barcelona, $1.5 \,\mathrm{km} \times 1 \,\mathrm{km}$
Path loss model	Empirical IEEE 802.11p radio shadowing [13]
Fading model	Rician (LOS) and Rayleigh (not in LOS)
Power transmission	23 dbm
Receiving sensing	-82 dbm ($\sim$400 m in LOS)
Mobility generator	SUMO [7]/C4R [3]
Mobility model	Krauss [8]
Max speed	60 km/h
MAC specification	IEEE 802.11 p
Bandwidth	6 Mbps
Simulation time	300 s
Inter-packet generation time	$T \sim \mathrm{U}(2,6)$ s $\mathrm{E}(T) = 4\,\mathrm{s}$
Packet size	1000 bytes
Routing protocol	GBSR [14]
Minkowski order parameter r	0.5, 1, 1.5, 2, 2.5, 3, 4, $+\infty$
GPS precision	10 m

All the figures are presented with confidence intervals (CI) of 95 %, obtained from 20 simulations per each density value and order parameter r using different movement traces per each simulation. Table 1 summarizes the main simulation settings.

4.2 Simulation Results

In this section, we present some results from comparing the simulations of GBSR using different values for the order parameter r. The evaluation is focused on three widely-used metrics applied to the performance analysis of VANET routing protocols. These metrics are the percentage of packet losses, the average packet delay and the average number of hops for the packets to reach destination. Figures 6, 7 and 8 depict these results for the two node densities under consideration.

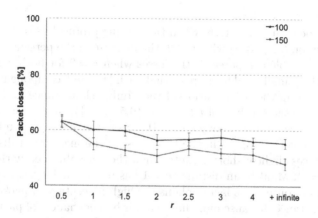

Fig. 6. Percentage of packet losses.

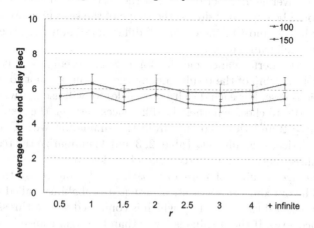

Fig. 7. Average end-to-end packet delay.

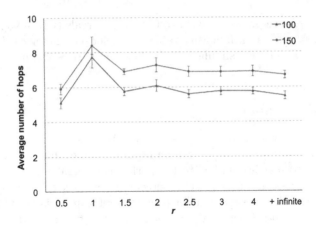

Fig. 8. Average number of hops.

As it can be seen from Fig. 6, when the routing protocol uses the Minkowski distance function (see Eq. 2) with $r < 2$, the increase in the percentage of packet losses is considerable compared to the losses when $r = 2$ for both vehicle densities. Notice that small r values implies that each $|x_i - y_i|^r$ component has a similar contribution in the computation of the Minkowski distance $\delta_r(x, y)$. Notice also that, for the these values of r (i.e., $r \in \{0.5, 1, 1.5\}$), the average end-to-end delay in Fig. 7 are similar among them. However, the averages number of hops are very different (see Fig. 8) in the three cases. The measure of distance with $r = 1.5$ produces slightly shorter routes than the ones obtained with Euclidean distance ($r = 2$). Manhattan distance $r = 1$ has by far the longest average number of hops in a route. This fact explains the high percentage of packet losses for Manhattan distance, because more hops entails higher chances of packet collision or packet error reception. On the contrary, the Minkowski distance with $r = 0.5$ has the shortest average number of hops, at the cost of the highest packet losses. These facts could be explained due to the shape of the searching area for $r = 0.5$ (see Fig. 2), which in most of the cases will differ more than any other searching area from the Euclidean circle.

To analyze the performance metrics for $r > 2$, we employ statistical tests because the relationship of the results among the distances is not so evident as it is in the previous case. For each density of vehicles we will use pairwise Wilcoxon statistical test [12] to check whether the differences between the results obtained with all the $r \geq 2$ and those coming from the simulation with Euclidean distances are statistically significant. Tables 2, 3 and 4 summarize the results of this test for the three metrics (i.e., percentage of packet losses, average end-to-end delay, and average number of hops in a path), and grouped by the two vehicle density. The outcome of a statistical test is a probability called the p-value (fourth column of Tables 2, 3 and 4), which is compared with a threshold named the significance level. If the p-value is lower than the significance level, then the difference between both performance metrics are statistically significant (fifth column in the tables). We employed a significance level on each test of 0.025, to obtain an overall error probability among the four pairwise comparison per metric of 0.10 (i.e., 0.025 × 4). The results of the statistical tests indicate that when there is a low vehicle density scenario (100 vehicles), there is no improvement or degradation on the percentage of packet losses and average end-to-end packet delay compared with the results obtained using the Euclidean distance (see Tables 2 and 3). However, there is a statistically significant difference in the average path length when the routing protocol GBSR employs a Minkowski distance with order $r = 2.5$ or the dominant distance ($r \rightarrow +\infty$), as can be seen in the fifth and eighth rows of Table 4. It means that the use of $r \in \{2.5, +\infty\}$ in our routing protocol GBSR for our low-density scenario provides the same quality of service (packet losses and delay) through shorter paths.

For the intermediate vehicle density scenario (150 vehicles), our results indicate that only when GBSR used the dominant distance to make the forwarding decision, the percentage of packet losses shows a statistically significant reduction (around 3 %, see Table 2) compared with GBSR employing classical Euclidean distance. This packet losses reduction is obtained without increasing the average end-to-end delay, which remains statistically equal (eighth row in Table 3). Moreover, this reduction of packet losses and similar delay, using the dominant distance comes with the use of shorter paths than the created by GBSR using Euclidean distance (around 0.18 hops, see Table 4). In the cases of $r = 3$ and $r = 4$, both distances do not have differences with the Euclidean in the percentage of packet losses. Nonetheless, regarding to the average end-to-end and path length, there are statistically significant improvements as shown in rows sixth and seventh in Tables 3 and 4. The Minkowski's order $r = 2.5$ in the intermediate vehicle density for the percentage of packet losses provides worse marks than the obtained with the classical Euclidean distance and only improve the average end-to-end packet delay.

Table 2. p-values of Wilcoxon signed rank test for a pairwise comparison of the effect of the Minkowski distance order r for the **packet losses metric**.

Vehicle density	Pairwise $(r,2)$	Standardized test statistic	p-Value 1 side	Is the difference significant (p-Value < 0.025)?	Median of differences
100	2.5	−0.336	0.378	No	1.088 %
	3	−0.896	0.194	No	2.52 %
	4	−0.485	0.324	No	0.158 %
	+∞	−1.381	0.088	No	−1.441 %
150	2.5	−2.091	0.018	Yes	2.549 %
	3	−0.971	0.174	No	1.024 %
	4	−0.299	0.392	No	1,738 %
	+∞	−2.24	0.012	Yes	−3.096 %

Table 3. p-values of Wilcoxon signed rank test for a pairwise comparison of the effect of the Minkowski distance order r for the **average end-to-end packet delay metric**.

Vehicle density	Pairwise $(r,2)$	Standardized test statistic	p-Value 1 side	Is the difference significant (p-Value < 0.025)?	Median of differences
100	2.5	−1.232	0.115	No	−0.483 s
	3	−1.307	0.101	No	−0.341 s
	4	−1.083	0.147	No	−0.158 s
	$+\infty$	−0.859	0.205	No	0.037 s
150	2.5	−2.427	0.007	Yes	−0.500 s
	3	−2.763	0.002	Yes	−0.584 s
	4	−2.203	0.013	Yes	−0.409 s
	$+\infty$	−1.269	0.108	No	−0.186 s

Table 4. p-values of Wilcoxon signed rank test for a pairwise comparison of the effect of the Minkowski distance order r for the **average number of hops metric**.

Vehicle density	Pairwise $(r,2)$	Standardized test statistic	p-Value 1 side	Is the difference significant (p-Value < 0.025)?	Median of differences
100	2.5	−2.837	0.002	Yes	−0.367 hops
	3	−1.680	0.049	No	−0.1635 hops
	4	−1.867	0.03	No	−0.228 hops
	$+\infty$	−3.173	0.0005	Yes	−0.515 hops
150	2.5	−1.829	0.035	No	−0.337 hops
	3	−2.165	0.015	Yes	−0.0136 hops
	4	−1.979	0.024	Yes	−0.66 hops
	$+\infty$	−3.323	0.0005	Yes	−0.11 hops

To conclude with, the simulation results show that it is possible to improve some performance metrics of our geographical routing protocol GBSR, if a different distance equation is used by the routing protocol. Particularly, the dominant distance ($r \to +\infty$) equation outperforms the traditional results ($r = 2$) in terms of packet losses and average number of hops for intermediate vehicle density and only the latter in low density areas. However, the result differences in the performance metrics between Euclidean and other distances are not high.

5   Conclusions and Future Work

In this work we have tested the impact of using different distance equations in the forwarding decision of a geographical routing protocol for VANETs. The distance equations were obtained through the Minkowski distance function, modifying the value of its order parameter. Our results in a realistic urban scenario, indicate that for low and intermediate vehicle densities, the use of the dominant distance $(r \rightarrow +\infty)$ in the routing decision leads to the creation of paths shorter than the ones obtained by the routing protocol employing the traditional Euclidean distance $(r = 2)$. Moreover, for the intermediate density (150 vehicles), the routing protocol improved its packet delivery ratio without increasing delay. Also, for intermediate densities, the Minkowski's order 3 and 4 were able to reduce the end-to-end packet delay keeping the same packet losses level. Nevertheless, our results show that the performance differences between euclidean distance are not far from the best ones obtained by other Minkowski r value.

Future work include performing this same comparison in other city topologies in order to find out whether the performance metric differences among the Minkowski's order depends on the layout of the city. Additionally, we are interested in developing a geographical routing protocol that combines some Minkowski distances like Manhattan, Euclidean and dominant to take the forwarding decision.

Acknowledgements. This work was partly supported by the Spanish Government through projects TEC2010-20572-C02-02 Continuity of Service, Security and QoS for Transportation Systems "CONSEQUENCE" and TEC 2013-47665-C4-1-R Emergency Response In Smart Communities "EMRISCO". Luis Urquiza-Aguiar is the recipient of a full scholarship from the Secretaria Nacional de Educación Superior, Ciencia y Tecnología (SENESCYT) with the sponsorship of Escuela Politécnica Nacional (EPN) (Ecuador). Carolina Tripp-Barba would like to thank the support of the "Universidad Autónoma de Sinaloa (Mexico)".

References

1. Borg, I., Groenen, P.: Modern Multidimensional Scaling - Theory and Applications, 2nd edn. Springer, New York (2005)
2. Estinet-Technologies: EstiNet 7 Network Simulator and Emulator (2015). http://www.estinet.com/products.php?lv1=13&sn=15
3. Fogue, M., Garrido, P., Martinez, F.J., Cano, J.C., Calafate, C.T., Manzoni, P.: A realistic simulation framework for vehicular networks. In: 5th International ICST Conference on Simulation Tools and Techniques, pp. 37–46. ACM, Brussels (2012). http://dl.acm.org/citation.cfm?id=2263019.2263025
4. Gerla, M., Kleinrock, L.: Vehicular networks and the future of the mobile internet. Comput. Netw. **55**(2), 457–469 (2011). http://dx.doi.org/10.1016/j.comnet.2010.10.015
5. Hartenstein, H., Laberteaux, K., Ebrary, I.: VANET: vehicular applications and inter-networking technologies. Wiley Online Library, Chichester (2010)
6. Karp, B., Kung, H.T.: GPSR Greedy perimeter stateless routing for wireless networks. In: 6th Annual International Conference on Mobile Computing and Networking, pp. 243–254. ACM Press, New York (2000). http://dl.acm.org/citation.cfm?id=345910.345953
7. Krajzewicz, D., Erdmann, J., Behrisch, M., Bieker, L.: Recent development and applications of SUMO - Simulation of Urban MObility. Int. J. Adv. Syst. Meas. **5**(3&4), 128–138 (2012)

8. Krauss, S., Wagner, P., Gawron, C.: Metastable states in a microscopic model of traffic flow. Phys. Rev. E **55**(5), 5597–5602 (1997). http://link.aps.org/doi/10. 1103/PhysRevE.55.5597

9. Lee, K., Lee, U., Gerla, M.: Survey of routing protocols in vehicular Ad Hoc networks. In: Advances in Vehicular Ad-Hoc Networks: Developments and Challenges, pp. 149–170. Information Science Reference (2009)

10. Naumov, V., Baumann, R., Gross, T.: An evaluation of inter-vehicle Ad Hoc networks based on realistic vehicular traces. In: 7th ACM International Symposium on Mobile Ad Hoc Networking and Computing, pp. 108–119. ACM Press, New York (2006). http://dl.acm.org/citation.cfm?id=1132905.1132918

11. OpenStreetMap: (2015). http://www.openstreetmap.org/

12. Sheskin, D.: Handbook of Parametric and Nonparametric Statistical Procedures, 2nd edn. Chapman and Hall/Crc, Boca Raton (2000)

13. Sommer, C., Eckhoff, D., German, R., Dressler, F.: A computationally inexpensive empirical model of ieee 802.11p radio shadowing in urban environments. In: Eighth International Conference on, Wireless On-Demand Network Systems and Services, pp. 84–90. IEEE Press (2011)

14. Barba, C.T., Aguiar, L.U., Igartua, M.A.: Design and evaluation of GBSR-B, an improvement of GPSR for VANETs. IEEE Lat. Am. Trans. **11**(4), 1083–1089 (2013)

15. Urquiza, L.: Developed code for Estinet simulator (2015). http://www.lfurquiza. com/research/estinet

Lossless Multicast Handovers in Proxy Fast Mobile IPv6 Networks

Bernd Meijerink[(⊠)] and Geert Heijenk

University of Twente, Enschede, The Netherlands
{bernd.meijerink,geert.heijenk}@utwente.nl

Abstract. There is a demand in the Public Protection and Disaster Relief (PPDR) community for high bandwidth services on mobile devices. Group communication is an important aspect of PPDR networks. In IP based networks multicast is the preferred method to efficiently transmit data to more than one receiver simultaneously. It is important PPDR users can switch seamlessly between wireless networks. This paper describes improvements to multicast in Fast handovers for Proxy Mobile IPv6 (PFMIPv6) to provide seamless mobility to its users. We also identify and explore the specific problems stemming from difference in end-to-end delay between the old and new path during handovers for multicast traffic. A novel mechanism to determine the delay difference between two paths in a PFMIPv6 system is described and an implementation of this system is evaluated. It is shown the proposed approach can prevent multicast packet loss during a handover.

Keywords: Fast Handovers for Proxy Mobile IPv6 · Multicast · Seamless mobility

1 Introduction

There is an increasing demand within the Public Protection and Disaster Relief (PPDR) community for high bandwidth mobile connections for services like streaming video and audio. PPDR systems are communication systems for public services like the police and fire department. Requirements for PPDR systems are different from the requirements for consumer systems in that they have to be highly resilient and provide strong security. Losing communication in a crisis situation can lead to dangerous situations and in the Netherlands prompted some fire departments to replace part of the TETRA system with analog equipment [1]. These systems differ from the more well-known mobile communications systems such as 3G and Long Term Evolution (LTE) by providing group call functionalities and operating (in a reduced manner) without support from a base station. While consumer demand for high bandwidth is driven by services like YouTube, Netflix and Spotify the demand in the PPDR community is based on live video from emergency sites and voice communication with groups of other users.

© Springer International Publishing Switzerland 2015
M.C. Aguayo-Torres et al. (Eds.): WWIC 2015, LNCS 9071, pp. 341–354, 2015.
DOI: 10.1007/978-3-319-22572-2_25

Current PPDR implementations used in Europe are mostly based on the TETRA system. While the system provides reliable voice communication among users, there is very limited support for applications that require high bandwidth such as video streaming. For the future there is a desire from the PPDR community for more bandwidth and more services [2]. The logical step is to switch to newer technologies such as LTE and use existing infrastructure in the form of IEEE 802.11 networks (Wi-Fi) in buildings. To allow data services on the network, such as video and image sharing, a switch to a fully Internet Protocol (IP) based network is useful. This will allow better resilience due to packet switching and easier development of services and applications. Another benefit of a switch to IP is the general trend in mobile network technologies to switch to IP. The results are cost benefits and increasing availability in areas where it might not be efficient to deploy a private PPDR platform.

One of the problems for PPDR users on current networks is that seamless handovers between networks are difficult and lead to packet loss. Packet loss is problematic as it can lead to users missing important data, for example critical frames in a live video of a robbery. This problem exists when switching between similar network technologies (for example IEEE 802.11 to IEEE 802.11) and between different technologies (for example IEEE 802.11 and LTE). Another problem is that PPDR work is characterized by working in groups leading to a requirement for group communication on the network [2]. In traditional mobile networks this is problematic as a separate connection needs to be set up from some central point to all users in the group call. In IP based networks, multicast functionality allows data to flow from a sender to multiple receivers. This reduces network load and bypasses the need for a central server that connects all participants in a group. The lack of multicast support in wireless networks requires each user to send data separately to each other user in the group call, leading to inefficiencies.

Users of PPDR systems would like to be able to roam seamlessly between networks across borders [2]. Mobility in IP networks can be achieved with the Proxy Mobile IP (PMIP) standard [3]. There are also extensions to the standard such as Proxy Mobile IPv6 (PFMIPv6) that allow seamless handovers between two different networks (technology independent) [4]. Other extensions cover multicast support for these network architectures through the use of multicast proxies at the PMIP network devices.

Currently there are no implementations of the PFMIPv6 protocol or Proxy Mobile IPv6 (PMIPv6) with multicast support integrated available. Supporting seamless handovers for multicast flows puts special demands on the handover processes, as these flows are typically destined to multiple users at the same time. The lack of available PFMIPv6 implementations with multicast support leads us to the following research question. How can we optimize multicast handovers in PFMIPv6 to allow minimal packet loss while minimizing the load on the wireless network?

The contributions of this paper are as follows. We present a method to determine the delay difference between two paths in a PFMIPv6 network. An implementation of the PFMIPv6 protocol supporting multicast listeners was made that makes use of the delay difference estimation. The implementation is evaluated on performance aspects based on measurements taken in a test environment.

The following section will provide background information on the technologies related to PFMIPv6, multicast and related work. Its parts can be safely skipped by anyone who feels confident in their knowledge in these areas. Section 3 describes the timing problems surrounding multicast fast handovers and a solution to this problem. In Sect. 4 our implementation is validated by measurements in real wireless environment and finally we draw conclusion in the final section.

2 Background and Related Work

This section will explain the technologies used and built upon for this project and describe related work.

2.1 PFMIPv6

Fast handovers for Proxy Mobile IPv6 (PFMIPv6) is an IP mobility technology. It allows mobile devices to move through a network and switch attachment point without the device noticing this on the IP layer (Fig. 1). To explain the way this system works we will start with explaining basic Mobile IP and build up to the more complex systems. It is interesting to note that Proxy Mobile IP is also an optional part of the 3GPP LTE specification, in which it replaces the GPRS Tunnelling Protocol (GTP) when used.

MIP. Mobile IP (MIP) works by having a fixed point in the (mobile) network that acts as a mobility anchor for mobile devices. In MIP this entity is called the Home Agent and it will tunnel packets for a Mobile Node (MN) to the network that node is currently on. In MIP the MN knows about the mobility and actively helps maintain it.

PMIPv6. PMIPv6 works by adding an Local Mobility Anchor (LMA) to the provider core network [3]. This LMA is the anchor point for the MNs in the domain (All IP routes for the MNs lead to the LMA). The LMA tunnels the data for the MN to the Mobile Access Gateway (MAG) that serves as the MNs point of attachment. The main improvement over MIP is that the MN has no knowledge of the IP mobility, it always thinks it is connected to the same network and will have the same IP address.

When a handover is performed, the serving MAG lets the LMA know the MN has disconnected. The new MAG (nMAG) lets the LMA know the MN has connected to it and a tunnel is set up between the LMA and the nMAG. Because the nMAG will have the same link layer address as seen from the node it does not know that is it actually on a different link and keeps the same IP address (If the MN requests a new IP address it would also receive the same one it had before).

Fast Handovers. Proxy mobile IP does not reduce the handover times by itself. An extension called "Fast Handovers for Proxy Mobile IPv6" (PFMIPv6) enables faster handovers by changing the handover procedure in the MAG (The LMA is not changed) [4]. When a handover occurs, the MAG (pMAG) will set up a tunnel to the nMAG and forward all traffic it still receives for the MN to the nMAG. The nMAG will buffer all traffic that is receives for the MN until it connects. Once the MN is connected the nMAG will flush all buffered traffic towards it. The PFMIPv6 protocol covers two handover situations: (i) Predictive handover, in which the network knows about the movement of the MN beforehand. (ii) Reactive handover, in which the network does not know about the movement beforehand.

2.2   Related Work

The IETF has a working group on multicast mobility [5]. Several informational and experimental RFCs have been released that deal with multicast handovers. Implementing multicast functionality in Proxy Mobile IP networks is not straightforward. Simply enabling multicast routing on the MAGs and LMA would not lead to the desired results, as multicast traffic would be routed over the normal network instead of the MAG-LMA tunnels. To solve this problem the IETF multicast mobility working group has released several experimental status RFCs regarding this issue. RFC 6224 [6] explains the deployment of Multicast Listener Discovery (MLD) proxies at the MAG and LMA. These proxies query and listen for incoming MLD reports from mobile nodes. These reports are forwarded from MAG to the LMA, which in turn can subscribe to the multicast traffic on the greater network it is connected to. Multicast traffic is forwarded to the MN in a reverse fashion. When it arrives at the LMA it is forwarded to the MAGs which have subscribed MNs. The MAGs in turn forward it to the interfaces with these MNs.

For fast handovers, RFC 7411 [7] contains an extra option for the Handover Initiation and Handover Acknowledgement messages. This option contains all the multicast groups the MN is subscribed to. The nMAG can already subscribe

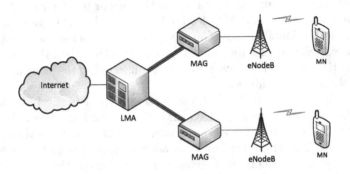

Fig. 1. Proxy Mobile IPv6 architecture

to these groups while the handover is happening. As with unicast traffic it is also possible to buffer multicast traffic being tunnelled from the pMAG preventing packet loss. This RFC does not deal with the problem of synchronizing multicast flows after the handover. There are also no reference implementations available of multicast fast handover systems.

A member of the IETF multicast mobility working group has published a multicast proxy implementation that can be used in PMIP networks [8]. The system is mainly built as a demonstration for peering between proxies to improve efficiency in situations where the MNs are also multicast senders. Enabling better support for multicast senders is not covered in this paper as the focus is multicast handovers. The application from [8] does however not integrate with fast handovers as is the goal in this paper. Integration with the PFMIPv6 system is vital as multicast subscriptions need to be transferred to the nMAG.

There is a large amount of work available on optimizing handovers for MIP. The main downside of MIP is the modified MN that needs to communicate with the network for mobility management. In [9] the performance of fast handovers in MIP enabled IEEE 802.11 networks is evaluated. It is shown that handover times can still be several seconds with up to 10 s in busy networks.

The authors of [10] show that PMIP provides significant improvements over MIP in that it improves handover performance, is link layer agnostic, and reduces the usage of wireless resources. While the paper does not look specifically at multicast all these improvements are also relevant to multicast traffic.

Work has been done on PMIP handovers that lead to the RFC 5949 standard for Fast Handovers for Proxy Mobile IPv6 [4]. This standard describes the handover procedure and how messages between the PFMIPv6 entities should be formatted. This standard will be used to implement fast handovers.

To make a handover appear seamless to a user it is very important that handovers occur as fast as possible. To reach this goal the handover delay needs to be minimized. In [11] it is shown through analytical modelling that using Media Independent Handover (MIH) can greatly improve the handover delay of PMIPv6 networks. The paper does however not cover fast handover situations with multicast. It is shown in [12] that multicast extensions for PFMIPv6 will greatly reduce handover delay for multicast traffic, but the authors did not test an actual implementation and all results were obtained analytically. In [13] it is shown that packets reordering during the buffer flush at the nMAG can be prevented by tagging the last packet sent from the LMA to the pMAG. While this method is shown to work well for unicast traffic, there is no potential end to multicast traffic streaming towards the pMAG, making this method unsuitable for multicast handovers.

3   Multicast Handover Timing

Handovers involving multicast traffic are different than those involving unicast traffic. With a unicast only handover the LMA can simply stop forwarding the traffic to the pMAG and start forwarding to the nMAG. With multicast traffic, and especially in a PPDR context, there is a high chance that there are still MNs on the pMAG that want to receive this traffic. The result is that the LMA needs to keep forwarding this traffic to the pMAG, and there is no point at which the traffic forwarding can simply stop.

When performing a handover with multicast using PFMIPv6 there are temporarily two interfaces at which multicast traffic arrives on the nMAG. Multicast traffic arrives at the nMAG from the pMAG-nMAG tunnel and the LMA-nMAG tunnel. Because the data on one tunnel takes a different route than traffic from the other tunnel, there can be a difference in arrival time of the same packet on both tunnels. This time difference can lead to problems during the handover. When the MN connects to the nMAG and the traffic buffer is flushed, the traffic should continue flowing from the LMA tunnel. When for example the LMA-nMAG tunnel has less delay than the pMAG-nMAG tunnel, this might lead to packet loss as these packets have not yet arrived on the LMA-nMAG tunnel. The nMAG needs to make a decision on when to start forwarding from the LMA-nMAG link. The packets themselves cannot be expected to contain information such as sequence numbers, so the nMAG needs a separate mechanism to make a forwarding decision.

Due to the possible differences in delay between the two tunnels there can be 3 different situations at the nMAG: (i) The delay is identical for both routes (Fig. 2a), (ii) The LMA-nMAG route is faster than the pMAG-nMAG route (Fig. 2b), (iii) The LMA-nMAG route is slower than the pMAG-nMAG route (Fig. 2c). Below, we describe the consequences of the scenarios for multicast handovers and their possible resolutions.

No Delay Difference. When the tunnels have the same delay, no special action needs to be taken. The application can simply flush the multicast traffic buffer that has built up during the handover, and switch to the data coming

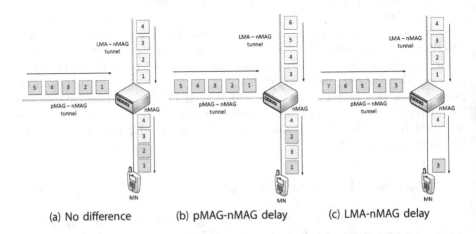

(a) No difference   (b) pMAG-nMAG delay   (c) LMA-nMAG delay

Fig. 2. Multicast synchronization

from the LMA-nMAG tunnel once it has arrived there (see Fig. 2a). In this figure the numbered boxes represent packets travelling to the nMAG. Packets coming from the pMAG are replaced by the packets coming from the LMA. In this case the switch can occur at any moment because there is no difference in the delay between the two tunnels. While this situation is ideal it is not very likely to occur during normal operations as it requires the delay on the direct LMA-nMAG tunnel to be equal to the delay on the LMA-pMAG-nMAG route.

LMA-nMAG Tunnel is Faster. In this situation the multicast packets coming through the pMAG-nMAG tunnel arrive behind those from the LMA-nMAG tunnel. The result, as can be seen in Fig. 2b, is that the MN is still receiving packets that would have already arrived over the LMA-nMAG tunnel. A useful solution in this scenario is to simply forward the packets when they arrive at the nMAG, and stop the pMAG-nMAG tunnel forwarding once all the data that was still missing from the LMA-nMAG tunnel has arrived. The duration that data still needs to be forwarded from the pMAG-nMAG tunnel is the delay difference between the two tunnels. This switching procedure 'mixes' packets from both tunnels until all packets that were missing on the LMA-nMAG tunnel have been transmitted to the MN.

pMAG-nMAG Tunnel is Faster. In this situation the new LMA-nMAG tunnel contains older data than the LMA-pMAG-nMAG tunnel. It is possible to simply send all the packets from the LMA-nMAG tunnel onto the network, but this would waste wireless bandwidth. A solution in which the traffic is simply not forwarded until the LMA-nMAG tunnel is caught up with the LMA-pMAG-nMAG route is most efficient in terms of network resources. In the example (Fig. 2c) the packets from the pMAG-nMAG tunnel are stopped forwarding once the LMA-nMAG tunnel is established and the packets from that tunnel start forwarding once there is new data for the MN on that tunnel.

3.1   Delay Difference Estimation

To make the correct decision on how to perform the multicast handover, the nMAG needs to know the difference in arrival time between the two tunnels. Traditional methods to determine one way delays are based on precise clock synchronization [14]. The delay estimation problem here is unique in that there is identical traffic arriving on two different interfaces and we are not interested in the delay of the link itself, but in the relative delay between the links.

We propose to send special timing packets from the LMA over all the LMA-MAG tunnels on a fixed interval. A timing packet consists of a UDP datagram containing a 16 bit sequence number and 32 bit timing interval. Timing packets are multicast down all tunnels. When the pMAG initiates the pMAG-nMAG tunnel for a handover, it will forward the incoming timing packets from the MN's LMA over this tunnel. The nMAG will now receive timing packets on the LMA-nMAG and pMAG-nMAG links. It can use the difference between the received time and the difference in sequence numbers on each link to calculate the difference in transmission times between both links. The delay difference between the two tunnels TD in ms is given by:

$$TD = (SeqN_{Tunnel1} - SeqN_{Tunnel2}) \times I - \left(T_{Tunnel1}^{arrival} - T_{Tunnel2}^{arrival}\right)$$

In this formula $SeqN_{tunnel}$ is the sequence number of the last received packet on that tunnel. I is the timing interval the packets are sent on in ms (taken from the timing packet). $T_{tunnel}^{arrival}$ is the arrival time of the last packet for that tunnel in ms Unix time. Calculating the delay difference in this manner only requires us to store the last received sequence number and arrival time per link, greatly simplifying the system.

Once the nMAG knows the delay difference between the tunnels, decisions on how to switch the two multicast tunnels can be made based on the difference between them. The data on the difference is at most I ms old, the accuracy of the data is thus dependent on how often the timing packets are transmitted. In very congestion networks with a high variation in delay the value for I should be reduced to compensate possible sudden changes in the delay.

The benefit of this solution, over more traditional methods such as Internet Control Message Protocol (ICMP) echo requests, is that it does not take a round trip time to measure the delay. The timing packets are always arriving when a tunnel exists. Other active methods to find the one way delay require precise time synchronization between the sender and receiver. The maximum time that is required to measure the transmission delay between two tunnels is the transmission interval I, with an average of $\frac{1}{2}I$.

4   Validation

This section will present the validation of the PFMIPv6 and delay estimation implementation. The goal is to measure how effective the implemented system is in measuring the delay difference between two paths on the network and performing lossless multicast handovers. In order to validate the proposed approach, we extended an existing PMIPv6 implementation [15] with fast handover and multicast functionality. We also implemented the described time difference and handover optimization mechanism for multicast traffic.

4.1   Measurement Network

The validation was done based on measurements taken from a PFMIPv6 network built for this purpose. Figure 3 shows the different devices in the network and how they are implemented on physical hardware. The LMA, MAGs and Corresponding Node (CN) are virtual machines running in VMWare (The box in Fig. 3). The CN will multicast packets to the MN. The MAGs are each connected to physical IEEE 802.11 interfaces that are connected to the host computer using USB. The USB devices are shared with the MAG VMs to enable direct access to

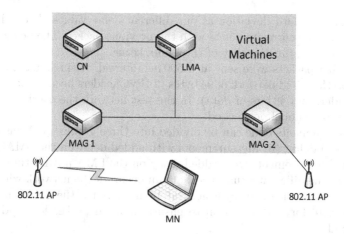

Fig. 3. PFMIPv6 experiment network

the IEEE 802.11 hardware. The MN (A laptop with an IEEE 802.11 interface) will connect to the MAGs through the MAGs wireless interface. This laptop is running a recent Ubuntu Linux distribution with a kernel that was compiled with Optimistic Duplicate Address Detection (DAD). While Optimistic DAD decreases the time need for a layer 3 handover significantly, there is still a delay of above 2 s for the handover on the layer 2 level. It is outside the scope of this paper to attempt to further reduce this delay. It should be noted that our PFMIPv6 implementation transmits buffered multicast packets as unicast link layer packets to the MN. This is done to allow for higher data rates than would be possible using unicast, and to prevent other nodes from receiving packets they already have. This approach also reduces losses during the buffer flush.

4.2 Measurement Method

Measurements were done using UDP multicast traffic flowing from the CN to the MN for 20 s. The handover trigger is sent exactly 5 s after the CN starts sending multicast traffic. The layer 2 handover takes 2.4 s on average after which the buffered traffic is flushed to the MN. Different packet loads will be used to measure the effect of the number of packets per second on the performance of multicast handovers.

In a larger network it would be common to find differences in the one way delay between the connections of the PFMIPv6 devices, due to delays in the routing and the distances involved. To simulate these delays on the measurement network, delay was added to specific tunnels. For this experiment several delay values will be used with or without an added variance in the delay. The delay between consecutive packets is distributed normally. It was shown in [16] that a normal distribution approximates real world packet delay. We will use 50 ms with 10 ms standard deviation, 100 ms with a 20 ms standard deviation and 200 ms with a 40 ms standard deviation as our different delay values. The delay given to a packet will be correlated 50 % with the previous packet. The delay is added using the NETEM functionality of the Linux kernel [17].

The timing packets were sent at a 500 ms interval. A single packet gives an overhead on the wired network of 94 bytes (2 IPv6 headers because of tunnelling, a UDP header, and 48 bits of data). In the test network the overhead amounts to 188 bytes per tunnel per second.

The measurements done can be divided into three groups: (i) Measurements with no added delay, (ii) Measurements with added delay on the pMAG-nMAG tunnel, (iii) Measurements with added delay on the LMA-nMAG tunnel. These groups cover the different situations that can occur on the network with respect to delay differences. If the delay is accurately measured at the nMAG it can take the appropriate forwarding action to ensure minimal packet loss and wireless network load.

When a handover occurs the nMAG will output its delay difference estimate. We will take all measurements of a single group (For example all measurements where the LMA-nMAG tunnel has 100 ms delay with 20 ms standard deviation) and calculate their average and standard deviation. We will compare these measured results to the delay settings the link was configured with. Each group of measurements will contain at least 30 measurement points.

For each measurement the packet loss will be recorded on the MN. Because multicast traffic is transmitted as broadcast packets on IEEE 802.11 networks, there is no retransmission mechanism as with unicast packets. The result of this unreliable delivery method is packet loss for multicast packets on the wireless interface. Because this background loss is not caused by the handover process itself, and we measure over a period longer than the handover, we try to compensate for this loss in the results. The packet loss measured surrounding the handover will be used to compensate for background losses during the handover. This compensation is done by subtracting the packet loss during the first 5 s of the measurement to compensate for losses before the handover. Compensating for losses after and during the handover is done by taking the number of packets lost from seconds 14 until 19 and multiplying them by 3 to compensate for losses that would otherwise have occurred during seconds 5 until 20. In an ideal scenario the packet loss will be close to 0. Each measurement will be run at least 10 times for each variable. The average of each measurement set will be reported with its 95 % confidence interval.

4.3   Results

In Fig. 4 we can see the delay that our measurement method reported at the nMAG during the handover. The measurement points are the mean calculated over all the measurements done at that specific delay. The bars around the measurement points represent the standard deviation of these results. We can see that the standard deviation correlates with the values used by NETEM to add delay to the links. A more detailed view of a single point in this graph (100 ms delay on the pMAG-nMAG link relative to the LMA-nMAG link) can

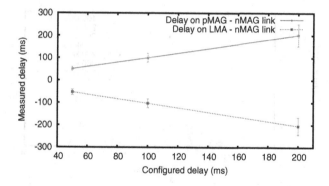

Fig. 4. Measured delay

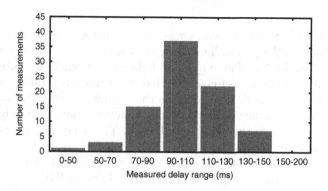

Fig. 5. Distribution of measured delay

be seen in Fig. 5. In this graph we see the amount of delay measurements that fell within a certain range. We can see this represents a normal distribution which can be attributed to the delay variation added in the experiment. Based on these results we can conclude that our system accurately finds the delay at the specific point in time the measurement is taken.

Figure 6 shows a graph of the throughput during the entire measurement process for PFMIPv6 handovers with different traffic loads with no added delay. The first 5 s the MN is connected to the pMAG and the throughput is around the value the data is sent at. At the 5 s mark the handover is initiated, and the throughput drops to 0 during the time the MN is disconnected from the network. After the handover is completed there is a visible spike in the throughput as the pMAG flushes the packet buffer to the MN.

The results for the packet loss during the measurements can be seen in Fig. 7. In this graph the y-axis shows the packets lost during the handover and the x-axis shows the traffic load. The labels are marked with the component that added the delay with the delay distribution that was used (LMA (50,10) means that 50 ms delay with a 10 ms standard distribution as variance was added on the LMA-nMAG link). Compensating for losses that occur due to the unreliable nature of

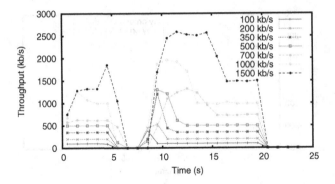

Fig. 6. Throughput during measurement

multicast on IEEE 802.11 networks was not as successful as hoped, leading to negative values on the y-axis. The cause of this results has three components: (i) Compensating for loss due to link unreliability only works well when the loss occurs equally over the measurement period. We cannot control the loss during the measurement as it fully dependent on the wireless channel. (ii) More importantly, the delay difference estimation does sometimes not accurately represent the actual delay due to the delay distribution. The delay measurement in the current system only occurs every 0.5 s. If the delay of one or both of the timing packets is an outlier this will cause the system to think the delay is much higher or lower than is actually the case in this timeslot. We can see this effect on the results with 0 variance in the delay as they are closer to 0. Decreasing the interval on which the delay is estimated and taking into account previous measurements can potentially lead to a better estimate for the current situation with high delay variance. (iii) As the buffer is unicast towards the MN these packets are less likely to be lost. Packets arriving during the buffer flush are however transmitted using multicast during this period so we still have to compensate for this loss, leading to overcompensation in most cases. The effect is

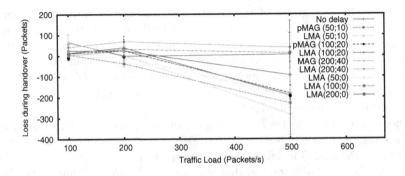

Fig. 7. Compensated packet loss during handover

exaggerated at higher packet rates, because the loss surrounding the handover are higher than during the handover.

5 Conclusions and Future Work

This paper describes optimizations to the multicast handover process in PFMIPv6. We presented a mechanism to determine the delay difference between two paths in a PFMIPv6 network. The values found with this method are used to optimize the multicast handover process. The optimizations and delay finding mechanism were implemented and validated with measurements done in an actual deployment with IEEE 802.11 networks. It was shown that our delay estimation mechanism can accurately find the delay difference between two paths in a PFMIPv6 network.

We avoid transmission of duplicate packets on the wireless network during a handover by switching the interface the multicast packets are forwarded from at the right moment. The decision of when to switch between the pMAG-nMAG and LMA-nMAG tunnels is based on the difference in delay between the two tunnels. This prevents multicast packets from being transmitted twice, reducing the load on the wireless network.

The interval the timing packets are sent on needs to be tuned. Increasing the time between timing packets puts less load on the network, but makes the estimated delay between tunnels less accurate. In a network with high amounts of congestion or large variances in delay, it could be beneficial to have the timing packet interval much lower than on a low congestion network. Previous measurements will also need to be taken into account. A single timing packet can currently cause a handover to perform sub-optimally if it was delayed more or less than the average delay during the handover. Our current PFMIPv6 implementation is still missing reactive handover support. Handovers that are made without initiating them first are performed as normal PMIP handovers. Support for multicast senders needs to be added to the implementation. While it is already possible for a MN to act as a multicast sender improvements are possible to allow multicast traffic to flow from MAG to MAG directly, skipping the LMA and reducing latency.

Multiple MNs listening to the same group on a MAG present extra synchronization problems. These mainly occur on the air interface. If MN A performs a handover to a MAG that already has a MN B listening to the same multicast group, it becomes difficult to deliver the same data on the air interface twice. On IEEE 802.11 networks this is a problem as the multicast packets from both sources (pMAG-nMAG tunnel and LMA-nMAG tunnel) might be broadcast at the same time. The same problem occurs when two nodes from different LMAs are connected that listen to the same multicast group.

Acknowledgement. The authors would like to thank the financial support provided by the SALUS project, co-funded by the EU under the 7th Framework Programme for research (grant agreement no. 313296).

References

1. Computable: Brandweer vervangt C2000-portofoons (2013). http://www.computable.nl/artikel/nieuws/telecom/4923768/1276977/brandweer-vervangt-c2000portofoons.html
2. Critical Communications Broadband Group: The Strategic Case for Mission Critical Mobile Broadband. Technical report, TCCA (2013)
3. Gundavelli, S., Leung, K., Devarapalli, V., Chowdhury, K., Patil, B.: Proxy mobile ipv6. Technical report, RFC 5213, August 2008
4. Yokota, H., Chowdhury, K., Koodli, R., Patil, B., Xia, F.: Fast Handovers for Proxy Mobile IPv6. Technical report, RFC 5949, September 2010
5. IETF Multicast Mobility Working Group: Multimob status pages (2014). http://tools.ietf.org/wg/multimob
6. Schmidt, T., Waehlisch, M., Krishnan, S.: Base deployment for multicast listener support in Proxy Mobile IPv6 (PMIPv6) Domains. IETF RFC6224, April 2011
7. Koodli, R., Waehlisch, M., Fairhurst, G., Schmidt, T., Liu, D.: Multicast Listener Extensions for Mobile IPv6 (MIPv6) and Proxy Mobile IPv6 (PMIPv6) Fast Handovers (2014)
8. Schmidt, T.C., Wölke, S., Wählisch, M.: Peer my proxy - a performance study of peering extensions for multicast in proxy mobile IP domains. In: Proceedings of 7th IFIP Wireless and Mobile Networking Conference (WMNC 2014), pp. 1–8. IEEEPress, Piscataway, May 2014
9. Montavont, N., Noel, T.: Handover management for mobile nodes in ipv6 networks. IEEE Commun. Mag. **40**(8), 38–43 (2002)
10. Kong, K.S., Lee, W., Han, Y.H., Shin, M.K., You, H.: Mobility management for all-ip mobile networks: mobile ipv6 vs. proxy mobile ipv6. IEEE Wirel. Commun. **15**(2), 36–45 (2008)
11. Magagula, L., Chan, H.: Ieee802.21 optimized handover delay for proxy mobile ipv6. In: Military Communications Conference, MILCOM 2008, pp. 1–7. IEEE, November 2008
12. Lee, J.H., Ernst, T.: Fast pmipv6 multicast handover procedure for mobility-unaware mobile nodes. In: 2011 IEEE 73rd Vehicular Technology Conference (VTC Spring), pp. 1–5, May 2011
13. Quoc, A.K., Kim, D., Choo, H.: A novel scheme for preventing out-of-order packets in fast handover for proxy mobile ipv6. In: 2014 International Conference on Information Networking (ICOIN), pp. 422–427, February 2014
14. De Vito, L., Rapuano, S., Tomaciello, L.: One-way delay measurement: state of the art. IEEE Trans. Instrum. Measur. **57**(12), 2742–2750 (2008)
15. Open Air Interface: Open air interface proxy mobile ipv6 (OAI PMIPV6) (2011). http://www.openairinterface.org/openairinterface-proxy-mobile-ipv6-oai-pmipv6
16. Elteto, T., Molnar, S.: On the distribution of round-trip delays in tcp/ip networks. In: Conference on Local Computer Networks, LCN 1999, pp. 172–181. IEEE (1999)
17. Linux Foundation: netem (2009). http://www.linuxfoundation.org/collaborate/workgroups/networking/netem

Wireless and Wired Networks

Unifying Web Services Communities Modelling Through a UML Profile

Hela Limam[1][(⊠)] and Jalel Akaichi[2]

[1] Institut Supérieur d'Informatique, Université Tunis El Manar, Tunis, Tunisia
hela.limam@isg.rnu.tn
[2] Institut Supérieur de Gestion, Paris, France
jalel.akaich@isg.rnu.tn

Abstract. Many works were interested in studying the ways of organizing Web services into communities which allowed the onset of a variety of definitions and models. The new paradigm, launched by the use of Web services communities models was adopted by users in various fields such as those related to marketing, commerce, health care, etc. However, the proposed conceptual models suffer from dispersed points of view that have to be unified in order to offer generic conceptual support for experts and clerical users. The purpose of this work is to propose a unified conceptual model able to unify different points of view through a generic UML description profile of Web services communities characteristics well adapted to new concepts imposed by the use of communities. Thanks to the proposed unified model, users will be able to build themselves their communities regardless the case of study involving Web services.

Keywords: Web services · Communities · Profile · Modelling

1 Introduction

The emergence of Web services in the information space raises many difficulties. Web services are developed by different entities and there is no consensus on the way to use services descriptions. In this context, the concept of community offers a solution for structuring and a organizing a large set of unstructured Web services sharing the same area of interest. Indeed, the community infrastructure contributes to improving the availability of Web services and provides centralized access to distributed Web services, the organization into communities raises a modelling problem resulting from the lack of a generic tool for the specification and the modelling of Web services communities. We propose in this work a unified model for representing different aspects of Web services communities through a UML profile. We illustrate the usefulness of the proposed profile notation using a health care community example designed with the proposed modelling tool.

The paper proceeds as follows. In Sect. 2 we argue our choice of the notion of the community and we situate our approach regarding the others proposed in the literature. The methodology for Web services communities modelling is described in Sect. 3. The unified model is detailed in Sect. 4. In Sect. 5 we propose the Web services community model. In Sect. 6 we illustrate our approach by a running example related to a health

© Springer International Publishing Switzerland 2015
M.C. Aguayo-Torres et al. (Eds.): WWIC 2015, LNCS 9071, pp. 357–366, 2015.
DOI: 10.1007/978-3-319-22572-2_26

care community. Finally Sect. 7 concludes our work and gives future directions of our research.

2   State of the Art

According to Wan et al., 2010, communities of Web services are defined as virtual spaces that can dynamically gather different Web services having complementary or related functionalities [1]. In this context, an approach is used to verify Web services communities modeled in UML activity diagram [2]. The first step consists on translating the activity diagram into an interpreted system model using predefined transformation rules. Then, specifications are expressed as formulae in a logic extending the Computation Tree Logic CTL with agent commitments needed for their communication. Finally, both the model and formulae are used as inputs for the multi-agent symbolic model checker. Yahyaoui et al., 2013 go beyond the definition of the concept of Web services communities and give some direct benefits that out of the adoption of communities of Web services [2]. Another approach for modeling Web services communities [3], is proposed by Sellami et al., 2013. It organizes Web service registries into communities according to the functionalities of the Web services in order to address the problem of the growing number of Web service registries and their poorly organized network.

Benharref et al., 2010 [4] proposed a managerial community of Web services for managing communities of Web services. This community is able to monitor, certify and assess the quality of Web services from other communities. A Web service will be allowed in the community if the quality of service is high or rejected if the quality of service is low. In this paper, the authors focused on the use of the managerial community in the selection of web services based on quality of service. In [5] Bouchaala et al., 2011 proposed a graph-based approach for managing communities of Web services registries. This approach consists of a set of algorithms and operations management. Management operations are verified at each stage of the life cycle of the community (create, delete, merge, split). Authors in [5], use communities to group records of Web services. Indeed, a community of Web services registries is a set of records with Web services that provide similar functionality. The concept of Web services community highlights the importance of management and organization of Web services in a community.

To conclude, Web services communities modeling issues have been addressed in different ways according to several approaches. However, few studies have focused on proposing a comprehensive conceptual modeling of various aspects of functioning of communities of Web services.

3   Methodology for Web Services Communities Modelling

In order to provide a formal description of the Web services community, we adopted the Model-driven architecture (MDA). In fact, MDA offers a conceptual framework that separates the organizational process from the technology platform decision [6].

A significant feature of the MDA is the use of automated tools and services to define the models (abstractions) and facilitates the transformations between different models. A UML profile for abstracting business information and business service specification was proposed [7], along with XMI's profile for selecting XML production options, exemplifying the MDA approach. Generators based on mappings of these languages to XML, WSDL, and other implementation technologies form the other crucial piece of an MDA framework for Web services. To cope with the specific aspects of Web services several design notations have been proposed [8–10]. While most of the proposed notations agreed on a set of concepts specific to Web services, none of them addresses the issue of Web services communities. This shortage motivated our work in proposing a Web services communities modelling approach which increases the expressiveness of UML for Web services communities and guides their design. Stereotypes and graphical annotations have been added to UML diagrams in order to distinguish between the different aspects in a Web services community.

4 The Unified Model

The design process of profile consists on defining a set of stereotypes and icons appropriate to Web services communities, then attaching constraints to profile elements in order to enhance its expressiveness. Our conceptual model provides a high level of abstraction and is completely software or hardware independent.

4.1 The Unified Model Visual Elements

A UML profile is a package that belongs to the extension mechanism. This package is stereotyped <<profile>> and the extension mechanism is allowed thanks to UML characteristics. In fact, the latter serves as foundation for building domain specific languages by specifying stereotypes, which introduce new language primitives by subtyping UML core types and tagged values, which represent new properties of these primitives. Model elements are assigned to such types by labeling them with the corresponding stereotypes.

The main modeling element of our system is the class stereotyped <<community>> used to represent a Web services community as a collection of Web services related to the same area of interest. A community is identified by a stereotype <<ID-parameter>> representing an abstract definition of the data used to identify a community. Data used to identify the community is essentially its category which describes the area of interest of the community.

The stereotype <<Web service>> is an abstraction of services providers which become members of the community while accomplishing the registration process. The community is accessible via a set of operations.

The stereotype <<operation>> represents abstract operations that summarize the major functions needed by community members. Community providers define generic operations based on their expertise on the corresponding area of interest.

Quality of Service specifies a set of quality requirements on the behavior of a community. To model this aspect, we used a class stereotyped <<quality of services>> that offers run time, business and security attributes.

In addition to proposed stereotypes, we attached an icon to each of them in the behavioral, structural and interactional diagrams as described in Table 1. Stereotypes and icons associated to them constitute the core of our proposed design language.

Table 1. Web services community notation

Icon	Stereotype	Concept
	<<community>>	Community of Web services
ID	<<ID-parameter>>	Identification parameter of the community
WS	<<web service>>	Web service
OP	<< operation >>	Operations of the community
QoS	<<quality of service >>	Quality of services related to the community

In order to cover specific perspectives related to Web services communities, we defined a UML based metamodel using the design notation introduced in the profile elements. This includes attaching a stereotype for each needed element inside a package named "profile". Only extended elements shall be represented as stereotypes. The proposed metamodel is given in (Fig. 1).

We have extended the class diagram to represent the structure of a community of Web service. A community is associated with a specific domain and is identified by a category and an identifier. It dynamically collects different Web services with similar functionality. The Web service providers, who register their Web services in a community, represent the communities' members.

A community is accessible via a set of generic operations. Community services providers define these operations based on their expertise in the field of community. A generic process is defined by a set of functional and non-functional attributes. Functional attributes describe the syntactic functions, which represent the structure of a generic operation, and semantic features, which refer to the significance of the operation or its messages. The semantic attributes are static or dynamic. The quality of operation is based on a set of qualitative attributes which are transverse to the overall operations such as cost and the response time.

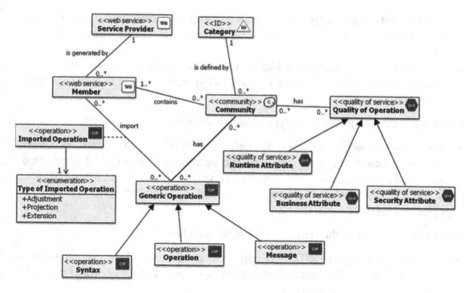

Fig. 1. Web services community metamodel

4.2 The Profile Constraints

For instance, constraints should be added to the aforementioned stereotypes to govern the metamodel structure.

In fact, constraints can be associated to stereotypes imposing restrictions on the corresponding metamodel elements. In this way, a designer can define the properties of a "well formed" model. In our work we adopted OCL (Object Constraint Language) for expressing constraints since it is a declarative language that describes constraints on UML metamodels [11].

As a constraint language, OCL allows to specify among other invariants on classes and types data in a UML model to express the pre and post conditions of operations and methods, defines invariants on stereotypes of a UML profile.

In our work, we mainly use the OCL invariant type to express constraints on meta-level UML stereotypes profile. An OCL invariant (keyword inv) is defined in the context of a class or a stereotype and specifies the conditions that must be met by its instances.

The context of this constraint definition is the class (keyword context). The keyword self is used in OCL to reference the current object of the specified class in the context; Implies the operator corresponds to the logical implication.

Using stereotypes, icons and constraints, we define a profile that helps us in the design of the Web services community.

In the following, we used the OCL syntax to describe some constraints associated to the presented metamodel in order to enhance its expressiveness while modeling a Web services community.

We express in the following constraints attached to the stereotype <<community>>

- A community has exactly one category: `context Community inv: self.ownedMember- > select(m|m.oclIsTypeOf (Category)) > size () = 1`
- A community has exactly one Identifier: `context Community inv: self.ownedMember- > select(m|m.oclIsTypeOf (Identifier))- > size () = 1`

Constraints attached to the stereotype <<web service>>

- The class <<web service>> is only associated to the class <<community>> or <<web service>> or <<generic operation>>: `self.allOpposite-AssociationEnds- > forAll(participant.oclIsTypeOf or oclIsTypeOf(web service) or oclIsTypeOf(generic-operation))`

Constraints attached to the stereotype identifier <<ID>>

- The class stereotyped <<ID>> is only associated to the class <<community>>: `self.allOppositeAssociationEnds- > forAll(participant.oclIsTypeOf (community))`

Constraints attached to the stereotype <<generic operation>>

- Class <<generic operation>> is only connected to <<community>> or <<web service>>: self.allOppositeAssociationEnds- > forAll(participant.oclIsTypeOf (Community) or oclIsTypeOf(web service))
- An element imported operation is an association between a departure element member and a receiver element generic operation: `context Imported Operation inv :(self.client.oclIsKindOf (member)) and (self.supplier.oclIsKindOf (generic operation))`

Constraints attached to the stereotype <<quality of service>>:

- The class <<quality of service>> can be only associated to the class <<community>>: `self.allOppositeAssociationEnds- > forAll(participant.oclIsTypeOf(Community))`

After the definition of the metamodel with its OCL constraints, we propose in the next step to instantiate the metamodel in order to generate a model of a Web services community.

5 The Web Services Community Model

The Web services model is built upon the Web services community classes. To represent the Web services community classes, the current prototype allows the user to draw class diagrams according to the language notation presented in Table 1. We begin with loading the UML meta-model. This later offers an editor for viewing and editing UML models. The edited model for the representation of the Web services community classes and description of relationships is given in the Web services community class diagram (Fig. 2).

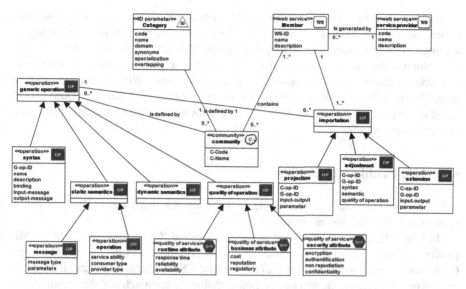

Fig. 2. Extended UML Web services community class diagram

The community is defined by an identifier, a category and a set of generic operations. All Web services that belong to community class have the same category. The category of a community is formally defined by a set of attributes (Domain, Synonyms, Specialization, Overlapping). Domain gives the area of interest of the community (e.g., "healthcare"). It takes its value from taxonomy for domain names. For flexibility purposes, different communities may adopt different taxonomies to specify their category. Specialization is a set of characteristics of the community domain. For example, "Patient Administration Services" and "Patient Care Services" are specialization of "healthcare". Communities are generally not independent. They are linked to each other via association relationships. These relationships are specified in the Overlapping attribute.

The community is accessible via set of operations called generic operations. Community providers define generic operations based on their expertise on the corresponding area of interest. A generic operation is defined by a set of functional and non-functional attributes. Functional attributes describe syntactic and semantic features of generic operations. Syntactic attributes represent the structure of a generic operation. An example of syntactic attribute is the list of input and output parameters that define the operation's messages. Semantic attributes refer to the meaning of the operation or its messages. We consider two types of semantic attributes: static and dynamic semantic attributes. Static semantic attributes (or simply static attributes) describe non-computational features of generic operations. Those are semantic attributes that are generally independent of the execution of the operation.

An example of static attribute is the operation's category. Dynamic semantic attributes (or simply dynamic attributes) describe computational features of generic operations. They generally refer to the way and constraints under which the operation is executed. An example of dynamic attribute is the business logic of the operation i.e., the results returned by the operation given certain parameters and conditions.

Service providers can, at any time, select a community of interest based on categories and register their services with it. The registration process requires giving an identifier (WS-ID), name, and description for the Web service. Multiple Web services that belong to the same community may import the same generic operation. Hence, it is important to define a set attributes that help select the "best" Web service supporting a given functionality. For this purpose, we define a Quality of Service (QoS) model based on a set of qualitative attributes that are transversal to all operations such as the cost and response time.

6 UML Profile Realization

A UML profile is a package belonging to the extension mechanism. This package is stereotyped "Profile" and is written in XML.

In StarUML platform we added an approach called 'CSW Approach' and a UML profile for Web services community composed of three models or diagrams are: CSWClassDiagram and CSWUeCaseDiagram and CSWSequenceDiagram. Indeed, we created two XML files, the first one is used to define the approach and the second one is used to create the profile. When we start StarUML, the 'New Project by approach' appears to select the desired approach. Our proposed approach called 'CSW Approach' is integrated in the platform. Consequently, it can be selected as all the approaches of the platform (Fig. 3).

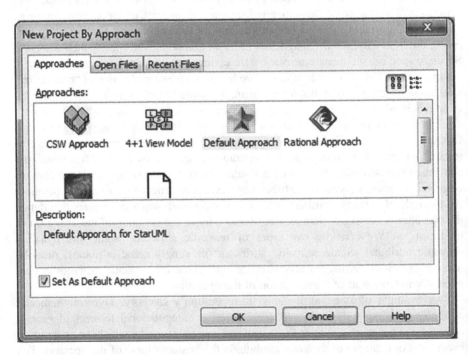

Fig. 3. CSW approach

After selecting the approach, we find in the "Model Explorer" of StarUML models called behavioral CSW model, structural model CSW and interactional CSW Model representing the functional, structural and interactional aspects of a Web services community.

In order to exemplify how the previously described model can be applied to a specific field we choosed a running example related to a health care community. In our work, we followed the UML profiling mechanism

Figure 4 describes the general class diagram for the health care community called 'CSWClassDiagram HealthCareCommunity'. The main domain classes are community health care, community members and health care provider health services.

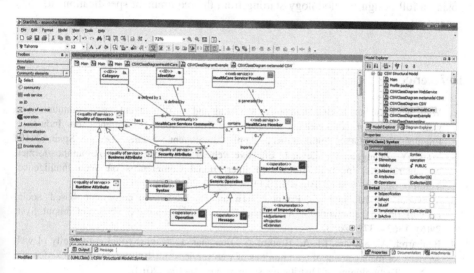

Fig. 4. CSWClassDiagram HealthCareCommunity

A Health care community is designed to combine data from the large ancillary services, such as pharmacy, laboratory, and radiology, with various clinical care services. It has an identifier and is described by a set of attributes. It is composed of a set of Health care Web services: Insurance Service, Care Service, Patient Referral Service, Physician Referral Service and scheduling Service. Web services inside a community are associated to each other's with peer relationships.

Each Web service is modelled as a class in the extended class diagram and is described by a set of attributes as shown in Fig. 4. The number of integrated Web services involved in the Health care community is dependent upon the data structures and has to provide an interface that allows clinicians to access the systems through a portal.

The Health care community portal must be able to schedule patient visit with physicians. The system also records drugs prescribed during the visit. Additionally patient referral services should be permanently updated and the information is used to track the visit.

7 Conclusion

In this work, we proposed a generic model of Web services communities. It consists on a UML profile destined to describe Web services communities using specific and well-adapted stereotypes and notations. Based on the general structure of the proposed model, we described a community of health care Web services necessary to ensure the community main requirements. The modelling of Web services communities was performed using a UML profile based on enriched diagrams; however enhancing the model with other behavioural diagrams and context-aware components, such as activity diagrams extended with mobility and context-aware features, is necessary for proposing a full design methodology starting from the requirement specifications to code generation.

References

1. Wan, W., Bentahar, J., Ben Hamza, A.: Modeling and verifying agent-based communities of web services. In: Proceedings of the 23rd International Conference on Industrial, Engineering and Other Applications of Applied Intelligent Systems, Cordoba, Spain (2010)
2. Wang, Y., Zhang, J., Vassileva, J.: Effective web service selection via communities formed by super-agents. In: IEEE/WIC/ACM International Conferences on Web Intelligence, Toronto, pp. 549–556 (2010). doi:10.1109/WI-IAT.2010.221
3. Yahyaoui, H., Maamar, Z., Erbin, L., Thiran, P.: Towards a community-based, social network-driven framework for Web services management. Future Generation Comput. Syst. 29(6), 1363–1377 (2013)
4. Benharref, A., Serhani, M.-A., Bouktif, S., Bentahar, J.: A managerial community of web services for management of communities of web services. In: 10th International Conference on New Technologies of Distributed Systems, pp. 97–104 (2010)
5. Bouchaala, O., Sellami, M., Gaaloul, W., Tata, S., Jmaiel, M.: Modeling and managing communities of web service registries. In: Filipe, J., Cordeiro, J. (eds.) WEBIST 2011. LNBIP, vol. 101, pp. 88–102. Springer, Heidelberg (2012)
6. Frankel, D., Parodi, J.: Using Model-Driven Architecture to Develop Web Services. OMG Series. Wiley, New York (2002)
7. Provost, W.:UML for Web services (2003). http://www.xml.com/pub/a/ws/2003/08/05/uml.html. Accessed
8. Ortiz, G., Hernandez, J.: Toward UML profiles for web services and their extra-functional properties. In: IEEE International Conference on Web Services Chicago, pp. 889–892 (2006). doi:10.1109/ICWS.2006.130
9. Belouadha, F., Roudiès, O.: Un profil UML de spécification de services Web composites sémantiques. In: 1ère Conférence Internationale Systèmes d'Information et Intelligence Economique, Tunisia, pp. 14–16 (2008)
10. Skogan, D., Gronmo, R., Solheim, I.: Web service Composition in UML. In: Proceedings of the Enterprise Distributed Object Computing Conference, Washington, pp. 47–57 (2004)
11. Warmer, J., Kleppe, A.: The Object Constraint Language: Getting Your Models Ready for MDA. Addison-Wesley, Boston (2003)

Towards Information-Centric Wireless Multi-hop Communication

Carlos Anastasiades[✉] and Torsten Braun

Institute of Computer Science and Applied Mathematics,
University of Bern, 3012 Bern, Switzerland
{anastasiades,braun}@iam.unibe.ch

Abstract. Information-centric networking (ICN) addresses drawbacks of the Internet protocol, namely scalability and security. ICN is a promising approach for wireless communication because it enables seamless mobile communication, where intermediate or source nodes may change, as well as quick recovery from collisions. In this work, we study wireless multi-hop communication in Content-Centric Networking (CCN), which is a popular ICN architecture. We propose to use two broadcast faces that can be used in alternating order along the path to support multi-hop communication between any nodes in the network. By slightly modifying CCN, we can reduce the number of duplicate Interests by 93.4 % and the number of collisions by 61.4 %. Furthermore, we describe and evaluate different strategies for prefix registration based on overhearing. Strategies that configure prefixes only on one of the two faces can result in at least 27.3 % faster data transmissions.

1 Introduction

With emerging community networks and social networking services, communication networks have shifted from resource interconnection to content sharing networks. In this context, information-centric networking (ICN) has gained much attention in recent years, because it addresses shortcomings of current host-based communication, namely scalability, flexibility to changing routes and security. In ICN, requests for content do not need to be sent to specific servers but nodes can express Interests and receive matching Data from any nearby node in response. The exchanged messages do not contain any source or destination addresses, which supports caching in any node. This is beneficial in multi-hop communication and communications with multiple requesters, because content does not need to be (re-)transmitted over the entire path but can be retrieved from the nearest cache. Because content is signed, integrity and authenticity of retrieved content is ensured and it is not important which node provided the content copy.

To transmit Interests towards content sources, forwarding tables need to be configured. In fixed ICN Internet communication, prefixes can be configured with the help of routing protocols [7,15] and nearby copies can be found via cache synchronization [17] or redundant random searches [4]. In wireless networks,

© Springer International Publishing Switzerland 2015
M.C. Aguayo-Torres et al. (Eds.): WWIC 2015, LNCS 9071, pp. 367–380, 2015.
DOI: 10.1007/978-3-319-22572-2_27

topologies may change and periodic exchange of routing information may over-
load the network. Existing works [1,10], therefore, exploit the broadcast nature
of the wireless medium. Requests are flooded and content prefix are overheard
to learn distances to available content sources similar to existing routing protocols like AODV [12]. To learn distances to content sources, endpoint identifiers
and hop distances are added to all messages. However, when adding endpoint
identifiers to messages, communication is not strictly information-centric anymore, which means that it loses its flexibility because it matters from which
node content is retrieved (endpoint specified in messages). As a consequence,
complicated handoff mechanisms are required as in current host-based communication. Current works in wireless information-centric communication do not
consider forwarding tables to route Interests and either consider only one-hop
communication to wired infrastructure [6,16] or consider routing on a high-level
[14] with endpoint identifiers [1,10].

In this work, we investigate a different approach without endpoint identifiers.
Nodes overhear broadcast content transmissions to configure prefixes in the forwarding tables. Routing can then be based on the same forwarding structures
as for wired information-centric networks, which facilitates interoperability. We
describe and evaluate different strategies for prefix registration and evaluate
optimizations to improve multi-hop communication in case of multiple potential
forwarders.

The remainder of this paper is organized as follows. Related work is described
in Sect. 2. In Sect. 3 we describe overhearing and forwarding strategies to support
opportunistic content-centric multi-hop communication. Evaluation results are
shown in Sect. 4 followed by a discussion in Sect. 5. Finally, in Sect. 6, we conclude
our work and give an outlook on future work.

2   Content-Centric Networking

2.1   Basic CCN Concepts

We base our investigations on the Content-Centric Networking (CCN) architecture [8]. It is based on two messages: *Interests* to request content and *Data* to
deliver content. Files are composed of multiple segments, which are included in
a Data message, and users need to express Interests in every segment to retrieve
a complete file. CCNx [3] provides an open source reference implementation of
CCN. The core element of the implementation is the CCN daemon (CCND),
which performs message processing and forwarding decisions. Links from the
CCND to applications or other hosts are called *faces*. A CCND has the following three memory components:

1. The Forwarding Information Base (FIB) contains forwarding entries to direct
   Interests towards potential content sources. Every entry contains a prefix,
   the face where to forward Interests and a lifetime value. To avoid loops, an
   Interest is never forwarded on the same face from where it was received.

2. The Pending Interest Table (PIT) stores pending forwarded Interests together with the face on which they were received. If Data is received in return, it can be forwarded based on face information in the PIT. Existing PIT entries prevent forwarding of similar Interests. Duplicate Interests are identified by a Nonce in the Interest header. Therefore, PIT entries form a multicast tree such that each Interest is only forwarded once at a time over a certain path.
3. The Content Store (CS) is used as cache in a CCN router storing received Data packets temporarily. It is used as short-term storage that can be used to reduce delays for retransmissions in multi-hop communication.

Prior to transmission, content is included and scheduled for transmission in a queue. To avoid duplicate content transmissions, an additive random delay (data_pause) is considered during content scheduling. If a node overhears the transmission of the same content from another node, it removes the scheduled content from the content queue (duplicate suppression). The *freshnessSeconds* field in content headers specifies how long a segment stays in the CS after its reception. Content can also be stored persistently in repositories of content sources. The *AnswerOriginKind* in Interest headers specifies from where the content should be retrieved, e.g., content store or repository.

2.2 CCN Forwarding and Routing

OSPFN [15] and NLSR [7] are routing protocols for large multi-hop networks. Link state advertisements (LSAs) are propagated throughout the entire network and each router builds a complete network topology. These protocols, therefore, target static networks without frequent topology and content availability changes to avoid many LSAs. To detect routes to content sources closer to the requester, which may not be on a configured path to the original content source, optimizations are required. Bloom filters [9,17] have been proposed to exchange caching information among neighbors. However, nodes would need to guarantee minimal cache validity times in order to be useful. Other optimizations [4,5] use an exploration phase, where Interests are flooded into the network to find new content sources closer to the requester. In [18] the concept of adaptive NDN Interest forwarding is investigated. Based on successful Data retrievals, forwarding nodes can select which FIB face to use in the next transmission. Routers inform downstream nodes if they cannot forward Interests due to missing FIB entries by Interest NACKs. Therefore, the approach targets unicast networks and requires the configuration of FIB entries in the first place.

Earlier works [1,10] in wireless ICN communication use flooding to learn content reachability via additional information in message headers. The Listen First, Broadcast Later (LFBL) [10] algorithm adds additional header fields to both Interest and Data messages including the communication end-points and hop distances. Nodes perform flooding if they do not know endpoints and learn distance information via overhearing. Forwarding is based on hop distance to the endpoints. E-CHANET [1] is a similar approach, which also adds endpoint (providerIDs) and distance (hop count) information to messages. To avoid multiple content sources responding to Interests, not only content names but also providerIDs in Interest and Data messages need to match. Mobility handoffs and provider selection are proposed to enable communication to the "closest" content source. However, both approaches circumvent one of ICN's fundamental design goals of avoiding endpoint identifiers. Aggregating requests for the same content becomes much more challenging in case of multiple redundant content sources. Additionally, Data messages, which are returned from cache, may hold imprecise provider and distance information. Furthermore, forwarding based on hop distance, i.e., using only the distance as path selection criterion, may not work efficiently in dense environments if multiple nodes may have the same "hop distance" to the endpoints. Both approaches are similar to AODV to learn distances to content sources, but they do not investigate name-based routing. In this work, we describe a different approach without endpoint identifiers, where content prefixes are configured in the FIB. This enables Interest aggregation to support multiple concurrent requests.

3   Multi-hop Communication with Overhearing

Information-centric multi-hop communication requires a mechanism to configure forwarding prefixes in the FIB and selecting forwarders out of multiple potential options to avoid duplicate transmissions. We consider the extraction of content names in overheard broadcast Data packets and include it temporarily into the FIB such that Interests can be forwarded towards the content source. To enable overhearing without configured FIB entries (and in the absence of other nodes requesting content), Interests from local applications can always be forwarded to a broadcast face to probe for content in the environment. We call this *pass-through* of local Interests. Interests from other nodes are only forwarded if a matching FIB entry exists. Interests forwarded via pass-through always ask for content from repositories but not from caches. Additionally, we add a hop counter to Interest messages to limit the propagation of Interests. A hop counter in Interest messages is also compliant with the new CCNx 1.0 protocol [11].

3.1   Prefix Registration and Forwarding Strategies

Since Interests can not be forwarded on the face from where they have been received, multi-hop communication requires at least two (broadcast) faces for communication: one for receiving and one for transmitting/forwarding messages. To receive messages on either face, both broadcast faces need to be configured. In addition, to forward Interests towards content sources, eligible prefixes need to be configured to those faces in the FIB. If a node receives Interests on one face, they should be forwarded on the other face.

We describe three different strategies for prefix registration below. All forwarding strategies require the configuration of two broadcast faces to receive content. The difference between the strategies is how prefixes are associated to those faces.

Two Static Forwarding Faces (2SF): Every prefix needs to be configured on both broadcast faces such that Interests can be forwarded on the opposite face on which they were received. In this strategy, we do not apply any overhearing mechanisms. All prefixes need to be configured to both broadcast faces in an initial phase because no feedback can be received from the network. This may result in large FIB tables to route all potential prefixes (even if the corresponding content is never requested). In addition, it is more difficult to adapt to changing topologies since routing protocols are required for periodic updates. Please note that we use 2SF only for reference purposes.

Two Dynamic Forwarding Faces (2DFo): In this strategy, overheard prefixes are added to both broadcast faces similar to *2SF*. However, in contrast to *2SF*, prefixes are only added dynamically to the FIB if the content is available, i.e., it has been overheard. The approach uses pass-through and hop counters. Pass-through works as follows: if a request on face 1 has not been successful, the Interest is automatically transmitted via face 2. To avoid that forwarders discard it as duplicate, the requester needs to change the nonce in the retransmitted Interest.

One Dynamic Forwarding Face (1DFo): In contrast to *2DFo*, overheard prefixes are only registered on the face on which content transmission has been overheard, but not on both faces. Similar to *2DFo*, pass-through and a hop counter is used.

We explain forwarding with the help of Fig. 1, which shows four nodes and their transmission ranges (dashed circles). Nodes in transmission range of the content source can broadcast an Interest on face 1 (pass-through) and all nodes in range of the content source can overhear Data transmission to configure the prefix in the FIB, i.e., they can configure the prefix on face 1 denoted by the solid grey circle in the figure. Nodes further away need to send Interests on face 2 so that nodes near the content source can forward it via face 1. Since they receive Data on face 2, they can configure the prefix on face 2 denoted by the white circular ring. As shown in the figure, only two broadcast faces are required to forward Interests from a requester multiple hops away by alternating the forwarding faces in the nodes along the path.

3.2 Configure Prefixes via Overhearing

Prefixes are configured by extracting the content name from overheard (broadcast) content transmissions. Only new content is registered in the FIB, i.e., only if the content is not already stored in the content store or the local repository. To limit message processing, only every n-th content message can be processed. By applying modulo operations on the received segment number, no additional state information is required.

If the 2DFo strategy is used, the prefix is registered to both broadcast faces. If the 1DFo strategy is used, the prefixes are only registered to the face from

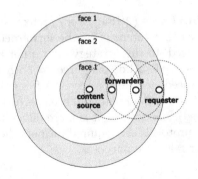

Fig. 1. Forwarding via alternating faces.

which the content has been received and to 1 face at maximum. If no prefixes are configured, Interests from local applications can be forwarded via pass-through. If an Interest needs to be forwarded via pass-through, the header field *AnswerOriginKind* is set to 0, which means that no cached answer from content store is accepted.

3.3   Interest and Data Forwarding

To avoid duplicate Interest (and Data) transmissions, the propagation of Interest messages needs to be controlled. The basic idea is the following: every node delays Interest transmissions randomly by an *Interest Forwarding Delay (IFD)*. Based on overheard Interest and Data messages, the IFD is increased or decreased. If a forwarder continuously receives Data to its transmitted Interests, it assumes to be a *preferred forwarder*.

Interest Forwarding Delay: To avoid duplicate Interest transmissions, every Interest is forwarded with a delay, which is randomly selected within a specified interval $[0, IFD_{max}]$. Based on overheard Interest or Data messages, IFD_{max} is modified. If Interests are transmitted and Data is received in return, IFD_{max} is decreased. By this, we can minimize the influence of large forwarding delays and reduce the time until the next Interest can be sent resulting in higher throughput. If the same Interest is overheard from another node before it has been transmitted, the Interest transmission is delayed once, i.e., *delayed send*, and the interval is slightly increased. If another Interest is overheard during that time, the Interest is discarded. The values are configurable but in our current implementation, we set IFD_{max} initially to 100 ms. We halve IFD_{max} if a Data message is received in return and no other Interest has been overheard. If an Interest has been overheard IFD_{max} is slightly increased by 1 ms.

Preferred Forwarders: Interests are forwarded based on the IFD. At some point, a forwarder may receive a Data message for which no Interest has been forwarded locally. Then, the forwarder knows that there is another node that forwarded the Interest faster. It assumes that it is *non-preferred* and adds a fixed delay (in our implementation 100 ms) to every Interest transmission. Due to the fixed delay, non-preferred forwarders will only attempt to forward Interests if preferred forwarders have not retrieved content already. If preferred forwarders have moved away or their Interests collide, non-preferred forwarders can forward their Interests (*delayed send*). To avoid unnecessary switching, e.g., due to occasional collisions, a non-preferred forwarder can only become preferred, if it has performed a delayed send for N (in our implementation: N = 3) subsequent times.

Data Transmission: Data is transmitted similarly to CCN with an additive random delay and Interests can be satisfied from cache. However, there is one modification: Data messages are only forwarded if the corresponding Interest has been forwarded and not only scheduled for transmission.

3.4 Data Structures

Our proposed approach uses the existing CCN data structures, namely the FIB, the PIT and the CS. For efficient multi-hop communication, we use the following additional hash tables:

Interest Table (IT): The IT points to the corresponding PIT entry and includes additional information for Interest forwarding. The information includes the number of times the Interest has been overheard, a list of faces where the Interest has been forwarded and multiple flags to specify whether: (1) a pass-through was required, (2) the Interest has been sent or only scheduled for transmission and (3) a delayed send was required due to an overheard Interest. An IT table entry is created whenever an Interest is received and forwarded. Cleanup can be performed at the same time as for the PIT table, i.e., when an Interest has been consumed or expired depending on the Interest lifetime.

Content Flow Table (CFT): The CFT is used to maintain the current IFD_{max} value and to remember whether it is a preferred node or not. It is created the first time when an Interest has been forwarded for an existing FIB entry. Similar to the FIB entries, CFTs have an expiration time, which can be regularly updated and checked at the same time as the FIB expiration. In our implementation, we set the expiration time to 500 s but also larger values are possible. CFT entries keep track of existing forwarding faces and unsuccessfully forwarded Interests: if S (in our implementation: S = 16) subsequent Interest transmissions have been detected over a specific face, the corresponding dynamically created FIB entries can be unregistered and removed from the content flow. If the content flow does not specify another outgoing face, the content flow is deleted.

4   Evaluation

We performed evaluations by simulations using our CCN framework based on OMNeT++ [13]. The simulation framework is based on CCNx and provides a complete CCN implementation including all memory components such as the Content Store (CS), Pending Interest Table (PIT), Forwarding Information Base (FIB) as well as content queues with the same delays and flags like CCNx. The framework allows us to process and store information as in CCNx (except signature calculations and verifications) but facilitates network setup, MAC layer observations and enables high scalability.

4.1   Simulation Scenario

The evaluation topology is shown in Fig. 2. The small solid circles represent network nodes and the dashed circles denote different network partitions. All network nodes inside a network partition can directly communicate with each other. The white solid circles are only part of one partition and can not directly reach nodes in other partitions. Black solid circles in the intersections between partitions are potential forwarding nodes that can relay between white solid nodes. In total, there are 150 nodes: 25 nodes within each partition (white circles) and 10 potential forwarders (black circles) in each intersection A, B, C, D, M of neighboring partitions. The content source is always placed in partition 1 and a requester (white node) in partition 1 requests content such that forwarders (black nodes) in the intersections A, B and M can overhear it. This step is only used to populate the FIB in partition 1. The common evaluation parameters are listed in Table 1.

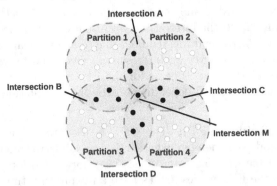

Fig. 2. Network with four partitions: all nodes in the same partition can see each other but not nodes from other partitions.

All network nodes have one 802.11g network interface and two broadcast faces configured to enable multi-hop communication. The broadcast data rate is set to 2 Mbps. The segment size corresponds to the effective CCN payload without CCN headers and the content lifetime defines how long content stays valid in the content store, i.e., corresponding to *freshnessSeconds* in CCNx. We set

Table 1. Common simulation parameters.

Parameter	Value
Interface	1x 802.11 g
Data rate	Broadcast: 2 Mbps
Segment size	4096 Bytes (RTS/CTS disabled)
Content size	4 MB (1000 segments)
Pipeline size	16
Content lifetime CL	600 s
Data_pause	100 ms
Request interval RI	2000 s, 30 s
Interest lifetime	4 s (default)
Prefix validity time in FIB	40000 s

data_pause, i.e., a random CCN delay for every Data transmission, to 100 ms. We evaluate multiple requests from different partitions and the request interval denotes the time interval between the requests. For a request interval of 2000 s, content cannot be found in the nodes' caches anymore. To evaluate competing concurrent flows, where part of the content can be found in the cache, we also evaluate a request interval of 30 s. Requesters are always selected among the "white nodes" within the corresponding partition to enforce multi-hop communication. We use the default CCNx Interest lifetime of 4 s. For the 1DFo, 2DFo and 2SF strategies, message processing is implemented as described in Sect. 3. The validity time of overheard prefixes in the FIB can be much larger than content lifetimes in the cache because name prefixes are significantly smaller than the content objects (multiple segments with payloads). Therefore, we set the validity time of overheard prefixes in the FIB to 40000 s but delete entries after 16 (consecutive) unsuccessful Interest forwardings. For every configuration, 100 simulation runs have been performed.

4.2 Multi-hop Communication with Interest Table

In this subsection, we evaluate the performance gain of IT/CFT compared to regular CCN message processing. To populate the FIB entries for the 1DFo and 2DFo strategies, a requester in partition 1 requests content from a content source in the same partition. After 2000 s, a requester in partition 2 is requesting the same content. Although the content does not exist in caches anymore, the FIB entries in intersections A and M are still valid. In Fig. 4a, we compare 1DFo, 2DFo and 2SF in terms of transmission times and transmitted Interests. The file size is 4 MB, which corresponds to 1000 segments. The left y-axis shows the requester's transmission time in seconds and the right y-axis the transmitted Interest messages by listeners, i.e., nodes that do not actively request content, in partition 2. Figure 4a shows that the 1DFo strategy results in 6.4 % shorter transmission times than 2DFo and 8 % shorter transmission times than 2SF with

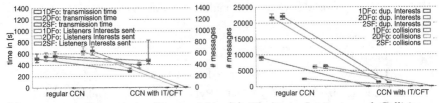

(a) Requester's Transmission Time and Listeners' transmitted Interests in partition 2 (b) Duplicate Interests and Collisions at Content Source in partition 1

Fig. 3. Comparing CCN to CCN with IT/CFT.

regular CCN. However, when applying IT/CFT, the transmission times of 1DFo can be drastically reduced by 47 %. The differences compared to other strategies become larger with applied IT/CFT, i.e., 1DFo performes 27.3 % faster than 2DFo and even 38.2 % faster than 2SF.

1DFo performs better than 2DFo and 2SF because all "white" nodes in partition 2 have only one face configured. Because Interests can not be forwarded on the face of reception, Interest forwarding in partition 2 could be effectively avoided with 1DFo. As Fig. 4a shows for the 1DFo strategy, listener nodes in partition 2 that do not have a direct connection to the content source do not forward Interests but only forwarders (black nodes in Fig. 2) do. When applying IT/CFT, transmitted Interests by listeners could be reduced for 2DFo and 2SF because listeners realize that they are non-preferred nodes. However, because forwarding via two faces results in more forwarded Interests and overheard Interests, Interest forwarding delays IFD_{max} of 2DFo and 2SF are higher than with 1DFo, which explains the longer transmission times.

Figure 3b shows the number of received duplicate Interests and collisions at the content source in partition 1. With regular CCN, the number of duplicate Interests is high because all forwarders in intersections A and M receive the Interests at the same time and forward it almost immediately before overhearing forwardings of other nodes. In the 1DFo strategy, every forwarder transmits on average 636 Interests, while with the 2DFo and 2SF strategy 934 Interests are forwarded by forwarders and 440 Interests by listener nodes in partition 1. As a result, a content source receives 48.2 % fewer duplicate Interests and experiences and 61.4 % fewer collisions with the 1DFo strategy compared to 2DFo and 2SF. With IT/CFT, the number of duplicate Interests can be drastically reduced by at least 93.4 % because non-preferred forwarders transmit only a few Interests, but duplicate transmissions cannot be avoided completely.

We would like to emphasize that multiple forwarders are beneficial for multihop forwarding with IT/CFT. Recall that forwarders delay Interest transmissions if they overhear the same Interest. Because these forwarders can transmit Interests via *delayed send* if they do not receive content, the communication can recover faster from collisions on the path. For example, in the current scenario with 20 potential forwarders in intersections A and M, content can be retrieved 20.7 % faster with 1DFo compared to a scenario with only 1 forwarder.

4.3   Multi-hop Communication with Multiple Requesters

In this subsection, we evaluate the influence of multiple concurrent requesters to multi-hop communication. We only show evaluation results with IT/CFT because it performed better than regular CCN. In addition, we only show evaluation results with concurrent requesters in different partitions, i.e., partitions 2, 3, 4. Concurrent requesters in the same partition would receive the content without any efforts due to broadcast communication and caching. Similar to the last subsection, a requester in partition 1 requests content such that FIB tables at forwarders are filled. The concurrent requests start after a delay of 2000 s to ensure that no content is cached. Then, requests in partitions 2, 3, 4 (in this order) start with an interval of 30 s, which means that some content can be retrieved from cache but requesters quickly catch up resulting in concurrent request streams.

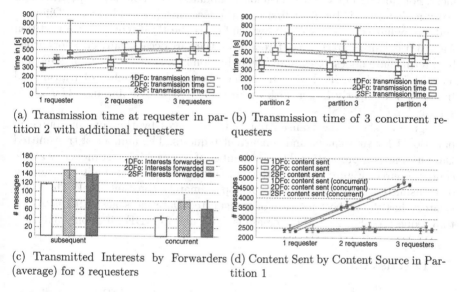

(a) Transmission time at requester in partition 2 with additional requesters

(b) Transmission time of 3 concurrent requesters

(c) Transmitted Interests by Forwarders (average) for 3 requesters

(d) Content Sent by Content Source in Partition 1

Fig. 4. Performance of concurrent requests.

Figure 4a shows the transmission time of a requester in partition 2 if there is one concurrent stream from partition 2, two concurrent streams from partition 2 and 3 or three concurrent streams from partitions 2, 3 and 4. Figure 4a shows that a requester in partition 2 needs 22.8 % more time if there is a concurrent stream in partition 3. Please note that only nodes in intersection M can receive Interests from both partitions 2 and 3, while nodes in intersections A only receive Interests from partition 2 and nodes in intersection B only from partition 2. Two concurrent requesters in partition 2 and 3 can, therefore, result in two competing streams, which may result in slightly longer Interest forwarding delays IFD_{max} and consequently, slightly longer transmission times. Another requester in partition 4 does not further increase the transmission time with 1DFo. Thus, the increase in transmission time does not grow linearly with increasing number of requesters. All concurrent requesters finish their transmission at the same time, which means that effective transmission times of requester 2 and 3 are approximately 30 s and 60 s shorter as Fig. 4b shows.

Figure 4c shows the Interests transmitted by the forwarders in intersections A, B, M on average when using the 1DFo, 2DFo and 2SF strategy with three requesters in partition 2, 3 and 4. The bars on the left side show the transmitted messages if the requests are subsequent with an interval of 2000 s such that requesters cannot profit from each other. The bars on the right side show the transmitted messages if requesters concurrently retrieve content in an interval of 30 s. Figure 4c shows that with 1DFo, the transmitted messages can be reduced by 64.0 %, i.e., to almost a third of the traffic of three requesters. This shows that 1DFo can efficiently handle concurrent multi-stream communication. For 2DFo and 2SF, the reduction is smaller because forwarders can forward Interests on two faces. Forwarding in CCN is continuously updated based on past experience and every node forwards Interests first over the face that it considers best. Different nodes may have different views on which face is "best". If requesters in partition 2 and 3 transmit Interests on different faces, they are occasionally both forwarded by intermediate nodes. Therefore, the reduction is only 46.74.5 % with 2DFo and only 54.73 % with 2SF. Please note that the absolute number of transmitted Interests is a slightly larger with 2DFo compared to 2SF because IDF_{max} is slightly larger with 2SF.

Figure 4d shows the transmitted Data messages by the content source in partition 1 for subsequent and concurrent requests. The number of transmitted Data messages is proportional to the number of received Interest messages at the content source. Figure 4d shows that all three strategies can limit the number of transmitted Data messages at an approximately constant level. The 2DFo strategy has the highest increase of transmitted Data messages of 9.1 % from 1 to 3 requesters. For 2SF, the increase is 5.6 % and for 1DFo, it is only 3.3 %.

5   Discussion

It would be possible to use only one forwarding face and enable FIB forwarding on the same face of reception. However, this would have implications on PIT processing because Interests would be forwarded on the same face from where they were received. To avoid inefficiencies, the number of Interest forwardings would need to be limited. If each received Interest could only be forwarded once (minimum for multi-hop), it would be similar to our 2DFo strategy. Our evaluations have shown that 1DFo outperforms 2DFo, which justifies the use of two forwarding faces, which may be artificially created on the same wireless interface.

One may argue that nodes need to overhear content (for prefix registration) before Interests can be forwarded over multiple hops towards a content source. However, the same applies to existing approaches that use endpoint identifiers [1,10], i.e., each intermediate node needs to know the content source in order to forward content. To address this issue, we see three approaches. First, one could advertise prefixes, but in contrast to current routing protocols [7,15], nodes should not learn the entire topology but only the immediate neighborhood via broadcast. Second, one could add an additional message flag to enable flooding over a limited number of hops (pass-through) if no forwarding entry is configured. Third, agent-based content retrieval [2] may be used for content retrieval in delay-tolerant networks over multiple nodes.

The validity time of overheard prefixes in the FIB is still subject to more investigations and may depend on network dynamics. We believe that negative acknowledgements (NACKs) as proposed in [18] to indicate unavailability of content would not be a good option in broadcast environents: although one node can not forward the Interest, another might be able to do so. Listening to NACKs from single nodes may, therefore, not be meaningful. Therefore, in this work, we tracked content responses for transmitted Interests and deleted forwarding entries if a consecutive number of Interests has timed out.

6   Conclusions and Future Work

In this work, we have described a new approach for information-centric wireless multi-hop communication based on overhearing. In contrast to existing approaches, no endpoint identifiers are used but overheard prefixes are registered in the FIB. Evaluations have shown that the current CCN architecture does not work well for wireless multi-hop communication if multiple paths (forwarders) are available. Every node that receives a message and has a forwarding entry, will forward it immediately resulting in many duplicate transmissions. Additional data structures to maintain Interest forwarding delays can reduce the number of duplicate Interest transmissions by 93.4 % and reduce the number of collisions by 61.4 %.

We have implemented two dynamic prefix registration and forwarding strategies based on overhearing, i.e. 1DFo and 2DFo, and compared it to a static strategy, i.e., 2SF. Evaluations have shown that 1DFo outperforms both 2DFo and 2SF in terms of both transmission times and transmitted messages. The 1DFo strategy results in 27.3 % faster transmission times than 2DFo and even 38.2 % faster transmission times than 2SF. Interest aggregation and caching works efficiently even in case of multiple concurrent streams. However, Interest aggregation is more efficient with 1DFo than with 2DFo or 2SF because Interests are forwarded over the same faces. As a consequence, the number of transmitted Data messages stay approximately constant for an increasing number of requesters.

The main challenge of the described approach is the fact that content needs to be overheard to configure forwarding prefixes. While this works well for popular content, it may be more difficult for unpopular content that is requested infrequently. As part of our future work, we will investigate options to address unpopular content in wireless multi-hop environments.

References

1. Amadeo, M., Molinaro, A., Ruggeri, G.: E-CHANET: routing, forwarding and transport in Information-Centric multihop wireless networks. Comput. Commun. **36**, 792–803 (2013)

2. Anastasiades, C., El Alami, W.E.M., Braun, T.: Agent-based content retrieval for opportunistic content-centric networks. In: Mellouk, A., Fowler, S., Hoceini, S., Daachi, B. (eds.) WWIC 2014. LNCS, vol. 8458, pp. 175–188. Springer, Heidelberg (2014)

3. CCNx: http://www.ccnx.org/ (April 2015)

4. Chiocchetti, R., Perino, D., Carofiglio, G., Rossi, D., Rossini, G.: INFORM: a dynamic INterest FORwarding Mechanism for information centric networking. In: Proceedings of 3rd ACM SIGCOMM ICN, Hong Kong, pp. 9–14, August 2013

5. Chiocchetti, R., Rossi, D., Rossini, G., Carofiglio, G., Perino, D.: Exploit the known or explore the unknown? Hamlet-like doubts in ICN. In: Proceedings of ACM SIGCOMM ICN, Helsinki, Finland, pp. 7–12, August 2012

6. Grassi, G., Pesavento, D., Pau, G., Vuyyuru, R., Wakikawa, R., Zhang, L.: VANET via Named Data Networking. In: Proceedings of IEEE INFOCOM NOM, Toronto, Canada, pp. 410–415, April-May 2014

7. Hoque, M., Amin, S.O., Alyyan, A., Zhang, B., Zhang, L., Wang, L.: NLSR: named-data link state routing protocol. In: Proceedings of 3rd ACM SIGCOMM ICN, Hong Kong, pp. 15–20, August 2013

8. Jacobson, V., Smetters, D.K., Thornton, J.D., Plass, M.F., Briggs, N.H., Braynard, R.L.: Networking named content. In: Proceedings of 5th ACM CoNEXT, Rome, Italy, pp. 1–12, December 2009

9. Lee, M., Cho, K., Park, K., Kwon, T., Choi, Y.: SCAN: scalable content routing for content-aware networking. In: Proceedings of IEEE ICC, Kyoto, Japan, pp. 1–5, June 2011

10. Meisel, M., Pappas, V., Zhang, L.: Listen first, broadcast later: topology-agnostic forwarding under high dynamics. In: ACITA, London, UK, pp. 1–8, September 2010

11. Mosko, M.: CCNx messages in TLV format, January 2015. http://tools.ietf.org/html/draft-mosko-icnrg-ccnxmessages-00, Internet Draft

12. Perkins, C.E., Royer, E.M.: Ad-hoc on-demand distance vector routing. In: Proceedings of 2nd IEEE WMCSA, New Orleans, LA, USA, pp. 90–100, February 1999

13. Varga, A.: The OMNeT++ discrete event simulation system. In: ESM, Prague, Czech Republic, June 2001

14. Varvello, M., Rimac, I., Lee, U., Greenwald, L., Hilt, V.: On the Design of Content-Centric MANETs. In: Proceedings of 8th WONS, Bardonecchia, Italy, pp. 1–8, January 2011

15. Wang, L., Hoque, M., Yi, C., Alyyan, A., Zhang, B.: OSPFN: An OSPF Based Routing Protocol for Named Data Networking. Technical report, NDN Technical Report, July 2012

16. Wang, L., Wakikawa, R., Kuntz, R., Vuyyuru, R., Zhang, L.: Rapid traffic information dissemination using named data. In: Proceedings of ACM NOM, Hilton Head, SC, USA, pp. 7–12, June 2012

17. Wang, Y., Lee, K., Venkataraman, B., Shamanna, R., Rhee, I., Yang, S.: Advertising cached contents in the control plane: necessity and feasibility. In: Proceedings of IEEE INFOCOM NOMEN, Orlando, FL, USA, pp. 286–291, March 2012

18. Yi, C., Afanasyev, A., Wang, L., Zhang, B., Zhang, L.: Adaptive forwarding in named data networking. ACM SIGCOMM Comput. Commun. Rev. **42**(3), 62–67 (2012)

Formal Approach for Modeling, Verification and Performance Analysis of Wireless Sensors Network

Sajeh Zairi[(✉)], Anis Mezni, and Belhassen Zouari

LIP2 Laboratory, University of Tunis El Manar, 2092 Manar II, Tunis(ia)
{sajeh.zairi,belhassen.zouari}@fst.rnu.tn,
mezni.anis@gmail.com

Abstract. The Control of energy consumption by sensor networks and the maximization of the sensor network lifetime are the most fundamental issues. Due to the variety of protocols dedicated to the different sensor's layers and the difficulty of a real network deployment, designers need some mechanisms and tools to validate the energy consumption and to observe its impact on the network's lifetime before deployment. In this context, we have proposed a modeling approach considering the global behavior of a sensor network and allowing the estimation of the network's energy consumption. This approach is based on the concept of components oriented modeling and the expressiveness of Colored Petri Nets (CP-NET). Thus, the global model representing sensor behavior is obtained by interfacing different models each one representing the behavior of a particular component of the sensor. In this work, our interest was firstly focused on the radio because it's the most energy consumer. When observing the node functioning, we show that the radio behavior is mainly controlled by the MAC component. Therefore, we were also interested in MAC component. The generated model has been used to estimate the energy consumption and to evaluate the network lifetime. Adopting the oriented components modeling approach, we may obtain two global models, where only MAC protocol change. Obtained models, representing the behavior of mostly used MAC protocols, allow comparing the impact of these two protocols on the network's global behavior and particularly on its lifetime.

Keywords: Wireless sensor networks · Energy consumption · Network global behavior · Components oriented modeling · Colored petri nets

1 Introduction

A wireless sensor network (WSN) is a wireless network consisting of spatially distributed autonomous devices using sensors to cooperatively monitor physical or environmental conditions, such as temperature, sound, vibration, pressure, motion or pollutants, at different locations [10]. The nodes are small in size and communicate wirelessly in short distances. These tiny nodes can perform sensing, data processing and communicating. A large amount of node's energy is used when sensing the field and uploading or communicating the sensor nodes readings to a central user location known as base station.

© Springer International Publishing Switzerland 2015
M.C. Aguayo-Torres et al. (Eds.): WWIC 2015, LNCS 9071, pp. 381–395, 2015.
DOI: 10.1007/978-3-319-22572-2_28

In addition to their application diversity, sensor networks may be deployed in a variety of physical media, including air [10], liquids [4], and physical structures. Providing efficient network functioning in different situations requires nodes collaboration. Many protocols have been developed to adapt the WSN performance to a subsets of sensor network scenarios. Selecting the appropriate protocols to a particular network scenario is a challenge in itself. Thus, given the increasing sophistication of WSN algorithms - and the difficulty of modifying an algorithm once the network is deployed - there is a clear need to use formal methods to validate system performance and functionality prior implementation.

Advanced WSN algorithms present a set of challenges to formal analysis tools:

(1) Modeling time-dependent behavior. WSN algorithms may use timers; message transmission may be subject to message delays, etc. In addition, lifetime of the network is often a crucial goal, requiring power consumption modeling which is time depending.
(2) Considering different geometric entities such as locations, distances, etc.
(3) Modeling different forms of communication. The frequently used model of communication is the broadcast where only nodes within a certain distance from the sender receive the signal with sufficient signal strength. In addition, the broadcast may be subject to transmission delays. The details that need to be modeled depend on the algorithm and its level of abstraction.
(4) Incorporating probabilistic behaviors.
(5) Simulating and analyzing systems with a large number of sensor nodes scattered randomly in a sensing area.
(6) Analyzing correctness and performance are critical aspects.

Furthermore, the formalism should be intuitive and should support specifying appropriate abstraction level. In this paper, we advocate the use of Colored Petri Nets (CP-nets) [3] for the formal specification, simulation, and further analysis of WSNs behavior. CP-nets were choose as they allow to model events driving behavior (message sent, environment sensing…). They also allow to take into account all WSN's aspects in the same formalism: the hardware that implements a single node; the protocol layers; the application code and the physical environment as viewed by nodes. A WSN is composed of a set of identical node. Thus, it's interesting to model the behavior of a specific node and then instantiate it, based on the number of the nodes composing the studied WSN, to obtain a global model of the WSN. CP-nets allow such instantiation so easily using colored tokens. Moreover, CP-nets authorize hierarchical modeling, possibly with different levels of details. Thus, the global model may be modularly built. Such possibility allow to easily substitute sub-models specifying the same component functioning. Based on such ability, it will be possible to compare the impact of specific component on the same context. Another advantage, and not least, is that the numerous existing CP-nets analyze tools may be exploited to formally validate the model. Exploiting the proposed model, we can formally analyze the global safety properties of the network.

In a previous work [16], we have presented a CP-nets model representing the global behavior of a specific WSN. The difference, compared to the work presented in this paper, is that the new work introduces a generic modeling approach which may be adapted to model any considered WSN. Moreover, energy model has been introduced in this new model since energy aspect is very important for WSN.

The remain of the paper is organized as follows: Sect. 2 presents a survey of existing approaches considering the WSNs validation and particularly works based on Petri nets. Section 3 presents the proposed generic CP-nets model representing the WSN behavior. Section 4 shows experimentation and performance analysis of the proposed model. Finally, Sect. 5 concludes the paper.

2 Related Works

Due to the increasing sophistication of the algorithms dedicated to WSN and the difficulty of modifying an algorithm once the network is deployed, there is a clear need to validate system functionality and performance prior to implementation.

Different existing approaches based on simulation [1] enable rapid exploration and validation of system designs before deployment. The formal validation of the WSN performance has also been considered by existing works. Based on the considered requirements (performance evaluation or model checking purposes), a specific modeling technique is selected and employed. Petri nets were one of the adopted models for WSN modeling. In [8], Petri nets were used to model the validity of an encryption scheme applied to WSNs. In [4], a CP-net model was exploited to analyze the behavior for one of the routing protocols (Vector Based Forwarding) in WSN. The authors of [6] described the data flow of WSN using generalized stochastic Petri nets (GSPN). Obtained model was used to analyze the impact of data aggregation on network latency and consequently in sensor's battery life. However, the proposed model didn't show a real estimation of node's energy consumption. In [10] authors proposed two methods to model the processor's energy consumption: Markov chains, and Petri nets. They demonstrate that the use of Petri nets is more accurate than the use of Markov chains. Using Petri nets they developed a model of a node that can accurately estimate the processor energy consumption. The global WSN model can be obtained by the composition of the node models. This paper has only focused on the processor energy consumption and didn't consider the other components consumption.

There are many other works related to the modeling and the analyzing of WSN [2, 6].

The major drawback is that most of existing works [13] have considered specific modeling problem. Generally, they represent the behavior of a specific protocol (routing, MAC...). In most case, the proposed model is based on an ordinary Petri net which not exploit the CP-nets features to obtain more compact model.

By observing the behavior of the various nodes' components, we can notice that they are too dependent on each other. Thus, to observe the real impact of a specific component on the network behavior, a global model must be used.

To our knowledge, Glonemo [9] is the only existing approach modeling the global behavior of a WSN based on a formal model. Moreover, it is the first work interesting to formally prove the maximization of the networks lifetime. In the presented model, each component of the node is modeled by a dedicated automaton. The overall model of each node results on the product of the different automaton representing the behavior of the various components of the node. Similarly, the model representing the global WSN behavior is the product of all nodes automaton. The problem of the state explosion is the major constraint of this approach. In this case, generating all the system's states and above checking the desired properties is too difficult even impossible.

To avoid state explosion constraint, we present a formal generic modeling approach, based on CP-nets, allowing to represent the global WSN behavior. The use of CP-nets allows defining a generic model representing the behavior of a specific component. The global model of the studied WSN is obtained be instantiating the CP-net model associated with each specific component. Such initiation is made using the initial marking of a subset of places. Using such approach, interfacing (synchronizing) all models, representing the behavior of the WSN components, is directly made based on the CP-nets semantic.

3 Proposed CP-Net Model Representing WSN Behavior

Based on the WSN characteristics, a components oriented modeling approach may be adopted during the development of the proposed model. Indeed, the behavior of a particular node is defined through a synchronization of all its sub-components. Hence, modeling separately each sub-component behavior and then interfacing interacting components seems to be a convenient method. Consequently, the global model is built more easily. Based on such approach, we can easily alter and obtain a global model where only a subset of components changes. The generated global models allow comparing two solutions where only a subset of component changes (such as the MAC protocol, for example) in a realistic context. Based on the obtained results, designers may choose the most suitable components according to the application's objectives. The proposed model must also allow studying properties related to energy consumption and their impact on the network lifetime before the deployment of the WSN. Thus, proposed model must include appropriate techniques to reliably estimate energy consumption.

The proposed approach which may be followed to obtain the global model of the WSN will be introduced based on two components of the node's behavior: radio and MAC components. In fact, as previously shown one of the major objectives of this work is the study of energy consumption and its impact on the network lifetime before deployment. Our interest was firstly focused on the radio because it's the most energy consumer. Seen that the radio behavior is mainly controlled by the MAC component. Therefore, we were also interested in this component. The proposed model was developed based on a hierarchical approach. The decomposition of the global component model is performed according to a functional approach. A local sub-model is associated with each function detailing its achievement. The high-level of the model represents the basic functions as standalone modules. It is simplified and gives an overview of the system that is being modeled. In the high-level model, each sub-module is represented by a substitution transition. Each module (specifically each of the substitution transitions) is associated with a CP-net describing its realization.

Models associated with those different modules are synchronized through fusion places.

All presented modeling specificity is fairly general, so they could be applied to various WSN applications and protocols. For constructing and analyzing the model, CPN-Tools is used.

3.1 CP-Net Modeling the Radio Component

By observing the functioning of the radio component (transmitter and receiver), we distinguish four states:

- Idle state: where the radio is on, but it is not really exploited. In other words, the node is not currently receiving or transmitting. This state induces a great waste of energy due to the passive listening of the channel.
- Sleep state: where the radio is turned off. In this state, energy is saved.
- Transmission state: where the radio is transmitting a packet.
- Reception state: where the radio is receiving a packet.

When functioning, the radio component transit from one state to another based on input events. While it is in a particular state, the radio consumes energy. To consider this consumption, a power value is associated with each state. By multiplying this value to the time spent in the specific state, we obtain the energy consumed during the period of stay in this state. We have also associated with each transition, between two different states, the time and the amount of energy required for its firing. By multiplying these two parameters, we obtain energy consumed for the achievement of the state's transition. To calculate the energy required to reach destination state from a source state, we have defined the following function:

$$Eng = (CT - TE) * PE + (PT * TT) \tag{1}$$

Where

- CT: the current time
- TE: time of entry to the starting state
- PE: power value associated to the current state
- PT: the power associated with the transition
- TT: time needed to transit from the source state to the destination state.

The first term of this equation computes the amount of energy consumed in the previous state. The second term represents the amount of energy required to reach the destination state from the source state. So, the residual energy of node may be updated by subtracting the energy consumption devoted to both: the state and the transition (calculated based on Eq. 1). Such abstraction allows to easily model a real estimation of the nodes residual energy. More elaborate equation can also be considered. Only in this paper, we are interested in the modeling approach and not in the energy consumption estimation.

As described above, the model representing the generic behavior of the radio component includes four substitution transitions as shown in Fig. 1 (the high-level of the radio model). Each substitution transition models a generic function:

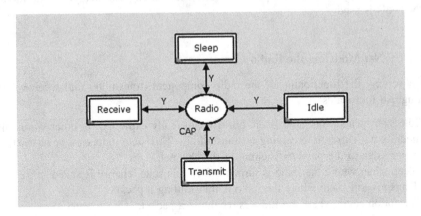

Fig. 1. The CP-net modeling the behavior of Radio component

- The substitution transition "*Sleep*" models the passage to the state "Sleep".
- The transition to the state "Idle" is modeled by the substitution transition "*Idle*".
- The transition to state "Transmission" is modeled by the substitution transition "*Transmit*".
- The substitution transition "*Receive*" models the transition to state "Reception".

A substitution transition is enabled when at least one of its internal transitions is enabled. A sub-CP-net is associated with each of these substitution transitions refining its realization. Due to the paper limitation, we will not detail all the subnets associated with those transitions. Note that each sub-net included a place "*SensorEng*" associating with each node its residual energy. Those places are fused. Thus, they handle the same tokens providing a real estimation of the nodes remaining energy.

3.2   CP-Net Radio Transmit

The subnet associated with the substitution transition "*Transmission*" is represented by Fig. 2.

The occurrence of a token in the place "*Order to send*" indicates that the node has a message to send and it has already found the Channel Free. Therefore, the node will fire the transition "*S-trans*", "*I-trans*" or "*R-trans*" depending respectively whether it was in the state "*Sleep*", "*Idle*" or "*Receive*". The place "*Order to send*" allows interfacing the transmission radio model with external models particularly the MAC model. Indeed, when the application generates a message to be send, the MAC layout first verifies that the channel is free. If it is the case, the MAC component will order the radio to transit to the transmission state. Thus, the input place "*Order to send*" in the

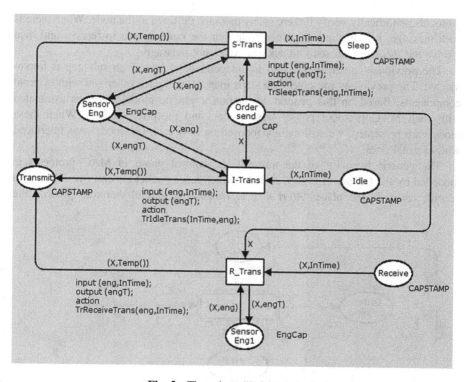

Fig. 2. The subnet *"Transmission"*

transmission radio model must be fused with the equivalent output place in the MAC component model.

Firing each of those transitions consumes time and energy. Thus, we have associated with each of those transitions a function computing this consumption as described above (Sect. 3.1). We can then update the residual energy of the node modelled by a token in the place *"SensorEng"*. This computation is modelled by the functions *"TrSleepTrans"*, *"TrReceiveTrans"* and *"TrIdleTrans"* associated respectively with the transitions *"S-trans"*, *"R-trans"* and *"I-trans"*. When the node enters each of these states, the time of entry will be memorized in the token indicating the state of the node.

3.3 CP-Net Modeling the MAC Layer

The radio functioning is the main source of energy consumption and the activity of this component is widely controlled by the MAC layer. The activity of MAC protocols may be divided in two phases: transmission and reception control. These two phases are independent on how they are implemented by the specified MAC protocol.

For transmission control, the MAC protocols verify that the channel is free for transmission, reserve it, alert the destination node of the message and really transmit the message when the destination is able to receive. For reception control, the MAC protocols periodically verify if there is any message destined to the node. When there is such message, inform the transmitter node that the node is able to receive and then receive the message and send an acknowledgement message.

The previously given description is independent of how each sub-step is implemented. The previously presented sub steps interact with each other and with external components. Based on this generic description a generic model has been associated with each MAC protocol phase: transmission and reception control. When these models are presented, we will mainly focused on how each sub-model was interfaced with external ones.

The generic behavior of the transmission control phase in MAC protocols is modelled by the CP-net of Fig. 3. A node, which has a packet to send (modelled by a specific token in the place "Alert msg to transmit"), should therefore precede the

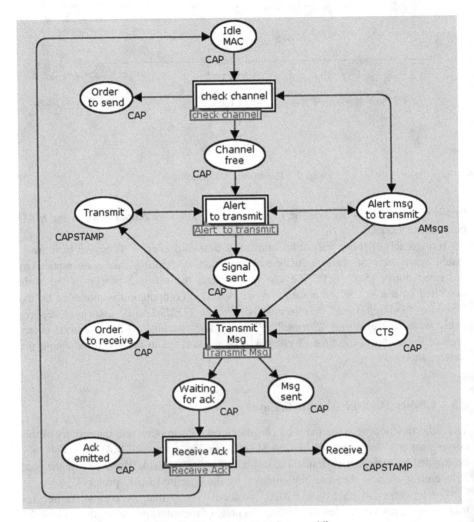

Fig. 3. The subnet "MAC transmit"

transmission of its packet by an alert phase. During this phase, the transmitter node must inform the destination node that it has a message destined to it. All nodes not concerned by this message may switch off their radio, during the transmission period, to save energy. Alert phase should be longer enough to ensure that the destination node will be informed. This sub-step is modelled by the substitution transition *"Alert to transmit"*. The input of this transition is that the channel is free and the transmitter node is already in transmission state. The first information is modelled by the tokens in place *"Channel free"*. This place is fused with the equivalent place in a model representing the verification of the channel and its allocation to the asker node (substitution transition *"Check channel"*). The second information is modelled by the tokens in the place *"Transmit"* fused with the same place of the subnet Transmission. The output of this substitution transition is the authorization of the transmission modelled by a token in the place *"CTS"*.

When alert phase is achieved, the MAC component begins message transmission (modelled by the substitution transition *"Transmit Msg"*) when it has already received the permission from the destination node.

At the end of the transmission phase, the transmitter node waits for an acknowledgement message before returning to the MAC idle state. Reception of the acknowledgement message and its processing is modelled by the substitution transition *"Ack reception"*. The implementation of each substitution transition will depend on the specificities of the chosen MAC protocol. Due to the paper limitation, we will not detail them. However, the interface places are always the same.

The generic behavior of the reception control phase in MAC protocols is modelled by the CP-net represented by Fig. 4. The first sub-step of this phase models the nodes wake-up and the channel probation. Indeed, nodes are assumed to be the most of time in a radio sleep states to save energy. Periodically, each node wakes-up and probes the channel. If it detects a signal on the channel informing that there is a message destined to it, the node remains listening in order to receive the data packet after sending a clear to send control message to the transmitter node. Message reception represents the second sub-step of the reception phase. At the end of the reception, the receiver node sends an acknowledgement message to the transmitter node to accuse the correct reception of the data packet.

In the CP-net model *"Mac Receive"*, the first sub-step is modelled by the substitution transition *"Wake up and probe"*. The second sub-step is modelled by the substitution transition *"Receive Msg"*. The last sub-step is modelled by the substitution transition *"Transmit Ack"*. In the same way as MAC transmission phase, the implementation of each substitution transition, modeling MAC reception sub-steps, will depend on the specificities of the chosen MAC protocol. The places described in Table 1 allow interfacing this model with the models of external components.

Adopting the oriented components modeling approach and based on the expressive power of CP-nets, we presented global and hierarchical generic models representing the behavior of two particular components of a node: radio and MAC components. The high level subnets are independent of the modelled components specificities. Indeed, all radio components despite their diversity, transit between four states. In the same way, all MAC protocols distinguish two phases: transmission and reception control. Each of these phases includes the same subset of sub-steps as shown above. However, the

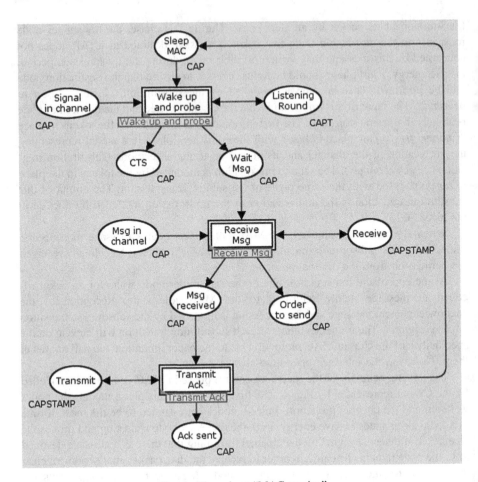

Fig. 4. The subnet "MAC receive"

Table 1. Interfacing places

Place	External component	Equivalent place
CTS	MAC transmit	CTS
Signal in channel	MAC transmit	Signal sent
Msg in channel	MAC transmit	Msg sent
Ack sent	MAC transmit	Ack emitted
Transmit	Radio transmission	Transmit
Order to send	Radio transmission	Order to send
Receive	Radio reception	Receive

subnets modeling the achievement of each sub-step will depend on the chosen components. Based on such properties only subnets associated with substitution transition will be modified to model the specificities of chosen components. Interfacing places are always the same as described above.

All presented models may be instantiated according to the number of nodes composing the final network to be studied. The instantiation is made through the initial marking of the CP-net. For example, to model a WSN including 5 nodes, the place "*Sensor*" will handle 5 tokens specifying the identities of the nodes. While place "*SensorEng*" will handle 5 tokens associating with the identity of each sensor its initial energy reserve. Thus, we note that obtaining a global model representing the WSNs behavior is very simplified. We don't need to duplicate or to synchronize the subnets, as it is the case with Glonemo model. Therefore, the presented model is not constrained by the problem of states space explosion.

4 Model Exploitation

As the model is executable, it may be simulated. The simulated network is composed of 6 nodes including the base station. Nodes were deployed randomly in a rectangle area of 500*500 m². Table 2 presents the different parameters used to evaluate our network's performance.

Table 2. Simulation's parameters

Deployment region	500*500 m^2
Number of nodes	5
Initial energy reserve	1 joule
Transceiver (Tx, Rx, Sleep)	27 mA/18 mA/1 mA
Packet transmission's time	160 ms
Ackittement transmission's time	32 ms
Back off duration before each transmission	160 ms

During the simulation, we can observe the energy spent and the correct messages transmission from the source node to the base station. A set of monitors can be integrated to the CP-net model to observe its simulation and produce output files which may be used for drawing curves. Simulation may be also used to estimate the network lifetime and to compare and choose the appropriate protocols (routing, MAC, activity scheduling…) to prove their efficiency regarding the considered application.

4.1 Impact of MAC Protocols on Sensor's Energy Consumption

In order to observe the influence of MAC protocols, we simulate two network models where only the MAC subnets change. The topology of the simulated WSN is represented by Fig. 5. In the simulated WSN, we assume that initially all nodes have the same energy reserve. We assume that node 1 has two data message to transmit to the base station. Simulations stop when the second message sent by the node 1 reached the base station. Table 3 shows the simulation results.

The first MAC protocol simulated is the B-MAC [17]. This protocol uses the preamble sampling technique to reduce power consumption during idle listening. In

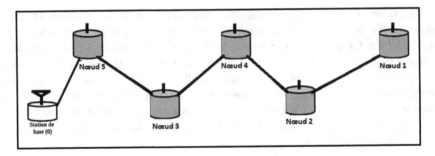

Fig. 5. Simulated WSN

Table 3. Energy consumption for two messages transmission

	Energy spent during the transmission of Msg 1	Energy spent during the transmission of Msg 2
B-MAC	(node 1,68078)	(node 1,68078)
	(node 2,64276)	(node 2,64276)
	(node 3,98527)	(node 3,98527)
	(node 4,100654)	(node 4,100654)
	(node 5,53143)	(node 5,53143)
Global Consumption	384 678	384 678
WiseMAC	(node 1,68078)	(node 1,15129)
	(node 2,64276)	(node 2,30463)
	(node 3,98527)	(node 3,19594)
	(node 4,100654)	(node 4,20473)
	(node 5,53143)	(node 5,1081)
Global Consumption	384 678	86 740

other words, the transmitter should precede the sending of its packet by a long preamble in order to ensure that its receiver is waked. WiseMAC [15] is the second MAC protocol simulated. Based on the information of the sampling schedule of directs neighbors, transmitter node may use a shorter preamble. The sleep schedules of the neighboring nodes are updated based on specific information included in the acknowledgment message (ACK).

This simulation results show that the two models behave similarly during the transmission of the first message. Such result is predictable, as for the first transmission, the use of a long preamble is necessary to both models (for WiseMAC sampling schedule information is not already known). These transmission costs 384678 µjoules. For the second transmission, the cost of energy remains the same using the B-MAC. However, it decreased to 86740 µjoules using the WiseMAC protocol. Indeed, knowing the wake-up period of its direct neighbor, the transmitter avoids sending a long preamble consuming a lot of energy as it is always the case with the protocol B-MAC. Figure 6 shows the different level of energy consumption for each node after the reception of the second packet by the sink node. Noting that, we measure the energy consumption only during the transmission of an event. However, if we simulate our network model for a long period we may show an important difference between the two protocols.

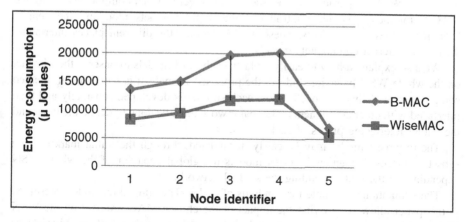

Fig. 6. Energy consumption of each node after the second packet's transmission

4.2 Calculating Worst Case of the WSN Lifetime

The developed CP-net may be also used to estimate the worst case of the WSN lifetime which corresponds to the shortest network's lifetime. Whereas, we must first choose the criteria that defines the loss of this network. Indeed, the life of a network is always determined relative to a particular criterion: either the first node is dead or when no more nodes have remaining energy or when the network is no longer connected. For our simulation, we choose the first criterion. In other word, we will stop simulation just after the first node's battery exhaustion.

In our case, only the node 1 is assumed to have alert message destined to the base station. We suppose that the initial energy reserve of all nodes is equal to 1 Joule. For this simulation, we study the impact of chosen MAC protocols on the network lifetime.

Based on these results, we show that the use of WiseMAC protocol increases the lifetime of the network compared to the B-MAC protocol. In addition, observing previous results, we see that the total number of messages sent by node 1 during its lifetime when using the WiseMAC is much greater compared to B-MAC protocol. So, we can conclude that the WiseMAC guarantees the network efficiency as it ensures a long lifetime (Table 4).

Table 4. The Arrangement of channels

Model MAC Used	Number of Messages sent	Network lifetime
B-MAC	9	167300
WiseMAC	12	227544

5   Conclusion

This paper has presented a CP-net modeling approach considering the global behavior of a WSN. We have particularly focused on two specific WSN components: radio and MAC component. We have introduced the high-level nets modeling the generic behavior of these components. These models include the different places interfacing them with external components models.

We also explained how to easily replace a subset of models to observe their impact on the whole WSN behavior. Indeed, the proposed formalism is based on an oriented components modeling approach. Thus, each sub-net is developed separately and then interfaced with other components. The major work must be done to define the input and the output interfacing places of each model.

The proposed model may be easily instantiated, through the initial marking of a subset of places. Instantiated CP-net models the global behavior of the whole WSN depending on the nodes madding the studied network.

The simulation is feasible for hundreds of nodes. The simulation studies presented in this paper allowed verifying the impact of the chosen MAC protocol on the WSN lifetime. The comparison of two models, where only the sub-net of the MAC layer changes, helped to see that WiseMAC protocol increases the lifetime of the network by 36 % compared to B-MAC protocol. Moreover, since the model is based on a formal model, formal validation techniques may be exploited. We are working on the exploitation of existing formal verification tools, to validate the behavior of the studied model.

References

1. Chandrasekaran, V., Anitha, S., Shanmugam, A.: A research survey on experimental tools for simulating wireless sensor networks. Int. J. Comput. Appl. **79**(16), 1–9 (2013)
2. Despaux, F., Song, Y.-Q., Lahmadi, A.: Modelling and performance analysis of wireless sensor networks using process mining techniques: ContikiMAC use case. In: DCOSS 2014, pp. 1–8 (2014)
3. Jensen, K., Kristensen, L.: Colored Petri Nets – Modeling and Validation of Concurrent Systems. Springer, Heidelberg (2009)
4. Ibrahim, D., et al.: Coloured petri net model for vector-based forwarding routing protocol. In: International conference on Computing Technology and Information Management (2014)
5. Jurdak, R., Lopes, C.V., Baldi, P.: Battery lifetime estimation and optimization for underwater sensor networks. IEEE Sens. Netw. Oper. **2006**, 397–420 (2004)
6. Lacerda, B., Lima, P.U.: Petri nets as an analysis tool for data flow in wireless sensor networks. In: 1st Portuguese Conference on WSNs, Coimbra, Portugal, pp. 1–6 (2011)
7. Venkatesan, L., et al.: A survey on modeling and enhancing reliability of wireless sensor network. Wireless Sens. Netw., 41–51 (2013)
8. Rodriguez, H., Carvajal, R., Ontiveros, B., Soto, I.: Using petri net for modeling and analysis of an encryption scheme for wireless sensor network. In: Pawlewski, P. (ed.) InTech (2010)

9. Samper, L., Maraninchi, F., Mounier, L., Mandel, L.: Glonemo: global and accurate formal models for the analysis of ad-hoc sensor networks. In: Proceedings of the First International Conference on Integrated Internet ad hoc and Sensor Networks. ACM (2006)
10. Shareef, A., Zhu, Y.: Energy modeling sensor nodes based on petri nets. In: Parallel Processing, pp. 101–110 (2010)
11. Xu, N.: A survey of sensor network applications. IEEE Commun. Mag. **40**(8), 102–114 (2002)
12. Yu, Z., Liu, Y., Cai, Y.: Design of an energy-efficient distributed multi-level clustering algorithm for wireless sensor networks. In: Wireless Communications, Networking and Mobile Computing, WiCOM 2008 (2008)
13. Ben-Othman, J., Diagne, S., Mokdad, L., Yahia, B.: Performance evaluation of a medium access control protocol for wireless sensor networks using petri nets, HET-NETs 2010 (2010)
14. Azgomi, M.A., Khalili, A.: Performance evaluation of sensor medium access control protocol using colored petri nets. Electron. Notes Theor. Comput. Sci. **242**, 31–42 (2009)
15. El-Hoiydi, A., Decotignie, J.-D.: WiseMAC: an ultra low power MAC protocol for multi-hop wireless sensor networks. In: Nikoletseas, S.E., Rolim, J.D. (eds.) ALGOSENSORS 2004. LNCS, vol. 3121, pp. 18–31. Springer, Heidelberg (2004)
16. Zairi, S., Niel, E., Zouari, B.: Global generic model for formal validation of the wireless sensor networks properties. In: 18th IFAC World Congress Milano (Italy), August 28–September 2 (2011)
17. Polastre, J., Hill, J., Culler, D.: Versatile low power media access for sensor networks. In: Proceedings of the Second ACM Conference on Embedded Networked Sensor Systems (SenSys), November 3–5, 2004

Optimization and Verification of the TR-MAC Protocol for Wireless Sensor Networks

Sarwar Morshed$^{(\boxtimes)}$ and Geert Heijenk

University of Twente, Enschede, The Netherlands
{s.morshed,geert.heijenk}@utwente.nl

Abstract. Energy-efficiency is an important requirement in the design of communication protocols for wireless sensor networks (WSN). TR-MAC is an energy-efficient medium access control (MAC) layer protocol for low power WSN that exploits transmitted-reference (TR) modulation in the physical layer. The underlying TR modulation in TR-MAC provides faster synchronization and signal acquisition without requiring channel estimation and complex rake receiver in the receiver side. TR modulation also enables multiple access for a pair of nodes using different frequency offsets. This paper introduces an explicit expression that allows the TR-MAC protocol to minimize its energy consumption, depending on the experienced traffic load. Furthermore, an implementation of the protocol in the OMNeT++ simulator with MiXiM simulation framework is introduced, and analytical results introduced in [13] are verified by simulation results obtained using the simulator.

Keywords: Energy-efficiency · MAC protocol · Energy-driven · TR modulation · TR-MAC

1 Introduction

Low-power wireless sensor devices have gained popularity in past decade. These low-power devices have to deploy an efficient medium access control protocol together with an efficient modulation technique in the underlying physical layer to enable low power operation. TR modulation is such a low-power spread-spectrum technique [7] where the transmitter sends the unmodulated carrier signal together with the modulated signal in the wireless medium separated by a frequency offset already known to the receiver. The receiver restores the original signal using the known frequency offset by performing self-correlation with the frequency shifted version of the same signal [11]. Hence the receiver enjoys faster synchronization with reduced signal acquisition time without the need of a complex rake receiver or channel estimation or power-hungry stable oscillators. Moreover, multiple frequency offsets using TR modulation can provide implicit addressing as link identifiers. As a result, the TR modulation with its simplified receiver architecture enabling low power, low data rate and low duty cycle operations provides more flexibility to the upper MAC layer for WSNs.

© Springer International Publishing Switzerland 2015
M.C. Aguayo-Torres et al. (Eds.): WWIC 2015, LNCS 9071, pp. 396–410, 2015.
DOI: 10.1007/978-3-319-22572-2_29

The radio transceiver dominates the energy consumption of a node in a WSN. To offer low power consumption, TR-MAC employs duty cycling by an asynchronous preamble sampling strategy where each node is allowed to switch off its transceiver as much as possible and switch it on periodically to sense channel activity. After the first time communication, the nodes can remember other nodes next wake up time and can communicate at that time to reduce energy consumption, which is suitable for a low duty-cycle based protocol operation. Even though the receiver architecture is simplified significantly with many attractive advantages to exploit in MAC layer, the transmitter consumes more power to transmit individual bits since the reference signal is also sent. This motivated the authors to design a new energy-efficient MAC protocol for this context as minimizing energy consumption is always a big challenge in WSNs. This paper optimizes the energy-efficient low-power TR-MAC protocol introduced in [12,13], which exploits the TR modulation characteristics in the MAC layer for WSNs. In addition, this paper provides an implementation of the TR-MAC protocol using OMNeT++ simulator and MiXiM simulation framework described in [9] and also provides a validation of the analytical models.

The contributions of this paper are as follows: (1) we provide an explicit optimization for the previously introduced TR-MAC protocol depending on the experienced traffic load; (2) we introduce the detailed design of TR-MAC by means of a finite state machine and implement the protocol in the OMNeT++ simulator using the MiXiM simulation framework; (3) we provide a verification of the analytical models of TR-MAC protocol introduced in [13] to analyze the energy consumption using simulated results obtained from the simulator.

This paper is structured as follows: related work in Sect. 2 is followed by TR-MAC protocol design in Sect. 3. Later on, Sect. 4 presents the TR-MAC modeling and optimization and Sect. 5 details the implementation in simulator. Finally, Sect. 6 gives the results and analysis followed by the conclusions and future work in Sect. 7.

2 Related Work

Energy-efficiency in MAC protocols for WSNs has been studied extensively in the past decade by researchers, see e.g., [1,3]. As the transmitter using TR modulation has a power penalty, we focus on energy efficient MAC protocols for our research. Contention-less TDMA-like MAC protocols, such as [8], are good for high traffic load but energy inefficient for low data rate WSNs because of its requirement of network-wide time-slot synchronization. Protocols with common active period, like [4,15], are good for periodic traffic but they also require a certain amount of network-wide active period schedule synchronization. Asynchronous preamble sampling protocols allow the node to sleep most of the time without the need of any network-wide synchronization, thus they are the most energy efficient category of MAC layer protocols, as confirmed in [3].

The simple preamble sampling protocol B-MAC [14] makes the transmitter to send a long preamble covering two consecutive channel sampling of the receiver, and the receiver listens the rest of the preamble before receiving the data packet. WiseMAC [6] takes this basic preamble sampling technique to operate in unsynchronized state and adds a synchronized state using receiver-driven communication strategy where the transmitter adapts the preamble length by remembering the receiver's next periodic wake up time. However, per packet overhead in low traffic increases the energy consumption in unsynchronized link state since the potential receiver and all the overhearers has to listen the complete preamble before receiving the data packet. Furthermore, WiseMAC lacks a transmitter-driven strategy in synchronized state and has to use long preambles for broadcasting instead of short ones in unsynchronized state since the protocol does not adapt duty cycles depending on the changing traffic pattern.

The packetized preamble sampling protocols, like X-MAC [2], enables the transmitter to send a packetized preamble and listen for an acknowledgement and repeat this process till an acknowledgement is received from the receiver. However, X-MAC does not adapt its preamble-listen duration by taking any advantage of the previous communication to shorten its preamble-listen iterations length. Also X-MAC does not send any acknowledgement after successful data packet transmission. CSMA-MPS [10] and ContikiMAC [5] also packetizes the preamble and iterates with listen cycles to optimize the unsynchronized link communication. Furthermore, both these protocols communicate in receiver-driven way by remembering the receiver's next wake up time but they lack the transmitter-driven strategy.

X-MAC and WiseMAC are very common protocols for asynchronous preamble sampling category of protocols. Thus TR-MAC protocol is compared with these two protocols.

3   TR-MAC Protocol Design

Our proposed TR-MAC protocol uses the asynchronous preamble sampling technique to exploit TR modulation characteristics in the underlying physical layer, to mitigate the power penalty of the transmitter side and to ensure energy-efficiency. The TR-MAC protocol has three basic states: (1) first time communication; (2) unsynchronized link state; and (3) synchronized link state, as given in Fig. 1. The first time communication is presented as a separate link state although communication takes place in unsynchronized fashion; because the protocol initializes in this state by performing neighbor discovery, exchanging MAC address and establishing link identifiers using frequency offsets.

As a preamble sampling protocol, the nodes in TR-MAC unsynchronized link state sleep most of the time and have periodic duty cycling to sense activity in the channel. The receiver using TR modulation saves energy by shortening its idle listening with the capability of detecting a very small preamble since it requires small signal acquisition time and enjoys faster synchronization. Thus we packetize the preamble and add a small data packet with the preamble and refer to it as preamble-data for the rest of this paper. Big data packets will be segmented and sent with an indication to

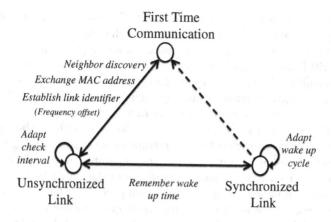

Fig. 1. TR-MAC: Three link states

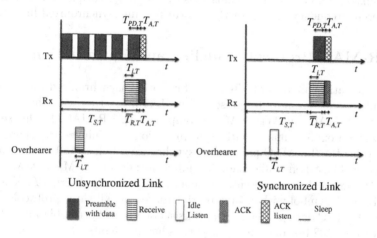

Fig. 2. TR-MAC protocol operation

the receiver to continue listening, but at this moment are out of scope of this paper. The transmitter using TR modulation transmits a preamble-data using the default frequency offset, then waits for the receiver acknowledgement and repeats this cycle until an acknowledgement is received. Receiving an acknowledgement from the receiver marks a successful communication. Thus the transmitter saves energy by shortening its preamble length. Potential overhearers can return to sleep after detecting one preamble-data packet and decoding the link identifier based on the type of preamble and the used frequency offset. The protocol operation is presented in Fig. 2.

In order to move to synchronized state, the transmitter and receiver pair has to agree on future communication time instance and frequency offset. This can happen in two ways: using a receiver-driven or a transmitter-driven strategy. For the receiver-driven case, the receiver sends its future periodic channel sampling time based on optimizing the check interval for a given traffic load in the acknowledgement packet. Thus the transmitter will delay the next packet transmission till the receiver's next periodic channel sampling time, meaning that the transmitter will follow the receiver; hence the term receiver-driven communication. For transmitter-driven case, the transmitter proposes a time instance and receivers adds an extra channel sampling time. Thus the receiver follows the transmitter and hence the term transmitter-driven communication.

The MAC layer enjoys tremendous flexibilities because of the options to communicate in either receiver-driven or transmitter-driven strategy for both link layer and multi-hop communication. For example, one node having less energy can transfer energy burden by requesting other node to follow its lead and can effectively operate like an energy-driven protocol. Efficient broadcasting can take place where one node makes its first-hop neighbors to follow its lead. Furthermore, TR-MAC protocol provides an efficient multiple access scheme to avoid collisions and costly retransmissions by enabling multiple pairs of nodes to use different frequency offsets for their corresponding synchronized link states.

4   TR-MAC Protocol Modeling and Optimization

The mathematical models of TR-MAC for both unsynchronized and synchronized link states were initially presented in [12,13] together with the analytical models for X-MAC and WiseMAC to compare with TR-MAC. In this section, we present an explicit mathematical optimization to minimize the energy consumption for the TR-MAC protocol unsynchronized link state by adapting the check interval based on traffic load. A symbol specific for TR-MAC, X-MAC and WiseMAC protocol are represented by comma separated subscript T, X and W respectively. A symbol without a subscript represents all three protocols.

The TR-MAC data packet $T_{PD,T}$, consists of 8 bits of preamble $T_{P,T}$, 16 bits of header $T_{H,T}$, 32 bits of data $T_{Data,T}$; thus having 56 bits. Data rate of 25 kbps is chosen for measurements. The sleeping time and power are represented by $T_{S,T}$ and $P_{S,T}$ respectively. The sampling interval or check interval $T_{W,T}$ includes the sleeping time between two consecutive periodic listening intervals of a node and one periodic listen cycle $T_{i,T}$; hence $T_{W,T} = T_{S,T} + T_{i,T}$. The switching time and power consumption to switch the transceiver among sleeping, sending and receiving states are much smaller compared to other values; thus are neglected in our modeling. The symbols and values for TR-MAC, X-MAC and WiseMAC are given in Table 1. Figure 2 also depicts the relevant notations.

A. Unsynchronized link state: The energy consumption for the TR-MAC protocol in unsynchronized link state is given by

$$E_T^{unsync} = \lambda(E_{Tx,T}^{unsync} + E_{Rx,T}^{unsync} + (n-2)E_{OH,T}) + nE_{PL,T} \qquad (1)$$

where E_T^{unsync} represents energy consumption of the total system that uses TR-MAC protocol, λ being the packet arrival rate, $E_{Tx,T}^{unsync}$ is energy to transmit a packet, $E_{Rx,T}^{unsync}$ is energy to receive a packet, $E_{OH,T}$ is overhearing energy

Table 1. System parameters

Symbol	Description	TR-MAC	X-MAC	WiseMAC
T_P	Preamble	8 bits	65 bits	T_W
T_{Data}	Data	32 bits	32 bits	32 bits
T_H	Header	16 bits	16 bits	16 bits
T_A	Acknowledgement	24 bits	65 bits	80 bits
T_i	Periodic listen	40 bits	195 bits	8 bits
P_{Tx}	Tx power	2 mW	1 mW	1 mW
P_{Rx}	Rx power	1 mW	1 mW	1 mW

and $E_{PL,T}$ is energy for periodic listening. We assume n nodes where one node transmits, another node listens and $(n-2)$ other nodes act as overhearers. The energy spent for packet transmission is characterized by the number of times the packet has to be transmitted until the receiver is awake and acknowledges it, multiplied with the energy spent for a transmission. The energy spent for packet reception is characterized by the additional time the receiver is listening beyond the periodic listening together with the energy for transmitting an acknowledgment. An overhearer receives one iteration of the preamble-data only, then sleeps without sending acknowledgement after realizing it was not the target node. The energy to send a packet, receive a packet, periodic listening and overhearing are given respectively by Eqs. 2, 3, 4 and 5

$$E_{Tx,T}^{unsync} = (\frac{1}{2}\frac{(T_{S,T} + T_{P,T})^2}{(T_{i,T} + T_{S,T})(T_{PD,T} + T_{A,T})} + 1) \\ * (P_{Tx,T}T_{PD,T} + P_{Rx,T}T_{A,T}), \tag{2}$$

$$E_{Rx,T}^{unsync} = P_{Rx,T}(\overline{T}_{R,T} - T_{i,T}) + P_{Tx,T}T_{A,T}, \tag{3}$$

$$E_{PL,T} = \frac{P_{Rx,T}T_{i,T} + P_{S,T}T_{S,T}}{T_{S,T} + T_{i,T}}, \tag{4}$$

$$E_{OH,T} = P_{Rx,T}(\overline{T}_{R,T} - T_{i,T}). \tag{5}$$

Here $\overline{T}_{R,T}$ represents the expected value of extended listening duration for the receiver. All these equations for TR-MAC unsynchronized link state are explained together with the expressions for X-MAC and WiseMAC protocols in [12,13] and are valid for at most one packet arrival per check interval duration.

B. Optimization of unsynchronized link state: The energy consumption for unsynchronized link state of TR-MAC protocol depends on the chosen check interval. We observed that the energy consumption reaches its minimum value if the protocol can optimize its check interval. Therefore we derive a mathematical expression to find the optimum check interval for the TR-MAC protocol. We use the well known technique to find out a minimum value by first differentiating the equation with respect to the respected variable, then evaluating the differentiated result for that variable. Thus we take the mathematical expressions of Eq. 1 and differentiate with respect to the check interval $T_{W,T}$, which is given by Eq. 6

$$
\begin{aligned}
\frac{dE_{Tx,T}^{unsync}}{dT_{W,T}} = {} & \frac{nP_{S,T}}{T_{W,T}} - \frac{n(P_{Rx,T}T_{i,T} - P_{S,T}(T_{i,T} - T_{W,T}))}{T_{W,T}^2} \\
& - \left(\frac{(T_{P,T} - T_{i,T} + T_{W,T})^2}{2T_{W,T}^2 \, (T_{A,T} + T_{PD,T})} - \frac{2(T_{P,T} - T_{i,T} + T_{W,T})}{2T_{W,T} \, (T_{A,T} + T_{PD,T})} \right) \\
& * \lambda \, (P_{Rx,T}T_{A,T} + P_{Tx,T}T_{PD,T}) .
\end{aligned}
\tag{6}
$$

Afterwards, we find out the optimized check interval $T_{W,T}^*$ by evaluating Eq. 6 and the result is given by Eq. 7

$$
\begin{aligned}
T_{W,T}^* = {} & [\lambda(P_{Rx,T}T_{A,T} + P_{Tx,T}T_{PD,T}) * \{\lambda(P_{Rx,T}T_{A,T} + P_{Tx,T}T_{PD,T}) \\
& * (T_{i,T}^2 + T_{P,T}^2) + 2n(T_{A,T}T_{i,T} + T_{PD,T}T_{i,T})(P_{Rx,T} - P_{S,T}) \\
& - 2\lambda T_{P,T}T_{i,T}(P_{Rx,T}T_{A,T} + P_{Tx,T}T_{PD,T})\}]^{1/2} \\
& / \, \lambda(P_{Rx,T}T_{A,T} + P_{Tx,T}T_{PD,T}).
\end{aligned}
\tag{7}
$$

This expression can be evaluated by supplying individual input values for respective variables to optimize the check interval. We also derived similar expressions for X-MAC and WiseMAC for optimizing the check interval but left the derivations for the lack of space.

C. Synchronized link state: In the synchronized link state of the TR-MAC protocol, a transmitter and receiver pair communicates at a previously agreed time and frequency offset. Using a known time for future communication allows the transmitter to shorten its data-listen iterations. And using a different frequency offset will avoid the overhearers. However, the transmitter in the synchronized link state might have more than one data-listen iterations depending on the precise wake-up time of either the transmitter or the receiver. Because of the potential clock drifts of the nodes, the receiver might wake up earlier than the transmitter or vice-versa, as represented in Fig. 3. The total energy of the system in the synchronized link state for TR-MAC protocol is given by

$$
E_T^{sync} = \lambda(\mathbb{E}[E_{Tx,T}^{sync}] + \mathbb{E}[E_{Rx,T}^{sync}]) + nE_{PL,T}
\tag{8}
$$

where $E_{Tx,T}^{sync}$ represents the expected energy to transmit a packet (Eq. 9) and $E_{Rx,T}^{sync}$ represents the expected energy to receive a packet (Eq. 10) respectively

$$
\mathbb{E}[E_{Tx,T}^{sync}] = \int_{d=d_{min}}^{d=d_{max}} P(D = d) \, E_{Tx,T}^{sync}|(D = d) \, d(d),
\tag{9}
$$

$$\mathbb{E}[E_{Rx,T}^{sync}] = \int_{d=d_{min}}^{d=d_{max}} P(D = d)\, E_{Rx,T}^{sync}|(D = d)\, \mathrm{d}(d). \qquad (10)$$

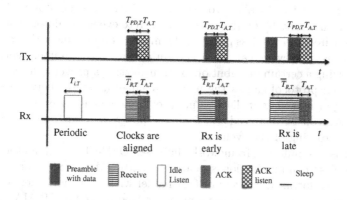

Fig. 3. TR-MAC synchronized link state

The equations to calculate energy consumption for the transmitter or receiver of Eqs. 9 and 10 has an energy part and a probability part. The energy part calculates the energy consumption to transmit or receive a packet for individual clock difference and the probability part represents the possible clock difference of the communicating nodes. The respective clock differences are modeled with random variable D with individual realization d. We assumed uniform distributions for the clock differences for both the transmitter and the receiver. The difference between two uniformly distributed clock drifts results in a convolution that further produces a triangular distribution. This triangular distribution will eventually determine the probability of the transmitter and receiver being awake to communicate at a previously agreed time.

The transmitter does not need to transmit any extra data-listen iterations if the receiver wakes up earlier than the transmitter or at the same time. However, if the receiver wakes up late than the transmitter, then the transmitter needs to send more than one data-listen iterations and the receiver needs to extend its receiving; which results in much energy consumption for both the transmitter and the receiver. This motivated us to experiment with an intentional clock offset. The measurement results showed that the energy consumption is not minimized for zero clock offset, rather at a point when the receiver is little early. Therefore we optimized the synchronized link state energy consumption by waking the receiver little early than the transmitter. The detailed equations and experiment results with the optimization are available in [13] together with the mathematical modeling for the synchronized state of WiseMAC protocol with which TR-MAC was compared.

5   Implementation in Simulator

Simulation is an important technique to evaluate the mathematical model since the system can be realized and tested in a controllable manner in a simulator. Thus we implement TR-MAC protocol in OMNeT++ simulator with MiXiM simulation framework [9]. OMNeT++ is a discrete event simulator that helps to analyze the wired and wireless protocols by means of events occurring at discrete time instances. An event can be a certain action, for example, generating a packet following a certain distribution, or transmitting a packet at a certain time. The simulated protocol causes the node to change its states between sleeping, transmitting or receiving at discrete point of time depending on the events. All these changes can be analyzed based on the progression of time together with the relative ordering of the events.

MiXiM is a simulation framework that uses OMNeT++ simulator for simulating wireless communication scenarios [9]. MiXiM provides some example protocol stacks for all the layers of OSI model with battery elements for computing energy consumption. Since we are interested to see the TR-MAC protocol behavior, thus we remodeled the MAC layer according to TR-MAC protocol and used the default implementation for the rest of the layers. The individual battery parameters are configured in MiXiM together with power levels where the transmitter uses double power than the receiver. The default network layer is used and the sensor application layer is configured with Poisson packet arrival with exponential inter-arrival times between packets. The physical layer uses simple path loss models without any specific channel effects or propagation delays.

We present a finite state machine for the TR-MAC protocol implementation in Fig. 4 with the possible states and events causing the node to change between its states. Here CCA represents clear channel assessment, CI represents check interval and FO represents frequency offset. After initialization in INIT, the node starts in unsynchronized link state and goes to SLEEP. First we explain the finite state machine from the point of receiver. The node wakes up to sense the channel for periodic listening by moving from SLEEP state to CCA state. If the node detects communication during CCA, then it goes to WAIT_DATA state; otherwise goes back to SLEEP. The node receives rest of the data packet in WAIT_DATA state and sends an acknowledgement back to the sender node if the received packet is a data packet and is meant for this node. The node also decides whether to move to synchronized link state by setting syncBit to one, or remain in unsynchronized link state by setting syncBit to zero in the acknowledgement packet before going to SLEEP. Next time this node will wake up for periodic listening or for an agreed time instance for synchronized case or if it has a packet to send; depending on which comes first.

Now a transmitter node having a packet to send in the finite state machine will first check whether it is operating in unsynchronized or synchronized link state. For unsynchronized link, the node moves to CCA state from SLEEP state and further moves on to send the packet right away if no communication is detected during CCA. For synchronized link state, the node continues to SLEEP delaying its wake up to the previously agreed time. If the desired time is reached

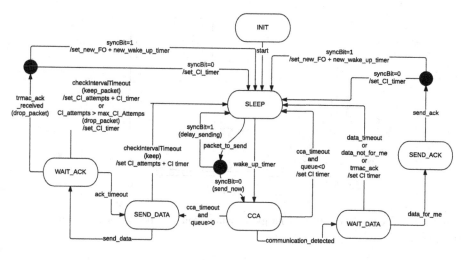

Fig. 4. Finite state machine of TR-MAC protocol implementation

for the synchronized case, then the node wakes up again and performs CCA. The node will move to SEND_DATA if no communication is detected during CCA, then to WAIT_ACK and iterate in these two states until it receives an acknowledgement or until the default check interval time is reached. After receiving an acknowledgement, the node will again decide about going to synchronized state or not by setting the syncBit to one or zero respectively. The node will drop the packet after a maximum number of failing attempts when it is unable to receive an acknowledgement for several check interval durations.

6   Results and Analysis

In this section, we evaluate the analytical models together with the simulation results for TR-MAC, X-MAC and WiseMAC protocol from the context of energy consumption. We simulate TR-MAC protocol using MiXiM framework in OMNeT++ and present the simulation results with 95 % confidence interval. For generating simulation results, we run each simulation to generate and transmit approximately 100 packets and the consumed energy is averaged for the number of packets. Afterwards 100 such simulation runs are used to average the result. We present the energy consumption results with respect to the following parameters, namely the check interval and the packet arrival rate. We consider Poisson packet arrival with exponential inter-arrival times between packets. The parameters and their corresponding representing symbols and values are given in Sect. 4 and in Table 1.

The total energy consumption for unsynchronized link state includes the energy to transmit or receive a packet, for periodic listening and for overhearing. At this moment, we focus on 1-hop link with a network of twelve nodes where one node is transmitting, another one node is receiving and ten other

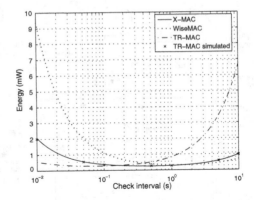

Fig. 5. Unsynchronized state: Energy consumption for packet arrival rate = 0.1 packet/s

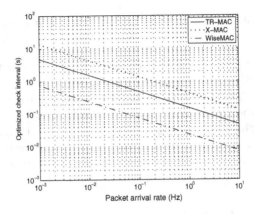

Fig. 6. Unsynchronized state: Optimized check interval for varying packet arrival rates

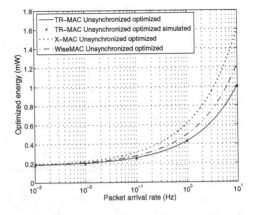

Fig. 7. Unsynchronized state: Energy calculated using optimized check interval for varying packet arrival rates

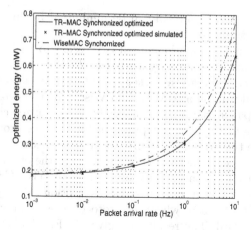

Fig. 8. Synchronized state: Energy consumption for varying packet arrival rates

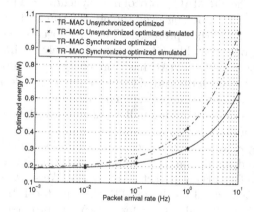

Fig. 9. TR-MAC: Unsynchronized and synchronized state comparison

nodes are overhearing. We present the energy consumption in unsynchronized link state for all three protocols with respect to varying sampling interval for a traffic load of $\lambda = 0.1$ packets/s in Fig. 5. We present and explain the energy consumption results for a particular packet arrival rate since we examined similar system behavior for given packet arrival rates. The TR-MAC simulation results, presented on top of the analytical results with 95 % confidence interval, matches to the analytical ones. The standard deviation from the mean value is very small, thus the simulation results coincide with the analytical results. We also see that periodic listening dominates the energy consumption for smaller check interval whereas packet transmission dominates the energy consumption for larger check interval. The results shows that the energy consumption for TR-MAC is lower than X-MAC but higher than WiseMAC for a small check interval. But the scenario turns around when the check interval increases. Therefore the energy consumption for TR-MAC protocol can be minimized by optimizing the check interval for a given traffic load.

In Sect. 4, we present a mathematical expression to find out the optimum check interval to minimize the unsynchronized link state energy consumption for TR-MAC protocol for a given packet arrival rate. We also derived the optimized check interval values for X-MAC and WiseMAC protocol but left out the derivations in this paper. Hence Fig. 6 presents the optimized check interval values calculated using mathematical expressions for all three protocols for a given traffic load. We see that WiseMAC can have smaller check interval because the receiver node only needs to detect the preamble. On the other hand, TR-MAC and X-MAC need to have longer check intervals than WiseMAC.

Next we calculate the overall energy consumption in unsynchronized link state for a range of traffic loads where the protocols use the previously calculated optimized check interval. The results are given in Fig. 7 where the simulation results for TR-MAC protocol with 95 % confidence interval verifies the analytical results. We see that the TR-MAC protocol in unsynchronized link state performs better than the reference protocols even though the transmitter using TR-MAC uses double power than other protocols. TR-MAC overhearers can return to sleep after receiving one preamble-data packet, effectively minimizing its periodic listening. On the contrary, WiseMAC has more energy consumption because the overhearers have to listen till the end of the preamble before deciding whether to receive the data packet or return to sleep. The difference between TR-MAC and WiseMAC protocol decreases with small number of overhearers and increases with large number of overhearers.

Afterwards, Fig. 8 presents the energy consumption calculated from both analytical models and simulation measurements for the optimized TR-MAC synchronized link state for varying packet arrival rates. We see that the simulation results confirm the analytical results for TR-MAC protocol. In the same figure, we also present the analytical results for WiseMAC protocol for comparison. We find that optimized TR-MAC performs better than WiseMAC protocol. We leave out X-MAC here since it does not have any synchronized state.

Finally, the overall energy consumption of the TR-MAC protocol for both unsynchronized and synchronized link state with respect to packet arrival rate is illustrated in Fig. 9. The protocol uses optimized check interval for individual traffic loads also in synchronized link state. Here we see the TR-MAC protocol synchronized link state has better energy consumption than unsynchronized link state. Thus the protocol will try to switch to synchronized state if the offered traffic is known. However, the protocol will operate in unsynchronized link state if the packet arrival rate is unknown or a priority packet has to be sent with shorter waiting time. The reason is the TR-MAC protocol in unsynchronized state will wake up more often if per packet delay needs to be minimized.

7   Conclusions and Future Work

This paper presents an implementation of TR-MAC protocol by applying a finite state machine using MiXiM simulation framework and OMNeT++ discrete event driven simulator. Furthermore, an enhancement to minimize the energy consumption for unsynchronized link operation of the TR-MAC protocol has been proposed. We found an explicit expression to optimize the check interval of preamble sampling TR-MAC protocol that will contribute to lower energy consumption. Simulation results with 95 % confidence intervals correspond to the analytical results generated for the similar scenario for both the unsynchronized and synchronized link states. The TR-MAC protocol has both transmitter-driven and receiver-driven communication possibilities together with efficient multiple access mechanism using different frequency offsets for different pair of nodes. The analytical and simulation results compared with X-MAC and WiseMAC protocols show that TR-MAC protocol is energy-efficient and suitable for low-power and low data rate WSNs.

For our future work, we will focus on the multiple channel access scheme for TR-MAC protocol. Furthermore, we will extend the protocol for network-level multi-hop communication and evaluate the protocol performance for scalability, throughput and other QoS parameters. Finally, our plan is to include a model for energy harvesting that will enable the TR-MAC protocol to operate based on available energy on the node.

Acknowledgement. This research is supported by the Dutch Technology Foundation STW, which is part of the Netherlands Organization for Scientific Research (NWO), and partly funded by the Ministry of Economic Affairs in the context of STW project 11317 - Walnut: Hard to Crack - Wireless Ad-hoc Links using robust Noise-based Ultra-wideband Transmission.

References

1. Bachir, A., Dohler, M., Watteyne, T., Leung, K.K.: MAC essentials for wireless sensor networks. IEEE Commun. Surv. Tutorials **12**(2), 222–248 (2010)
2. Buettner, M., Yee, G.V., Anderson, E., Han, R.: X-MAC: A short preamble MAC protocol for duty-cycled wireless sensor networks. In: Proceedings of the 4th International Conference on Embedded Networked Sensor Systems, SenSys 2006, pp. 307–320. ACM, New York (2006)
3. Cano, C., Bellalta, B., Sfairopoulou, A., Oliver, M.: Low energy operation in WSNs: A survey of preamble sampling MAC protocols. Comput. Netw. **55**(15), 3351–3363 (2011)
4. van Dam, T., Langendoen, K.: An adaptive energy-efficient MAC protocol for wireless sensor networks. In: SenSys, pp. 171–180. ACM (2003)
5. Dunkels, A.: The ContikiMAC Radio Duty Cycling Protocol. Technical report T2011:13, Swedish Institute of Computer Science, Dec 2011
6. El-Hoiydi, A., Decotignie, J.-D.: WiseMAC: an ultra low power MAC protocol for multi-hop wireless sensor networks. In: Nikoletseas, S.E., Rolim, J.D.P. (eds.) ALGOSENSORS 2004. LNCS, vol. 3121, pp. 18–31. Springer, Heidelberg (2004)
7. Hoctor, R., Tomlinson, H.: Delay-hopped transmitted-reference RF communications. In: IEEE Conference on Ultra Wideband Systems and Technologies, pp. 265–269 (2002)

8. van Hoesel, L., Havinga, P.: A lightweight medium access protocol (LMAC) for wireless sensor networks: Reducing preamble transmissions and transceiver state switches. In: 1st International Workshop on Networked Sensing Systems, INSS 2004, pp. 205–208. Society of Instrument and Control Engineers (SICE), Tokio (2004)

9. Köpke, A., Swigulski, M., Wessel, K., Willkomm, D., Haneveld, P.T.K., Parker, T.E.V., Visser, O.W., Lichte, H.S., Valentin, S.: Simulating wireless and mobile networks in omnet++ the mixim vision. In: Proceedings of the 1st International Conference on Simulation Tools and Techniques for Communications, Networks and Systems and Workshops, Simutools 2008, pp. 71:1–71:8. ICST (Institute for Computer Sciences, Social-Informatics and Telecommunications Engineering), ICST, Brussels, Belgium, Belgium (2008). http://dl.acm.org/citation.cfm?id=1416222.1416302

10. Mahlknecht, S., Bock, M.: CSMA-MPS: a minimum preamble sampling MAC protocol for low power wireless sensor networks. In: Proceedings of the 2004 IEEE International Workshop on Factory Communication Systems, pp. 73–80 (2004)

11. Meijerink, A., Cotton, S., Bentum, M., Scanlon, W.: Noise-based frequency offset modulation in wideband frequency-selective fading channels. In: 16th Annual Symposium of the IEEE/CVT. IEEE/SCVT, Louvain-la-Neuve, Belgium (2009)

12. Morshed, S., Heijenk, G.J.: TR-MAC: an energy-efficient MAC protocol for wireless sensor networks exploiting noise-based transmitted reference modulation. In: 2nd Joint ERCIM eMobility and MobiSense Workshop, St. Petersburg, Russia, pp. 58–71. Bern, Switzerland, June 2013

13. Morshed, S., Heijenk, G.: Tr-mac: An energy-efficient mac protocol exploiting transmitted reference modulation for wireless sensor networks. In: Proceedings of the 17th ACM International Conference on Modeling, Analysis and Simulation of Wireless and Mobile Systems, MSWiM 2014, pp. 21–29. ACM, New York (2014). http://doi.acm.org/10.1145/2641798.2641804

14. Polastre, J., Hill, J., Culler, D.E.: Versatile low power media access for wireless sensor networks. In: SynSys, pp. 95–107 (2004)

15. Ye, W., Heidemann, J., Estrin, D.: An energy-efficient mac protocol for wireless sensor networks. In: Proceedings of the Twenty-First Annual Joint Conference of the IEEE Computer and Communications Societies, INFOCOM 2002, vol. 3, pp. 1567–1576. IEEE (2002)

A New Hierarchical Key Management Scheme for Secure Clustering in Wireless Sensor Networks

Mohamed-Lamine Messai[1,2]([⊠]), Hamida Seba[2], and Makhlouf Aliouat[3]

[1] Department of Computer Science, Faculty of Exact Sciences, University of Bejaia,
06000 Bejaia, Algeria
messai.amine@gmail.com
[2] University of Lyon 1, CNRS, LIRIS, UMR5205, 69622 Lyon, France
hamida.seba@univ-lyon1.fr
[3] Department of Computer Science, Faculty of Sciences, University of Setif 1,
19000 Setif, Algeria
aliouat_m@yahoo.fr

Abstract. In Wireless Sensor Networks (WSNs), clustering is the suitable topology to save the energy of sensor nodes. In this paper, we provide a secured cluster formation by proposing a new symmetric key management scheme for hierarchical WSNs. The new scheme is called EAHKM (Energy Aware Hierarchical Key Management in WSNs). EAHKM needs the pre-distribution of only three keys in each sensor node before deployment, and it ensures a secure cluster formation after deployment. EAHKM assures the establishment of a pairwise key between each sensor node and its cluster head, thus the establishment of a broadcast key in each cluster in the network. Simulation results show that EAHKM provides an energy-efficient, flexible and scalable solution to the key management problem in hierarchical WSNs, and it presents a good resilience to node compromising attacks than other hierarchical key management schemes.

Keywords: Secure clustering · Hierarchical wireless sensor networks · Key management · Energy saving

1 Introduction and Motivation

Nowadays, Wireless Sensor Networks (WSNs) become the key technology for ubiquitous computing. They can be integrated in any application that collects data in environments [1]. A WSN consists of many tiny sensing devices called sensor nodes. A great number of sensor nodes are deployed in the field of interest either randomly or in predefined positions. Each sensor node has a sensing and a wireless communication capabilities, which enable it to sense data from the environment and send them to other sensor nodes in the network or to a base station (BS) [1].

© Springer International Publishing Switzerland 2015
M.C. Aguayo-Torres et al. (Eds.): WWIC 2015, LNCS 9071, pp. 411–424, 2015.
DOI: 10.1007/978-3-319-22572-2_30

A sensor node is equipped with limited resources and is manufactured to be a low cost device. As a result of its resource constraints, applying existing security solutions that are applied in wired networks or mobile ad hoc networks is infeasible. Security in this context becomes a challenging task and requires the design of appropriate key management schemes [2,3]. In WSNs, most proposed key management schemes are based on symmetric cryptography for its resource savings [4]. However, the challenge in using the symmetric cryptography is how to distribute, maintain and refresh pairwise keys between communicating sensor nodes in a network. The pairwise key establishment is needed to provide the authentication, the confidentiality and the integrity of exchanged messages between each neighboring sensor nodes. Key pre-distribution is the technique used to ensure key sharing after deployment of sensor nodes. It consists of pre-loading symmetric keys into memories of sensor nodes before their deployment. It is a practical method to deal with the key distribution problem in WSNs [5].

For energy saving purpose (in particular in long lived WSNs), a WSN is usually organized into a cluster-based topology that forms an hierarchical network. Hierarchical WSNs are more often used in real applications because they can improve the network scalability and reduce the energy consumption [6,7]. Therefore, the hierarchical organization is a promising technique in WSNs to ensure the key management process.

An example of hierarchical topology of a WSN is illustrated in Fig. 1. In a cluster-based topology, sensor nodes are randomly scattered in the sensing area and transmit their messages to a BS through cluster heads. Each sensor node in the network is either selected as cluster head (CH) or it is a cluster member by choosing a neighboring sensor node as a CH.

The existing hierarchical key management schemes [8–14] suppose that the WSN is previously organized into clusters by applying one of the existing clustering algorithms. So, the proposed key management solutions relay on hierarchical WSNs and do not take into account the security of cluster formation where an attacker can easily disturb this phase. As a result, existing schemes of key management do not ensure a secure cluster formation phase.

This paper propose a new scheme called EAHKM (Energy Aware Hierarchical Key Management Scheme for Wireless Sensor Networks) with a secure phase of cluster formation. EAHKM has two phases; (1) key pre-distribution phase and (2) cluster formation and key establishment phase. In the first phase, each sensor node S_i is pre-distributed with three keys: $K_{BS,i}$, $K_{i,BS}$ and K_N. $K_{BS,i}$ and $K_{i,BS}$ are two pre-distributed keys to encrypt messages (e.g. node readings) from sensor node S_i and the BS. K_N is the network key shared by all sensor nodes. This key will be deleted after cluster formation and key establishment phase. EAHKM uses a symmetric crypto-system and supports in the second phase an energy efficient formation of clusters with the establishment of two keys: K_{c_i} is a cluster key shared between sensor nodes of a cluster i, and K_{i,CH_j} is the pairwise key between a sensor node S_i and its cluster head S_j.

The rest of the paper is organized as follows. Section 2 discusses the related works on hierarchical key management schemes in WSNs. Section 3 details our

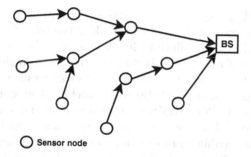

Fig. 1. An example of an hierarchical WSN.

proposed scheme EAHKM. Section 4 presents the security analysis of EAHKM. In Sect. 5, we compare and evaluate by simulation EAHKM with some existing hierarchical key management schemes. Conclusion is presented in Sect. 6.

2   Related Work

Recently, several key management schemes using symmetric crypto-systems and based on key pre-distribution have been proposed to establish secure communications between sensor nodes in WSNs. However, few works consider key management in an hierarchical topology of WSNs.

In this section, we discuss some proposed hierarchical key management schemes in WSNs. We classify the existing schemes into centralized and distributed as presented in Fig. 2.

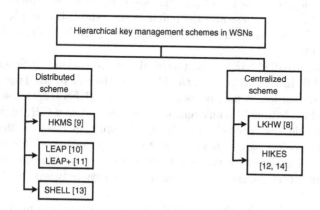

Fig. 2. Classification of existing hierarchical key management schemes in WSNs.

Among the first proposed centralized hierarchical key management schemes in the literature, we find LKHW [8]. This scheme is based on a logical key hierarchy. In LKHW [8], the BS distributes keys over a previously constructed tree. The BS is the root of the tree and it plays the role of a key distribution center to nodes. LKHW [8] is flexible, it allows new nodes to join the network. The main drawback of this scheme is that the BS is the single point of failure. If the BS of the network fails, key management cannot take place.

In [9], authors presented a distributed hierarchical key management named HKMS for clustered WSNs. HKMS [9] is designed for homogenous WSNs, it does not employ special sensor nodes (e.g. sensor nodes with high energy or high computational capability) to distribute or to establish keys. In HKMS [9], sensor nodes are pre-distributed with an initial key before their deployment. The selection of CHs is done according to an algorithm proposed in [15] without any security mechanism. HKMS [9] limits the size of clusters by using a TTL (Time To Leave) for broadcasted messages. The CHs broadcasts their messages encrypted by the pre-distributed initial key. The authors fix the value of the TTL to three without any argument or justification. The security of HKMS [9] is based on an initial key. If an adversary compromises a sensor node immediately after its deployment and discovers the initial key, he can compute any established pairwise key in the network.

In [10,11], a distributed hierarchical key management scheme called Localized Encryption and Authentication Protocol (LEAP) is proposed. LEAP [10,11] establishes five keys for each node: a global key, a pairwise key, a cluster key, an individual key and a group key. Each sensor node is initially pre-distribute with a global key K_I, an individual key shared with the BS, and pseudo-random function f. Using K_I and f, a sensor node can generate its master key and those of other sensor nodes. LEAP [10,11] is a scalable scheme but it has a low resilience to node compromising attacks. The entire security is based on a global initial key K_I. Once a sensor node is compromised before a threshold time, an adversary can obtain all pairwise keys. K_I is erased immediately after the neighbor discovery phase and the pairwise key establishment phase, it is not possible to add new sensor nodes to the network. Therefore, LEAP [10,11] has a poor flexibility.

A new scheme called HIKES (Hierarchical Key Establishment Scheme) is proposed in [12,14]. In HIKES [12,14], the BS plays the role of the Trust Authentication (TA) and assigns a part of its role to CHs. HIKES [12,14] uses a partial key escrow table that enables any sensor node, selected as a CH, to generate all the cryptographic keys needed to authenticate other members within its cluster. However, storing partial key escrow table requires an additional memory space. When an adversary obtains a partial key escrow table through a node compromise of a CH, he can deduce the pairwise keys between this CH and its members.

In order to underwrite the scalability metric, the authors in [13] proposed a scheme called SHELL (Scalable, Hierarchical, Efficient, Location-aware, and Lightweight). SHELL [13] employs the Exclusion Basis System (EBS) method [16] and performs location-based key assignment in the clusters to decrease the number of keys revealed by a node compromising attack. According to EBS [16], there are $k+m$ keys and each sensor node knows a distinct set of k keys. When a sensor node is compromised, the m keys (not known to the compromised sensor node) are used to replace the k compromised keys. It is notable that a large k increases the storage requirements at the sensor node, while a large m increases communication overhead for the revocation of compromised keys.

Above schemes are applied in hierarchical WSNs. They do not consider the security aspect in the phase of cluster formation of deployed nodes. This phase is the first step to perform by the deployed nodes. For this reason, we propose EAHKM to secure the cluster formation and ensure the key management in clustered WSNs.

3   Energy Aware Hierarchical Key Management for Wireless Sensor Networks

3.1   Network, Energy and Threat Models

The following properties are assumed in regard to the WSN model:

- Each sensor node has a unique identifier S_i.
- N homogeneous sensor nodes are randomly dispersed in a $m \times m$ field.
- Sensor nodes are homogeneous: they have the same capabilities of processing, memory and battery.
- The sensor nodes can use power control to change the amount of transmit power.
- The sensor nodes and the BS are static after deployment.
- The sensor nodes are unaware of their locations after deployment.
- The BS has no constraint on energy.
- Communications are symmetric: meaning if a node S_i can listen to a node S_j, S_j can listen to S_i.

In our work, we use the radio model proposed in [17]. According to this model, the energy cost to transmit or receive k *bits* between two sensor nodes that are separated by a distance d is given by the following equations:

$$E_{Tx}(k, d) = k \times E_{elec} + k \times \varepsilon_{fs} \times d^2, d \le d_0 \tag{1}$$

$$E_{Tx}(k, d) = k \times E_{elec} + k \times \varepsilon_{amp} \times d^4, d > d_0 \tag{2}$$

$$E_{Rx}(k) = k \times E_{elec} \tag{3}$$

Equations 1, 2 and 3 present the energy consumption of the radio module. Depending on the transmission distance d_0 (the threshold distance), both the free space channel ϵ_{fs} and the multi-path fading channel ϵ_{amp} models are used. When receiving, the radio expends E_{Rx} according to Eq. 3.

We assume that an adversary can listen to all broadcasted messages in the network. However, in the bootstrapping step (immediately after deployment of sensor nodes) adversaries cannot be present in all regions. When a sensor node is compromised, we assume that all its security material (keys, cryptographic algorithm, etc.) will be disclosed to the adversary. The BS cannot be compromised.

3.2   Proposed Scheme

Our approach has two phases: a key pre-distribution phase, and a cluster formation and key establishment phase. The notations used in our work are listed in Table 1.

Table 1. Notations.

Notation	Description
S_i	i^{th} sensor node in the network
$\{M\}_k$	Encryption of the message M with the key k
$BS \longrightarrow * : M$	The BS broadcasts the message M
$MAC_k(M)$	Message Authentication Code of M using the key k
K_{c_i}	Cluster key when the sensor node S_i is the CH
K'_N	Refreshed key of K_N
N_i	A nonce generated by the sensor node S_i
CH_i	Cluster head S_i
$H_k(M)$	A one-way hash function applied to M using the key k

Key Pre-distribution Phase: Sensor nodes are pre-distributed with the following three keys before their deployment into the sensing area: K_N, $K_{S_i,BS}$ and K_{BS,S_i}. K_N is the key shared by all sensor nodes in the network. This key is deleted from memories of nodes after the second phase. $K_{S_i,BS}$ and K_{BS,S_i} are two keys shared between S_i and the BS for encryption of messages. S_i uses $K_{S_i,BS}$ to encrypt its messages sent to the BS. Similarly, the BS uses K_{BS,S_i} to encrypt messages sent to S_i. By employing these two pairwise keys, a cryptanalysis attack becomes very hard to do. The BS stores K_N and $2 \times n$ pairwise keys in its memory where n is the number of nodes.

Cluster Formation and Key Establishment Phase: After deployment, the BS initiates the construction of clusters by broadcasting a Hello message as follows:

$$BS \rightarrow \{Hello, BS, Level = 0, Energy = \infty, MAC_{K_N}(BS, 0, \infty)\}_{K_N}.$$

Then, each sensor node executes the steps of cluster formation and key establishment given by Algorithm 1. When a sensor node receives the Hello message of the BS, it chooses the BS as a CH. If the node receives Hello messages from its neighbors, it chooses as CH the node with the lowest level that has the highest energy value. The selection of CHs is modified at regular intervals.

After the cluster formation and key establishment phase, each CH generates a cluster key K_{c_i} and sends it to each member node of its cluster encrypted by the established pairwise keys. So, each sensor node in the network stores a cluster key K_{c_i} and a pairwise key employed to secure the communication with its CH in addition of the three pre-distributed keys.

After key establishment, the CH generates a Time Division Multiple Access (TDMA) schedule for its members. The schedule message is encrypted with the shared cluster key K_{c_i}. Each sensor node transmits its messages to its CH in its assigned time slots encrypted with K_{i,CH_j} and it keeps its state in sleep mode during the remained slots. The CHs and the BS exchange messages by using a Code Division Multiple Access (CDMA).

Algorithm 1. Cluster formation and key establishment

Receive $\{Hello, Sender\_ID, Sender\_Level, E_{Sender\_ID},$
$CH_{Sender\_ID}, MAC_{K_N}(Sender\_ID, Sender\_Level, E_{Sender\_ID})\}_{K_N}$
If $(Sender\_ID := BS)$
$CH_i := BS$; /* cluster head is the identifier of the BS. */
$Level_i := 1$;
/*A shared key already exists.*/
Else
Begin
Repeat
Add E_{Sender_ID} to E_List_i
Add $Sender\_Level$ to $Level\_List_i$
Receive $\{Hello, Sender\_ID, Sender\_Level, E_{Sender\_ID},$
$CH_{Sender\_ID}, MAC_{K_N}(Sender\_ID, Sender\_Level, E_i)\}_{K_N}$
Until (receiving all neighbors messages)
$CH_i := $ The identifier of the node with the greatest ratio $E_{Sender}/Level_{Sender}$;
$Level_i := $ Level of its cluster head $+ 1$;
/* Compute a pairwise shared key with the cluster head */
$K_{S_i,CH_i} := H_{K_N}(S_i||CH_i||Level_i)$;
end;
EndIf
$S_i \rightarrow \{Hello, S_i, Level_i, E_i, CH_i, MAC_{K_N}(S_i, Level_i, E_i)\}_{K_N}$

Addition of Sensor Nodes. In most cases, new sensor nodes are added by a post-deployment to a deployed WSN to assure network connectivity, to replace dead nodes or to cover more regions in an area of interest. EAHKM is flexible by allowing addition of new sensor nodes. New sensor nodes will be able to establish pairwise keys with previously deployed sensor nodes. Adding a new node S_n is achieved as follows:

1. Before deploying S_n, the BS sends a new generated K'_N to all nodes in the network over the CHs.
2. S_n is pre-distributed with $K_{S_n,BS}$, K_{BS,S_n} and the current K'_N.
3. After being deployed, S_n generates a nonce N_n and broadcasts a Join message as follows: $S_n \rightarrow \{JOIN, S_n, N_n, MAC_{K_N}(S_n, N_n)\}_{K'_N}$. The Join message is encrypted with K'_N, the shared key by all sensor nodes.

4. When receiving the join message, every cluster head CH_i in the transmission range of the new sensor node generates a nonce N_i and responds with the following message: $\{JOIN-Ack, S_i, N_n, N_i, Level_i, E_i, MAC_{K_N}(S_i, N_i)\}_{K'_N}$.
5. S_n declares its CH, the source of the received message with high ratio $E_{CH_i}/Level_{CH_i}$ and diffuses the following message: $\{CH\_ID, S_n\}_{K'_N}$.
6. The CH node adds S_n in its cluster member list.
7. The CH and S_n compute their shared keys: $K_{S_n,CH_i} := H_{K'_N}(S_i||CH_i|| Level_i)$;
8. The CH sends to S_n the cluster key K_{c_i} encrypted with K_{S_n,CH_i}.

Key Refresh. To prolong the lifetime of the network, it is necessary to change the CH role among the sensor nodes. In EAHKM, the rekeying operation refreshes the clusters and the keys. Key refresh is on demand and it is initiated by the BS. Before key refresh, the BS sends to all sensor nodes through CHs a new generated network key K'_N. Then, it broadcasts the same diffused message after the initial deployment of sensor nodes encrypted by K'_N:

$$BS \rightarrow \{Hello, BS, Level = 0, Energy = \infty, MAC_{K_N}(BS, 0, \infty)\}_{K'_N}.$$

All sensor nodes re-execute Algorithm 1 (cluster formation and key establishment) given above. After the end of the algorithm execution, we will get new clusters with new established keys.

4 Security Analysis

In this section, we analyze the security of our solution. An outsider adversary, who does not know the key K_N, cannot discover the meaning of broadcasted messages by the BS and sensor nodes after their deployment. Nevertheless, an adversary can compromise one or more sensor nodes, so he becomes an insider adversary. The keys of compromised sensor nodes can be used to forge wrong useless messages to waste the energy of nodes. We note here that the compromised nodes cannot induce any damage on other communications in the network. Inside a cluster, the established pairwise keys and the cluster key are used to encrypt and authenticate messages. Therefore, adversaries who do not know these keys cannot obtain the clear messages. In the following, we present how EAHKM prevents specific attacks in WSNs; Hello flooding, Sybil and node replication attacks.

Hello flooding attack: in EAHKM, sensor nodes discover their neighbors by sending Hello messages encrypted with the key K_N. An attacker cannot launch a Hello Flooding attack without knowing the key K_N.

Sybil attack: in the cluster formation and key establishment algorithm, a MAC of the sensor node identifier, its level, and its CH identifier is calculated to authenticate the sender and the receiver. Therefore, a sensor node cannot play a role of an other sensor node.

Node replication attack: this attack is detectable by the CH if the replication is in the same cluster. However, node replication may affect EAHKM when an adversary duplicates compromised sensor nodes in different clusters.

5   Comparison and Simulation Results

In this section, we first define the metrics for performance evaluation. Then, we present a comparison of EAHKM and the schemes discussed in Sect. 2. After that, we use simulation to compare EAHKM, LEAP+ [11] and HKMS [9].

5.1   Evaluation Metrics

The aim of a key management scheme is to provide the basic security objectives in terms of integrity, confidentiality and authentication. In addition to these objectives, a key management scheme is evaluated in accordance to the following metrics:

- Efficiency: It refers the energy consumption, storage requirement and calculation needed by the key management scheme.
- Flexibility: It is the adaptability of the key management scheme to add and revoke sensor nodes.
- Resiliency or resistance to node compromising attacks: It measures the impact of capturing nodes on the links of non-compromised nodes in the network.
- Key connectivity (KC): It is the probability that two adjacent sensor nodes share a key after their deployment.
- Scalability: It measures the ability of the key management scheme to support a large number of deployed sensor nodes.

5.2   Comparison

In EAHKM, each sensor node is pre-distributed initially with three keys before deployment. After deployment, if the sensor node is a CH, it computes a number of keys that is equal to the number of its cluster members. The analysis of the communication complexity for the construction of clusters is measured by the number of messages received and issued by each sensor node. Each sensor node sends a message, receives d messages from its neighbors and receives (or sends, if this sensor node is CH) a message containing the cluster key, that is, $d + 2$ messages by each sensor node. Table 2 shows that EAHKM has a low communication complexity over other schemes. In addition, EAHKM ensures a secure cluster formation phase that makes it adaptable for real-world applications. Table 3 summarizes whether the scheme supports: key refresh, cluster key establishment, addition of new sensor nodes and if the scheme necessitates that sensor nodes are aware of their locations after deployment.

EAHKM allows key refresh and nodes addition which makes it dynamic and flexible. The establishment of a cluster key allows a secure broadcast of messages in the cluster and sensor nodes are unaware of their locations after deployment.

Table 2. Comparison 1.

Schemes	Communication complexity	Memory efficiency	KC	Secured clusters formation
LKHW [8]	Tree formation	h+1	1	No
HKMS [9]	m (depend on TTL value)	d'+1	1	No
LEAP [10]	(2xd)+1	(3xd)+2+key chain of TESLA	1	No
LEAP+ [11]	(2xd)+1	(3xd)+2+key chain of TESLA	1	No
HIKES [12]	6xd	partial key escrow table+7 keys+encrypted nonce	1	No
SHELL [13]	d+1	k keys+key's identifier	1	No
EAHKM	d+2	4 + number of cluster members	1	Yes

d: number of neighbors. d': number of neighbors within the same cluster. h: height of the tree.

Table 3. Comparison 2.

Schemes	Key refresh	Node addition	Cluster key establishment	Location acknowledgment
LKHW [8]	Yes	Yes	Yes	No
HKMS [9]	Yes	No	Yes	No
LEAP [10]	Yes	No	Yes	No
LEAP+ [11]	Yes	Yes	Yes	No
HIKES [12]	No	No	Yes	No
SHELL [13]	Yes	Yes	No	Yes
EAHKM	Yes	Yes	Yes	No

5.3 Simulation Results

We implemented EAHKM, LEAP+ [11] and HKMS [9] using the MATLAB framework[1]. Simulation parameters are cited in Table 4.

Figure 3 shows the communication overhead for different networks size, which consists of the average number of received messages by each sensor in the key establishment phase. For instance, in EAHKM each node receives 49 messages in a WSN of 200 nodes, which is a less cost than LEAP+ [11] and HKMS [9]. In LEAP+ [11], each sensor node broadcasts a message, receives d messages from its neighbors and then sends d messages to its neighbors to establish a cluster key. For HKMS [9], each CH broadcasts a number of messages that depend on

---

[1] MATLAB for MATrix LABoritory is a matrix-based system for scientific and engineering calculation.

Table 4. Simulation parameters.

Network area	250 m × 250 m
Base station location	(50 m, 50 m)
Initial energy	0,5 J
Packet size	4000 bits
E_{elec}	50 nJ/bit
E_{amp} ($\alpha = 2$)	$10\,pj/bit/m^2$
E_{amp} ($\alpha = 4$)	$0.0013\,pj/bit/m^4$
Distance d_0	87 m
Key size	128 bits

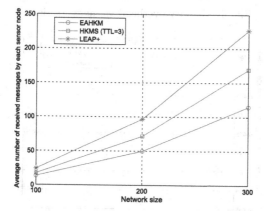

Fig. 3. Communication overhead.

the TTL value and receives d messages from its neighbors. Also, a node that is not a CH receives different messages from surrounding CHs and sends one message to a chosen a CH.

Figure 4 presents the total storage requirement in different networks size. From this Figure we can see that EAHKM has a nearly total memory value than HKMS [9] and a very small value compared to LEAP+ [11]. In EAHKM, each sensor node has to store only three keys in its memory before deployment. After deployment, in a cluster of m nodes there are $m - 1$ established keys. EAHKM is a memory-optimal scheme adapted to sensor nodes. When the network size increases, the total memory space in the network linearly increases in EAHKM.

Due to the energy constraint of sensor nodes, key management schemes should be energy-efficient. Figure 5 evaluates energy consumption during key establishment by calculating the average remaining energy in a sensor node. In HKMS [9], a cluster member node sends its messages to its CH through several hops which consumes more energy than a one hop transmission. However, in EAHKM each sensor node conserves its energy by choosing as a CH the sensor

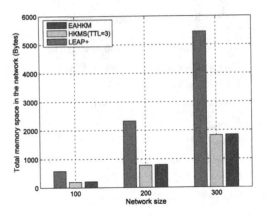

Fig. 4. Memory overhead vs. network size.

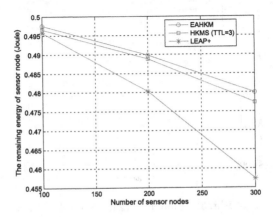

Fig. 5. Average energy consumed by sensor node during key establishment (including cluster heads).

node S_i with the highest value $E_{S_i}/Level_{S_i}$, this means choosing the nearest to the BS (in number of hops) and the highest energy node to be a CH.

CHs perform more encrypt and decrypt operations and receive more messages than cluster member nodes. In EAHKM, sensor nodes with high energy budgets are selected as CHs, this prolongs the lifetimes of low energy sensor nodes which extends the lifetime of the network.

Suppose an adversary that captures randomly sensor nodes in a network of 100 nodes. Resiliency is measured by the fraction of compromised links on the rest of communications in the network. Figure 6 illustrates the resiliency of EAHKM, LEAP+ [11], and HKMS [9] against node compromising attacks when an adversary captures randomly 1 to 5 sensor nodes. It is noted that EAHKM outperforms the other schemes. In EAHKM, if a compromised node is a cluster member, it does not affect other communications within its cluster and if the node is a CH, it does not affect communications in other clusters.

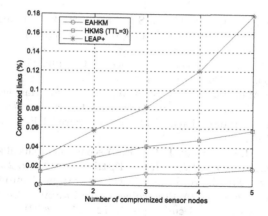

Fig. 6. Resilience to node compromising attack.

From the presented comparison and simulation results, EAHKM not only ensures a secure cluster formation, but also provides better performance in terms of energy efficiency, communication overhead, memory overhead, scalability and resilience to node compromising attacks.

6 Conclusion

Organizing WSNs in hierarchical topologies is a promising technique to save energy. This organization needs to be constructed in a secure way. Nevertheless, the use of wireless channels, the energy-constraint and the large number of deployed sensor nodes complicate the task of key management in WSNs. This work proposed a new hierarchical key management scheme called EAHKM. Our comparison and simulation results indicate that EAHKM presents a better performance than other key management schemes. In addition, EAHKM offers a secure bootstrapping to sensor nodes. This desired feature is not warranted by the discussed schemes.

References

1. Zhou, Y., Fang, Y., Zhang, Y.: Securing wireless sensor networks: a survey. IEEE Commun. Surv. Tutorials **10**(3), 6–28 (2008)
2. Cardei, M., Ibriq, J., Ilyas, M., Mahgoub, I.: Encyclopedia of wireless and mobile communications (2007)
3. Chen, C.Y., Chao, H.C.: A survey of key distribution in wireless sensor networks. In: Security and Communication Networks (2011)
4. Messai, M.L., Aliouat, M., Seba, H.: Tree based protocol for key management in wireless sensor networks. EURASIP J. Wirel. Commun. Networking **2010**, 59 (2010)
5. Cheng, Y., Agrawal, D.P.: An improved key distribution mechanism for large-scale hierarchical wireless sensor networks. Ad Hoc Netw. **5**(1), 35–48 (2007)

6. Ya-nan, L., Jian, W., He, D., Li-jun, S.: Intra-cluster key sharing in hierarchical sensor networks. IET Wirel. Sens. Syst. 3(3), 172–182 (2013)
7. Reegan, A.S., Baburaj, E.: Key management schemes in wireless sensor networks: A survey. In: 2013 International Conference on Circuits, Power and Computing Technologies, pp. 813–820. IEEE (2013)
8. Di Pietro, R., Mancini, L.V., Law, Y.W., Etalle, S., Havinga, P.: Lkhw: A directed diffusion-based secure multicast scheme for wireless sensor networks. In: Proceedings of the International Conference on Parallel Processing Workshops, pp. 397–406. IEEE (2003)
9. Zhang, Y., Li, X., Liu, J., Yang, J., Cui, B.: A secure hierarchical key management scheme in wireless sensor network. Int. J. Distrib. Sens. Netw. 2012 (2012)
10. Zhu, S., Setia, S., Jajodia, S.: Leap: efficient security mechanisms for large-scale distributed sensor networks. In: Proceedings of the 10th ACM Conference on Computer and Communications Security, pp. 62–72. ACM (2003)
11. Zhu, S., Setia, S., Jajodia, S.: Leap+: Efficient security mechanisms for large-scale distributed sensor networks. ACM Trans. Sens. Netw. (TOSN) 2(4), 500–528 (2006)
12. Ibriq, J., Mahgoub, I.: A hierarchical key establishment scheme forwireless sensor networks. In: 21st International Conference on Advanced Information Networking and Applications, pp. 210–219. IEEE (2007)
13. Younis, M., Ghumman, K., Eltoweissy, M.: Location-aware combinatorial key management scheme for clustered sensor networks. IEEE Trans. Parallel Distrib. Syst. 17(8), 865–882 (2006)
14. Ibriq, J., Mahgoub, I.: Hikes: Hierarchical key establishment scheme for wireless sensor networks. Int. J. Commun. Syst. 27(10), 1825–1856 (2014)
15. Chen, J.S., Hong, Z.W., Wang, N.C., Jhuang, S.H.: Efficient cluster head selection methods for wireless sensor networks. J. Netw. 5(8), 964–970 (2010)
16. Eltoweissy, M., Heydari, M.H., Morales, L., Sudborough, I.H.: Combinatorial optimization of group key management. J. Netw. Syst. Manage. 12(1), 33–50 (2004)
17. Min, X., Wei-Ren, S., Chang-Jiang, J., Ying, Z.: Energy efficient clustering algorithm for maximizing lifetime of wireless sensor networks. AEU-Int. J. Electron. Commun. 64(4), 289–298 (2010)

Author Index

Printed in the United States
by Book...

Printed in the United States
By Bookmasters